THE ARMY OF
ROBERT E. LEE

THE ARMY OF ROBERT E. LEE

Philip Katcher

ARMS AND
ARMOUR

Arms and Armour Press
A imprint of the Cassell Group
Wellington House, 125 Strand, London WC2R 0BB

Distributed in the USA by Sterling Publishing Co. Inc.,
387 Park Avenue South, New York, NY 10016-8810.

Distributed in Australia by Capricorn Link (Australia) Pty. Ltd.,
2/13 Carrington Road, Castle Hill, NSW 2154.

British Library Cataloguing-in-Publication Data: a catalogue record
for this book is available from the British Library

ISBN 1-85409-375-4

Designed and edited by DAG Publications Ltd.
Designed by David Gibbons; edited by Michael Boxall;
Printed and bound in Great Britain by
Hartnolls Limited, Bodmin, Cornwall

Contents

Introduction

'The Confederate service was a personal service. The 1st Virginia Brigade, for instance, glorious at First Manassas and on other fields, was never anything but the Stonewall Brigade. There were Benning's Georgians and Law's Alabamians and Pickett's Division was so designated; and the I Corps was Longstreet's Corps – and your old men always said "Lee's Army".'

John W. Thomason, Jr., *Lone Star Preacher*

MOST GREAT MILITARY LEADERS COMMANDED A VARIETY of troops. Wellington commanded Portuguese in Spain and Dutch in Belgium. Napoleon had French, Italian, Polish and Germans under him in his various campaigns throughout Europe. Julius Caesar had legions made up of men recruited throughout the Empire which he led in Gaul, Britain, Egypt and Italy. Marlborough led a force of Dutch and Germans as well as British against the French. And Eisenhower led Americans, British, French and soldiers from a dozen other countries during the Second World War.

But Robert E. Lee, remembered as much as the best of them, is forever linked with one small force that fought in one small area of the globe for a fairly short time. It is true that he commanded other Confederate units in 1861 and technically had overall military command of Confederate Army forces by the end of the war, but for most of the war he commanded one army, an army entrusted with the defence of the South's leading city, in every sense of the word. The titles 'Lee's Army' and the 'Army of Northern Virginia' will be forever synonyms for the same organization.

Although booksellers reckon that books with Confederate themes are the most popular of Civil War literature, it is surprising that far fewer books about the Southern forces have been published than ones dealing with Union soldiers and organizations. In part this is because those who returned to the North were the victors, anxious both to publish their own exploits and read of those of their neighbours.

Confederate veterans, on the other hand, felt that they had little to boast of, especially in those hungry years just after the surrender of their forces in the field. Initially they were too busy trying to rebuild their homes and lives and re-adjusting to a vastly changed society. There was, too, some shame, no matter how well disguised, at having been on the losing side. Losing is just not the American way. Unlike

7

the civilians in the North, Southern civilians frequently treated their veterans badly, considering them to have been failures. It was not for many years that, with time softening the edges of memory, both Southern civilians and soldiers alike were able to recall those memories and begin to create a series of myths of the 'Old South' and of the Confederacy as having been its finest hour.

It should be noted, too, that most publishing houses were in the North, which may account for the fact that fewer Confederate than Union accounts were published during the post-war years.

With the next generation came an outpouring of Confederate titles, but even today there are great gaps in Confederate as compared to Union studies. There has yet to be an historian to do for the Confederate armed forces what the late Francis Lord did for the Union soldiers and sailors. No one has done for the Confederate cavalry what Stephen Z. Starr did so well for that of the Union. As yet there has been no attempt to spell out the Confederate Army's organization at high command levels in the way that Frank J. Welcher has done for that of the Union.

The Confederate forces deserve better. Putting aside legal or even moral questions about the Southern cause, the pure effort made by its men and women to create and sustain its military forces so as to bring about a victory in the field, is a study that is surely worth making. Their improvisation of equipment and organizations to meet changing needs was conducted not only while fighting an enemy on their fronts, but also with a political administration that seemed to be acting as if the war were over, and the Confederacy were already enjoying the peace they had known during the decades before the war began.

After the war, too, a tremendous system of myth-building began. Some of these myths were designed to place Lee on a pedestal as one of the greatest leaders in history, perfect in every aspect. Some were created to answer the inevitable question: 'If Lee were such a great general, why did he have to surrender his army?' So the myth of overwhelming Union resources was adopted.

Lee was an outstanding general, but he was only human, often in poor health, and he made mistakes. His contemporaries recognized many of his errors, even if men of later generations didn't. And Confederate veterans realized that they hadn't really been that much worse off than their enemies. Lieutenant Colonel W. W. Blackford, one-time cavalry staff officer and at times senior officer of 1st Regiment of Engineers, was to write later: 'In books written since the war it seems to be considered the thing to represent the Confederate soldier as in a chronic state of starvation and nakedness. During the last year of the war this was partially true, but previous to that time it was not any more than falls to the lot of all soldiers in an active campaign. Thriftless men would get barefooted and ragged and waste their rations to some extent anywhere and thriftlessness is found in armies as well as at home. When the men came to houses, the tale of starvation, often told, was the surest way to succeed in foraging.'

This book is an attempt both to shed light on and outline some of those actual qualities that made Lee's Army a unique organization. In some ways material on Lee's Army is valid for other Confederate armies, such as the Army of Tennessee, insofar as it relates to organization, pay, etc., which was mandated by the central government in Richmond.

Yet observers found much to distinguish Lee's from other Confederate armies, notably the fact that they simply looked different. Much of their clothing, supplied either by the Richmond Clothing Manufactory or by state governments, was superior in quality from that supplied to western units. Each individual Confederate field force adopted its own system of battle flags, Lee's Army being distinguished by its square red banners with a dark-blue Saint Andrew's cross and white stars. Eventually, the basic design of the Army of Northern Virginia battle flag was adopted throughout most of the Confederate's armies, but even then the design was never exactly as found in Lee's Army.

For some reason the men of the Army of Tennessee seem to have been better supplied with marked belt plates, often rectangular pieces of brass bearing the letters 'CSA', than those of the Army of Northern Virginia. A plain frame buckle was the most common style of belt plate worn by Lee's men. Lee's men tended to be better armed than soldiers in other Confederate armies, mostly because they were closest to the sources of arms, the factories in Richmond and the ports on the eastern seaboard.

Finally, there was the matter of morale. Lee's men thought that they could just about whip the world, being under the command of Lee and his generals. No other Confederate force ever had such confidence in itself. And Lee had just as much faith in the abilities of the men he commanded as they had in him, something that commanders of other forces often lacked. The result was possibly one of the finest field armies ever assembled and committed to battle.

As with any project so comprehensive, thanks are due to many people who helped with it in one way or another. These include Howard E. Bartholf, John M. Bighami, Roderick Dymott, Allen R. Hoilman, James Jacobsen, Don Johnston, Benedict Marynaik, John Ogle, Harry Roach, Lee A. Wallace, Jr. and Michael Welch. Individuals who helped to gather art include Marilyn W. Burke, William A. Frassanito and Michael J. Winey. Special thanks also go to that extraordinary researcher, buff and encourager, Sue Kerekgyarto.

1
The Mission of Lee's Army

ON 17 APRIL 1861, FOLLOWING A LEVY OF MEN BY THE FEDeral government on the State of Virginia for the purpose of putting down a rebellion among other Southern states, Virginia itself passed an ordinance of secession. Although Union sentiment was strong in Virginia, especially in the western part of the state where commercial ties to Northern states were great and slaveholding was rare, the majority of Virginians were more against fighting their fellow Southerners than for saving the Union. They would link their fate with the rest of the South who were already forming a new 'Confederate States of America' from what had been member states of the United States of America. Eventually there would be thirteen states in this new Confederacy.

Since the Federal government, under newly inaugurated President Abraham Lincoln, had already called for troops to march South against South Carolina and the other new Confederate states, it was obvious that Virginia too could expect invasion. After all, the state, or 'commonwealth' as it was properly termed, lay directly between the Northern states and the offending Carolinas.

So on the 17th another ordinance was passed, this one calling for the governor to accept as many volunteers as were needed 'to repel invasion and protect the citizens of the state in present emergency'.[1]

It would be an immense task to protect Virginia. The state was the fifth most populous in the United States and, indeed, the most populous in the South, numbering some 1,596,652 according to the 1860 census. Of these the large majority, 1,047,579, were whites, the remaining 549,073 being blacks, most of whom were slaves.

This was a mixed blessing. While the blacks were available for labour, both skilled and unskilled, they also presented a potential threat. Slave insurrections had been known in Virginia during the years before the war; in 1831 slave Nat Turner had led an uprising near Richmond in which 56 whites were killed and thousands more were terrified of what could happen to them as well. Therefore any troops defending the state's borders would have to keep an eye over their shoulders to be sure the slaves they left behind were behaving themselves.

Virginia was a large state; at some 67,230 square miles, her territory was about the same size as the six states of New England combined. The state was better developed than most Southern states, and had approximately 1,150 miles of railroad track.

Richmond, the capital city, was the obvious target for an invader. This was especially true in the early days of the war when geographic centres were the main targets of any military campaign. Some years were to pass before the most clear-thinking military men realized that the way to defeat an enemy was to destroy his armies in the field rather than simply to occupy some of his real estate. Prior to that, conventional military thinking called for the capture, preferably bloodlessly, of the enemy's major cities through skilful manoeuvring, after which negotiation would produce a peace treaty. In a civil war, as any war between North and South must be, however, nothing less than the destruction of an enemy's will and ability to fight would result in a victory. Negotiations were not possible: either the Union, in its 1860 form or a different form, would prevail, or the South would become independent. There could be no middle ground.

In 1861 this was little understood, save perhaps by America's leading military genius, Major General Winfield Scott, who proposed a plan to destroy the South slowly in order to win the war. At first his plan was not seriously considered as a single strategic concept, but it eventually won the war. It called tor the closing of all Southern ports, a drive South from Illinois to take the entire Mississippi River and an army to operate in Northern Virginia to threaten Richmond and tie down the Southern forces required to defend that city.

While the overall plan was not adopted immediately, some elements were. But whereas Scott wanted simply an army in being in Northern Virginia to threaten Richmond, it was decided to attempt to capture Richmond quite early on. Scott feared that an untrained Northern army would face defeat and demoralization in a premature attempt on the city, but the newspapers called for the city's quick capture and the politicians, including Lincoln, bowed to public opinion. Richmond was to be the first major target of the war.

So it would be Richmond rather than the troops defending it that would be the target of any army that invaded Virginia with the intention of forcing its return to the Union. But Richmond was far more than just a city in which government met. It was the leading industrial point in the entire South. It was a major rail centre from which the Richmond, Fredericksburg & Potomac line ran north, the Virginia Central line ran to the Shenandoah Valley, and the Richmond and Danville line ran south and west. Ships from both the North and South dropped anchor in the port at Rocketts, where deep water in the James River ended. The Tredegar Iron Works, which since 1850 had been building locomotives, cannon, anchors and anchor chains, was the only industrial plant in the South with this capability. The river bank was lined with cotton, paper and flour mills. The most difficult

11

aspect of defending this major city was that it lay within easy reach of an enemy based in Washington, DC, the capital of the United States. Indeed, it is only 104 miles from Richmond to Alexandria which lies just across the Potomac River from Washington.

Therefore, Virginia and the new Confederacy had to defend Richmond if for nothing else than to sustain its war effort.

However, the topography of Virginia helped protect Richmond from overland invasion from the general direction of Washington. Although the terrain was relatively flat, with only gently rolling hills and a fine network of roads on which to march, it was also cut up by a network of rivers and streams which ran generally from, if a clock were superimposed on a state map, 11 o'clock to 4 o'clock. Any army marching due south from Washington, hugging the west shore of the Potomac at first, before heading straight south, would cross the Aquila Creek, then the Rappahannock River, the Po River, the North Anna or Pamankey Rivers and the Chickahominy River. Each of these would present a potentially fine defensive line.

The city was tremendously vulnerable to any attack from due east, from the sea. The James River was virtually navigable by deep water ships up to the city's front steps. The York River, running parallel with the James, also afforded passage to deep water ships for some distance towards Richmond. And the US Army's old Fort Monroe sat at the end of the peninsula formed between the York and the James. Any army marching due north-west from that starting-point, which never passed into state control, would have a relatively short march before it was in Richmond. Chesapeake Bay, into which the York and James Rivers flowed, curved northwards towards the Northern ports and the US Navy facilities at Baltimore and Washington. It was certain to remain in US hands, which meant that the threat from this direction was certain to remain.

To the west the state was cut up by a series of what were called mountain ridges, although they were nothing like the great Rocky Mountains, being at best tall, tree-covered lines of hills. None the less they presented a formidable barrier to any invasion from the west. Indeed, various mountain chains on the west and the Blue Ridge Mountains on the east surrounded a very fertile area known as the Valley of Virginia or, sometimes, the Shenandoah Valley. Unlike the rivers, the Valley ran south-west/north-west, from the James River in the south to Harper's Ferry on the Potomac River in the north.

This area, connected to Richmond by the Central Railroad, provided much of the food that was consumed in the state. Whoever held the few passes or 'gaps' through which ran the rail and other roads, held the state. The only route for a large force moving east or west from or to the Valley across the Blue Ridge Mountains was through Ashby's Gap, just south of Harper's Ferry, and then, from north to south, through Manassas Gap, Carter Gap, Thornton's Gap, Fisher's Gap, Swift Run Gap (which had no main roads through it), Brown's Gap and, at the end near Waynesboro, Rockfish Gap. The distance from north to south was almost 150 miles. And the Valley would be cut off from the rest of the state by the closing of these gaps. Moreover, any force defending the Valley from an enemy already in the Valley would be limited in communications and support from a force near Richmond to whatever could get through gaps behind its front lines.

Also it is 108 miles from Richmond to the nearest major population centre in the Valley, Staunton, further than Richmond is from Alexandria. So that an army defending the city from the north would be much closer and much more in the eye of the city's population than would be forces operating in the Valley.

Besides distances, the differences in the defensive problems of these two areas, Richmond and the Shenandoah Valley, meant that the forces defending each area would be largely independent in command as well as mission, even though one general might technically have command over both areas.

On 21 April Governor John Letcher ordered every volunteer infantry, rifle and artillery company in the counties running west from Richmond, the state capital, to the Blue Ridge Mountains and in the Shenandoah Valley to the Tennessee line to be ready for action at a minute's notice. Command of Virginia's forces was given to a US Army colonel of engineers who had recently resigned his commission to share Virginia's fate: Robert Edward Lee.

Lee accepted his commission as major general commanding the 'Provisional Army of Virginia' on 23 April, and the army's organization was spelled out by the Virginia Convention on the 27th. The ordinance creating the army called for two artillery regiments, eight infantry regiments, a rifle regiment and one cavalry regiment.

Some of these forces were already in place and on 22 May Lee wrote to General Milledge Bonham, whose troops were at Manassas Junction on the line directly between Washington and Richmond, that 'the policy of the State at present is strictly defensive. No attack, or provocation for attack will therefore be given, but every attack resisted to the extent of your means.'[2] This, indeed, was the basic mission of the army defending Virginia, that force that became Lee's Army, in the early years of the war. Later, Lee's natural aggressiveness led him to go on the attack — note the words 'at present' in his letter to Bonham — but even then the official Confederate strategy was basically defensive.

In 1861 Virginia's forces were not wholly ready for the task before them. The old militia system, where each man was liable for service and had to maintain his own equipment and show up for an annual muster day, was pretty much a piece of ancient history. In its place, a patchwork system of volunteer companies, officially but often not actually organized into regiments and brigades, had sprung up. These were dependent more on individual desire for military glory than on a rational plan for overall state defence drawn up in Richmond.

Some of these volunteer companies, especially in the longer established eastern parts of the state, had been in service a long time and were well equipped, trained and organized. Some were more social than military organizations, with groups of similar people, such as Irish or First Families of Virginia scions, meeting every week or so to bend an elbow and impress the ladies with their elaborate military dress.

The 1st Regiment of Virginia Volunteers, as an example of a well-established unit, had actually been organized in 1851 from nine volunteer companies that were mostly much older than the regiment itself. The Richmond Light Infantry Blues, for example, had been organized on 10 May 1793, the Richmond Fayette Artillery in 1824 and the Richmond Greys in 1844.

But such antiquity was rare among Virginia's volunteer companies. Indeed there were few of any such organizations in most of the towns of the state until 1859. It was then that John Brown, an unhinged abolitionist who had been born in Connecticut 59 years earlier, led an armed band of followers into Harper's Ferry, then located in Virginia, in October 1859. Their goal was to cause a slave uprising and it failed, but only because Colonel Lee brought a company of US Marines from Washington and captured Brown.

After a trial for treason against Virginia, Brown was found guilty and hanged. His slave insurrection did not succeed, or even seriously begin for that matter; but the affair so unnerved Virginians that many of them began organizing volunteer companies in virtually every county in the state.

So it was that the annual inspection of the state's militia for the year ending 30 September 1860 showed on its rolls four major generals; 28 brigadier generals; one adjutant, inspector and quartermaster general; 20 aides-de-camp; 27 brigade inspectors; 20 brigade quartermasters; 173 colonels; 182 lieutenant colonels; 324 majors; 181 adjutants; 168 quartermasters; 148 paymasters; 45 chaplains; 172 surgeons; 160 surgeons' mates; 1,463 captains; 2,554 lieutenants; 155 sergeant majors; 139 quartermaster sergeants; 588 musicians; 40 buglers and trumpeters; 3,621 sergeants; 3,202 corporals; 129,740 privates. These were organized into five divisions, 28 brigades, 197 infantry regiments, 9 cavalry troops, 17 artillery companies, 73 light infantry companies, 72 rifle companies and 1,141 infantry companies.[3] The secession of South Carolina in December 1860 was a further spur to volunteering.

The result was that most of the state's regiments were made up of companies that had been in existence for relatively short periods of time and consequently their officers and men were generally poorly equipped and trained. Take, for example, the 5th Regiment Virginia

Volunteers. It included thirteen companies, one of which had been organized in 1855, one in 1858, two in 1859 and the rest in 1861.[4]

With all this volunteering came expanded orders for arms and equipment from Northern manufacturers, as most makers of this equipment were in the industrialized Northern states rather than in the agrarian South. The state was forced to attempt to bring its volunteer units up to mobilization status fairly quickly, but lacked much of the stuff necessary to do so. Indeed, an article in the Richmond *Examiner* of 17 April reported that the entire military stores of the state included only 200 kegs of powder, with another 240 on order. It went on to say that the state had some 60,000 longarms, but 54,000 of these were flintlocks, most of which had been manufactured by the long-closed Virginia Armory at Richmond during the early 1800s.

The state's adjutant general, William Richardson, made a more complete survey of the state's military condition and reported his findings to state governor John Letcher on 15 December 1860:

'There are undoubtedly at least 200,000 men in the State subject to military duty, yet the annual consolidated return gives nearly 60,000 short of that number.

'The volunteer force has increased rapidly and continues to increase. There are now in commission 92 troops of cavalry, 26 companies of artillery, 111 companies of light infantry and 113 companies of infantry ... These companies have been armed as follows:

'Cavalry — Twenty-four troops have been armed with sabers and pistols; twenty-six with sabers only.

'Artillery — Eleven companies with 6-pounder field guns, mounted (in all twenty-four pieces), with implements and artillery swords; one company with six 12-pounder howitzers, mounted, and with horse artillery sabers.

'Light Infantry — Six companies with rifled muskets; fifty-six companies with smooth-bore percussion muskets; twenty-six companies with flint-lock muskets.

'Riflemen — Three companies with long-range rifles and sword bayonets; twenty-three companies with percussion rifles; seven companies with flint-lock rifles.'[5]

On 24 April 1861 Virginia concluded a treaty of alliance with the new Confederate States. It had also promised that if a popular vote supported it, it would accept the Confederate constitution, a close copy of the Federal one, and become a Confederate state. Furthermore, it proposed that its capital city of Richmond become the new Confederate capital. On 25 May the vote was held, with ratification winning the day. A day later, the Confederate Congress voted to leave the small, crowded city of Montgomery, Alabama, and take up residence in the larger city of Richmond.

On 20 July the Confederate President, Jefferson Davis, reported to his Congress: 'I deemed it advisable to direct the removal of the several Executive Departments, with their archives, to this city (Richmond), to which you had removed the seat of government, immediately after your adjournment. The aggressive movements of the enemy required prompt and energetic action. The accumulation of his forces on the Potomac sufficiently demonstrated that his efforts were to be directed against Virginia; and from no point could the necessary measures for her defense and protection be so efficiently protected as from her own capital.'[6]

Scott's idea of having an army in being threatening Northern Virginia had paid off; the new Confederate government and, presumably, troops to defend it, were drawn to face this threat. On the whole, however, this may not have been the best idea for the Confederates in terms of defending the entire South. In all, the general Confederate government was responsible for defending some 3,500 miles of coastline stretching from Virginia south to the tip of Florida, then west to where Texas and Mexico met. This coast included several major ports, including New Orleans, Louisiana; Savannah, Georgia; Charleston, South Carolina; and Norfolk, Virginia. In addition, there were smaller ports in North Carolina, Alabama and Texas, which would be vital if the already existing US Navy attempted to cut off needed supplies from overseas. Then, too, the government needed to defend other industrial cities such as Nashville, Chattanooga, and Memphis, Tennessee, and Atlanta, Georgia.

The government decided early on that its efforts would be spent on defending every point that the North could threaten, regardless of its overall importance to the whole Confederacy. This despite the fact that it obviously could not physically do so, in terms of Southern versus Northern manpower and industrial strength.

This was partly a consequence of the insistence of the various state governors on having each point in their states defended regardless of the consequences. After all, the whole idea of the Confederacy was that the states were the major political bodies and no one political body would allow any of its territory to be given up. Priority ratings were not assigned to different points, so Confederate forces were to be tossed about in penny packets to defend any post about which a particular governor might be concerned.

The result was that in some places that virtually never heard a shot fired in anger there were important garrisons which, for political reasons, could not be spared for the defence of, for example, Richmond, whose industrial might demanded that it be defended first for the good of all.

Moreover, the idea was fixed that the Confederate forces would only defend against attacking Federal forces. Even if a quick assault into Northern states would break up enemy concentrations before they could get going, the plan was not to attack but to wait for the enemy. It would look better to the international audience. After all, then, the Confederacy would be only defending itself and its legitimate legal rights of peaceable secession.

Given this situation, the location of the government and especially its president, Jefferson Davis, whose US Military Academy education and military service convinced him that he was the best qualified for the post of commander-in-chief to which he was constitutionally appointed, would be fixed on the eastern Virginia front. After all, it would be troops from this front with whom they would be most acquainted. Naturally enough, the rest of the Confederacy's war effort would be only glanced at from time to time as needed. Placing the capital in some centrally located city such as Atlanta, or even leaving it in the too small but better situated Montgomery, Alabama, might overall have been a better plan. Be that as it may, the government was glad to pack up and leave Montgomery for Richmond. On 8 June 1861, General Order No. 25, Headquarters Virginia Forces, placed the state forces under command of all 'lawful' orders of the Confederate president. As many state units as the Confederates wanted could be transferred into Confederate national service. The 1st Battalion, Virginia Regulars was mustered into Confederate service on 30 June, with other state units following.

With the arrival of the Confederate government, Virginia was no longer solely responsible for the defence of the state. Troops from other Southern states, even as far away as Texas, arrived in the Richmond area. There they were organized into a new Confederate Army, not as yet called the Army of Northern Virginia, and given the task of defending Virginia's borders.

On 3 June, a clerk in the Confederate War Department in Richmond, John B. Jones, noted in his diary that: 'Troops are beginning to arrive in considerable numbers. The precincts of the city will soon be a series of encampments. The regiments are drilled here, and these mostly forwarded to Manassas, where a battle must soon occur, if the enemy, now in overwhelming numbers, should advance. The Northern papers say the Yankee army will celebrate the 4th of July [Independence Day] in Richmond.'[7] Four days later, he added, 'We have, I think, some 40,000 pretty-well armed men in Virginia, sent hither from other States. Virginia has I know not how many, but she should have at least 40,000 in the field. This should enable us to cope with the Federal army of 70,000 volunteers, and the regular force they may hurl against us.'[8]

Lee's Army was being born, its mission having already been decided.

2
Robert E. Lee

THE MAN NAMED COMMANDER OF VIRGINIA'S FORCES PRIOR to the arrival of the Confederate government, Robert Edward Lee, was well known in military circles before the war.

On 7 May 1861, War Department Clerk Jones noted in his diary: 'Col R.E. Lee, lately of the United States army, has been appointed major general and commander-in-chief of the army in Virginia. He is the son of "Light Horse Harry" Lee of the Revolution. The North can boast no such historic names as we, in its army.'[1]

Lee was indeed the fifth child of 'Light Horse Harry' Lee, a noted Revolutionary War cavalry leader. He was born in the family mansion, 'Stratford', in Westmoreland County, Virginia, on 19 January 1807. His father lost his fortune in unwise land speculation, and the family gave up its estate to move to Alexandria, Virginia. In 1812 he was in Baltimore on business when he was attacked by a mob. His injuries prevented him from accepting a general's commission in the American army fighting the War of 1812 in Canada, so he left for the West Indies in the hope of restoring his health. Robert was then eleven years old. His father died on the return voyage.

Robert E. Lee entered the US Military Academy at West Point, New York, in 1825. He was graduated in 1829 second in his class, with the amazing record of never having been given one demerit during the four years he was at the Academy. He received a commission as a brevet second lieutenant of engineers, the corps which accepted only the brightest Academy students, and served as an engineer at various seaboard fortifications.

On 30 June 1831 he married Mary Ann Randolph Custis, a daughter of one the first families of Virginia, the only child of George Washington Parke Custis, a grandson of the wife of George Washington by her previous marriage. Mary Ann had seven children; the eldest son was to become a Confederate major general, the youngest served as an artillery private.

However, theirs does not appear to have been an especially happy marriage. Lee was absent for long periods, not always on account of his military duties. His wife and children could have accompanied him, but she was a chronic invalid and preferred to stay at home in Virginia. While it is clear that Lee was fond of the ladies, no evidence has come to light of his having been unfaithful to his wife

18

despite the strained relationship. None the less, an unhappy marriage makes for an unhappy individual, one who often puts all the intensity he might have brought to marriage into other activities.

The outbreak of the Mexican War in 1846 found Lee holding the rank of captain. He was assigned to Texas as an assistant engineer on the staff of Major General John E. Wool. He was soon transferred to the staff of Major General Winfield Scott who led a sea-borne expedition to capture Mexico's capital city. His conduct in aiding Scott during this campaign was so outstanding that he received three brevets, which were temporary commissions for gallantry and distinguished service. At the end of the war in 1848 he was serving as a colonel of engineers.

After the war, he served as Superintendent of the US Military Academy from 1852 to 1855. He was then transferred to a line post by Secretary of War Jefferson Davis, as lieutenant colonel of the 2nd Cavalry Regiment in Texas where he was serving when the Civil War broke out.

As early as 5 December 1860, Lee saw, as most Americans did, that Southern secession was more than just a slight possibility. Indeed he wrote to his eldest son, Custis, to say that if the Southern states left the Union, he would return to Virginia. Moreover, in other letters home he expressed his conviction that the North was guilty of aggression against the South, although he personally hoped that the Union would not be dissolved. As of 23 January he was writing that in case of war he would return to Virginia to help defend that state.

He left Texas in February, arriving home on 1 March, only five days before the Confederate Congress authorized an army of 100,000 volunteers. Lee then had a long discussion with his old commander and mentor, now the US Army's commanding general, Winfield Scott. The result of this conversation was that on 30 March he accepted a commission as a colonel in the US Army.

However, Virginia's convention voted to secede from the United States on 17 April, and Lee followed his state, resigning his new commission on the 20th. On 22 April he was offered, and accepted, the commission as a Virginia major general and the state's commander-in-chief. His commission as a Confederate brigadier general, then the highest rank authorized, was dated 14 May.

He was now 54 years old. His entire life had been spent in the military, mainly on engineering projects and staff work. He had performed valiant service in one war, directly under one of America's top soldiers, but had never commanded a combat unit during that war.

Although he had been commander of Virginia's army, Lee was not immediately appointed commander of the Confederate army which was gathering just north of Richmond. His first job, after being promoted to the rank of full general on 31 August, was as special military adviser to his old superior, Jefferson Davis, who had been US Secretary of War when Lee was posted to the 2nd Cavalry.

While holding the position of Davis's adviser, Lee was sent to handle the defence of the area which is now the State of West Virginia. There, bothered by local loyalty to the Union instead of the new Confederacy, and bickering and infighting by his supposed subordinates, he was unable to succeed. The area fell to a Union general whose star was in the ascent, Major General George B. McClellan. Much criticism of Lee's performance was thereafter voiced in the Southern press and by the citizens generally, although not especially by the soldiers who had been under his overall command.

Thereafter Lee was sent on a mission to examine defences on the Georgia and South Carolina coasts, and prepare them against attack. He returned to Richmond in March 1862, taking up the advisory post once again.

McClellan, given command of the Union troops around the US capital city of Washington, began an assault on Richmond via the obvious route up the peninsula bounded by the James and York Rivers. The army that was organized to stop him was led by General Joseph E. Johnston, whose personal luck in battle was often bad. He was severely wounded in action and Lee was named to replace him on 31 May.

From now on, Lee's fate and reputation were tied up with this army, which he renamed the Army of Northern Virginia. On 6 February 1865 he was further named General in Chief of the Armies of the Confederate States, assuming overall command of all Southern military forces. But this appointment came too late for him to take personal charge of the Southern forces far from Richmond and Petersburg, where his Army of Northern Virginia lay besieged by a numerically superior Union army. On 9 April, forced out of their entrenchments and unable to break through Union forces to join up with the forces under Johnston in North Carolina, Lee surrendered this army.

Lee was not well-to-do; indeed much of his finances were tied up in worthless Confederate bonds and bills. Even so, he refused several offers to take advantage of his fame throughout the nation after the war by becoming involved in, for example, insurance companies. Instead, he accepted the presidency of a small Virginia college, Washington College, in Lexington. There he spent his few remaining years, active in the vestry of the local Episcopal Church and in training young southern boys to rebuild their part of the country. He died there on 12 October 1870.

Lee was an imposing man, both physically and intellectually, and his presence at any occasion was almost invariably noted and later recorded by those who met him. The stresses of command for so many years had taken their toll of him and many other Confederate commanders. One advantage of the Union Armies' constant replacement of inept commanders was that fresh, unworn soldiers were constantly taking up new commands with new ideas and untried spirits. The Confederacy had no such reserves of new blood.

In June 1861 a Maryland volunteer, McHenry Howard, saw Lee in Richmond: 'General Lee at that time wore a heavy brown moustache, with no beard, and was a very handsome man, looking, of course, very much younger than he was afterwards known and pictured.'[2]

A Tennessee enlisted man, Sam R. Watkins, saw Lee during his first campaign in West Virginia in 1861: 'He was a fine- looking gentleman, and wore a moustache. He was dressed in blue cottonade. I remember going up mighty close and sitting there and listening to his conversation with the officers of our regiment. He had a calm and collected air about him, his voice was kind and tender, and his eye was as gentle as a dove's. There was none of his staff with him; he had on no sword or pistol, or anything to show his rank. The only thing that I remember he had was an opera-glass hung over his shoulder by a strap.'[3]

Later, Lee went to Charleston, to work on fortifications, and a local man, Paul Hamilton Hayne, saw him, thinking him 'perhaps the most striking figure we had ever encountered — the figure of a man seemingly about fifty-six or fifty-eight years of age, erect as a poplar, yet lithe and graceful, with broad shoulders well thrown back, a fine, justly proportioned head posed in unconscious dignity, clear, deep, thoughtful eyes and the quiet, dauntless step of one every inch the gentleman and soldier.'[4]

Staff officer G. Moxley Sorrel saw him a little later: 'When General Lee took command it was my first sight of him. Up to a short time before Seven Pines he had worn no beard but only a well-kept moustache, which soon turned from black to grizzled. When he took us in hand his full gray beard was growing, cropped close, and always well tended. Withal graceful and easy, he was approachable by all; gave attention to all in the simplest manner. His eyes — sad eyes! — the saddest it seems to me of all men's — beaming the highest intelligence and with unvarying kindliness, yet with command so firmly set that all knew him for the unquestioned chief. He loved horses and had good ones, and rode carefully and safely, but I never liked his seat. The General was always well dressed in gray sack-coat of Confederate cloth, matching trousers tucked into well-fitting riding-boots — the simplest emblems of his rank appearing, and a good, large black felt army hat completed the attire of our commander. He rarely wore his sword, but his binoculars were alway on hand. Fond of the company of ladies, he had a good memory for pretty girls. His white teeth and winning smile were irresistible.'[5]

On 22 June 1862, while serving in Richmond as the president's adviser, Lee described himself in a bantering, flirtatious letter to one of his daughters-in-law, Mrs W. H. F. Lee: 'My coat is of gray, of the regulation style and pattern, and my pants of dark blue, as is also prescribed, partly hid by my long boots. I have the same handsome hat which surmounts my gray head (the latter is not prescribed in the regulations) and shields my ugly face, which is masked by a white beard as stiff and wiry as the teeth of a card.'[6]

A year later, a British observer, Colonel Arthur Fremantle, met Lee, whom he believed to be 'almost without exception, the handsomest man of his age I ever saw. He is fifty-six years old, tall, broad-shouldered, very made, well set up — a thorough soldier in appearance; and his manners are most courteous and full of dignity. He is a perfect gentleman in every respect. I imagine no man has so few enemies, or is so universally esteemed...

'He generally wears a well-worn long gray jacket, a high black felt hat, and blue trousers tucked into his Wellington boots. I never saw him carry arms; and the only mark of his military rank are the three stars on his collar. He rides a handsome horse, which is extremely well-groomed. He himself is very neat in his dress and person, and in the most arduous marches he always looks smart and clean.'[7]

On campaign, however, Lee did not wear the full double-breasted coat of his rank, instead, according to an officer of the Washington Artillery, 'He always wore during the campaigns a gray sack coat with side pockets like the costume of a business man in cities.'[8] Also, until his heart attack in the spring of 1863, he generally wore a standing collar with his coat; thereafter he wore a turned-down collar. By September 1864, when the regulation colour for trousers was changed from blue to grey, he apparently also switched to wearing grey trousers, all subsequent photographs showing trousers that match his coat in tone.

He also switched to his full dress uniform for his last major duty, that of surrendering the Army of Northern Virginia at Appomattox. An impressed Union officer, Horace Porter, saw him there: 'Lee ... was six feet and one inch in height, and erect for one of his age, for he was Grant's senior by sixteen years. His hair and full beard were a silver-gray, and thick, except that the hair had become a little thin in front. He wore a new uniform of Confederate gray, buttoned to the throat, and a handsome sword and sash. His top-boots were comparatively new and had on them near the top some ornamental stitching of red silk. Like his uniform, they were clean. On the boots were handsome spurs with large rowels. A felt hat which in color matched pretty closely that of his uniform, and a pair of long, gray buckskin gauntlets lay beside him on the table.'[9]

More than stress had aged Lee. Throughout the war he was struck, as too many Confederate generals were, by disease that not only wore him down, but also possibly led to bad decisions. His pinkish face gave evidence, unknown at the time, of the heart ailment that would eventually kill him. In April 1863 he was taken ill with what doctors now believe was acute pericarditis. He wrote to his wife on 5 April, describing his symptoms as giving him 'a good deal of pain in my chest, back, & arms. It came on in paroxysms, was quite sharp.[10] He suffered another attack in late August, admitting to his wife on 28 October that 'I have felt very differently since my attack of last spring, from which I have never recovered ... My rheumatism is better, though I still suffer.'[11]

Besides this chronic condition, which had set in early in 1863, Lee was in less than perfect physical condition during several periods throughout the war. On 31 August 1862 his horse, Traveler, suddenly leaped away from him while, dismounted, Lee was holding the reins. Jumping to prevent its escape, Lee fell heavily to the wet ground, breaking a small bone in one of his hands and straining both hands. He had to ride in an ambulance for two weeks, his hands being too swollen and painful to grasp a rein. For the duration of the first invasion of Maryland, then, he had to contend not only with the enemy, but with physical pain.

Six weeks after the accident he had a letter written home in which he said that only by now, 'with my left hand, I am able to dress and undress myself, which is a great comfort. My right is becoming of some assistance, too, though it is still swollen and sometimes painful. The bandages have been removed. I am now able to sign my name. It has been six weeks today since I was injured, and I have at last discarded the sling.'[12]

During the height of the fighting along the North Anna River in 1864, he fell victim to an acute intestinal disorder which put him out of action for a week. Moreover, according to one of his staff officers, Walter Taylor, and his corps commander, Jubal Early, for most of the 1864 spring campaign he was far from physically fit; age and stress were gaining on him.[13] The result was that during each major action, from Sharpsburg to Chancellorsville and Gettysburg until the end of the war, Lee was in a state of physical discomfort, often acute, and this would almost certainly have affected his thinking.

Other influences also affected him. Like most Virginians of prominent families, he was a devout Episcopalian, a faith characterized by a strong recognition of civil, as well as theological, authority. A tendency to obey commands without a rebellious attitude is encouraged in that faith, and only such an attitude could allow one to graduate from West Point without a demerit. At the same time, he accepted whatever life, or the Union Army, forced upon him as being simply the will of God, something that could not nor should not be contested. Lee felt that he could only do his duty to God and his country, or state, and that God would do as He willed.

He stressed the role of the Lord in his own life and that of his army on an almost daily basis. Indeed, his order suspending military duties in the Army on 21 August 1863, a day which the president had set aside as a day of fasting and prayer, was taken directly from his Church's *Book of Common Prayer*: 'Soldiers! we have sinned against Almighty God. We have forgotten His signal mercies, and have cultivated a revengeful, haughty, and boastful spirit. We have not remembered that the defenders of a just cause are pure in His eyes; that "our times are in His hands", and we have relied too much on our own arms for the achievement of our independence. God is our only refuge and our strength. Let us humble ourselves before Him. Let us confess our many sins, and beseech Him to give us a higher courage, a purer patriotism, and more determined will; that He will convert the hearts of our enemies; that He will hasten the time when war, with its sorrows and sufferings, shall cease, and that He will give us a name and place among the nations of the earth.'[14]

Lee's family was a source of real concern. His wife was always in poor health and he was always solicitous of her. In October 1862 his daughter Annie died. He had been especially devoted to her. His faith helped him accept her death, but he was deeply saddened by it. Within six months he suffered his first heart attack. Then, in June 1863, his second son, W. H. F. 'Rooney' Lee, was severely wounded. He was sent to recuperate at home, where he was captured by a Union raiding party. He was not exchanged until March 1864, another concern for a loving father.

The amazing thing is, therefore, that Lee was not only able to keep his mind on his job, but to do it so well as to win the almost universal love of his officers and men from the highest to the lowest. Indeed, most of them, flushed by constant success, believed that Lee's Army would win despite any odds. And he returned the compliment, believing that there was little or nothing that his men could not do.

Lee cared deeply for his officers and men. A story which found wide circulation among his troops in West Virginia was that one dark, rainy night a new private, worn-out by arduous duties, had fallen asleep whilst on guard. The regimental officers felt that the offence deserved the death penalty. But Lee asked the captain of the guard how he and his fellows would think if the sleeper been one of them. The captain replied that he had not thought of it that way. Lee told the offending private to return to his quarters and warned him never to sleep on guard duty again. The affair would be forgotten.

During cold winter months when rations were constantly hard to come by, he concerned himself with the functioning of the commissariat, on one occasion suggesting that they swap their sugar for bacon from the local inhabitants. In February 1863 he wrote to his wife saying that they were 'up to our knees in mud & what is worse on short rations for men & beasts. This keeps me miserable. I am willing to starve myself, but cannot bear my men or horses to be pinched.'[15]

Nor did Lee allow his position to make him unapproachable. He dealt with every man in a calm, cool manner, sometimes mistaken for coldness, but each was treated equally, without regard for the chevrons on their sleeves or gold embroidery on their collars.

Once, in 1864, when Lee was by a roadside, watching his troops heading towards Hanover Junction, an old private stepped out of the ranks and went up to him. He introduced himself, to the probable consternation of the staff officers, and the two shook hands like old friends. As the troops passed by they could see the two talking, the private with his musket in one hand and the other on the neck of Lee's horse.

When staff officers brought messages to Lee's small headquarters, which was almost always maintained in tents rather than the local houses which most generals preferred, Lee would invariably invite them to dinner and talk with them as if they were his equal in rank.

Not every Confederate soldier felt that Lee was wholly without faults. A number of middle-grade officers, colonels and generals in particular, questioned his actions on many occasions. Lieutenant General Richard Taylor, who had served under Lee as a brigade commander, was not a professional soldier and his criticisms, although not without validity, reflect this:

'In truth, the genius of Lee for offensive war had suffered by a too long service as an engineer,' he wrote. 'In both the Antietam [Sharpsburg] and Gettysburg campaigns he allowed his cavalry to separate from him, and was left without intelligence of the enemy's movements until he was upon him. In both, too, his army was widely scattered, and had to be brought into action by piecemeal.'[16]

Staff officer Sorrel, later a brigadier general in the Army of Northern Virginia, disagreed. 'Some in the army were given to speak of him as the "King of Spades" who would never allow us to show fighting,' he wrote, of the period in late 1862. 'The past fourteen months had indeed opened the eyes of these sneerers.'[17]

In fact, if anything, Lee tended to be too offensive-minded, splitting his army for a flank attack which luckily worked at Chancellorsville, and going for a killing thrust to the heart at Gettysburg, which did not work. Brigadier General E. Porter Alexander, one of the Confederacy's finest artillerymen and, judging from his memoirs, one of its leading military analysts, believed that: 'Military critics will rank Gen. Lee as decidedly the most audacious commander who has lived since Napoleon, & I am not at all sure that even Napoleon in his whole career will be held to have overmatched some of the deeds of audacity to which Gen. Lee committed himself in the 2 years & 10 months during which he commanded the Army of Northern Va.

'On two occasions, I am quite sure, he will be adjudged to have overdone it. He gave battle unnecessarily at Sharpsburg Sep. 17th 1862...

'Then perhaps in taking the aggressive [*sic*] at all at Gettysburg in 1863 & certainly in the place & dispositions for the assault on the 3rd day, I think, it will undoubtedly be held that he unnecessarily took the most desperate chances & the bloodiest road.'[18]

However, the mention of the cavalry being away from the body of his army is a valid point, and was a consequence of his often giving his subordinates too free a hand to pursue their own agendas. In the case of the cavalry during the Gettysburg campaign, this was the fault of Major General JEB Stuart who was attempting to gain glory by repeating his stunt of riding around the Union army during the Peninsula Campaign, and ignoring Lee's vital need for intelligence.

Indeed, when Stuart finally did join Lee's main army on the afternoon of 2 July, well after the battle had been joined, all Lee is supposed to have said to him was, 'Well, General Stuart, you are here at last.'[19] Admittedly, officers quailed from even such a mild rebuke when administered by Lee, from whom harsh words were virtually unknown, but Stuart's failures probably merited something rather more severe.

Lee's failure adequately to order his generals to perform specific actions or discipline them if they failed was probably his greatest character defect. General Alexander pointed out that at the Seven Days one of the problems was that Lee simply gave orders and expected them to be carried out. 'No commander of any army does his whole duty who simply gives orders, however well considered. He should *supervise their execution*, in person or by staff officers, constantly, day & night, so that if the machine balks at any point he may be most promptly informed & may most promptly start it to work.[20]

One of his staunchest defenders agreed: 'He had a reluctance to oppose the wishes of others, or to order them to do anything that would be disagreeable and to which they would not consent.[21]

John Cheeves Haskell, who had been a college student when the war broke out and thereafter rose to the rank of colonel of artillery under Lee, also had some adverse opinions of the general. 'He had an apparent antipathy to anything partaking of pomposity and the vanity of war, but he had an utterly undue regard for the value of the elementary teaching of West Point and for the experience gained by the very small police duty of our (US) miniature regular army. He failed to realize that while a military school is excellent for the training of drill masters, who are most necessary, it teaches little of military science in comparison with the hard experience of a single campaign. When an army is confined for military leaders to a handful of lieutenants, who have never seen more than a regiment, probably not more than a company, in action, and have never had to deal with a harder problem in the

26

maintenance of their men than how to get a wagon train from the nearest railroad station, it is apt to be hurt by the restriction.

'But General Lee never went outside, and was apparently resolute against doing so, the regular grades to find officers, who might have been very Samsons to help him multiply his scant resources.'[22]

In much the same way, Longstreet, who was born in South Carolina, objected to their being 'too much Virginia' among the high command of the Army of Northern Virginia.[23] Both criticisms have validity, but neither can be wholly laid at Lee's door. Jefferson Davis, himself a West Point graduate, closely monitored promotions to the general grade and tended to prefer fellow West Point graduates. Even had Lee wanted to, he could not have overridden any of Davis's appointments, even in his own army.

However, Lee did have complete tactical ontrol of his army and Davis never ignored any suggestion from Lee as to its strategic deployment. And, on that point, a very real criticism of Lee is that while he managed to defend Richmond for almost three years, he allowed the rest of the Confederacy to be slowly eaten away. Instead of eagerly releasing forces from his inactive front while Vicksburg was being besieged in early 1863, he resisted any transfer of troops. Instead, he proposed an offensive by himself into Pennsylvania which, at best, would not be apt to slow down the Vicksburg offensive to any great extent. It should have been fairly evident that, while the Union Army may have felt that it had to transfer troops to the east during a Confederate offensive against Pennsylvania, those troops would have come from the Tennessee rather than the the Mississippi theatre. His action sealed not only Vicksburg's fate, but in many ways that of the Confederacy.

It has been argued that this was not Lee's responsibility, and, of course, it was not. But he, more than any other Confederate military man, had Davis's ear, and to win Davis to one's idea was to have it done, regardless of the intelligence of the move. Since Lee chose always to emphasize his theatre over the other theatres, despite what was happening in them overall, he appears to have been little better than any other theatre commander, Bragg in Tennessee or Kirby Smith across the Mississippi, in placing the Confederacy above his own army.

In the end, one wonders if Lee thought that it would have made any difference. He is supposed to have said to John S. Wise, son of a Virginia governor, after the Battle of Sayler's Creek, 'A few more Sayler's Creeks and it will all be over — ended — just as I have expected it would end from the first.' And, Army of Northern Virginia artillery commander Brigadier General William N. Pendleton later said that Lee told him: 'I have never believed we could, against the gigantic combination for our subjugation, make good in the long run our independence unless foreign powers should, directly or indirectly, assist us.'

Since he wrote to his wife on 25 December 1861 that, 'We must make up our minds to fight our battles & win our independence alone. No one will help us,' it looks as if he expected to lose from the very start.[24] It is difficult to win if one expects to lose, and one must question Lee's very motivation.

Be that as it may, his troops expected to win, and in large part because Lee was in command. Lee and the Army of Northern Virginia was one of those very rare marriages of an outstanding commander and a top-notch force that fight their way into the pages of history. Probably neither would have amounted to as much apart as they did together — a form of military synergy.

3
Lee's Generals

W HILE AN ARMY CAN BE NO BETTER THAN ITS COMMAND-
ing general, in fact the record of that general can be little
better than those of his immediate subordinates. It is they
who interpret his orders and carry them out, it is their initiative or lack
of it that drives an army on to success or allows it lapse into failure. On
the whole, Lee, and the Army of Northern Virginia, were well enough
served, especially in the early years before disease and combat wounds
deprived him of his most able generals. Thereafter, some corps commands had to be filled by officers who were less capable at such a high
level.

Lieutenant General Thomas Jonathan 'Stonewall' Jackson
Lee's most able general was another Virginian, 'Stonewell' Jackson. He
was born on 21 January 1984 to a Scottish-Irish family in the small
town of Clarksburg in what is now West Virginia. Orphaned at an early
age and raised by an uncle, Jackson received an appointment to West
Point in 1842. Grinding hard work enabled him to overcome his lack
of previous education, and he graduated 17th in a class of 59 – 24 of
whom earned general's commissions on either side during the war.

An artillery officer, Jackson served in a heavy artillery company
which fought as infantry during the Mexican War where he earned two
brevets, ending the war as a brevet major. After several years of peace-
time work in New York and Florida, where he became a convinced
Christian, he resigned from the army to accept the post of Professor of
Natural and Experimental Philosophy and Artillery Tactics at Virginia
Military Institute. The school, supported by the state, was essentially a
four-year private military academy organized along the lines of the public academy at West Point, and awarded degrees of Bachelor of Science.

Jackson was present at the hanging of John Brown, as commander of the Corps of Cadets from VMI who were sent there. When the
war broke out, he was commissioned a colonel in Virginia's forces and
sent to Harper's Ferry. Later, General Joseph E. Johnston was given
overall area command, while Jackson himself was promoted on 17 June
to the rank of brigadier general and given an all-Virginia brigade to
command.

At first many of his men thought that at best he was a bit daft.
He had a habit of going about with his right hand raised, 'to improve

the circulation in his arm', having been slightly wounded in the hand at the First Manassas. From time to time he could be seen sucking lemons for their medicinal properties.

He led a Sunday school for blacks as part of his Presbyterian faith; yet he respected all Christian faiths, even studying that of the Roman Catholic Church while he was in Mexico, apparently free from the typical bias of the period. His, however, was both a personal and a very demanding God; he would never fight on the Sabbath if it could be avoided. He had little use for disbelievers, regardless of their military abilities, preferring to surround himself with men of faith. 'Tom Fool Jack' was one of his more polite nicknames.

'In face and figure Jackson was not striking,' one of his aides later wrote. 'Above the average height [Longstreet said that he was 5 feet, 10 inches tall], with a frame angular, muscular, and fleshless, he was, in all his movements from riding a horse to handling a pen, the most awkward man in the army. His expression was thoughtful, and, as a result I fancy from his long ill health, was generally clouded with an air of fatigue. His eye was small, blue, and in repose as gentle as a young girl's. With high, broad, forehead, small sharp nose, thin, pallid lips generally tightly shut, deep-set eyes, dark, rusty beard, he was certainly not a handsome man.

'He was quiet, not morose. He often smiled, rarely laughed. He never told a joke but rather liked to hear one, now and then. He did live apart from his personal staff, although they were nearly all young; he liked to have them about, especially at table. He encouraged the liveliness of their conversation at meals, although he took little part in it. His own words seemed to embarrass him, unless he could follow his language by action. As he never told his plans, he never discussed them. He didn't offer advice to his superiors, nor ask it of his subordinates.'[1]

Sent to reinforce the Confederates under attack at the First Manassas, Jackson arrived near Henry Hill where his troops were standing solidly under attack. Nearby, South Carolina Brigadier General Bernard Bee pointed to where his men stood like a 'stone wall' from where both Jackson and his brigade gained their nicknames during the battle. But it is still not certain whether Bee was admiring Jackson's stand or complaining about his lack of forward movement to support Bee's own men. Since Bee was killed in the battle, Stonewall's legion of admirers chose the former version, and that's the one that is accepted today.

Promoted on 7 August to the rank of major general, Jackson was given command of troops in the Shenandoah Valley, with orders to clear out that threat to the Virginian left flank. During a fast campaign in which he drove his infantry forward so rapidly that they adopted the name of 'Stonewall's Foot Cavalry', he smashed three separate Union forces under Banks, Fremont and Shields, and cleared the enemy totally from the valley by his last battle at Port Republic on 9 June.

On 23 June elements of his forces began arriving in the Richmond area as much-needed reinforcements for Lee's outnumbered army. McClellan's much larger Union army was then pressing within sight of Richmond's church spires.

Lee immediately set Jackson's forces to work as part of an overall assault on McClellan's lines. But the brilliant commander of the Valley was a lacklustre commander on the peninsula. Worn down by the stress of his recent campaign, in this unfamiliar territory Jackson again and again missed opportunities and muffed chances.

But he more than regained his reputation when, after McClellan had been forced into a defensive position, clearly never to advance again, Jackson was sent against another Union army. This, under Pope, was coming from the north and Jackson totally fooled the Union general, smashing him at Second Manassas. His troops were also vital in the defence at Sharpsburg, following a rapid march to rejoin Lee's main army after having being sent to capture Harper's Ferry. Following this action, Jackson was promoted to lieutenant general (10 October 1862), and given command of Second Corps of the Army of Northern Virginia. At Fredericksburg, he commanded the right wing.

'For quickness of perception, boldness in planning, and skill in directing, General Lee had no superior,' one of Lee's aides later wrote. 'For celerity in his movements, audacity in the execution of bold designs and impetuosity in attacking, General Jackson had not his peer.'[2] This estimate was shown to be highly accurate at Chancellorsville, where Lee unleashed Jackson in a wild gamble of a flank march against a much larger Union army.

Although the attack was a major success, rolling up the entire Union line and foiling an otherwise excellent Union battle plan, Jackson himself was wounded while making a mounted reconnaissance one dark, rainy evening. Although at first his wounds seemed relatively slight, his left arm had to be amputated and pneumonia set in. On 10 May 1863 he died. His funeral procession was the highlight of an outpouring of grief from the entire South, for whom he was the single greatest hero of the war. Indeed, his reputation overshadowed Lee's throughout the war and for some years afterwards.

'In my humble opinion', wrote one of the privates who served under him in the 21st Virginia Infantry, which was not in the original Stonewall Brigade, 'the army never recovered from the loss of Jackson. There was something about Jackson that always attracted his men. It must have been faith. He was the idol of his old soldiers, and they would follow him anywhere.'[3]

Yet he often made enemies of other generals, being quick to press charges against those whom he thought to have failed in the execution of his orders. During one march he made A. P. Hill ride behind his division because of what Jackson felt was laxity and negligence. He lodged charges against Brigadier General Richard B. Garnett, soon to die at Gettysburg, still under a cloud, for what he felt were flaws in his performance at Kernstown. Indeed, his style had made him a number of high-ranking enemies in the Army of Northern Virginia.

One of his brigadier generals, Richard Taylor, felt that Jackson had 'an ambition as boundless as Cromwell's, and as merciless. This latter quality was exhibited in his treatment of General Richard Garnett...'[4]

If this were true, Jefferson Davis, admittedly not the best judge of men's characters, was quite fooled. 'He was not seeking by great victories to acquire fame for himself,' Davis wrote, 'but always alive to the necessities and dangers elsewhere, he heroically strove to do what was possible for the general benefit of the cause he maintained. His whole heart was his country's, and his whole country's heart was his.'[5]

But, in the end, it was R. E. Lee who felt his loss the most. 'It is a terrible loss,' he wrote his son Custis. 'I do not know how to replace him. Any victory would be dear at such a cost. But God's will be done.'[6]

Lieutenant General James P. Longstreet

'I was born in Edgefield District, South Carolina, on the 8th of January, 1821,' wrote James Longstreet after the war.[1] His father, who had prompted him towards a military career from an early age, died when Longstreet was twelve. Thereafter his mother moved to Alabama. In 1828 he was admitted to West Point, graduating 60th out of a class of 62 in 1842. At first assigned to the 4th US Infantry Regiment, he served in the 8th Infantry during the Mexican War, winning two brevets for gallantry.

When the Civil War broke out, Longstreet was serving in Albuquerque, New Mexico, as a staff paymaster with the rank of major. He sought service in the same role when applying for a Confederate commission in late June 1861, but instead was appointed a brigadier general on 1 July, in command of a Virginia brigade near Richmond.

'General Longstreet is an Alabamian — a thickset, determined-looking man, forty-three years of age,' wrote an English observer in 1863.[2]

One of his staff officers later wrote that he was: 'a superb horseman and with an unsurpassed soldierly bearing, his features and expression fairly matched; eyes, glint steel blue, deep and piercing; a full brown beard, head well shaped and poised. The worst feature was the mouth, rather coarse; it was partly hidden, however, by his ample beard.'[3]

Having served with notable success at the First Manassas, he was promoted to the rank of major general on 7 October 1861. 'General Longstreet was published yesterday as a major general,' one of his soldiers noted in his diary on 14 October. 'We thereby have lost from the command one of the best brigadiers in the army.'[4]

While his troops were encamped near Richmond, Longstreet's headquarters was known to his officers as a place where a friendly poker game was often in progress. The general was one of the better players and was known to share in whatever liquid refreshments were available. But after watching three of his children die in one week during an epidemic of scarlet fever in Richmond, he was never the same again. He gave up poker and whiskey for the comforts of the Episcopal Church, and one of his staff officers said that it was years before he became anything like his old cheerful self.

In late 1862, Longstreet was suffering from a sore heel caused by a chafing boot, and the discomfort was such that during the Battle of Sharpsburg he had to wear a carpet slipper, which put him in no good humour at all.

One year and two days after being named a major general, he was promoted to lieutenant general and given command of First Corps of the Army of Northern Virginia, with which he largely served. But he was absent from the corps at Chancellorsville, when his troops were foraging farther south, and again in late 1863.

Commander of the right wing at Gettysburg, his actions there involved him deeply in the greatest controversy of the Civil War. Those who excused Lee from the defeat generally blamed Longstreet, an easy target given his politics after the war, when he became a supporter of the Republican Party, the party of Abraham Lincoln.

Essentially, the argument against Longstreet was that he disagreed with Lee's taking the offensive at Gettysburg, which is indisputable, and therefore acted in a passive manner, dragging his heels and failing to attack, although ordered to do so, when he could have won the battle and, quite possibly, the war.

'The Confederate commander, upon his arrival on the field after the battle of July 1st was over, had immediately seen the great importance of Little Round Top,' wrote a Maryland officer. 'I saw him sweep the horizon with his glass, and noted that he scanned that elevation with great attention. Accordingly General Longstreet was ordered to move the next morning "*as early as practicable with the portion of his command that was up*, around to gain the Emmitsburg road on the enemy's left" [Longstreet's statement]. This order he took the responsibility of disobeying [by his own confession], preferring to wait till the last of his brigades was up; and so the movement which should have been made early in the day [his troops were bivouacked within four miles of the battle-field the night before] did not take place until four p.m. Thus the golden opportunity was lost which would have given Lee the key of the battlefield.'[5]

On the other hand, artillery commander Alexander C. Haskell wrote: 'Longstreet had been blamed greatly for the delay on the second and third days. I can't say how justly. But I well remember that on the second day we — the First Corps, which Longstreet commanded — got on the field by dawn and lay there until four o'clock when we were ordered to attack. About noon I remember that Lee and Longstreet rode up together and sat for half an hour on the very spot where my guns opened the fight at 4 p.m. At that time the infantry was a quarter of a mile of the position where they began fighting that afternoon, and I have never understood why, if General Lee wanted the fight to begin, what delayed it then. Surely he could have begun it, had he so desired.'[6]

The controversy raged after the war, fanned by those who wanted to protect Lee's reputation and had to explain such a defeat as Gettysburg, and by Longstreet's increasingly intemperate explanations in print of how Lee and not he was responsible for the battle. The truth, as usual, seems to lie somewhere between the two. Lee may well have wanted Longstreet to attack sooner than he did. Longstreet appears to have felt that the Confederates should not have attacked at all, but remmained on the defensive and let the enemy come to them. However, Lee's generally aggressive nature wouldn't have let him do that.

The result was that Longstreet did act in a passive manner, accepting Lee's orders, but insisting on waiting for the rest of his troops to come up. Lee, who rarely overruled any of his generals, allowed Longstreet to do this — and for this Lee must receive much of the blame for the attack. Haskell was, after all, right: Lee could have ordered Longstreet forward sooner, but failed to do so. And Longstreet was wrong; he should have obeyed his general implicitly and without delay, ordering his men forward with all rapidity.

The argument as to whether Longstreet were responsible for the defeat at Gettysburg did not surface until after the war, however. Lee does not appear to have changed his opinion of him from that which he showed at Sharpsburg. When Longstreet joined him after the battle, he walked up as Longstreet dismounted, threw his arms around him and, in a rare departure from his usual reserve, said, 'Here's my old war-horse at last.'[7]

After Gettysburg, Longstreet talked the authorities into sending him and his corps west to help clear Tennessee of Union forces. There he hoped to achieve his long-term goal, independent command. Instead, however, he was assigned under Braxton Bragg, one of the most hated general officers in the Confederacy. Nevertheless, Longstreet and his men fought very well at Chickamauga where they are often said to have made the difference between defeat and victory.

Unable to get along with Bragg, however, he got his corps sent off to a siege of Knoxville, Tennessee, to the mutual delight of himself and Bragg. But Bragg was driven off from his siege of Chattanooga, however, and Longstreet's corps was threatened. Unsuccessful in his attempt to take Knoxville, and badly threatened by the victorious troops at Chattanooga, Longstreet withdrew. He and his men were then returned to the Army of Northern Virginia. Thereafter, although he may still have desired independent command, he never said as much and served apparently happily under Lee's command.

Shortly after his return, while leading his men towards an assault during the Battle of the Wilderness (6 May 1864), he was severely wounded in the throat and right shoulder by fire from his own men of the 6th Virginia Infantry Regiment who had become separated from the main body of troops, now hidden by the heavy brush in that area. Well loved by his men, according to artillery commander E. Porter Alexander, 'Longstreet's fall seemed actually to paralyse our whole corps.'[8] The assault he was leading, planned for noon, was not made until four o'clock, and it failed.

He was not sufficiently recovered to be able to return to command until November, and his right arm was completely paralysed so that he had to write with his left hand, a handicap that lasted for some years. But he remained with his corps in the Army of Northern Virginia until its surrender.

After the war he settled in New Orleans. A friendship with U. S. Grant, whom he had known at West Point, brought him into the Republican Party, which gained him the enmity of his erstwhile Confederate comrades in arms. He served as minister to Turkey in 1880, then as commissioner of the Pacific railroads. On 2 January 1904 he died at Gainesville, Georgia, the last of the Confederate high command.

And the last of the high command of the Army of Northern Virginia, a man who had been closer to Lee than anyone — even the brilliant, but hard-to-warm-to Jackson. 'The relations between him [Lee] and Longstreet are quite touching — they are almost always together,' Fremantle later wrote.[9]

But a staff officer who admittedly was never close to him, later summed him up: 'The reputation that Longstreet had as a fighting man was unquestionably deserved, and when in action there was no lack of energy or of quickness of perception, but he was somewhat sluggish by nature, and I saw nothing in him at any time to make me believe that his capacity went beyond the power to conduct a square hard fight. The power of combination he did not possess, and whenever he had an independent command he was unsuccessful. A better officer to execute a prescribed movement, and make such variations in it as the exigencies of the battle required, it would be hard to find, but he needed always a superior mind to plan the campaign and fix the order of battle.'[10]

Lieutenant General Ambrose Powell Hill

Another career army officer and Virginia native, Ambrose Powell Hill, usually referred to as A. P. Hill, was born in Culpeper on 9 November 1825. He graduated from the US Military Academy in 1847, just in time for the Mexican War. He should have graduated a year earlier, but the first of a variety of illnesses that would plague him for the rest of his life, caused him to lose a year.

An artillery officer, Hill saw service against the Mexicans and then against the Seminoles in Florida. In 1855 he was transferred from the artillery to the staff of the Superintendent of the Coast Survey. He resigned his commission on 1 March 1861 and accepted a commission as colonel of the 13th Virginia Infantry, even though personally he was deeply opposed to slavery.

In June 1861 Hill saw some success under J. E. Johnston in Western Virginia before his regiment was sent to the main army in time for First Manassas. During the winter of 1861/2, while still a colonel, he was seen by a South Carolina artillery officer, who noted: 'Hill was a very pleasant, attractive man, quite good looking and rather dandified in his dress, which was always a blue blouse shirt of broadcloth, with very conspicuous insignia of his rank and a treble row of large gold buttons. He was a stylish horseman, always well mounted, and presented a very pleasing appearance. I don't think very much was expected of him beyond being a creditable soldier, but he was the next year appointed major general in command of the Light Division of Jackson's Corps, and made for himself and his command a brilliant reputation.'[1]

Indeed, on 26 February 1862 Hill was promoted to the rank of brigadier general. Under his command his troops achieved an admirable record in the Peninsula Campaign. They captured some 160 prisoners, eight guns and seven flags at the Battle of Williamsburg alone. Hill's next promotion, to major general, naturally followed rapidly, on 26 May, largely because of his excellent handling of his men.

More as a matter of morale than of tactics or weapons, he nicknamed his division 'The Light Division'. The unit lived up to the designation, serving with distinction under Stonewall Jackson. It performed quite well indeed at Cedar Mountain, and saved the day at Sharpsburg.

At Chancellorsville, after he was wounded, Jackson turned over command of his corps to Hill, a mark of his confidence in the man although earlier the two had quarrelled. Hill was wounded shortly thereafter, but returned to duty in time to be promoted lieutenant general on 24 May 1863 and receive, as his command, the new Third Corps of the Army of Northern Virginia.

'Hill was a West Point man of medium height,' a staff officer wrote. 'A light, good figure, and most pleasing soldierly appearance. He surely handled his division on all occasions with good ability and courage and justly earned high reputation. When Lee created the Third Army Corps he placed him in command of it, and it was thought that Hill did not realize in that high position all that was hoped of him.'[2]

Indeed, the first action of his corps was to open the Battle of Gettysburg, a battle to which Hill contributed little since he was ill during most of the campaign. As the battle was beginning Lee found Hill in an ambulance at Cashtown, several miles from his troops. In October 1863, according to a company-grade officer who served under him, Hill fought badly at Bristow Station: 'While we were here, Gen. Lee and Staff came up to a little knoll a few yards in front of our line. The General seemed to be in no good humor and casting a glance over the field thickly strewed with dead Confederates sharply called to Gen. Hill to send immediately for his pioneer corps to bury his unfortunate dead. Gen. Hill recognized a rebuke in the tone and manner of his commander and replied, "This is all my fault, General."

"Yes," said Lee, "it is your fault. You committed a great blunder yesterday; your line of battle was too short, too thin, and your reserves were too far behind." Poor Hill, he appeared deeply humiliated by this speech and no doubt wished that he could sink out of sight in the lowest depths of his capacious cavalry boots, and there hide his diminished head.'[3] In fact, he had ordered an assault on Federal positions at Bristow Station without adequate reconnaissance, an assault that cost his regiments more than 1,300 casualties with nothing to show for their efforts.

Nevertheless he continued as Third Corps commander, serving at the Wilderness and the 1864 campaigns and at the Siege of Petersburg. But his bouts of illness, which appear to have been at least partially psychosomatic, forced him to be away from his troops fairly often. He missed important days of action during the Wilderness. During the Siege of Petersburg, General John Gordon later recalled: 'The commanding general directed that I build a fort at the left of my line, and that A. P. Hill construct a similar one near it on the opposite of the run. General Hill became ill after the order was received, and the construction of his fort was not pressed.'[4]

Hill rose from yet another of his sick beds on 2 April 1865 personally to reconnoitre the point where Federal troops had broken through his line. Accompanied by a single orderly, the same sergeant, George W. Tucker, Jr., who later accompanied Lee to Appomattox Court House, he came across two lone Pennsylvania infantrymen. With drawn revolver, he prepared to ride them down and to force their surrender, but he was shot from his horse by one of them and died instantly.

Lieutenant General Richard Stoddert Ewell

Although born in the suburb of Washington in Georgetown, DC, his family moved to Prince William County, Virginia, when he was nine, so Dick Ewell was virtually a native of that state. He graduated from the US Military Academy in 1840, 13th in his class, a high enough standing to earn him a commission in the 1st Regiment of Dragoons. Awarded a brevet captaincy for his conduct in the Mexican War, he was a serving officer at the outbreak of the Civil War, on sick leave in Virginia.

Resigning his captain's commission on 7 May 1861, he was quickly awarded a Virginia lieutenant colonel's commission. Soon promoted, he was assigned to command a camp of cavalry instruction. His commission of brigadier general in the Provisional Army of the Confederacy was dated 17 June 1861.

After notable service at the First Manassas, he was promoted to the rank of major general on 24 January 1862. John Gordon met him during those early days of the war. 'General Ewell', he later wrote, 'had in many respects the most unique personality I have ever known. He was a compound of anomalies, the oddest, most eccentric genius in the Confederate Army. He was my friend, and I was sincerely and deeply attached to him. No man had a better heart nor a worse manner of showing it. He was in truth as tender and sympathetic as a woman, but even under slight provocation, he became externally as rough as a polar bear, and the needles with which he pricked sensibilities were more numerous and keener than porcupines' quills. His written orders were full, accurate, and lucid; but his verbal orders or direction, especially when under intense excitement, no man could comprehend. At such times his eyes would flash with a peculiar brilliance, and his brain far outran his tongue.'[1]

Ewell went on to serve as a divisional commander during the Valley Campaign. It was there that he again met the then Colonel Richard Taylor, whom he had known many years earlier. Taylor wrote of him: 'Bright, prominent eyes, a bomb-shaped bald head, and a nose like that of Francis of Valois, gave him a striking resemblance to a woodcock; and this was increased by a bird-like habit of putting his head on one side to utter his quaint speeches. He fancied that he had some mysterious internal malady, and would eat nothing but frumenty, a preparation of wheat; and his plaintive way of talking of his disease, as if he were some one else was droll in the extreme. His nervousness prevented him from taking regular sleep, and he passed nights curled around a camp-stool in positions to dislocate an ordinary person's joints. With all his oddities, perhaps in some measure because of them, Ewell was adored by his officers and men.'

Taylor went on to say: 'Subsequently, alleging that he had small opportunity for study after leaving West Point, he drew from me whatever some reading and a good memory could supply; but his shrewd remarks changed many erroneous opinions I had formed, and our "talks" were of more value to me than to him.'[2]

Ewell went on to command during the Seven Days, but was badly wounded in the knee at the Battle of Groveton in August 1862. His leg was amputated, but he recovered quickly and had an artificial leg fitted. But, as Taylor later recalled, 'His absence of mind nearly proved fatal. Forgetting his condition, he suddenly started to walk, came down on the stump, imperfectly healed, and produced violent haemorrhage.'[3]

He was none the less able to return to active duty, being given command of Stonewall Jackson's Second Corps on 23 May 1863. Before assuming command, however, the old bachelor married a widowed cousin, Lizinka Campbell Brown, whom he always called 'Mrs Brown'. His marriage, as well as his serious wound, apparently changed him. Gordon noted that, 'He no longer sympathized with General Early, who, like himself, was known to be more intolerant of soldiers' wives than the crusty French marshal who pronounced them the most inconvenient sort of baggage for a soldier to own.'[4]

Ewell became less aggressive; one staff officer noted that 'He entered the war a blunt, undevout soldier; he went out of it an earnest and humble Christian.'[5] His fighting qualities diminished, not so as much as to make him incompetent, but enough to make him less of a fighter than before – the difference was significant in the high command of the Army of Northern Virginia, already stricken by Jackson's death, and Lee and Hill's illnesses, and his decline was yet another element that contributed to the loss of the army's edge.

None the less, 'Old Bald Head' as his men called him, continued to command the corps through Gettysburg, where his lack of aggression on the first day's fighting was a major cause of defeat. Had he moved more quickly and aggressively against the troops holding the areas around Gettysburg itself and Culp's Hill, Lee would have been in a much better position to fight the battle.

Ewell served on until Spotsylvania Court House. E. Porter Alexander described him during this period as, 'Dear, glorious, old, one-legged Ewell, with his bald head, & his big bright eyes, & his long nose [like a woodcock's as Dick Taylor said].'[6]

He was twice wounded. At the Bloody Angle at Spotsylvania he took a heavy fall from his horse, which prevented his assuming any further field command. Lee had hoped that his injuries would be only temporary, wanting to 'replace him in command of his corps after the present occasion for extraordinary exertion shall have passed'.[7]

Although he was no longer serving with the Army of Northern Virginia, at Lee's request he was re-assigned to the command of the defences of Richmond. After the fall of that city, he fled west with the army, but was captured at the Battle of Sayler's Creek and imprisoned at Fort Warren, outside Boston, until his release on 19 August 1865. After the war, he retired to a farm near Spring Hill, Tennessee, where he died on 25 January 1872. He was buried in the Old City Cemetery in Nashville.

Lieutenant General Jubal Anderson Early

Born in Franklin County, Virginia, on 3 November 1816, Jubal Early graduated from the US Military Academy in 1837. He was commissioned as a lieutenant of artillery and sent to Florida to participate in the Seminole War. A year after his graduation he resigned to study law, being licensed in early 1840.

During the Mexican War Early served as a major in the Regiment of Virginia Volunteers which was stationed in northern Mexico. He saw little action, and became seriously ill with a cold and fever which led to a chronic rheumatic condition. This painful affliction caused him to walk with a stoop in his later years. Early, too, would enter Confederate service in less than tip-top physical condition.

Although he opposed secession as a delegate to the April 1861 Virginia convention, when the measure was passed he helped organize and arm three regiments, the 24th and 28th Virginia Infantry and 30th Virginia Cavalry Regiments in Lynchburg. He was assigned command of the 24th, which he led with distinction at the First Manassas.

As a result of this service, he was promoted to the rank of brigadier general on 21 July 1861. He led his brigade in the Army of Northern Virginia's 1862 battles, being promoted to major general on 17 January 1863.

'Of all the generals who made for themselves a reputation in the Army of Northern Virginia,' wrote staff officer Henry Kyd Douglas, 'there was none of General Lee's subordinates, after the death of General Jackson, who possessed the essential qualities of a military commander to a greater extent than Early. With a mind clear, direct, and comprehensive, his opinion was entitled to that respect which it always received from his Commanding General. Quick to decide and almost inflexible in decision, with a boldness to attack that approached rashness and a tenacity in resisting that resembled desperation, he was yet on the field of battle not equal to his own intellect or decision. He moved slowly from point to point, but had he possessed the personal *vie* and dash of General John B. Gordon, he would have escaped such severe censure in his misfortune [in the 1864 Valley campaign].

'Moreover, he received with impatience and never acted upon, either advice or suggestion from his subordinates. Arbitrary, cynical, with strong prejudices, he was personally disagreeable; he made few admirers or friends either by his manners or his habits, and those who defend him now do so because of his patriotism, of his earnestness, and of his great ability. If he had a tender feeling, he endeavored to conceal it and acted as though he would be ashamed to be detected in doing a kindness; yet many will recall little acts of General Early which prove that his heart was naturally full of loyalty and tenderness.'[1]

This seems to have been a generally accepted view of Early. Another staff officer, Moxley Sorrel, felt that he 'was one of the ablest soldiers in the army. Intellectually he was perhaps the peer of the best for strategic combinations, but he lacked ability to handle troops effectively in the field; that is, he was deficient in tactical skill. His irritable disposition and biting tongue made him anything but popular, but he was a very brave and able commander. His appearance was quite striking, having a dark, handsome face, regular features, and deep piercing eyes. He was the victim of rheumatism, and although not old was bent almost double, like an aged man. Of high scholarly and fine political attainments, he never married, but led the life of a recluse in Virginia, apart from social and public affairs.'[2]

Early played an important role at Salem Church and Gettysburg. He went on to serve as an acting corps commander of Hill's Corps for a short time during the Wilderness Campaign. When Ewell was forced to retire from active duty at that time, Early was assigned command of Second Corps and given the rank of lieutenant general on 31 May 1864. 'Early proved himself a remarkable corps commander,' E. Porter Alexander later wrote. 'His greatest quality perhaps was the fearlessness with which he fought against all odds & discouragements.'[3]

The high regard in which Lee held Early can be seen from the fact that Early was given Stonewall Jackson's old job of distracting the Federal forces from around Richmond by attacking north through the Valley of Virginia. He rapidly cleared the Valley and then turned east, towards Washington, DC. His veterans were met by a patchwork force of Ohio National Guard units and other garrison troops at Monocacy, Maryland, where the Union troops bought precious time to rush reinforcements, the Union VI Corps, from Petersburg to the capital city. Although Early won that battle, he reached the outskirts of Washington only a day before the Army of the Potomac men.

Outside Washington, in July 1864, he paused for a day, then decided not to take on that city's formidable works and retired whence he came. However, he did strike north again, sending cavalry to raid Chambersburg, Pennsylvania.

The dwindling resources of the South prevented any such further raids, while Grant was able to send a new army under fighting general Philip Sheridan against Early's outnumbered men. The Confederates were beaten at Winchester and then at Fisher's Hill. A counterattack at Cedar Creek started successfully enough, but revitalized Union forces were able to reform and retake their old ground from Early's tired Confederates. The remainder of Early's force was wiped out by Custer's troops at Waynesboro, Virginia, in March 1865.

Early managed to escape and on 30 March 1865 was ordered to turn over what remained of his command to Brigadier General John Echols and return to his home. After Lee's surrender, Early donned a disguise, fearing Northern retribution, and escaped to Mexico. Later he went to Canada before returning to Virginia to resume his law career. He spent most of his later life building the myth of the invincible Lee, especially in his capacity as first president of the Southern Historical Society, by putting much of the blame for Gettysburg on Longstreet. He died in Lynchburg on 2 March 1894.

Lieutenant General Richard Heron Anderson

It is perhaps noteworthy that the least important of the holders of the command of a corps or above in the Army of Northern Virginia, Richard 'Dick' Anderson, was also the only one who survived the war without injury or major disease.

Grandson of a Revolutionary War hero, Richard Anderson was also the only South Carolinian to command a corps in the Army of Northern Virginia. He was born in Sumter County, South Carolina, on 7 October 1821. He finished number 40 in the US Military Academy class of 1842 which numbered 22 Civil War generals from among 37 graduates living in 1861. After graduation he was commissioned as a lieutenant in the Dragoons, serving in the Mexican War as well as against the Indians in the west.

In December 1860, upon the secession of South Carolina, Anderson resigned his commission to accept the colonelcy of the 1st South Carolina Infantry Regiment, in which capacity he was present at the bombardment of Fort Sumter. He was awarded the rank of major in the regular army of the Confederacy on 16 March 1861. His volunteer rank of brigadier general, however, was awarded to him on 18 July, together with command at Charleston, South Carolina. In August he was moved to Pensacola, Florida, under Braxton Bragg.

He joined the army in Virginia in early 1862, fighting with distinction under Longstreet at Seven Pines, Gaines' Mills and Malvern Hill. On 14 July 1862 he was promoted to the rank of major general and given a division. 'Maj.-Gen. Richard H. Anderson, of South Carolina, had been a captain of cavalry in the United States Army, and was rather an interesting character,' wrote a staff officer. 'His courage was of the highest order, but he was indolent. His capacity and intelligence excellent, but it was hard to get him to use them. Withall, of a nature so true and lovable that it goes against me to criticize him. He served well as a brigadier general, and now with Longstreet, commanding a division, had more to do. Longstreet knew him well and could get a good deal out of him, more than any one else.'[1]

Anderson served in First Corps until Chancellorsville, after which he was transferred to Third Corps. It was in this corps, at the Wilderness, that Longstreet was wounded and Anderson took over his command. He received the temporary rank of lieutenant general on 31 May 1864. 'Gen. Dick Anderson was as pleasant a commander to serve under as could be wished, & was a sturdy & reliable fighter,' recalled artilleryman E. Porter Alexander.[2]

During the Wilderness fighting, Moxley Sorrel wrote, Anderson 'had shown commendable prudence and an intelligent comprehension of the work in hand. He was a very brave man, but of a rather inert, indolent manner for commanding troops in the field, and by no means pushing or aggressive. My relations with him were uniformly pleasant. He seemed to leave the corps much to his staff, while his own meditative disposition was constantly smoothed by whiffs from a noble, cherished meerschaum pipe in process of rich coloring. He was a short, thick, stocky figure, with good features and agreeable expressions.'[3]

After Longstreet's return, Anderson was transferred to a command of troops in the Richmond area. He and his men retreated with the bulk of the Army of Northern Virginia on the loss of Petersburg. His command was virtually destroyed at Sayler's Creek on 6 April 1865. He escaped and returned to Richmond. Since there was no command available for a general of his grade, he was relieved as being supernumerary on 8 April 1865.

His post-war career was not particularly successful; he was just capable of taking in enough money to live. At his death in Beaufort, South Carolina, on 26 June 1879, he was serving as 'state phosphate agent'.

Major General James Ewell Brown Stuart (Chief of Cavalry)

Stuart, whose initials formed the letters of his better known nickname 'JEB', was born in Patrick County, Virginia, on 6 February 1833 to an old and well-established local family. At the age of 15 he entered Emory and Henry College, but dropped out in 1850 to enter the US Military Academy. He was graduated 13th in a class of 46 in 1854 and was appointed to the Regiment of Mounted Rifles.

Stuart saw service with the regiment in the south-west, earning sufficient distinction to be one of a handful of specially selected officers to serve in one of the new cavalry regiments created in 1855. Stuart served as regimental quartermaster of the 1st Cavalry, but also saw action in the field against Indians on the frontier, being seriously wounded in 1857.

On 1 November 1855 he married Flora Cooke, only fourteen days after meeting her. She was the daughter of Colonel Philip St. George Cooke, 2nd Dragoons, who would later command Union cavalry serving against Stuart's Confederate cavalrymen in Virginia.

In 1859, while on leave in Washington, attempting to interest the War Department in a detachable sabre sling that could be used with any ordinary waistbelt, Stuart happened to get pressed into service to defeat the abortive slave uprising led by John Brown. Stuart, who had served as a cadet under Robert E. Lee at West Point, served as an aide to him at Harper's Ferry where the two got to know each other better.

Appointed captain in April 1861, Stuart nevertheless resigned his US Army commission on 10 May 1861 after Virginia left the Union. He quickly accepted the commission of colonel of the 1st Virginia Cavalry, then organizing at Harper's Ferry. According to one of his officers, 'He wore at this time his blue United States army uniform, and a forage cap covered with a white "havelock," resembling a chain helmet, which made his head resemble that of a knight of the days of chivalry; and at the head of his troopers, as they moved through the spring forests, he was a romantic figure.'[1]

Another of his officers, John Mosby, first saw him at this time: 'At the beginning of the war he was just twenty-eight years old. His appearance — which included a reddish beard and ruddy complexion — indicated a strong physique and great energy.'[2]

He led his 'Black Horse Cavalry' with distinction at the First Manassas, smashing the 11th New York 'Fire Zouaves' Infantry at a key point of the battle. For this service he was promoted to the rank of brigadier general on 24 September.

In charge of reconnaissance in the area between the Chickahominy and Totopotomoy Rivers during McClellan's advance on Richmond via the Peninsula, on 12 June 1862 Stuart led his command of 1,200 men on a route march that entirely circled the Union forces. His 100-mile ride around McClellan's some 100,000 men cost him only one casualty, a Captain Latane.

But later in the campaign his enthusiasm allowed his artillery to open prematurely on Union positions at Malvern Hill, which alerted Union forces to the pending Confederate assault. Despite this command error, he was promoted to the rank of major general and given command of the Army of Northern Virginia's Cavalry Division (later corps) on 25 July 1862.

Fitzhugh Lee, another leading Army of Northern Virginia cavalry general, summed Stuart up at this point in his career: 'His brilliant courage, great activity, immense endurance, and devotion to his profession had already marked him as a cavalry commander of unquestioned merit. He had the fire, zeal, and capacity of Prince Rupert, but, like him, lacked caution; the dash of Murat, but was sometimes rash and imprudent; was as skillful and vigorous as Frederick the Great's celebrated cavalry leader, and, like Seidlitz, was willing to break the necks of some of his men by charging over rough ground if he made bold horsemen of the rest and gained his object. He would have gone as far as Cardigan, with "cannon to the right of him, cannon to the left of him, cannon in front of him". He was a Christian [an Episcopalian] dragoon — an unusual combination. His Bible and tactics were his text-books. He never drank liquor, having given a promise to his mother to that effect when a small boy, but when wet from the storm and wearied from the march he would drink, without cream or sugar, the contents of a tin quart cup of strong coffee. Duty was his guiding star.'[3]

It could also be added that he appears to have been personally somewhat insecure, always looking for fame and fortune, always concerned that he might miss it. He was very much aware of what newspapers said about him, more so than any other Confederate general, and some of his military actions appear to have been influenced by the hopes of getting good press notices that would add to his fame and, he hoped, earn him further promotion.

At the same time, he affected a distinctive dress and personal style designed to make him stand apart from his peers and subordinates. His own uniform was decorated to the full extent, with gold Austrian knots on each sleeve and the full wreath and stars on each collar. His grey trousers, with two gold stripes up each leg, were tucked into tall boots whose tops came up well over his knees.

In the field, as did many mounted officers, he wore a waist-length jacket. But his jacket was double-breasted, cut so that it could be buttoned back to expose his grey vest, with a wide yellow sash always wrapped around his waist under his sword belt. Early in his career he gave up his forage cap and havelock, as did most of his men, and instead wore a tannish broad-brimmed hat with one side turned up and pinned back with a gold embroidered star. A long black ostrich feather and a gold and black hat cord and tassel further decorated the hat.

Evidence of his youthful and innovative mind can be seen in the weapons he accumulated during his Confederate service. He owned a rare Calisher & Terry carbine, a British-made breech-loading carbine, and a LeMat revolver. The last was a strange affair, designed by a New Orleans citizen but made in France, with a single shotgun barrel in the centre and a normal revolving cylinder around it, and a barrel for the cylinder above it. The shotgun load, combined with the revolver rounds, should have made the weapon an ideal cavalryman's piece, but production quality was poor. Indeed, when Stuart fought in his last battle, at Yellow Tavern, he was armed with a Northern-made 0.36-calibre Whitney revolver, which was a reliable and solid if not exciting weapon.

Jeb apparently saw himself in the role of the romantic knight. On his staff was a banjo player who was a constant companion. 'This peerless Chief of Cavalry,' wrote one of Jackson's aides, 'never quiet, never depressed, whistling on the battlefield, singing in camp, laughing and dancing in the parlor, when he approached our Quarters was generally heard afar off.'[4]

Stuart served exceptionally well during the Second Manassas and Sharpsburg campaigns, not only gathering intelligence but raiding the enemy's rear. At Fredericksburg he personally directed his horse artillery batteries on the right flank and helped stop the attack on Jackson's corps. His troopers then foiled Stoneman's raid and protected the route of Jackson's march during the Chancellorsville campaign. When first Jackson and then Hill were wounded during the last days of that battle, Stuart took over temporary command of Second Corps.

Stuart's luck began to turn on 9 June 1863, however. During a large review, which many thought vainglorious, Union troopers, finally trained to the point of being man-for-man equals of their Southern counterparts, struck at Brandy Station. Although the Confederates held their positions in this, the largest cavalry battle ever fought in North America, Stuart's reputation was badly damaged.

Smarting from the adverse criticism of his review, Stuart cut loose, being given only the most general orders by Lee during the following campaign that took the war into Pennsylvania. Although he did capture a large Union wagon train and essentially replicated his Peninsula Campaign feat of riding around the Union Army, he and his men were not at Lee's side in the opening hours of Gettysburg. The result for Lee was a lack of much-needed information about the Union forces — intelligence usually gathered by cavalry reconnaissance — which led to faulty decisions and a major defeat.

Thereafter Stuart never repeated the mistake of the Gettysburg campaign, but stayed close to the main body of the Army of Northern Virginia. But superior Union weapons, including multi-shot, breech-loading Northern carbines against single-shot Southern-made muzzle-loading carbines, combined with better fed and trained Union men and horses, had taken their toll. Never again would Stuart's cavalry be able to stand off Union cavalry of equal numbers.

He did rise to the occasion during the campaign along the Rapidan when reports from his cavalry allowed Lee to follow and anticipate Grant's moves. On 11 May 1864 Stuart led some 4,500 Southern troopers against a force of 12,000 Union cavalrymen, under Major General Philip Sheridan, who were approaching Richmond. The two forces met at Yellow Tavern, where Stuart was shot by a dismounted Union cavalryman.

He died next day, before his wife could reach his bedside, and was buried with full honours in Hollywood Cemetery at Richmond.

'General Stuart was a great cavalry commander, taking him all in all, the greatest the war produced, unless Forrest was his equal,' Kyd

Douglas later wrote. 'He was a great soldier but a born cavalryman, dashing, fearless, clearheaded, enterprising, brilliant. He held Lee in the greatest reverence; he admired and studied Jackson as no other man did; both of them had a personal affection for him. Fond of show and with much personal vanity, craving admiration in the parlor as well as on the field, with a taste for music and poetry and song, desiring as much the admiration of handsome women as of intelligence, with full appreciation of his own well-won eminence — these personal foibles, if they may be called such, did not detract from his personal popularity or his great usefulness. He could not fail, in many things, to remind one of Murat.'[5]

But Lee had the last word on Stuart, being quoted as having said to another Confederate cavalryman, Wade Hampton, years after the war: 'General Stuart was my ideal of a soldier. He was always cheerful under all circumstances; and always ready for any work, and always reliable.'[6]

Brigadier General William Nelson Pendleton (Chief of Artillery)

Born in Richmond on 26 December 1809, Pendleton graduated from the US Military Academy, fifth in the class of 1830. But his army career was brief; he resigned after only three years of service to go into teaching. His teaching career was equally short, because he was ordained a minister in the Protestant Episcopal Church in 1838. He gave up teaching altogether in favour of the ministry in 1847, being named rector of Grace Church in Lexington, Virginia, in 1853. Save for the four years of the Civil War, he stayed in this post for the rest of his life.

When the war broke out Pendleton, already 51 years old, was the captain of the Rockbridge Artillery, which had been organized on 12 April 1861. He was soon promoted colonel in command of what was to be the 1st Regiment (Pendleton's) of Virginia Light Artillery, but only two companies were ever assigned to the regiment which had been disbanded by early 1862.

In the meantime, Pendleton went on to serve on Joseph Johnston's staff as colonel and chief of artillery. On 26 March 1862 he was promoted to the rank of brigadier general and given command of the reserve artillery of what became the Army of Northern Virginia. He served in this rank and title throughout the war. He was not a particularly dynamic artillery officer, his skills being mostly administrative and organizational.

Indeed, Pendleton was not highly regarded by his younger, more active subordinates. E. Porter Alexander, who had little or no use for him, later wrote: 'He was too old & had been too long out of army life to be thoroughly up to all the opportunities of his position. But I never knew that Gen. Lee himself fully appreciated it, until I read the correspondence which Gen. Johnston published. Gen. Lee sends Gen.

Pendleton to inspect Johnston's artillery, & says that, "if he wishes, he may keep Gen. Pendleton as chief". But Gen. [Johnston] did not wish.'[1]

Staff officer Moxley Sorrel was a bit more generous: 'There was also a strong body of reserve artillery [in the Army of Northern Virginia] under command (and indeed he claimed some authority over the rest) of Brig.-Gen. W. N. Pendleton. This officer had graduated from West Point, had changed the uniform to the cassock and was rector of an Episcopal church in Western Virginia. He was an especial friend of General Lee, and leaving his pulpit brought a good battery to Jackson's command. A well-meaning man, without qualities for the high post he claimed — Chief of Artillery of the Army.'[2]

After Jackson's death, when the army was reorganized into three corps, Pendleton's command, that of the reserve artillery, was abolished. What Lee thought of him can be seen from a letter he wrote to Jefferson Davis on 15 June 1864 in answer to a question of whom to use to replace another Episcopal clergyman, General and Bishop Polk, who had recently been killed: 'As much as I esteem & admire Genl Pendleton,' Lee wrote, 'I would not select him to command a corps in this army. I do not mean to say that he is not competent, but from what I have seen of him, I do not know that he is.'[3]

However, Pendleton retained his brigadier's rank and at least the title of the army's Chief of Artillery. His duties were thereafter administrative, his only active command being of the small amount of ordnance kept in reserve at army headquarters. In this job he was successful, as organization was always his strong point. In March 1864 he went to Dalton, Georgia, to inspect Johnston's artillery, as Alexander mentioned, but he returned to Lee's army thereafter.

He never gave up his religious calling even in the field. He took the opportunity to hold Morning Prayer and similar services whenever he could to whatever body of troops he could, wearing, according to eye-witness Arthur Fremantle, a surplice over his uniform. [4]

After the war, he returned to Grace Church, where General Lee served as a member of the vestry when he was president of the nearby college. Pendleton was rector of the church when he died on 15 January 1883.

Lee's Generals

The individuals listed in the following table were commissioned into the rank of general officer and served in the Army of Northern Virginia at some time. As their commands were generally designated by their names, i.e., Kershaw's Brigade, knowing the dates of their commissions, and if anything happened to them, and when, is of use in tracking the army's organizational history.

Name	Brig Gen	Maj Gen	Lieut Gen	Notes
Alexander, E. Porter	26 Feb 64			
Anderson, George B.	9 June 62			Died 16 Oct 62
Anderson, George T.	1 Nov 62			
Anderson, Joseph R.	3 Sept 61			Resigned 19 July 62
Anderson Richard H.	16 Mar 61	14 July 62	31 May 64 (temporary)	
Archer, James Jay	3 June 62			Captured 1 July 63
Armistead, Lewis A.	1 Apr 62			Died 5 July 63
Barksdale, William	12 Aug 62			Killed 2 July 63
Barringer, Rufus	1 June 64			
Barton, Seth M.	11 Mar 62			Captured 6 April 65
Battle, Cullen A.	20 Aug 63			Wounded at Cedar Creek
Beale, Richard L. T.	6 Jan 65			
Beauregard, P. G. T.	1 Mar 61			General, 21 July 61
Bee, Barnard E.	17 June 61			Killed 21 July 61
Benning, Henry L.	17 Jan 63			
Branch, Lawrence O.	16 Nov 61			Killed 17 Sept 62
Brafton, John	6 May 64			
Brevard, Theodore W.	28 Mar 65			Captured 6 April 65
Bryan, Goode	29 Aug 63			Resigned 20 Sept 64
Butler, Matthew C.	1 Sept 63	19 Sept 64		
Chambliss, John R., Jr.	19 Dec 63			16 Aug 64
Chilton, Robert H.	16 Feb 64			
Clingman, Thomas L.	17 May 62			
Cobb, Howell	12 Feb 62	9 Sept 63		
Cobb, Thomas R.R.	1 Nov 62			Killed 13 Dec 62
Cocke, Philip St-G.	21 Oct 61			Suicide 26 Dec 61
Colquitt, Alfred H.	1 Sept 62			
Colston, Raleigh E.	24 Dec 61			
Conner, James	1 June 64			
Cook, Philip	5 Aug 64			Captured 2 April 65
Cooke, John R.	1 Nov 62			
Corse, Montgomery D.	1 Nov 62			Captured 6 Sept 65
Cox, William R.	31 May 64 (temporary)			
Cumming, Alfred	29 Oct 62			Transferred west
Daniel, Junius	1 Sept 62			Killed 12 May 64
Davis, Joseph R.	15 Sept 62			
Dearing, James	29 Apr 64			Died 23 Apr 65
Dibrell, George G.	26 Jul 64			
Doles, George P.	1 Nov 62			Killed 2 June 64
Drayton, Thomas F.	25 Sept 61			
DuBose, Dudley M.	16 Nov 64			Captured 6 Apr 65
Dunovant, John	22 Aug 64 (temporary)			Killed 1 Oct 64
Early, Jubal A.	21 July 61	17 Jan 63	31 May 64	
Echols, John	16 Apr 62			
Elliott, Stephen, Jnr.	24 May 64			

Name	Date commissioned			Notes
	Brig Gen	Maj Gen	Lieut Gen	
Elzy, Arnold	Aug 61	4 Dec 62		
Evans, Clement A.	19 May 64			
Evans, Nathan G.	21 Oct 61			
Ewell, Richard S.	17 June 61	24 Jan 62	23 May 63	Captured 6 Apr 65
Field, Charles W.	Mar 62	12 Feb 64		
Fomey, William H.	15 Feb 65			
Fry, Birkett D.	24 May 64			
Gadand, Samuel, Jnr.	23 May 62			Killed 14 Sept 62
Gamett, Richard B.	14 Nov 61			Killed 3 July 63
Gary, Martin W.	19 May 64			
Godwin, Archibald C.	5 Aug 64			Killed 19 Sept 64
Goggin, James M.	4 Dec 64			Captured 6 Apr 65
Gordon, James B.	28 Sept 63			Died 18 May 64
Gordon, John B.	1 Nov 62			14 May 64
Gregg, John	29 Aug 62			Killed 7 Oct 64
Gregg, Maxcy	14 Dec 61			Died 15 Dec 62
Grimes, Bryan	19 May 64			15 Feb 65
Hagood, Johnson	21 July 62			
Hampton, Wade	23 May 62	3 Aug 63	14 Feb 65	
Harris, Nathaniel H.	20 Jan 64			
Hays, Harry T.	25 July 62			
Heth, Henry	6 Jan 62	17 Feb 64		
Hill, Ambrose Powell	26 Feb 62	26 May 62	24 May 63	Killed 2 Apr 65
Hill, Daniel Harvey	10 July 61	26 Mar 62	11 July 63	
Hoke, Robert F.	17 Jan 63	20 Apr 64		
Holmes, Theophilus H.	5 June 61	7 Oct 61	10 Oct 62	
Hood, John Bell	3 Mar 62	10 Oct 62	20 Sept 63	General (temp), 18 July 64
Huger, Benjamin	17 June 61	7 Oct 61		Relieved 12 July 62
Humphreys, Benjamin G.		12 Aug 63		
Hunton, Eppa	9 Aug 63			Captured 6 Apr 65
Imboden, John D.	28 Jan 63			
Iverson, Alfred, Jnr.	1 Nov 62			
Jackson, Thomas J.	17 June 61	7 Aug 61	10 Oct 61	Died 10 May 63
Jenkins, Micah	22 July 62			Killed 6 May 64
Johnson, Bradley T.	28 June 64			
Johnson, Bushrod R.	24 Jan 62	21 May 64		
Johnson, Edward	13 Dec 61	28 Feb 63		
Johnston, Robert D.	1 Sept 63			
Jones, David R.	17 June 61	10 Mar 62		Died 15 Jan 63
Jones, John M.	15 May 63			Killed 5 May 64
Jones, John R.	23 June 62			Captured 4 July 63
Jones, William E.	19 Sept 62			Killed 5 June 64
Kemper, James L.	3 June 62	19 Sept 64		
Kershaw, Joseph B.	13 Feb 62	18 May 64		Captured 6 Apr 65
Kirkland, William W.	29 Aug 63			

Name	Date commissioned			Notes
	Brig Gen	*Maj Gen*	*Lieut Gen*	
Lane, James H.	1 Nov 62			
Law, Evander M.	2 Oct 62			
Lee, Fitzhugh	24 July 62	3 Aug 63		
Lee, George W. C.	25 June 63	20 Oct 64		Captured 6 Apr 65
Lee, Robert Edward	14 May 61			General, 14 June 1861
Lee, Stephen D.	6 Nov 62	3 Aug 63	23 June 64	
Lee, William H. F.	15 Sept 62	23 Apr 64		
Lewis, William G.	31 May 64			Captured 7 Apr 65
Lilley, Robert D.	31 May 64			
Lomax, Lunsford L.	23 June 63	10 Aug 64		
Long, Armistead L.	21 Sept 63			
Longstreet, James	17 June 61	7 Oct 61	9 Oct 62	
McCausland, John	18 May 64			
McComb, William	20 Jan 65			
McGowan, Samuel	17 Jan 63			
McLaws, Lafayette	25 Sept 61	23 May 62		
MacRae, William	22 June 64			
Magruder, John B.	17 June 61	7 Oct 61		
Mahone, William	16 Sept 61	30 July 64		
Martin, William T.	2 Dec 62	10 Nov 63		
Moody, Young M.	4 Mar 65			
Moore, Patrick T.	20 Sept 64			
Morgan, John T.	16 Nov 63			
Paxton, Elisha F.	1 Nov 62			Killed 3 May 63
Payne, William H. F.	1 Nov 64			
Peck, William R.	18 Feb 65			
Pegram, John	7 Nov 62			Killed 6 Feb 65
Pender, William D.	3 June 62	27 May 63		Died 18 July 63
Pendleton, William N.	26 Mar 62			
Perrin, Abner M.	10 Sept 63			Killed 12 May 64
Perry, Edward A.	28 Aug 62			
Perry, William F.	21 Feb 65			
Pettigrew, James J.	26 Feb 62			Killed 14 July 63
Pickett, George E.	14 Jan 62	10 Oct 62		
Posey, Carnot	1 Nov 62			Died 13 Nov 63
Pryor, Roger A.	16 Apr 62			Resigned 18 Aug 63
Rains, Gabriel J.	23 Sept 61			
Ramseur, Stephen D.	1 Nov 62	1 June 64		Died 20 Oct 64
Ransom, Matt W.	13 June 63			
Ransom, Robert, Jnr.	1 Mar 62	26 May 63		Retired, autumn 63
Roberts, William P.	21 Feb 65			
Robertson, Beverly H.	9 June 62			Relieved, summer 63
Robertson, Jerome B.	1 Nov 62			
Rodes, Robert E.	21 Oct 61	May 63		Killed 19 Sept 64

Name	Date commissioned			Notes
	Brig Gen	Maj Gen	Lieut Gen	
Rosser, Thomas L.	28 Sept 63	1 Nov 64		
Sanders, John C.C.	1 May 64			Killed 21 Aug 64
Scales, Alfred M.	13 June 63			
Semmes, Paul J.	11 Mar 62			Killed 2 July 63
Simms, James P.	8 Dec 64			Captured 6 Apr 65
Smith, Gustavus W. —		19 Sept 61		Resigned Jan 63
Smith, William	31 Jan 63	12 Aug 63		
Sorrel, Gilbert M.	27 Oct 64			
Stafford, Leroy A.	8 Oct 63			Killed 5 May 64
Starke, William E.	6 Aug 62			Killed 17 Sept 62
Steuart, George H.	6 Mar 62			
Stevens, Walter H.	28 Aug 64			Chief Engineer,
Stuart, James E. B.	24 Sept 61	25 July 62		Killed 11 May 64
Taliaferro, William B.	4 Mar 62			
Terrill, James B.	31 May 64			Killed 30 May 64
Terry, William	19 May 64			
Terry, William R.	31 May 64			
Thomas Edward L.	1 Nov 62			
Toombs, Robert A.	19 July 61			Resigned 4 Mar 63
Toon, Thomas F.	31 May 64 (temporary)			Reverted Aug 64
Trimble, Isaac R.	9 Aug 61	17 Jan 63		
Walker, Henry H.	1 July 63			
Walker, James A.	15 May 63			
Walker, John G.	9 Jan 62	8 Nov 62		
Walker, Reuben L.	18 Feb 65			
Wallace, William H.	20 Sept 64			
Weisiger, David A.	31 May 64			
Wharton, Gabriel C.	8 July 63			
Wickham, William C.	1 Sept 63			Resigned 9 Nov 64
Wilcox, Cadmus M.	21 Oct 61	3 Aug 63		
Winder, Charles S.	1 Mar 62			Killed 9 Aug 62
Wise, Henry A.	5 June 61			
Wofford, William T.	17 Jan 63			
Wright, Ambrose R.	3 June 62			
York, Zebulon	31 May 64			

4
Lee's Staff

'THERE IS', WROTE ARTILLERYMAN E. PORTER ALEXANDER, 'A need of an abundance of competent staff officers by the generals in command. Scarcely any of our generals had half of what they needed to keep a *constant & close supervision on the execution of important orders*. And that ought always to be done. An army is like a great machine, and in putting it into battle it is not enough for its commander to merely issue the necessary orders. He should have a staff ample to supervise the execution of each step, & to promptly report any difficulty or misunderstanding.'[1]

The regulations themselves were fairly vague as to how many officers that should be. According to them: 'Staff officers and officers of engineers, and artillery, according to the nature of the service, are assigned to the headquarters of armies and divisions, and detached brigades, by order of the general commanding-in-chief, when the distribution of these officers has not been regulated by the War Department.'[2]

Lee himself preferred a small personal staff. When he assumed command of the Army of Northern Virginia only Walter Herron Taylor had served him from the beginning. Taylor was born on 13 June 1838 in Norfolk, Virginia. In 1852 he became a cadet at the Virginia Military Institute, but was forced to drop out during his junior year when his father died during an epidemic of yellow fever. Thereafter he went into finance, working as an auditor for the Norfolk and Petersburg Railroad and later as an officer of the Bank of Virginia.

Taylor had been a member of a Norfolk militia unit before the war broke out. He was commissioned as a lieutenant in the 3rd Virginia Infantry when Virginia left the Union. On 2 May 1861 he was promoted captain and assigned to Lee's staff, a position he never relinquished. He was promoted to major on 31 December 1861, and he received his final promotion to lieutenant colonel on 7 October 1863.

Initially Taylor's title was that of aide-de-camp, but he was much more than that, performing many of the functions of a military secretary and adjutant. At first Lee simply distributed papers to all his staff every morning at a staff meeting, telling each one what to do. These were often rather vague instructions, Lee depending on the judgement of his hand-picked personal staff officers. For example, according to Charles Venable, one of his personal aides, 'Written complaints of officers as to injustice done them in regard to promotion he would sometimes turn over to an aide-de-camp, with the old-fashioned phrase: " 'Suage him, Colonel, 'suage him," meaning thereby that a kind letter should be written in reply.'[3]

It soon became apparent that the system whereby Lee was his own chief of staff was quite inefficient, so he appointed Taylor to funnel all documents to the appropriate staff officers. Taylor was named acting assistant adjutant general in the spring of 1863, the 'acting' part of it soon being omitted.

His duties included not only the writing of reports and dispatches but the screening of documents and would-be visitors to Lee. According to Taylor, Lee 'had a great dislike to reviewing army communications: this was so thoroughly appreciated by me that I would never present a paper for his action, unless it was of decided importance, and of a nature to demand his judgment and decision.'[4]

Taylor was also responsible for handling the monthly strength returns, and, blessed with a near photographic memory, he assumed responsibility for many of the myriad details of running the army.

On Lee's surrender, while the other staff officers left the army at Appomattox to go home, Taylor accompanied Lee back to Richmond before returning to Norfolk.

When Lee took over the army from Johnston all Johnston's staff officers quit save Captain Arthur Pendleton Mason, a Virginian, who was serving as an assistant adjutant general. Lee, however, created only a small staff to replace them. 'His staff was small and efficient,' Moxley Sorrel later wrote. 'Four majors [afterwards lieutenant-colonels and colonels] did his principal work. Walter Taylor, from the Virginia Military Institute, was adjutant-general, and better could not be found for this important post.

'Charles Venable, a scholar and mathematician, and with some study of strategy, together with Charles Marshall, a distinguished lawyer by inheritance from his ancestor, the Chief Justice, and his own attainments, did much of the correspondence under dictation. Talcot [sic] was the engineer officer, and Long, of the old US Army, a close friend of the General, was ranked as military secretary and did various duties. At a later date Brig.-Gen. R. H. Chilton, A.A. G., was assigned to confidential duties with the General, and was sometimes called chief of staff. But Lee really had no such chief about him. The officer practically nearest its duties was his extremely efficient adjutant general, W. H. Taylor.

'Maj. H. E. Young was also attached later — an excellent officer. There were possibly one or two young lieutenants for personal aids [sic], but this was Lee's staff, although perhaps I have made some omissions. Of course it does not include the important administrative officers like Cole, chief commissary; Corley, chief quartermaster; Doctor

Guild, medical director, and his chiefs of ordnance and other organizations.'[5]

On 4 June 1862, the War Department assigned Robert Hall Chilton to Lee, and Lee actually did name Chilton the army's chief of staff, although the English visitor Colonel Fremantle in June 1863 believed that he was introduced to him as the army's adjutant general. Indeed, no one performed the duties expected of a modern chief of staff.

Chilton was born in Loudoun County, Virginia, on 25 February 1815. A member of the US Military Academy class of 1837, he had served gallantly in the Dragoons in Mexico, actually saving Jefferson Davis's life at Buena Vista, before switching to the Pay Department in 1854. On quitting the US Army, he was commissioned a lieutenant colonel in the Regular Confederate Army's Adjutant and Inspector General's Department. It was as such that he was assigned to Lee's Army.

Chilton was soon promoted to the rank of colonel and should easily have been promoted to brigadier general, but in his position as chief of staff he had clashed with a number of Lee's field commanders, notably Brigadier General John B. Magruder. Their influence caused the senate to reject Chilton's nomination which would have ranked from 20 October 1862. He was finally confirmed in that rank on 16 February 1864.

Chilton continued in his position until April 1864 when, at his own request, he left Lee's field headquarters to operate as the army's inspector general out of Richmond. He also held a brief combat command in May 1864 in the defence of Richmond. Although he did well in this fight along the Richmond & Petersburg Railroad, he returned to the inspector general's post which he held until the war's end.

Armistead Lindsay Long, mentioned by Sorrel as one of Lee's pre-war friends from the US Army, was born in Campbell County, Virginia, on 3 September 1825. He was an 1850 graduate of the US Military Academy, serving in the artillery until resigning on 10 June 1861 to join the Confederate Army. He was commissioned a major of artillery in that army.

His first service was in Western Virginia on the staff of Brigadier General William Loring before being sent to join Lee's staff in Charleston, South Carolina, as his military secretary. In fact, he often performed the duties of the army's chief of artillery, since General Pendleton was found somewhat wanting.

Performing well in that activity, he was promoted to brigadier general and on 21 September 1863 was assigned command of Second Corps' artillery which he held until the end of the war.

Charles Scott Venable, a Virginian, was Lee's third personal aide. Considered brilliant by his peers, Venable spent much of his time on inspections for Lee's headquarters. His entire military career was spent on Lee's staff, and he ended the war as a lieutenant colonel.

Charles Marshall, the sole staff officer to accompany Lee when he met Grant at Appomattox Court House, was another Virginian, but he had been a lawyer in Baltimore before the war. His strong point was writing, and Lee made much use of him to draft and write dispatches, reports and orders. It was he who drafted the famous farewell address of Lee to the Army after Appomattox, General Order Number 9, Lee only striking out one paragraph, which he said could lead to continued hard feelings between North and South, and making a few other minor changes.

Thomas Mann Randolph Talcott was a fellow engineer officer and son of one of Lee's old friends, Colonel Andrew Talcott, who was also an engineer. He served as an aide-de-camp on joining the army in June 1862, but was promoted to lieutenant colonel on 4 April 1864 and given command of a newly formed engineer regiment.

Finally, the only other officer who lived with and shared the table at Lee's headquarters from the beginnning was Captain Mason. The sole survivor of Johnston's command, he left early in 1863 to rejoin Johnston who had recuperated sufficiently to resume command.

As officers like Mason and Talcott left his personal staff, Lee replaced them gradually, chosing members of the overall Army headquarters staff. But eventually he did add other staff members. Major Henry B. McClellan, who was Stuart's adjutant when the general was killed, served as one of Lee's aides after Stuart's death. Major Giles Buckner Cooke became an assistant adjutant general on Lee's staff in November 1864 and served until the war's end. Others who ended up serving Lee personally, having come from headquarters, included Major Henry Edward Young (a South Carolinian who was later the army's judge advocate general) and Major Henry E. Peyton. Lieutenant Colonel Edwin J. Harvie joined Lee's staff in June 1862, but soon left to rejoin Johnston's staff. Colonel George W. Lay served during March 1863. And Lieutenant Colonel Edward Murray served from 30 December 1862 to 31 August 1863 and then again in November 1864.

This relatively small personal staff led a simple life at Lee's headquarters. He generally refused to take shelter in buildings near the army, preferring to set up seven or eight tents, with the three or four wagons used to carry them and headquarters luggage nearby. Lee and the staff were accompanied by several slaves who performed household duties such as cooking, and some mounted enlisted men who served as couriers. Lee carried relatively little personal baggage, only an iron-framed camp-bed and a set of tin messware, which all the staff shared, together with trunks for clothing and camp equippage. Each staff officer was allowed only one trunk for his own kit. Lee's aides slept two men to a tent. Indeed, in West Virginia, before joining the

Army of Northern Virginia, Lee and Taylor shared a single tent. The slaves and couriers had no tents, but found shelter in and under the headquarters wagons.

Lee's headquarters was marked by a cotton bunting first national flag, measuring 79 by 48½ inches. Nine five-pointed stars were arranged in an arc in the canton, with the letter 'A' being formed by four stars placed between the first and second stars from the bottom — the whole forming the 'arc of the covenant'.

The broader staff of the Army of Northern Virginia was made up of the heads of its various non-combatant arms. These officers did not generally live near Lee's headquarters, staying instead where they could be of more use to their various departments. These department chiefs were the Chief of Ordnance, Chief Commissary, Chief Quartermaster, Medical Director, Chief of Artillery, Judge Advocate General and Chief Engineer. The posts were filled by: Lieutenant Colonel Edward Porter Alexander, Chief of Ordnance until November 1862 when he was replaced by Lieutenant Colonel Briscoe Gerard Baldwin; Lieutenant Colonel Robert Granderson Cole, Chief Commissary; Lieutenant Colonel James Lawrence Corley, Chief Quartermaster; Surgeon Lafayette Guild, Medical Director; Brigadier General William Nelson Pendleton, Chief of Artillery; and Major Henry Edward Young, Judge Advocate General.

The post of Chief Engineer was filled by Colonel Jeremy Francis Gilmer from 4 August 1862 to 4 October 1862; Lieutenant Colonel William Proctor Smith in the summer of 1863, save for the Gettysburg Campaign when the post was held by Captain Samuel Richards Johnston; Major General Martin Luther Smith from 16 April 1864 to July 1864; and Brigadier General Walter Husted Stevens, in June-July 1862 and again from August 1864 until the war's end.

Lee considered these officers and their assistants of great importance in running his army, more so than his own personal staff. On 21 March 1863 he wrote to President Davis that the overall staff structure should be reorganized. 'Our armies are necessarily very large in comparison with those we have heretofore had to manage. Some of our divisions exceed the army General Scott entered the City of Mexico with, and our brigades are larger than his divisions. The greatest difficulty I find is in causing orders and regulations to be obeyed. This arises not from a spirit of disobedience, but from ignorance. We therefore have need of a corps of officers to teach others their duty, see to the observance of orders, and to the regularity and precision of all movements. This is accomplished in the French service by their staff corps, educated, instructed, and practiced for the purpose. The same circumstances that produced that corps exist in our own Army. Can you not shape the staff of our Army to produce equally good results? Although the staff of the French army is larger than that proposed by

Senate bill, I am in favor of keeping ours down, as it is so much easier to build up than to deduct if experience renders it necessary. I would therefore assign one general officer to a general commanding an army in the field, and give to his inspector-general, quartermaster-general, commissary-general, chief of ordnance, and medical director the provisional grade of colonel of cavalry. I would reduce his aides and give to his chief of staff and inspector-general assistants, or they will never be able to properly attend to their outdoor and indoor work, which from the condition of our Army, as before stated, is very heavy. I would apply the same principles to the division and brigade staff, placing their chiefs on an equal footing and giving each a complete organization in itself, so that it can maneuver independently of the corps or division to which it is habitually attached and be detached with promptness and facility when required. Each, therefore, in addition to its general staff, should have a surgeon, quartermaster, commissary, and ordnance officer. If you can then fill these positions with proper officers, not the relatives and social friends of the commanders, who, however agreeable their company, are not alway the most useful, you might hope to have the finest army in the world.'[6]

While the central government did not act on Lee's suggestion until a new staff organization — virtually the same as he had described — was adopted on 29 April 1864, Lee went ahead and ordered basically this staff system in the Army of Northern Virginia during the winter of 1862/3.

Officially, the new staffs authorized by General Order No. 44 authorized an army staff to include a senior assistant adjutant and inspector general and an assistant adjutant and inspector general, each ranking no higher than a colonel and each being assisted by two assistant adjutant and inspector generals, one a lieutenant colonel and the other a major. One of these two was especially to examine court-martial records. Also there were to be a surgeon, acting as medical drector, with another surgeon as his assistant, and another surgeon as a medical inspector.

A corps was authorized a senior assistant adjutant and inspector general and an assistant adjutant and inspector general, ranking no higher than lieutenant colonel. Each one was aided by an assistant adjutant and inspector general ranking no higher than a major. There was also a surgeon to serve as medical director and inspector.

A divisional staff was to include a senior assistant adjutant and inspector general and an assistant adjutant and inspector general, each ranking no higher than major, and a surgeon as chief surgeon and inspector who was in charge of the divisional field infirmary.

Each brigade staff was allowed an assistant adjutant and inspector general of captain's rank; a brigade quartermaster and a brigade commissary, each of major's rank; a surgeon serving as brigade surgeon and inspector, who was to be in charge of the field infirmary as well as acting as regimental surgeon.

Each general officer was allowed two aides-de-camp, except brigadier generals who had only one. Cavalry divisions and brigades were authorized an extra assistant adjutant and inspector general, ranking no higher than major.[7]

This system was revised by legislation approved on 14 June 1864 which created the final staffs. Lee was to be assisted by another general officer whose job was army administration, together with two assistant adjutants general, a chief quartermaster, a chief of ordnance, and a chief commissary, all of whom ranked as colonels. The medical director was a surgeon who ranked as a colonel, while Lee was also authorized two aides-de-camp, one ranking as a colonel and the other as a lieutenant colonel.

Each corps commander rated two assistant adjutants general ranking as colonels; a chief of ordnance, a chief quartermaster, and a chief commissary, each ranking as a lieutenant colonel; a surgeon who was the medical director and ranked as a lieutenant colonel; and two aides-de-camp, one ranking as a lieutenant colonel and the other as a major.

Each divisional staff included two assistant adjutants general, ranking as lieutenant colonels; a chief of ordnance, a chief quartermaster, a major, and a chief commissary, each ranking as a major, and two aides-de-camp, one a major, the other a captain.

The brigade staff included two assistant adjutants general and an assistant inspector general and a surgeon, all ranking as majors; an ordnance officer and an aide-de-camp ranking as captains; and an aide-de-camp ranking as a first lieutenant.[8]

During battle both Lee's personal staff and the Army staff had different tasks to perform. Lee described their activities in his report on the Battle of Fredericksburg: 'To the officers of the General Staff, Brig Genl Robert H. Chilton, Adjutant & Inspector General, assisted by Major Peyton, Lieut Col Corley, Chief Quartermaster; Lieut Col Cole, Chief Commissary; Surgeon Guild, Medical Director, and Lieut Col Briscoe G. Baldwin, Chief of Ordnance, were committed the care of their respective departments, and the charge of supplying the demands upon each. They were always in the field, anticipating as far as possible the wants of the troops.

'My personal staff were unremittingly engaged in conveying and bringing information from all parts of the field. Col Long was particularly useful before and during the battle in posting and securing the artillery, in which he was untiringly aided by Captain Samuel R. Johnston of the Provisional Engineers; Majors Talcott and Venable in examining the ground and the approaches of the enemy; Majors Taylor and Marshall in communicating orders and intelligence.'[9]

Corley, a South Carolinian, also had responsibility for the disposition and safety of the army supply wagons, which contained the clothing, equipment and even some foodstuffs. Indeed, although he was not responsible for the commissary's department, Lee specifically mentioned that Corley was responsible for getting corn to Jackson in the Valley in November 1862.[10] Corley was also responsible for regulating the order in which the wagon trains were to move when the army was on the march.

Baldwin, a Virginian and 1848 graduate of the Virginia Military Insitute, was not only responsible for issuing smallarms and ammunition, and keeping these in good repair, but for gathering ordnance from the battlefield for repair and reissue.

Army staff officers also had to liaise between the army and Confederate Army headquarters departments in Richmond. For example, on 15 August 1863 Lee sent Baldwin to Colonel Josiah Gorgas, Confederate Army Chief of Ordnance, to consult with him on the need of smallarms and, he hoped, obtain some that were in storage in Charleston for distribution to the Army of Northern Virginia. In much the same way, Cole was sent to Richmond on 8 February 1865 to try to get some meat, he having been obliged to report to Lee that none was on hand for issue to the weary, battleworn troops.

These staff officers in charge of departments also had their own staffs. Lee had a habit of getting rid of officers he considered inefficient, either posting them out west or to static posts farther south. It is a clear indication of the value in which he held his staff department officers, as well as his personal staff officers, that they tended to stay in their positions until the war ended, unless they had been promoted to higher commands.

It is therefore sad to note that after the war Baldwin, who moved to Texas, and Corley both suffered bouts of what was called insanity and finally committed suicide, perhaps victims of the Post Traumatic Stress Disorder syndrome which claimed the happiness and even the lives of so many Confederate veterans.

Finally, staff officers received the pay of cavalry officers holding the equivalent rank. As of 6 March 1861, general officers were paid $301 a month, while a brigadier general's aide-de-camp received $35 a month in addition to his lieutenant's pay.[11] Higher ranks were recognized with pay increases on 10 June 1864 when the monthly pay of a general was set at $500; of a lieutenant general $450; of a major general $350. Lee, as a general commanding an army in the field, received an extra $500 a month, while all other generals received an extra $50 a month when serving in the field.[12]

5
Lee's Soldiers

The Nature of Lee's Army

Armies reflect the societies from which they are created. The society out of which came Lee's Army was largely agrarian, rural, with relatively little education, and not a great deal of social intercourse with individuals beyond their immediate spheres. As a rule, before the war Southern states did not have systems of public education as did Northern states, so schooling was of mixed quality and quantity.

The men who would go into the Army of Northern Virginia were largely of British descent and Protestant. In Virginia and South Carolina the Protestant Episcopal Church had been the established church and a large number of officers and men from those states were members of that church. Presbyterians predominated in large parts of North Carolina and other areas, such as Charleston, South Carolina, where Scottish/Irish had settled. Roman Catholics came also from cities such as Charleston, and from Louisiana, but they made up only a small minority of the army. Larger cities presented a small number of Jews, but there were even fewer of them than of Roman Catholics.

In fact, there were relatively few city men in the army at all. Most soldiers came from small farms, often miles from any city. Over the years, inefficient agricultural methods such as not rotating crops had rendered the soil so poor in many areas that it would not support large farms or plantations. Farmers simply got enough out of the soil for their own basic needs with a small amount left over to sell.

Although the issue of slavery prompted the split between North and South, few of these farmers — adherents of slavery in fact if not conciously — were actually slave owners. Among those who were, most only owned one or two field hands. Almost half of all individuals who reported owning slaves owned five or fewer slaves. The type of soldier who left 'Tara' of *Gone With The Wind* fame was very rare.

In fact, only 385,000 families owned slaves, out of a white population in the slave states of 1,516,000 families. In Virginia and North Carolina, whence a great proportion of the army's troops were drawn, only a quarter of all families owned slaves in 1860. There were proportionately more slaveholders in the states that rebelled first, with some two-fifths of the families in Georgia holding slaves and a third of those in Alabama, Louisiana and Florida with slaves. And, of course, in South Carolina, where secession began, about half the families owned slaves. But the majority of soldiers in the Army of Northern Virginia did not come from families that had a direct personal stake in the right to own slaves.[1]

Men of the South had been raised to consider themselves the equal of any man — which was one of the reasons why they had so much disdain for the blacks whom they saw as having allowed themselves to become enslaved and therefore could not be wholly human. The white Southerner was proud of himself and of his heritage. He had been brought up on tales of how a rag-tag American 'Continental' army, untrained in the sophisticated ways of 18th-century warfare, had beaten one of the world's finest standing armies, the British Army, in the Revolution and earned independence for its countrymen. He was well aware that a Virginian, George Washington, led that army, supported by such men as Virginia's Daniel Morgan.

The people who lived in the wilderness exhibited different traits from city dwellers. Rural Southerners were good shots for the most part, having hunted all their lives. They were good riders and could handle horses. They could live on relatively poor rations.

At the same time, they were more vulnerable to such childhood diseases as mumps and chickenpox than city children. Having been used to living alone or in small groups and families, they were used to fending for themselves, and discipline did not come naturally; they had to be convinced of its importance, and this was never wholly achieved, much to the dismay of leaders such as Lee.

In the years before the war, Southerners of all walks of life were becoming increasingly concerned about what they saw as a tendency of Northerners to interfere in their business. They felt uneasy in the presence of Northerners, most of whom tended to be quite different from their own comfortable crowd. Northerners were city people, often from different European countries such as Germany, many of whom who were educated and much better off than the Southerners. Many came from suspect religious backgrounds, ranging from Unitarians to Jews. They were louder, quicker in speech and action, less friendly, apparently overly concerned with such notions as fashion, and the getting and spending of money.

Some of these Northerners came South as teachers, unconsciously flaunting their better education. Some were lawyers, who are rarely loved no matter what they do. Many were merchants, another rarely loved group, who bought what products Southerners had to sell at prices Southerners felt were too low. What was worse, these merchants were the only source for many goods that Southerners needed but did not produce themselves; ranging from agricultural equipment such as ploughs down to less important items such as pins and photographic chemicals. For a people who took pride in their independence, having to acquire goods from people of a wholly different culture was difficult to swallow.

So when groups of Northerners began speaking out loudly about the South's 'peculiar institution', slavery, Southerners grew defensive, even if they owned no slaves themselves. After all, slavery was the major thing which set the South apart from the North — indeed, from most of the civilized world, Brazil being the only major exception.

But at the bottom of it all, it was not the issue of slavery for which the average officer or enlisted man went to war. In fact, after some years of abolitionist propaganda, most of them felt at least some discomfort about the subject and some felt guilty. What really motivated them was their tremendous pride in their own land and what they and their fathers had achieved, combined with a general dislike of Northerners stemming from most superficial knowledge of the real people who inhabited the northern states.

So it was that when slavery was threatened, and Southern leaders spoke out against the threatening of their own cherished rights, Southerners from all walks of life drew together in opposition to the North. When Northerners such as John Brown, leading his abortive slave insurrection, threatened some Southerners, they threatened all Southerners, and it was easy to get them all to band together.

In many areas defence organizations were already in place. For example, in Richmond there were a number of volunteer militia companies that had been formed years before the war. These included the Richmond Light Infantry Blues, which had been formed in 1793; the Richmond Light Dragoons, of 1807; the Richmond Fayette Artillery, of 1824; and the Richmond Greys, of 1844. Georgia's Liberty Independent Troop, of Liberty County, was first organized in 1791. In South Carolina, the Charleston Ancient Battalion of Artillery was organized in 1756 and the city's German Fusiliers traced their history back to 1775, while the newer Scottish Union Light Infantry was organized in 1807.

Many more such volunteer militia units were formed as the prospect of war became ever more imminent. Indeed, after John Brown's hanging in 1859, volunteer militia companies filled up all over the South, and new ones were formed. These companies, old and new, were made up of local citizens who had time enough to spend on weekly drill and money enough to acquire uniforms, at least in the more formal organizations where uniforms were authorized. Weapons and equipment were usually, although not always, supplied by the various states.

The units were usually, but not necessarily, authorized by the various states. At times they would be included in paper militia organizations, sometimes up to divisional level, which allowed the state's governor to appoint various generals and their staffs. However, the units rarely if ever came together to drill as integrated organizations.

They held their own drills, designed their own uniforms, and participated in their own events.

For the most part these paper organizations were largely quickly forgotten when war broke out. Some volunteer companies quickly disappeared as volunteers discovered that they were too old for active service or joined other volunteer companies. None the less, in the year 1852, whose figures were closest available to those of 1860, there were some 736,000 members of various militia organizations in the states that went on to make up the Confederacy.[2] These men would form the bulk of the Confederacy's initial forces; in all, the number of men who served in the Confederacy's armed forces about equalled that number, although the exact figure is unknown and subject to much debate.

Then, in 1860, the new Republican Party, a Northern-based political party, nominated Abraham Lincoln from Illinois as its presidential candidate. Today Lincoln would be considered a moderate. Although he never called for the abolition of slavery, he did not want it to spread to western territories.

Working on the principal that one step against slavery would lead to its eventual total outlawing — and the eventual destruction of the entire Southern way of life — Southerners began to feel that if Lincoln were elected the only way their society would survive would be to leave the Union. And there was precedent for such a move, at least on paper. Some years previously, South Carolinian John C. Calhoun had declared that each state that came into the Union should agreed to its laws only if its own laws and way of life were protected, and if that condition were violated, the Union between state and general government should be dissolved.

'No one now not living at the time, can realize the excitement that prevailed throughout the south, immediately following the election of Lincoln to the presidency, in the fall of 1860,' Texas volunteer John W. Stevens later wrote. 'The secession of South Carolina followed very soon after, which spread from state to state until in due course of time, the whole slave section of the Union had taken similar action. Excitement was at white heat, the public mind was soon wrought up to such a pitch that every man had to align himself with the secession movement or stand as an enemy of the South. A middle ground status was impossible.'[3]

So it was that volunteer companies, either pre-war or organized when war broke out, offered their services to state governors. These companies were gathered at major posts, usually outside urban areas, where the governors had them organized into regular regiments. Then the regiments were placed into state service and from there taken into service as volunteer Confederate regiments.

The Confederate government also authorized a Regular Confederate Army, to include both officers and enlisted men. However, the regular officers who served with the Army of Northern Virginia served either as generals and other officers of volunteers, or as officers of Engineers. No regular army enlisted men served in the Army of Northern Virginia, which meant that the Army was virtually a wholly volunteer force.

The initial volunteer force did not need to seek recruits. These were men who had joined volunteer companies, elected their company-grade officers, and then gone on to their initial camps where they were organized into full regiments. Their field officers were largely appointed by state governors, often from the group of men who had resigned US Army commissions to return to their own states. Many, however, were local citizens who may have had some military training, perhaps as volunteers in the Mexican or similar war or in a pre-war volunteer company. Or they may simply have been local civic leaders.

Recruiting

It was readily apparent that the initial volunteer militia companies would not serve to fend off the might of the volunteer armies that the Union's President Lincoln called for to restore the nation. Therefore, the Confederate Army began recruiting additional men from the beginning. On 6 March 1861 Congress called for an army of no more than 100,000 men with one-year enlistments. After the First Manassas showed that the war was apt to be long and bloody, another 400,000 volunteers were requested.

After the initial force of pre-war volunteer militia companies had taken the field, the units that would replace and augment them were to be formed by individuals organizing units among their friends and neighbours, either from pre-war volunteer units or as wholly new units. Under a Congressional act dated 8 May 1861, the President was authorized to commission individuals directly to recruit regiments, squadrons, battalions or companies. The individual had only a provisional commission until his unit reached minimum numbers; he had two months in which to muster enough men to fill a company and four months for a larger organization.[1] Indeed, this was the most common method of creating and filling the initial Confederate Army units.

Once set up, these units began losing men almost immediately, usually more to disease than to the enemy, although, of course, battles like First Manassas took their toll. Some way of keeping units up to regulation strength was required. The system that Congress set up for doing this, on 19 December 1861, called for each regiment and independent battalion, squadron and company to detail a subaltern and an enlisted man to be stationed for recruiting purposes in the area where the organization was raised. Each recruiting party was so detailed for a period of no longer than 30 days, after which they had to return with their recruits to their parent organizations.[2]

An example of how this would work can be seen from the notes of a commander of a battery in Louisiana's Washington Artillery. In December 1862, he recalled, 'Sargeant [sic] J. R. McGoughy and myself were detailed to proceed to Jackson, Miss. and there to establish head-quarters for recruits.

'In Summit, Mississippi, I secured several recruits. Some New Orleans friends were located at this point. Time's up! Back to old Virginia!'[3]

Going further, the Confederate Congress authorized the recruitment of men from slave states outside the Confederacy — Kentucky, Missouri, Maryland and Delaware — as early as 30 August 1861.[4] Delaware never furnished more than a handful of men to the Confederacy, but the other states provided a hard core of some of the South's best fighting men. Virtually all Maryland's volunteers ended up in Lee's Army, not only in Virginian regiments, but also in units that served with the state name and under its flag.

After the first wave of volunteer units, which were taken into the new army for only one year's service, new units were to be recruited for three years or for the duration of the war. Also recruits for the units that had volunteered for only one year were only taken if they accepted a term of three years or the duration.

On 28 January 1863 the Army published its official regulations which changed the recruiting system from one in which each unit took care of its own needs to an army-wide system under the direction of the Adjutant and Inspector General's Department. According to the regulations, the country was divided into recruiting districts, each under command of a field-grade officer. These officers would set up recruiting stations at important towns with a team of personnel at each station. The team consisted of the station commander, a lieutenant, a non-commissioned officer, two privates, a drummer and a fifer. The latter, parading through the town, attracted potential recruits.

According to the regulations, recruiters were to accept:, 'Any free white male person above the age of eighteen and under thirty-five years, being at least 5 feet 4½ inches tall, effective, able-bodied, sober, free from disease, of good character and habits, and able to speak and understand well the English language.[5] Recruits under 21 had to have the written consent of a parent, guardian or master. On 27 September 1862 Congress raised the upper age limit to 45.

The age requirement was often ignored. For example, 15-year-old Frank Mixson was turned down as under age by Colonel Johnson Hagood when he tried to join the colonel's 1st South Carolina Volunteers in April 1861. A couple of months later, however, feeling left out of things, according to Mixson, 'I went to Charleston and over to the Regiment and joined Company I, commanded by Capt. J. J. Brabham, in which my brother, J. S. Mixson, was First Lieutenant. When Hagood saw me down there he again ordered me home, and I told him I had already joined. Besides, if he drove me away I would go somewhere else and join. He let up, and I was happy beyond measure.'[6]

Not only was young Mixson allowed to join although under age, but his story suggests that his recruiting was against all regulations in that he apparently never received a medical examination. According to the initial Act of 19 December 1861, every new recruit was to be examined by a commissioned Confederate Army, or Navy surgeon or assistant surgeon before he joined a unit. Army regulations spelled out that: 'In passing a recruit the medical officer is to inspect him stripped; to see that he has free use of all his limbs; that his chest is ample; that his hearing, vision, and speech are perfect; that he has no tumors, or ulcerated, or extensively cicatrized legs; no rupture or chronic cutaneous affection; that he has not received any contusion, or wound of the head, that may impair his faculties; that he is not a drunkard; is not subject to convulsions; and has no infectious disorder, nor any other that may unfit him for military service.'[7]

A cicatrix was a scar over a healed wound or ulcer; hence cicatrized legs would show healed scars. Why healed wounds in the legs would prevent service is not readily apparent, but most likely officials were concerned that a network of extensive scars might hide weak, previously broken bones or badly healed ulcers.

Within six days of being recruited, the new Confederate soldier was to have been read, and have had time to consider, the 20th and 87th Articles of War. The 20th Article called for the punishment of death for desertion, while the 87th Article said that the death penalty had to be approved by at least two-thirds of the members of the general court-martial which tried the offender.

If the recruit was acceptable to the surgeon and he still wanted to join, even knowing the possible punishment if he decided to desert, he was sworn in by a commissioned officer. The oath he took read: 'I, A—- B—-, do solemnly swear or affirm (as the case may be), that I will bear true allegiance to the Confederate States of America, and that I will serve them honestly and faithfully against all their enemies or opposers whatsoever, and observe and obey the orders of the President of the Confederate States, and the orders of the officers appointed over me, according to the rules and articles for the government of the armies of the Confederate States.'[8]

Initially, little more than patriotism — aided by many women who taunted those who did not rush to the colours — was sufficient to keep the army by and large up to authorized strength. After the first year's glow of successes, however, recruiting slowed down. In order to encourage recruiting, the Confederate Congress authorized a $50 bounty and a furlough of no more than 60 days to each enlisted man who enlisted for three years or the duration of the war as of 11 December 1861. This included not only new recruits, but men who had enlisted for twelve months originally but now re-enlisted for the full term.[9]

At first there was some question as to when this money should be paid. After all, if the men got their money in a lump sum when they initially joined, might they not desert immediately, perhaps to enlist again elsewhere, under a different name? The men, on the other hand, wanted the money at once, both to serve present needs and perhaps aware of the shoddy way the Continental Congress had treated their grandfather veterans of the Revolution, who received only worthless paper certificates when they were finally discharged. Congress gave in to the wishes of the men as of 17 February 1862, authorizing payment immediately after each man passed his physical examination. Also, each civilian or soldier who brought in a recruit who was accepted was authorized a two dollar bounty.

By July 1861 the entire Confederate Army mustered some 112,040 officers and men, of whom 33,752 were in the Armies of the Potomac and Shenandoah, the force which formed the nucleus of what became Lee's Army.[10] At about the same time, however, the Union Army had on its rolls a total of 152,354 officers and men, of whom 43,284 were threatening northern Virginia.[11] With an army one-third again as large as that fielded by the Confederacy — 10,000 more in the Virginia area alone — the Union should be able to prevail easily. Moreover, the Union still had a large number of recruits coming forward, encouraged, to be sure, by even larger bounties than those offered by the Confederacy, but good men none the less. Something had to be done.

The initial move was to repair the folly of accepting enlistments for only one year. Many of the units that had come into the Confederate Army in the early months of 1861 were getting ready to go home by 1862. Of course, 30- and even 60-day furloughs, as authorized by Congress, and the bounty were offered to every man who would re-enlist for the rest of the year. While a fair number did re-enlist, many more felt that they had done their duty and prepared to muster out and let others take over the defence of the Confederacy. After all, they'd won the major battles, Richmond was apparently safe, and there was spring planting to do.

But Congress was well aware that there weren't enough men available to take over the South's defence, and in particular there were not sufficient men with the training and seasoning that these men had received. So, on 16 April 1862, Congress extended the service of all its men in the field, tacking another three years, unless the war ended sooner, to their enlistments. To make their lives a bit easier, however, the men were given a further option. They were free to elect new officers to their units; so they often got rid of officers who enforced discipline, choosing ones who were popular instead. Also, they were entitled to the bounty and furlough. The result was to place the army in a state of virtual chaos during the opening months of 1862, mostly in about April in Lee's Army.

But Congress did more than simply retain the army they had in the field. They also resorted to something that every defender of states' rights had to hate — mass conscription by the general government.

Despite protests, they allowed the President to place any man who could pass the physical examination and was not exempt from military service for any other reason into the army or navy for a term of three years. Conscripted men were allowed to produce a substitute, usually hired for the purpose, which would get them out of serving themselves.[12] Substitution quickly became a whole new business. Most substitutes at first received about $150 in Confederate paper currency, or $50 in gold, from their hirer. Their price soon soared as the manpower pool diminished. By the end of 1862 prices of $1,000 were commonplace, while a year later substitutes were demanding and getting about $4,000, and payments of as much as $10,000 were not unknown.

Even compared to the evils of substitution, conscription proved a mixed blessing at best. Immediately it brought in a flood of volunteers who wished to avoid being stigmatized with the label of 'conscript'. On the other hand, many others spent much time trying to avoid the draft which could have been more profitably spent supporting the war effort. Large bands of men who had fled their homes to avoid the draft gathered in encampments in areas such as northern Alabama and western North Carolina. These men terrorized local inhabitants since they supported themselves largely by robbery.

There was also a legal way of avoiding the draft for those who did not want to leave their homes but could not afford to hire substitutes. Telegraph operators had been exempted from military service by the central government even before conscription went into effect. The states were given quotas of men to fill, and they were free to exempt from conscription pretty well anyone they pleased — at least at first. For example, on 7 March 1862 South Carolina listed the following types of men as not liable to conscription: members of both branches of the general assembly; the state secretary of state, surveyor general, and comptroller general; ordinaries; court clerks; masters, commissioners, and registers in equity; clergymen; doctors; the faculty of incorporated colleges and seminaries; schoolmasters of 20 or more students; students under 18; branch pilots; one white man per each ferry, toll bridge, and toll grain mill; the president, cashier, and a teller from each bank; policemen in Charleston and Columbia; most of the fire departments of those cities; railroad company employees; state military officers and cadets; the superintendent and keeper of the lunatic asylum; Confederate government office-holders; and aliens.[13] And, this is a relatively short list. In states like Georgia, where the Governor really resented general conscription and made life difficult for Confederate conscription officials, even more men managed to get exemptions.

Eventually the general government got many of the exemptions removed, but only with much difficulty and never completely. State governors fought their every move. For example, wrote War Department Clerk J. B. Jones, 'Gov. Vance is furious at the idea of conscripting magistrates, constables, etc. in North Carolina. He says it would be an annihilation of States Rights — nevertheless, being subject to militia duty by the laws of the State, they are liable under the Act of Conscription.'[14]

In October 1862 the upper limit for exempt men was raised to 45 years of age. 'This', wrote War Department Clerk Jones, 'will furnish, according to the Secretary's estimate, 500,000, after deducting the exempts. A great mistake.'[15]

Resistance to conscription came from two sources, state governments and the people themselves. Judge Richmond Person, the chief justice of North Carolina, ruled that the law was unconstitutional, and this ruling led, Confederate government officials believed, to a large number of desertions from troops of that state — troops who made up a large percentage of Lee's Army. 'The local judiciary are doing what they can to defeat the conscription and encourage desertion in many places, especially Georgia, North Carolina and Tennessee,' wrote the head of the Confederate Bureau of War on 20 May 1863. 'These states have the largest infusion of dissatisfaction, the former source of Unionism, a great deal of faction, and the two latter any quantity of Reconstructionism [a movement urging the re-entering of the Union]. I mistrust that these feelings have a good deal to do with these decisions by which they thwart and obstruct the execution of the conscription.'[16]

The result was that far too often, once the initial rush of volunteers had joined up to avoid being conscripted, and those who did not wish to serve in the military had made arrangements to avoid the draft through other means, legal or otherwise, conscription did not produce the number of men needed. War Department Clerk Jones wrote in his diary in March 1863 that one conscription call in Eastern Tennessee enrolled 25,500 men, but produced only 6,000 new soldiers.[17] By mid-July the head of the Bureau of War had noted in his diary 'The prospect for recruiting our wasted armies is very poor. The conscription up to 40 is about exhausted. Between 40 and 45 it will not yield probably over 50,000 men and will take 6 months to get them out. We are almost exhausted.'[18]

Finally, all too often the men who finally were drafted were not the best material needed by the army. Indeed, on 13 October 1862 Clerk Jones noted that 'Gen. Lee does not want any more raw conscripts. They get sick immediately, and prove a burden instead of a benefit. He desires them to be kept in camps of instruction, until better *seasoned* (a term invented by Gen. Wise) for the field.'[19]

For all of this, conscription filled a real need. Wrote Colonel John Mosby afterwards, 'The conscription law increased the numbers but impaired the *esprit de corps* of the volunteer army that won the victory of Manassas — the flower of Southern manhood that had been gathered there. But the law saved the Confederacy from the danger of collapse without another battle through the disbandment of its army. After the war I heard severe criticism of the Conscription Act which, in fact, saved the Confederacy — for a time.'[20]

Even so, Lee also had great problems in assigning conscripts within his army. He wanted to place them in units that needed men; they demanded to be assigned to units that had been recruited, and were posted, near their homes. 'The evil complained of is greater in South Carolina than in any other State, though it exists to some extent in all,' he wrote to Jefferson Davis on 19 January 1864. 'The South Carolina regiments in this army are much reduced by hard service, and it has been found impossible to recruit them, principally, if not entirely, on account of the encouragement given to men to volunteer in regiments engaged in the defense of the Department of South Carolina, Georgia, and Florida, and the measures adopted in that department to retain conscripts.'[21]

Finally, even with conscription, bounties and extending the terms of the original volunteers, Lee was never able to recruit his army to the level he needed. On 23 August 1864, with less than eight months of life left to his army, he wrote to the Secretary of War: 'The subject of recruiting the ranks of our army is growing in importance and has occupied much of my attention. Unless some measures can be devised to replace our losses, the consequences may be disastrous.' Time was growing short, he was all too aware. 'Our numbers are daily decreasing, and the time has arrived in my opinion when no man should be excused from service, except for the purpose of doing work absolutely necessary for the support of the army. If we had here a few thousand men more to hold the stronger parts of our lines where an attack is least likely to be made, it would enable us to employ with good effect our veteran troops. Without some increase of our strength, I cannot see how we are to escape the natural military consequences of the enemy's numerical strength.'[22]

It was a problem that was never solved.

The Officer Corps

Initially, units coming into what became Lee's Army elected their own officers. This made total sense to all concerned; after all, if in a democracy one elects one's political leaders, why not one's military leaders also? And, generally, those who were elected had some credentials for the job, either previous military experience or education or social position.

Mississippi's militia at the outbreak of the war, for example, called for a biennial election for all militia officers, including general officers. These elections were typical of militia organizations throughout the USA prior to the Civil War, although in some areas officers had to submit to further screening. In Louisiana, for example, officers had to pass an examination by a board of state officers. The captains appointed by South Carolina's governor, he reported, had all but one been veterans of the Mexican War or were US Military Academy graduates, while lieutenants were either state military academy graduates, Mexican War veterans, or especially qualified civilians.

The Confederate Congress realized that it would have to base its own field forces on volunteer units already in existence, so in March 1861, when it authorized the acceptance of volunteer units into its army, it specifically stated that the officers of these units would be appointed according to the various state laws rather than a national law.[1] On the other hand, officers of the Regular Confederate Army were to be appointed by the President with the advice and consent of the Congress.[2] Regimental staff officers were also to be appointed by the President.

In May 1861, when Congress authorized the recruitment of a larger army than had been thought necessary, it called for Presidential appointments for all field as well as staff officers, while company-grade officers were still to be elected by the men they were to command. However, an additional proviso was added; the company-grade officers once chosen had to be 'acceptable' to the President or his representatives.[3]

For the most part, such an additional force was to be created by individuals who had been promised commissions of a specific rank in exchange for recruiting sufficient men to fill their units. However, regulations spelled out that even these individuals had to stand for election in their new units. Naturally, individuals who brought in personnel for a unit could generally expect to be elected to their command, and for the most part this is exactly what happened. There were, none the less, a few examples of individuals who had organized units, only to be rejected as commanders by the vote.

Generally the new units were organized as companies, commanded by captains. The army would then organize the new companies into regiments or battalions. The President was then authorized to appoint the regimental field and staff officers. These would-be officers came to the President's attention through the lobbying of congressmen or governors, or through their own attempts to get noticed. Throughout the war a fair number of men essentially hung around the government buildings hoping to attract the attention of some political leader who could obtain a commission for them.

Some early volunteer companies gathered themselves into regimental organizations while still in their states. Then usually the company-grade officers would elect the field-grade officers.

On 31 August 1861, Congress made further changes to the appointments process. As of that date, it provided that officers on a general's staff could be appointed directly from civilian life on the request of that general, with the President's approval. Also, regimental adjutants could be appointed at the colonel's request.[4]

While obtaining the President's approval for a commission sounds rather formidable, the actual process was often not complex at all. For example, John Mosby, before the war a college student and in 1861 a cavalry private, later recalled: 'I had scarcely reached our camp when a message came from the commander of the regiment, Colonel Jones, to come to his tent. I went, and he offered me the position of adjutant. I was as much astonished as I had been the night before to be asked to sit at the table with generals. Of course I was glad to accept it, and Jones wrote to the War Department requesting my appointment. The Journal of the Confederate Senate shows that I was confirmed to take rank from February 17, 1862.'[5] In much the same way, an Englishman, who had come to the South to fight her battles, served as a volunteer in Purcell Battery when he received a first lieutenant's commission. 'I learned afterwards that Willie Pegram had been so good as to recommend my appointment on account of my behaviour at Mechanicsville,' he wrote, 'and his recommendation was vigorously sustained by his uncle, Captain Robert B. Pegram, and my Navy friends. The Confederate government had no power to appoint company officers for the volunteer forces; and for this reason I did not receive a commission in the line. My appointment was under an Act of the Confederate Congress, which authorized the appointment of forty First Lieutenants of Artillery for assignment to duty as Ordnance officers.'[6]

When the army was reorganized in early 1862, all officers faced new elections. Even those who had been appointed by the states, under state laws, had to be elected to their posts in the Confederate Army. Naturally, many of those who had been stern disciplinarians, but otherwise excellent officers, were booted out of the army, much to their disgust, and the disgust of many of the better of their fellow officers.

'There may have been inefficient officers in the army, and doubtless there were, but they could have been gotten rid of in other ways,' complained an officer who had lost his post in his company's election. 'To introduce the element of democracy into an army, and to strike down numbers of the best men in it, was an injury to the morale of the troops they never got over. If one set of officers had become unpopular by establishing discipline and had been turned out by a reorganization, why might not another set be served in the same way in the future? The lesson was taught: Keep in with your men, whatever the consequences, if you don't want to be turned out some day. The officer felt that he owed his place to certain of the men who voted for him, and these men felt they had made him an officer. Could anything have been more destructive to discipline?'[7]

Indeed, this was a major revolution that turned Lee's Army in the field upside down. Some 155 field officers in about 200 infantry regiments failed to be re-elected.[8] This meant that during early 1862 about three-quarters of Lee' infantry regiments had at least one important command change, involving the replacement of an experienced field officer by one new to the job.

None the less, most officers were apparently sufficiently qualified for their jobs. Out of some 1,763 individuals who served in the rank of colonel in Lee's Army, only 72 had been professional soldiers before the war, but 157 had attended the Virginia Military Institute; 78, the US Military Academy; 40, the South Carolina Military Academy; 16, the Georgia Military Academy; four, the US Naval Academy; and one, the LaGrange Military Academy.[9]

Even so, some men who had managed to obtain commissions were found, after some service, to be clearly unsuitable; incompetent, too old or infirm for active field service, or with personality problems. In May 1862, therefore, the army set up a procedure to get rid of its undesirables. An officer accused of being in this group was to go before a board of no less than three officers of equal or superior rank who would question him and report back to the War Department.

One sentence of the order which set up these boards officially, at least, finally formalized the method by which all officers would obtain their commissions. It stated that the order creating the boards would 'apply to all persons not yet commissioned or recognized as in commission by the Department'.[10] In other words, individuals seeking commissions had to have board approval to obtain them.

What were the qualifications needed to hold a Confederate commission? According to orders issued in the Western Department on 6 May 1862, which did not differ significantly in their requirements from those of the army in Virginia, each board was to ensure all officers were 'to be of good physical and mental ability and of fair moral character. All field officers must be able to maneuver or drill a battalion in the "school of the battalion", and be found acquainted with the Articles of War and the Army Regulations touching their duties, especially in the camp, on the march, and on outpost service, as prescribed from these headquarters. And all company officers must be able to drill a company in the "school of the company" and "soldier", and be acquainted with the duties of a company officer and officer of the guard, as prescribed in the Army Regulations.'[11]

Moreover, as of 13 October 1862, the Army was given not only the authority to get rid of its deadweight officers, but also the ways to detect them on a regular basis. Congress ordered monthly reports on every officer to be sent to the War Department. These were to include such information as periods of absence, for whatever reason, occasions when the officer had been especially efficient, or when he had been held to be negligent and inattentive to his duties.[12]

The Congressional Act that set the system of efficiency reports in motion also called for officer examining boards to get rid of officers with continuously poor reports. And it put a stop to the business of unit elections by ordering that a vacancy be filled by the officer next in rank, if competent, or, if not, by the officer next below. And if there were no competent officers, the President would appoint an officer to fill the position.

In August 1863 Lee himself issued orders flatly forbidding elections of even junior second lieutenants, and requiring that field officers whose competence was in question be examined by such a board.[13] By that time, and thereafter, officers generally were being commissioned from the ranks, usually for valour or special skills. However, by law, if a vacancy occurred, these men were only allowed to be promoted within their own unit, and could not be promoted out of the unit.

'This limits the promotions for valour & skill to such an extent that it renders the law almost a dead letter,' Lee wrote to the Secretary of War on 8 February 1864. 'I would earnestly recommend that if this is the true interpretation of the law that it be modified so as to permit promotions on this account to any company or regiment from the same State, or at least to any company in the regiment to which the private or officer belongs. It is very important to increase the number of these promotions and to render them more certain.'[14]

Such a letter merely continued the process which had been evolving, that of making a truly national Confederate Army officers' corps, rather than a collection of state officers under a general overall command. This did not sit well with state governors, of course. They tended to consider all troops raised within their states as part of their militia and therefore officers' commissions should be awarded by them. 'It is mortifying', North Carolina's Governor Vance told his legislature in November 1862, 'to find entire brigades of North Carolina soldiers in the field commanded by strangers, and in many cases our own brave and war-worn colonels are made to give place to colonels from distant States, who are promoted to the command of North Carolina troops over their heads to vacant brigadierships.'[15]

The question of state vs. general government commissions was never resolved to everyone's satisfaction, but on the whole Lee's Army had become, after several years in the field, an efficient selector of the best qualified officers, who were generally promoted from the ranks.

There was, however, one final source of commissioned officers into Lee's Army, and that was through the Corps of Cadets. Originally, cadets were to be stationed at a military school, such as the Corps of Cadets of the US Military Academy at West Point. But there was no such school available, nor would there be one throughout the war, so instead each cadet was attached to an army unit in the field as a supernumerary officer, usually on the commander's staff. Each received the pay, and wore the uniform, of a second lieutenant.

On 7 April 1863, it having become obvious that no suitable military academy would be set up during the war, it was ordered that once a cadet reached the age of 21 he was to be examined by a board of officers in his branch of service. If he passed the examination he would be commissioned as a second lieutenant. If he failed he would be sent home. Once commissioned, successful officers were promoted in the normal way, up to the highest rank of general. Company-grade officers were: second lieutenant, first lieutenant, and captain, who commanded a company or battery. Also, an ensign, who wore the insignia of a first lieutenant and whose sole duty was to carry the regimental Colour, was authorized on 17 February 1864. The Act that created the rank of ensign was amended on 31 May, restricting it to infantry battalions only, and the rank was abolished on 23 February 1865, a distinguished enlisted man being given the task of Colour-bearer from then on.

Field-grade officers, majors, lieutenant colonels and colonels, served at regimental level. In the pre-war US Army, where those in charge of Lee's Army had received their training, generals were few and far between. Indeed, the highest actual rank was that of brigadier general, although major generals were authorized. The US Army's commanding officer was only a major general.

Logically, however, if a brigadier general were to command a brigade, which he did, a division should have a major general in command of it, a corps should have a lieutenant general, and an army should rate a full general. The Confederate Congress, less wary of military ranks than the old highly democratic pre-war US Congress, agreed with this logic and authorized those ranks. Hence, Lee was a full general, while corps commanders such as Longstreet and A. P. Hill became lieutenant generals — even though the US Army maintained its pre-war system until quite late in the war. Even then, U. S. Grant, at this juncture in charge of the largest army the nation had ever known, was still only a lieutenant general at the war's end.

The system of rank insignia made each group of officers quite clear. Company-grade officers were distinguished by embroidered gold bars, ½-inch by ¾-inch, worn on the collar. A second lieutenant wore his in the centre of the collar; a first lieutenant, two; a captain, three.

Field-grade officers wore gold embroidered five-pointed stars of 1¼-inch diameter on each collar. A major wore one; a lieutenant colonel, two; a colonel, three. Generals all wore the same insignia, devised when it was believed that there would be no long war or large Confederate Army. It consisted of a gold embroidered wreath encircling three gold stars, the centre one of 1¼-inch in diameter and the two outer ones of ½-inch diameter.

Originally this insignia was to be worn with an elaborate system of gold lace Austrian knots on each sleeve. Generals were to wear four braids of lace in this fashion, field-grade officers three, captains two, lieutenants, one. The combination of Austrian knot and collar insignia made officers easy targets in the field, however, and as of 3 June 1862, officers were allowed to wear plain coats with appropriate collar insignia.

The coat on which this insignia was to be worn, according to the Army's dress regulations of 6 June 1861, was a grey double-breasted tunic, with two rows of seven brass buttons, and a standing collar of a colour varying according to branch of service. The collar colour for generals and staff officers, except medical officers, was buff.

The pointed cuffs under each Austrian knot, fastened with three small brass buttons, were also of the branch of service colour. Brigadier generals were to wear eight buttons, in pairs, on each row down the coat front. This was the same as in the pre-war US Army so, following that example, major generals and above often placed their nine buttons in each row in groups of three.

The tunic, which came only a little way below the waist, was not popular. 'The officers would have none of it. They took the familiar frock coat with a good length of tail,' wrote Moxley Sorrel. 'Longstreet and two of three of us tried the tunic, but it was not popular.'[16]

Trousers for generals were officially dark-blue with two gold lace ⅝-inch-wide stripes on each outer seam, one inch apart. Staff officers had the same trousers with a single 1¼-inch wide gold stripe down each leg. Regimental officers were to wear sky-blue trousers with a branch of service colour stripe, 1¼-inch wide, down each leg.

The original headgear included cocked hats for generals and staff officers, but only Major General John Bankhead Magruder was photographed wearing such a worthless device. Otherwise, a copy of the French kepi was the official cap, its design being promulgated on 24 January 1862.

According to the orders issued then, the kepi was to be dark-blue for generals and staff officers. Artillery, infantry and cavalry officers had dark-blue bands around the base of their forage cap, but the tops were to be of branch of service colours. The cap was to be decorated with gold lace braid on front, sides and back, and in the centre of the crown, in the same number as Austrian knot lace stripes on each cuff.

So much for regulations.

In reality, there was great latitude in what officers wore. At first, many officers retained their old pre-war US Army or militia uniforms. Rank insignia on them was worn as gold-edged shoulder-straps in branch of service colours. Even after the regulation Confederate rank insignia system was described, many officers continued wearing the old shoulder-straps, sometimes together with the new collar badges. On 21 March 1862 the Richmond *Daily Dispatch* warned against doing this, as shoulder-straps distinguished the officer and might make him particularly vulnerable in the field. But as late as May 1863, staff officer Henry Kyd Douglas was photographed while in Richmond for Jackson's funeral, still wearing his old shoulder-straps on an otherwise plain grey, double-breasted coat.

Many officers, especially in permanent posts, preferred the comfort of a turn-down collar, even on the double-breasted frock coat. These collars, usually of grey piped with the branch of service colour, had the proper collar insignia sewn down on them.

Basic uniform colours quickly went by the wayside. Coats were generally some variant of grey, ranging from an almost light-blue to an almost brown shade of grey. Often they were made of one colour, without the regulation branch of service colours. Lee himself preferred a plain grey coat. Otherwise, narrow cloth piping around the cuffs, collar and front was popular. After all, a coat with narrow piping was easier to keep clean than one with wide buff collar and cuffs.

Trousers came in all sorts of colours rather than the stipulated blue – in fact blue was rather rare. Grey was the most common and by September 1864 was the colour of trousers issued by the Quartermaster Department. Lee started out wearing blue trousers, but by 1864 was photographed in grey. Officers often wore their trousers with stripes down each leg, but sometimes with narrow welts inset into the outer leg seams, as were worn by US Army regimental officers. And, even more often, they wore plain trousers, especially in the field.

While the frock coat looked nice, it was not particularly practicable, and the wearer, in a group of enlisted men wearing waist-length, single-breasted jackets, stood out as an easy target. Why merely remove the sleeve lace when the entire coat was a dead giveaway as to the wearer's importance? So officers took to wearing waist-length jackets in the field, with little more than the appropriate collar badge of rank. At times they also wore branch of service piping on each sleeve, as well. The entire Austrian knot, sometimes in branch of service colour piping rather than gold lace, on each sleeve of an otherwise plain jacket, was not unknown, but was rare. Mounted officers, even generals such as 'Stonewall' Jackson, habitually wore such a jacket for comfort in the saddle.

In the same way, but generally to preserve expensive cloth and buttons, single-breasted coats were worn in the field from time to time.

Lee himself often wore a blouse-style coat, made like a civilian male day coat, with an open front, turn-down collar, and outer pockets. The rank insignia was sewn on the collar. This type of coat was especially popular among staff officers, it being convenient and comfortable in the office.

The regulation French kepi was also less worn than other types of headgear. When it was worn, it usually had a grey, rather than branch of service coloured, crown and sides. For some reason artillery officers were more apt to wear branch of service coloured crown and sides on their cap than officers of the staff or other combat arms. Bands were often still dark-blue — always with the artillery red cap — but more often of the branch of service colour. Just as often, however, officers wore a plain grey cap, with crude leather peak and chinstrap.

The most popular officer's headgear was a plain felt, broad-brimmed hat known as a 'slouch hat'. At times these featured ostrich feather plumes, and gold embroidered or stamped brass insignia on one side, pinning the brim up. Plaited black and gold hat cords and tassels, as worn by US Army officers on their dress hat, were popular but not easily obtainable. In the field, the plain hat, usually nothing more than a civilian hat, was by far the most popular and widely worn officer's hat in the field. In summer, a natural coloured straw hat was sometimes worn in place of the thicker felt hat.

Officers on duty were to be further distinguished by a silk sash worn around the waist and knotted at the left hip, under the sword-belt. The sash was to be buff for generals; red for staff, artillery and infantry officers; yellow for cavalry officers. While common at first, particularly in permanent camps, the sash was quickly packed away when officers in Lee's Army took the field. Lee himself rarely wore a sash (although he did do so on the day he surrendered the Army), and virtually never in the field, and his officers followed his example.

Officers had to provide their own uniforms. This was fine when material was readily available and costs were commensurate with officers' salaries. But as the Confederate dollar plummeted in value, and material became scarce, there was a growing demand for clothing to be issued, or at least made available, through the Quartermaster Department, as it was for the enlisted men. On 16 January 1865, therefore, Congress authorized an annual uniform issue to officers.

The issue was to include a coat and a pair of trousers, or four yards of double-width material and trimmings for the outfit, a pair of shoes, a hat or cap, three pair of drawers, three cotton shirts, two flannel shirts and four pairs of socks.[17]

Non-Commissioned Officers

Traditionally, non-commissioned officers are said to be the 'backbone of the army'. It is they, more than the officers, who are in constant contact with the privates who do the dirty work. It is they who must keep those privates to their tasks no matter how unpleasant. 'During the fight the officers and non-commissioned officers keep the men in the ranks, and enforce obedience, if necessary,' Confederate Army Regulations read.[1]

At the first gathering of men into units for what became Lee's Army, non-commissioned officers were elected as well as officers. 'After a short service as private,' wrote Captain Charles Squires of New Orleans' Washington Artillery, 'I was elected Corporal, Sergeant and First Sergeant.'[2]

Once units had been formed and seasoned in the field, however, non-commissioned officers were appointed by the commanding officers of their units. Generally, captains chose non-commissioned officers up to their first, or orderly, sergeant — the highest non-commissioned grade in a company —while regimental commanding officers chose the regimental sergeant major and staff non-commissioned officers. The regimental commander had the final say on appointments to all non-commissioned grades. The grades could just as easily be taken away for such misdemeanours as absence without leave or drunkenness.

There were no schools, or even formal appointment processes, for non-commissioned officers. The man whom the commander thought the best qualified was chosen. If he failed in the job he could just as easily be replaced.

Squires listed all the basic company non-commissioned officer grades. The first grade above private was that of corporal, the next was sergeant. Both these grades were listed in order within each company. For example, the roster of Co. H, 30th Georgia Infantry, listed Fifth Sergeant M. Hudson, Fourth Sergeant W. M. Sewell, Third Sergeant J. P. Baker, Second Sergeant P. M. Rimble, and First Sergeants J. H. Tatum and G. J. Smith, who apparently served at different times.

In theory, and usually in practice, one progressed up the non-commissioned officer ranks as vacancies occurred. If the third sergeant were no longer able to perform his duties, the fourth sergeant would receive that grade (officers had ranks, non-commissioned officers had grades) until he reached the grade of first sergeant. In the same way, one worked his way through corporal grade to first corporal, then began again at the bottom of the sergeant ladder.

First sergeants were high in the non-commissioned officer grades, with the responsibility of maintaining order among the company or battery's enlisted men. They were the ones who filled out the daily Morning Reports and kept the duty rosters. Above them were the staff non-commissioned officers. The highest of these was the sergeant major, to whom all the company first sergeants reported and who was responsible for the behaviour of all the enlisted men in the regiment.

Each regiment also had a regimental quartermaster sergeant, who assisted the regimental quartermaster, a lieutenant.

Also, Confederate Army dress regulations called for an ordnance sergeant. Ordnance sergeants were a rather different breed of non-commissioned officer. They were appointed directly by the Secretary of War from among recommended, well-behaved sergeants. Thereafter, they were assigned directly to a specific post and functioned under the orders of the post commander directly, although assigned by the Adjutant and Inspector General and reporting to the Chief of the Ordnance Department.

Ordnance sergeants were to wear the uniform and insignia of the artillery corps. This included, officially, a double-breasted grey coat such as that worn by officers, with branch-of-service coloured pointed cuffs and standing collar. In the case of Ordnance Sergeants, as well as artillery non-commissioned officers, the branch-of-service colour was red. Grade insignia consisted of large, branch-of-service coloured chevrons on each sleeve. The Ordnance Sergeant was to wear three chevrons, points down, above both elbows, with a five-pointed star in the apex of the chevrons. Theoretically, this was to be of silk, but in the resource-starved Confederacy, cotton tape was more common.

Similar chevrons were worn by other non-commissioned officers. These included three chevrons and three arcs for sergeant majors, and three bars and three ties for a quartermaster. Both these staff non-commissioned officer grades were to be distinguished by silk chevrons. Company-grade non-commissioned officers were to wear worsted tape chevrons. They included three chevrons and a diamond, or lozenge, for a first sergeant, sometimes called an orderly sergeant because he kept the 'orderly room' where company orders were filed. The sergeant had three chevrons, the corporal only two.

Odd, non-regulation chevrons were worn from time to time; but, in the absence of any documentation of the time, we can make no sense of them today. One cavalryman was photographed with outlined horses, probably in yellow, on each sleeve where chevrons would normally be worn. Was he a farrier or guidon-bearer or something of that sort? We simply don't know. In much the same way, a single chevron (perhaps a 'leading private' in imitation of the British Army's lance-corporal) was sometimes worn. Colour sergeants, especially in North Carolina regiments, apparently often wore the single five-pointed star, officially designating an ordnance sergeant, above their chevrons. Fife- and drum-majors sometimes wore crossed drumsticks or crossed fifes or batons above three chevrons.

The Maryland Infantry Regiment/Battalion apparently had its non-commissioned officers wear their chevrons on one sleeve only. 'The mark of a rank of a corporal was two chevrons, I think of black braid, on the left sleeve of the jacket, at the elbow; a sergeant had three chevrons, and the first sergeant put a small square or diamond in the angle of the chevrons,' recalled McHenry Howard, a veteran of the unit.[3] Randolph McKim, another unit veteran, also recalled wearing sergeant's chevrons on his left arm, although at least one photograph shows the chevrons clearly on the right arm. Either way, in that unit, chevrons were a single-arm affair. But these were all regimental practices and did not apply to Lee's Army as a whole.

Some Confederate quartermaster sergeants apparently followed the unofficial Union Army practice of wearing two bars with the three chevrons for a battalion quartermaster sergeant and one bar with three chevrons for a company quartermaster sergeant. Officially only the regimental quartermaster sergeant had distinctive chevrons, with his three bars. Chevrons of these designs first began appearing in the Union Army as early as May 1863, and it is likely that some Confederates adopted the practice fairly soon thereafter.

Chevrons worn in the Confederate Army were usually pieces of tape sewn directly to each sleeve. Often they were black, as was noted in the Marylanders, since branch-of-service coloured tape was expensive and difficult to obtain. More often, however, non-commissioned officers simply didn't wear chevrons in the field. 'When my sisters knew that I had been appointed a sergeant nothing would do but that they should put on the stripes on my sleeves. I didn't care to have it done, but they put them on anyway,' wrote a 1st South Carolina sergeant of a leave in 1864. 'The space between the works and the quarters was used for a drill ground and a general street. Down this street I had to go. I had not gone far before some fellow cried out, "There goes the dominecker sergeant", and in no time you could hear it for a mile ahead, "Here comes the dominecker sergeant." Then it was that I cursed myself for having on those stripes.'[4]

In a would-be democratic army, the wearing of non-commissioned officer's chevrons was seen as putting on airs, and privates would be suitably derisive. One would expect it of officers, after all they were nothing but 'brass buttons' and 'chicken guts' (after the Austrian knots on their sleeves), but non-coms were one's 'pards'. In most of Lee's units, the concept of a non-commissioned officers' mess was quite unknown; a sergeant was simply another ranker with a slightly different job and a few more bucks in his pay packet every month.

Officially, however, they had one further distinction. Their sky-blue trousers, changed to grey by September 1864, had a branch-of-service coloured stripe, 1¼-inch wide, down each leg. In practice, however, these were rarely if ever seen.

Training
'We drilled every good day and took our first lessons in skirmish drill, as well as the bayonet exercise, or Zouave drill,' wrote 21st Virginia

Infantry Private John Worsham, about his first experiences in camp as a new soldier. 'Before we left, we became very drilled in each.'[1]

As each company was organized, it was sent to a nearby town where it was formed into a regiment and began its process of changing from a mob of civilians into a unit of soldiers. This meant drill, drill and more drill. Not only was the drill necessary to get men to obey without thinking, but the drill systems were actually used in combat to get units on to the field and control them once there.

Since most of the officers and non-commissioned officers knew little more about military practice than did their men, regimental colonels and other field officers usually held classes in Army Regulations and branch-of-service drill manuals every evening to prepared the unit for war.

As units were thinned by disease and battle, recruiters returned home to sign up new soldiers. These men, having been accompanied to their new units at the front or in camp, were then assigned to their permanent duty stations. There was no formal place for them to be trained; they learned their skill from the non-commissioned officers and their fellow soldiers.

Conscripts and recruits for the general army, however, were sent to Camps of Instruction where they were instructed in the fundamentals of soldiering; handling their equipment, learning the differences in ranks, and the basic drills. There they received their first uniforms. Each Camp of Instruction had a hospital where the men were vaccinated. At first many of the recruits were housed in tents, but these were eventually replaced by huts. In cities the men were housed in pre-war barracks such as the South Carolina Military Academy.

Each camp was commanded by a major, assisted by a staff that included a quartermaster and a commissary, each a captain, and an adjutant who was a first lieutenant.

In the Camps troops were trained in all the combat arms. For example, the training staff of drill-masters at Camp Randolph, Calhoun, Georgia, included seven first lieutenants and seven second lieutenants of infantry, two first lieutenants of artillery, and one first lieutenant of cavalry. Only recruits who brought a horse with them were authorized to be trained as cavalrymen.

Camps were not considered a top priority for arms and equipment. Indeed, as late as the end of November 1862 the camp commandant at Talladega, Alabama, who had been authorized 500 stands of arms, with all equipment and ammunition, was begging for his allotment, having been able to obtain 180 muskets, without a bayonet or cartridge, by that date.[2] Just how well his recruits could be trained with this equipment can be imagined.

Basically, Camps of Instruction were located in major cities in each state. Units from that state sent copies of their rosters, indicating their needs, to the appropriate camp commander. When he had recruits for their units, he would notify the unit commanders. They would then send an officer to the camp to escort their newly assigned troops to the front.

By early 1862, Lee's Army was being supplied by recruits trained at Camp Lee, Richmond, and Dublin Station for Virginia units; Camp Holmes, Raleigh, for North Carolina units; Columbia for South Carolina units; and Camp Randolph for Georgia units. Alabama's camps were in Talladega and Macon County. The state capital of Florida, Tallahassee, was the site of that state's camp.

There was no regulation length of time or course of instruction for recruits or conscripts at the camps; each one was sent on to a unit in the field as soon as two conditions were met: 1. The commandant, through his drill-masters, was satisfied that the recruit was ready for service, and 2. a unit in the field requested a replacement.

In the first five months of its existence, some 1,200 men passed through the Camp of Instruction at Talladega. On 17 February 1863 its commandant reported that he had 149 men in his camp, including his permanent garrison of guards. Many of the men were as yet without uniforms and, indeed, only 33 could be forwarded to the front. Even these, he said, were not properly 'prepared for the field'.[3]

A detailed report on Camp Holmes, a Camp of Instruction near Raleigh, North Carolina, dated 16 June 1864, described how a typical camp worked. As each conscript or recruit entered the camp his name, age, county, and the officer by whom enrolled, was listed in a master book. His next duty stations were recorded in the same book when he left. Each recruit was quartered in a log hut. He was vaccinated for smallpox; the medical facilities included an 18-bed hospital staffed by several medical officers, a hospital steward and a disabled conscript who served as a clerk.

On average, each recruit stayed at the camp for one week only, which scarcely sufficed to learn the basics of military life, let alone battlefield procedures. Many spent their time working in the 20-acre vegetable garden during their stay in the camp, although six conscripts unfit for active duty were permanently assigned this duty. In fact, at this particular camp, recruits were not drilled at all during their week's stay, other activities having been found for the assigned drill-masters. At the inspection date, there were 136 enlisted men in camp, of whom 64 were disabled soldiers in the camp's permanent garrison.[4] There were no formal schools for officers.

Once in the field, although there was often drill and some basic practice in the military arts such as target shooting, there was little formal training. Indeed, only occasionally were directives issued that were designed to further train the men. An example of one of these uncommon circulars was issued by Lee on 7 April 1864, and addressed the question of what to do if captured. 'We can not spare brave men to fill Federal prisons,' the circular read. 'Should, however, any be so unfortunate as to fall through unavoidable necessity into the hands of the enemy, it is important that they should preserve entire silence with regard to everything connected with the army, the positions, movements, organizations, or probable strength of any portion of it. I wish the commanding officers of regiments and companies to instruct their men, should they be captured, under any circumstances not to disclose the brigade, division, or corps to which they belong, but to give simply their names, company, and regiment, and not to speak of military matters even among their associates in misfortune.'[5]

Discipline

To the average small farmer, used as he was to living by his own efforts, or to the average well-to-do Southerner, used to bossing slaves, the idea of being disciplined by total strangers, who could issue all sorts of stupid orders solely because of the stripes on their sleeve or gold badges on their collar was difficult, if not impossible to accept.

At the beginning, virtually any sort of discipline was almost impossible to maintain. One Maryland enlisted man, for example, later recalled being on a march at about four in the morning during his first campaign: 'As we trudged along, with knapsack and musket, in a lonely part of the road, we were overtaken by a mounted officer, muffled up in a cloak, who gruffly demanded what we were doing ahead of our regiment, to which I hotly replied, "What business is that of yours?" One of my companions pulled me by the sleeve and said, "Man, that is General Elzey; you'd better shut up, or you'll be arrested and put in the guard-house, or shot for insubordination." I suppose I must have known he was an officer, and that my reply was a gross breach of discipline. But obedience and submission to military authority was a lesson I had not yet learned in my seven days of soldiering.'[1]

After several months in the field, however, this type of insubordination became less frequent, although enlisted men still automatically disliked officers — especially officers whom they did not know or who had not proved themselves worthy of the Austrian knots on their sleeves.

In several ways the Confederate Army never became a disciplined force comparable to European armies, or even the US Army. In 1863, for example, a Prussian officer noted: 'The extremely strict discipline on duty, on marches, and during the battle was definitely not to be seen in camp life. For example, nobody considered it an instance of insubordination at the time of the snow in April, when every stranger who passed through the camp, whether a general or a private soldier, was pelted with snowballs by the Texans, high-spirited as they were, though none the less renowned for their valour.'[2]

Throughout its existence there were disciplinary problems in Lee's Army, many caused by drink, although in some ways the drink problem was less acute than in the Northern army. The troops were usually posted fairly far from civilian centres, where saloons were commonplace, so soldiers had to make an extra effort to find their bottles of 'how come you this way'. In rural areas stills supplied much of the soldiers' wants, but they were illegal and were destroyed when discovered.

None the less, on 9 January 1862, the Adjutant and Inspector General's Office issued its General Order No. 3 which declared, in part, that drunkenness 'is the cause of nearly every evil from which we suffer; the largest portion of our sickness and mortality results from it; our guard-houses are filled by it; officers are constantly called from their duties to form courts-martial in consequence of it; inefficiency in our troops and consequent danger to our cause is the inevitable result.' So the bringing of any alcohol into camps, save for medicinal purposes, was banned. It was an order mostly observed in the breech.

Fighting was always a problem. Men forced to live together often get on one another's nerves, even in combat units where relationships are sometimes extraordinarily close, and trivial matters could set men off.

For the most part, minor disciplinary infractions such as fighting and drunkenness were handled within the company or battery. The first sergeant simply included the offenders on his mental list for unpleasant duties.

Theft from fellow soldiers was mostly dealt with in the company or battery concerned. Usually the offender was given a humiliating and painful punishment such as having to wear a barrel, often with a sign tacked to its front proclaiming its wearer a thief, or holding a log while balanced on top of a post or, especially in mounted units, having to ride a wooden 'horse' — a thin rail or log. Marching around the company area carrying a knapsack filled with stones was another punishment for minor crimes. For more serious crimes dealt with in the unit, punishments included being tied to the wheel of a gun caisson or suspended by the thumbs from a tree. A similar, and extremely painful, punishment was 'bucking and tying' in which the victim was gagged and his ankles and wrists tied together. A stick was thrust between his bent knees and out-thrust arms so that he could neither straighten his legs nor move his arms. Released after several hours in this state, the man was quite unable to move.

Courts-martial were held down to regimental level, and could award punishments that included stoppage of pay, demotion, public reprimand, confinement to the stockade — in informal camps often merely a staked-out area — and even branding for crimes such as cowardice in the face of the enemy or desertion. Flogging, which had been authorized. In the pre-war US Army, was not banned until after 13 April 1863.

Pillaging from local civilians was a more serious offence and was dealt with by special courts-martial that had been created on 9 October 1862 to handle such cases. They were made up of three colonels and a captain who was a judge advocate assigned at corps level, and were authorized to call civilian witnesses.

There were three areas in which the discipline in Lee's Army broke down to the point where it definitely affected the army's ability to fight.

The first was straggling. On every march, men fell out with sore feet, or to forage for food, or simply to chat with their fellows. At the end of the march these stragglers could take hours to rejoin their units. This may not have been too serious if the army were merely moving from one camp to another. It was disastrous if the army were moving into battle.

'The army is resting to-day on the Opeduon, below Martinsburg,' reported Lee to President Davis on 21 September 1862, after the Battle of Sharpsburg. 'Its present efficiency is greatly paralyzed by the loss to its ranks from numerous stragglers. I have taken every means in my power from the beginning to correct this evil, which has increased instead of diminished. A great many men belonging to the army never entered Maryland at all; many returned after getting there, while others who crossed the river kept aloof. The stream has not lessened since crossing the Potomac, although the cavalry has been constantly employed in endeavoring to arrest it. To give you an idea of its extent in some brigades, I will mention that, on the morning after the battle of the 17th, General Evans reported to me on the field, where he was holding the front position, that he had but 120 of his brigade present, and that the next brigade to his, that of General Garnett, consisted of but 100 men.'[4]

Most Confederate officers seemed to accept it as a fact of life that a certain percentage — at times quite a high percentage — of their men would simply drop out of any long march. Stonewall Jackson was one of the rare generals who did not. He even placed one of his chief officers, A. P. Hill, under arrest for neglect of duty in 1862 when Hill kept his division marching while men began to fall by the wayside. Jackson ordered the brigade to halt while the stragglers rejoined. Hill objected and was relieved of his command.

Even worse in terms of its effects on the army, was the second major disciplinary problem, that of desertion. Right from the start, especially after the initiation of conscription, the Confederacy had troubles with men simply quitting and going home. As early as 17 July 1862 the War Department sent each governor a copy of a confidential circular which began: 'Our armies are so much weakened by desertions, and by the absence of officers and men without leave, that we are unable to reap the fruits of our victories and to invade the territory of the enemy. We have resorted to courts-martial and military executions, and we have ordered all officers employed in enrolling conscripts to arrest both deserters and absentees, and offered rewards for the former. In Virginia the sheriffs, constables, and jailers have also been employed by the permission of the Governor, but still the evil continues, and unless public opinion comes to our aid we shall fail to fill our ranks in time to avail ourselves of the weakness and disorganization of the enemy.'[5]

The Secretary of War had put his finger on the main problem. In many areas public opinion was not against those who deserted. In fact, in many areas of the states which made up the Confederacy, popular opinion was definitely pro-Union and hence pro-deserter. These were usually hilly areas of small farms, with few slaves, and little popular support for slavery. The pro-Union areas included Western Virginia and North Carolina, north-eastern Georgia, and northern Alabama – areas which should have fed men into Lee's Army, rather than draw them away.

But they didn't. Large numbers of men from these areas deserted Lee's Army. Indeed, the 3rd Alabama Reserve Regiment deserted almost to a man, while most members of the 22nd and 54th Virginia Infantry Regiments were said to be members of a secret pro-Union organization. Finally, most of the 22nd also returned home — or took to the woods as outlaws — without benefit of formal discharge.

Others who may have been pro-Southern often deserted after their homelands had been overrun by the Union forces and their families left to fend for themselves. The pull of home and its immediate defence and needs, quite often clearly explained by wives in pleading letters, was stronger than the call of duty to a new flag. Even wives in areas not under enemy control were often too poor to feed and clothe themselves and their children on a soldier's pay in ever- devaluing Confederate paper currency. The natural instinct of the men who had joined Lee's Army was to give up and get home to care for their families. And, of course, many veterans simply grew tired of the war, especially when all the victories seemed to be Northern, and city after Southern city fell to the blue-coated enemy.

This problem plagued Lee and his officers throughout the war. 'The number of desertions from this army is so great and still continues to such an extent, that unless some cessation of them can be caused, I fear success in the field will be seriously endangered,' he wrote to Davis on 17 August 1863. 'Night before last thirty went from one regiment and eighteen from another. Great dissatisfaction is reported among the good men in the army at the apparent impunity of deserters.'[6]

Lee's figures were high indeed. Some 130,000 men were missing according to strength returns for April 1863. Of the men who should have been present, only 50 per cent were on duty by the end of 1864.

The penalty for desertion was death, and it was imposed time and again. But it did not stop the flow. Of the some 100,000 men who deserted from the armies of the Confederacy, only a handful were caught and shot. Others were pardoned, although Lee was unhappy about this because he felt that only stern discipline could stop the flood. Yet these examples were not enough to stop men from going home when they wanted.

On 16 August 1863 Lee attempted to stem the flow of deserters by granting furloughs to deserving soldiers, initially at a rate of two men for every hundred present for duty. Thereafter, one soldier was granted a furlough for every hundred present for duty. Since many of Lee's soldiers had to travel quite some distance to get home, the duration of the furlough varied: men from Virginia got 15 days; from North Carolina, 18; from South Carolina, 21; from Georgia and Tennessee, 24; from Florida, Alabama, Mississippi and East Louisiana, 30 days. Men from areas under enemy control were still allowed furlough, but were forbidden to pass through enemy lines to get home.

When the war was almost over, despite Lee's generous furlough policy, on 27 January 1865 he wrote to the Secretary of War: 'I have the honor to call your attention to the alarming frequency of desertions from this army. You will perceive, from the accompanying papers, that fifty-six deserted from Hill's corps in three days. I have endeavored to ascertain the causes, and think that the insufficiency of food and non-payment of the troops have more to do with the dissatisfaction among the troops than anything else. All commanding officers concur in this opinion.'[7]

What was worse was that many of these deserters were not going home — they were going over to the enemy. And this stemmed in large part from the third major flaw in discipline in Lee's Army — friendly relations with the enemy.

Such fraternization was bound to happen. After all, the Civil War was not a war between foreigners. Both Confederates and their enemies spoke the same language, shared the same history, belonged to the same religions, and had every major value system in common. Moreover, there were many times when the two sides were encamped quite close to each other, separated by only a thin line of pickets. Often only a river such as the Rappahannock separated the two sides. What could be more natural than for pickets on either side of the river to strike up at least a shouted conversation?

'Our pickets and the Yankey pickets are not more than about forty yards a part [sic] at a great many places on the line,' William E. Penn of the 4th Virginia Infantry wrote of the lines at the Siege of

Petersburg. 'They are very friendly on both sides in front of this divi-sion [*sic*], they very often meet in front of their posts on half way ground and talk and trade. It is against orders but they will do it, they are deserting also from both sides occasionally.'[8]

It would not take many contacts with an enemy whose rations were much better, whose clothes were warmer, and who were paid in money worth more, to convince some whose loyalties were, at best, lukewarm to begin with, to quit the war. Of course, this was especially so for men who had no families to return to and conscripts new to a unit with little loyalty to the men with whom they were serving.

Speaking later of trading with the enemy, and how that some-times led to desertions, Moxley Sorrel wrote: 'Our tobacco was always good for coffee and a Northern paper. It got to be too familiar and led to desertions of our men. Their rations were of the poorest ... their clothing and shoes worn and unfit for the field, and their work and duties of the hardest on our attenuated lines. Reliefs were few and far between. No wonder they sometimes weakened to better themselves, as

---

THE STRENGTH OF LEE'S ARMY

The size of Lee's army, as reported to the War Department on official strength returns, stayed fairly consistent in terms of the number of officers and men actually on hand, after a period of rapid growth to the end of 1862. The serious drop in December 1863 not only reflected losses during the summer, but also the detachment of Longstreet's corps, which had been sent to Tennessee three months earlier. The main problem was the number of absentees, which grew tremendously towards the end of the war. Some of the absences were legal, as men were on detached duties in manufacturing facili-ties, or on recruiting duties, or sick in hospital. But many were sim-ply desertions – a problem that Lee was never to solve.

Date	Officers	Enlisted Men	Aggregate Present	Present and Absent	Absent
21 July 1861	1,351	20,512	21,863	N/A	N/A
31 Dec 1861	4,039	57,859	76,331	98,050	21,719
30 June 1862	3,586	53,890	78,891	119,242	40,351
31 Dec 1862	5,827	70,972	91,093	152,842	41,749
30 April 1863	N/A	64,799*	77,379	109,859	32,480
30 June 1863	6,116	68,343	88,735	133,652	44,917
31 Dec 1863	3,530	42,966	53,995	90,055	36,060
30 June 1864	4,261	51,069	66,141	101,464	35,323
31 Dec 1864	N/A	60,334	71,854	150,373	78,519
20 Feb 1865	4,046	55,575	73,349	160,411	87,062

* Fit for duty.

they supposed, and stayed with the fat-jowled, well-clad, coddled up masses opposite them.'[9]

No doubt Grant's troopers across the field from Lee's men would not have seen themselves as either 'fat-jowled' or 'coddled up', but the point was clear. As the war wore on, Confederates began to stream away from Lee's Army, either back South or up North.

So it was that discipline was always a major problem in Lee's Army.

Clothing

The first arrivals at the camps where Lee's Army would be trained, wore their civilian clothes or, in the case of men who had served in pre-war volunteer militia companies, their old uniforms.

These uniforms varied tremendously in colour and cut. Old companies had tended to prefer cut-away style coatees, with waist-length fronts and long tails, liberally trimmed with heavy braid, often gold, on standing collars, cuffs and tails. Worsted fringed epaulettes and leather shakos were usual. Units formed just before the war often wore the frock-coat, as being more modern, and usually some version of the French kepi. The coat was often trimmed as was the earlier style tail-coat, with several rows of buttons down the front and elaborately trimmed standing collar and cuffs. While the US 'national colour' was blue, grey was often worn to distinguish volunteer status. Rifle companies, such as the Clinch Rifles, which later became Co. A, 5th Georgia Infantry, wore dark-green, the traditional rifles' uniform colour. Many volunteer companies also wore a waist-length jacket, usually single-breasted, for fatigue wear.

Variants of national dress were also worn by units such as the Germans, Scots and Irish of Charleston and the French of Louisiana. The French units, in particular, although often made up of more Irish than French, chose a variant of the Zouave dress, as worn by Berber natives in the French Army. This included baggy trousers, usually red, fez or turban, and short blue jacket trimmed with red braid and cut away in front to reveal an elaborate vest or shirt.

On 6 March 1861 Congress recognized that it was unable to provide uniforms quickly and authorized payment to each volunteer of a sum equal to the cost of a Regular Confederate Army uniform. On 22 April instructions from the Adjutant and Inspector General's Office stated that: 'The first issue of clothing to recruits will be one blue shirt (to be made into a blouse), three undershirts, two pairs of overalls, two pairs of drawers, two pairs of stockings, one pair of bootees, one blanket, one leather stock.'[1]

But a different and more complete uniform was described in regulations issued on 6 June 1861, which called for a double-breasted grey frock-coat with two rows of seven buttons down the front, with pointed cuffs and a standing collar of a branch-of-service colour. Trousers were to be sky-blue, and the cap, probably a black shako type, was to have a branch-of-service colour pompom. On 24 January 1862 the cap was simplified into a French kepi with a dark-blue band and branch-of-service coloured top and sides.

Trouser colour had been switched from blue to grey by September 1864, although for some time both colours were issued. A matron in a Richmond hospital recalled that in 1864: 'The men had their fashions, too, sometimes insisting upon having light-blue pants drawn for them, and other seasons preferring gray; but while the mania for either color raged, they would be dissatisfied with the other.'[2]

Officially, in the first year of his enlistment each Confederate soldier was to receive two caps, a cap cover, two coats, three pairs of trousers, three flannel shirts, three pairs of flannel drawers, four pairs of bootees or one pair of boots and two pairs of bootees, four pairs of stockings, one leather stock and one greatcoat. He was to receive a smaller, but sufficient quantity of these items every year thereafter. Regulations aside, the first uniforms of 1861 were supplied from old militia stocks and the folks back home. This led to problems of identifying units in the field and so field designations were ordered. Early in July some 6,000 wing badges were made in Richmond and distributed to the infantry and cavalry of the Army of the Potomac. Early's 6th Brigade were to wear their wings with the yellow sides out, except for artillerymen who were to wear red cap- or armbands, while Ewell's Brigade was to wear the wings red sides out. Cocke's Brigade was to have red flannel bands around the cap or upper arm. In November it was decided that troops of the Army of the Peninsula were to wear white cap-bands, while their scouts were to wear a white sash across the body.

Militia stocks did not last long; they were insufficient, and the uniforms for the most part were impracticable and not tough enough for field use. Mothers, wives and sisters scrambled to find enough material to make clothing to their soldiers' specifications.

For example, 2nd Georgia Infantry Private Henry Graves wrote home on 21 August 1861: 'I wish Ma would send me a coat; let her make it of that gray woolen cloth she once made me a hunting coat from... It must be a jacket, buttoning all the way up in front military fashion, with a short collar designed to stand up; buttons either brass or silver, oval shape, nearly half inch in diameter; put a short piece of white tape ¼-inch wide upon the shoulder, running front to back. Let it be warm; pockets inside and on both sides.'[3] This, minus the white tape, is a good description of the typical 1861 Confederate's jacket, although cotton mixture cloth was also quite commonly used.

Improvisation of this kind might have served if the war had lasted for perhaps three months, but it soon became obvious that the

Civil War would last much longer than that. On 7 August 1861, the Secretary of War issued a circular letter to the various governors. 'The war existing between this Government and that at Washington will probably be prolonged during the coming winter, and in view of the rigor of the climate at that season on the line of the seat of war it is desired that our soldiers shall be well supplied with clothing. You are therefore requested to cause the quartermaster's department to have made up at an early date, to the extent of your ability, woolen clothing to supply the needs of the Army, to be charged to this Government.'[4]

State responses to the challenge varied. North Carolina set up its own clothing factory in Raleigh where it produced 49,000 jackets, 68,000 pairs of trousers, 6,000 greatcoats, and 12,000 blankets during its first year.[5] Alabama went to outside suppliers, advertising on 31 August 1861 in the Montgomery *Weekly Advertiser* for uniforms that must include grey wool waist-length jackets with seven brass buttons down the front, a standing collar, shoulder-straps, and a strap on each side buttoned at the top and sewn down at the bottom through which the waistbelt passed. Trousers were to be plain grey, while shirts could be of either checked or striped cotton. South Carolina was probably unique in contracting for, probably grey, trousers and plain frock-coats as stipulated in the regulations; waist-length jackets were by far more common, as these conserved precious material.

Civilians of all the states, too, continued to produce clothing to meet this 'Great Appeal'. Local 'Ladies' Aid Societies' produced large quantities of clothing for their men in the field. 'Contributions of clothing, provisions, etc., are coming in in large quantities; sometimes to the amount of $20,000 in a single day,' reported a clerk in the War Department on 9 October 1861.[6]

The result was that the force that fought throughout 1861 and into 1862 to defend Virginia was not uniform in appearance, either as to cut, colour or quality of its dress. A Northern correspondent reported seeing captured troops during the Peninsula Campaign. 'Some were wrapped in blankets of rag-carpet, and others wore shoes of rough, untanned hide. Others were without either shoes or jackets, and their heads were bound in red handkerchiefs. Some appeared in red shirts; some in stiff beaver hats; some were attired in shreds and patches of cloth; and a few wore the soiled garments of citizen gentlemen; but the mass adhered to homespun suits of gray, or "butternut", and the coarse blue kersey common to slaves. In places I caught glimpses of red Zouave breeches and leggings; blue Federal caps, Federal buttons, or Federal blouses; these were the spoils of anterior battle, and had been stripped from the slain. In a corner, lying morosely apart were a major, three captains, and three lieutenants – young, athletic fellows, dressed in rich gray Cassimere, trimmed with black, and wearing soft black hats adorned with black ostrich-feathers. Their spurs were strapped upon elegantly fitting boots, and they looked as far above the needy, seedy privates, as lords above their vassals.'[7]

The 'butternut' colour to which the reporter referred was brown rather than the regulation grey and was imparted by a dye made from walnuts mixed with copperas. Experiments at the University of North Carolina showed that cloth dyed grey with vegetable dyes turns brown, or 'butternut', after a few weeks of exposure to sunlight. The colour produced by either method varied from an almost whitish tan to the dark-brown of black coffee, and sometimes even had a yellowish tint. These cheap dyes were often used on materials made into uniforms by soldiers' relatives when grey cloth was unobtainable.

By late summer 1861 the Quartermaster's Department set up its Clothing Bureau in Richmond to supply uniforms to all the troops, thus relieving the states of this responsibility. It also started a Clothing Manufactory and a Shoe Manufactory in Richmond, and eventually there were others in Athens, Atlanta, and Columbus, Georgia. But the Richmond enterprise remained the the main source of supply for Lee's Army.

Material used by the Richmond Manufactory came from four local sources and, from time to time, Great Britain. All wool cloth was supplied by the Crenshaw Woolen Mills in Richmond, while Kelly, Tackett & Ford of Manchester, Virginia, produced a variety of materials. Woollen jeans material came from Bonsack & Whitmore, Bonsack's Depot, Virginia, and the Scottsville Manufacturing Co., Scottsville, Virginia. And unbleached cotton Osnaburg made by the Battersea Mills, the Ettrick Manufacturing Co., and the Matoaca Manufacturing Co., was used for jacket linings and shirts.

The Richmond Manufactory began producing trousers, caps and jackets (rather than frock-coats) from these materials as early as February 1862. Apparently, the first type of jacket produced was cut waist-length, with nine brass buttons down the front, a standing collar, shoulder-straps, and belt loops sewn to each side. Branch-of-service coloured piping was sewn around the collar, shoulder-straps, and into a point on each cuff.

Trim, besides being a bit of unnecessary embellishment, was expensive and difficult to obtain, so that by the spring of 1862 the Manufactory had dicontinued its use on many of the jackets it turned out. In the field soldiers often cut off the belt loops and shoulder-tabs as being unnecessary and at times a nuisance.

Although caps were regulation and certainly made and issued throughout the war, the broad-brimmed slouch hat was by far the more common headgear. Many of these were obtained from civilian sources, but so many slouch hats, identified as having been worn by Confederate enlisted men, exist as to suggest that there was a fairly common pattern of issue. Indeed, on 21 September 1864, the Quartermaster General wrote to his agent in Liverpool that 'A cheap and serviceable felt hat would be very acceptable to the Army.'[8]

The most common type of hat known to have been worn in Lee's Army was made of black felt, with a brim about three inches wide, edged with a narrow ribbon binding on its top side only. A steel-grey cotton band almost an inch wide was worn around the crown. The brim was often hooked up on one side.[9]

Despite the manufacturing efforts undertaken by the Quartermaster's Department, there were many times in the 1862 campaign when Lee's men were poorly clothed. 'My opinion is that by the first of April the war will be very near an end,' wrote Corporal T. R. Stratten, Co. A, 6th New Jersey Volunteers, on 28 September 1862. 'I would like to see how the rebels are going to winter over they certainly are very near out of clothing for their appearance proves this fact. I have seen hundreds of prisoners and I never saw one who was half dressed. Some with no hat and in fact the most god forsaken individuals I ever saw.'[10]

A Maryland woman who saw Lee's men on their march to Sharpsburg at about the same time agreed, calling them 'a poor forlorn looking set of men who certainly had seen hard service. They were tired, dirty, ragged and had no uniforms whatever. Their coats were made out of almost anything that you could imagine, butternut color predominating. Their hats looked worse than those worn by the darkies. Many were barefooted; some with toes sticking out of their shoes and others in the stocking feet. Their blankets were every kind of description, consisting of druggets, rugs, bedclothes, in fact anything they could get, put up in a long roll and tied up at the ends, which with their cooking utensils, were slung over their shoulders.'[11] Of course, dirt-coloured clothes, devoid of trim, although uniform in style, would have hardly appeared to be true uniforms to eyes used to seeing elaborate volunteer, or differently cut, US Army uniforms.

In an endeavour to get enough clothing to keep the men warm through the winter of 1862/3, another 'Great Appeal' was launched, but it was less successful than the first. Less material was available, and it cost much more. Mistrusting their government, any clothing that relatives were able to make tended to be sent directly to their 'own' soldiers at the front rather than to the Quartermaster's Department to go into a general pool.

But the Quartermaster officials felt confident, and convinced Congress, that they could resolve the clothing problem. On 8 October 1862, Congress repealed the Act that authorized payment to soldiers for clothing, and directed the Secretary of War to clothe all the Confederacy's armies.

Thereafter, Lee's Army began to assume a more uniform appearance, although it could never be said to have had the uniformity associated with a modern military formation. When British Army observer

Colonel A. J. L. Fremantle first saw the men of Pender's Division in June 1863, he described them with the eye of a professional soldier: 'The soldiers of this division are a remarkably fine body of men, and look quite seasoned and ready for any work. Their clothing is serviceable, so also are their boots; but there is the usual utter absence of uniformity as to colour and shape of their garments and hats: grey of all shades, and brown clothing, with felt hats, predominate.'[12]

None the less, Lee's soldiers throughout the 1863-4 campaign largely reported home that they were well supplied with ample clothing. 'I am now as I stated in former letters abundantly supplied with clothes,' wrote Confederate cavalry Private William Wilson on 24 March 1864.[13]

By 1864, its production having continued to expand, the Richmond Manufactory again simplified its jacket by eliminating shoulder-tabs and belt loops. These last Manufactory-produced jackets were mostly made of cadet grey kersey, earlier jackets having been made from a variety of materials that included cotton mixtures, wool mixtures and cotton/wool mixtures. It would appear that the wool uniforms were often saved for winter issue, while cotton blend jackets were preferred for the heat of Southern summers.

'By using cotton clothing during the summer and spring and reserving the woolen goods for fall and winter, it is hoped and believed that enough may be to hand to prevent suffering next winter. We will get through this season without much trouble,' reported Quartermaster General A. R. Lawton to Congress on 27 January 1865. 'The supply of cotton clothing has heretofore been abundant, and is now ample.' Lawton also reported that his Department's goal was to issue a suit of jacket and trousers every six months to each soldier in the field and he felt that they would succeed in this.[14]

Although not specifically asked for by the central government, some supplies continued to arrive from the states, especially North Carolina and Georgia. The latter state, for example, issued 26,795 jackets, 28,808 pairs of trousers, 37,657 pairs of shoes, 7,504 blankets, 24,952 shirts, 24,168 pairs of drawers, and 23,024 pairs of socks in 1864 alone.[15] Since the Richmond Manufactory, even with some outside production, was unable to meet the goal of supplying all the army's clothing, the Quartermaster Department turned to Europe for clothing. These imported garments came ready made, although cloth for the clothing manufactories was also imported. Peter Tait of Limerick, Ireland, a uniform manufacturer who had supplied the British Army during the Crimean War, produced many thousands of jackets, caps and trousers, the vast majority of which went to Lee's Army.

Tait jackets were made of a fine dark-grey kersey with eight brass, usually British-made, regulation branch-of-service buttons down the front, a standing collar, and a tab on each shoulder. Many of these

Left: The symbol of Lee's Army was its distinctive battle flag, the blue Saint Andrew's cross on a red square. This specimen belonged to the 16th North Carolina and bears battle honours for (top triangle), Seven Pines, Cedar Run, Sharpsburg (right triangle), Mechanicsville, Manassas, Shepherdstown (bottom triangle), Gaines' Mill, Ox Hill, Fredericksburg (left triangle), Frasier's Farm and Harper's Ferry. (North Carolina Department of Archives and History)

Below: The area of northern Virginia which Lee's Army was to defend was largely rural, its small towns — like Centerville, seen here — dotting the landscape. Most of them consisted of a handful of scattered stone and wooden houses on gently rolling hillsides. (US Army Military History Institute)

Above: This post-war impression by a Confederate veteran, based on contemporary photographs, shows troops behind the stone wall at Fredericksburg, December 1862. Only the top buttons of the jackets are done up, and the hat brims are turned up. The canteens all appear to be of Union Army issue. (*Battles and Leaders of the Civil War*)

Robert E. Lee

Opposite page, left: General Robert E. Lee photographed after his heart attack in early 1863, wearing a coat with turned down collar and bearing the plain three stars of a colonel. (National Archives)

Opposite page, right: This photograph of Lee, taken at Lexington, Virginia, just after the war, shows how the stress of the conflict had aged him. (Author's collection)

Lee's Generals

Above: Lieutenant General Thomas J. 'Stonewall' Jackson. In the field he tended to wear a plain, waist-length jacket. (Library of Congress)

Above right: Lieutenant General James Longstreet, photographed in 1861. He is wearing the tunic-length coat that was the original regulation officer's coat, but which was eventually rejected by them in favour of the full-length frock-coat. His trousers are dark-blue with rank stripes up the legs, the sash is buff. He is holding the regulation dark-blue kepi. (Lee-Fendall House)

Right: Lieutenant General A. P. Hill, seemingly indifferent to regulations, always dressed informally. Here he is wearing what appears to be a loosely woven black-and-white double-breasted coat, cut along the lines of a civilian's day coat, over a checked shirt. He has the plain three stars of a colonel on each collar. (Library of Congress)

Top right: Lieutenant General Jubal Early. (Library of Congress)

Above: Lieutenant General Richard H. Anderson. (National Archives)

Left: Major General James Ewell Brown (JEB) Stuart seems to have worn the lapels of his double-breasted coat or jacket buttoned back to expose the waistcoat. (Library of Congress)

Lee's Staff

Right: On 26 April 1862 Colonel T. M. R. Talcott was appointed to Lee's staff as an engineer, with the rank of major. Cn 1 April 1864 he left Lee's staff to command the 1st Regiment of Engineers. He is wearing a plain grey coat bearing the three stars of his rank, with a darker waistcoat piped in the buff facing colour of an officer of engineers. (The Valentine Museum)

Far right: First Lieutenant James B. Washington was serving as an aide-de-camp to General Joseph E. Johnston when he was captured on 31 May 1862, while on a mission during the Seven Pines battle. His short jacket is typical of mounted staff officers, but his shoulder-straps are absolutely nonregulation, although they were worn by staff officers at least as late as May 1863. He is seen here seated next to an old US Military Academy classmate, George A. Custer. (US Army Military History Institute)

Above: According to regulations, staff officers were to wear copies of the French *chapeau de bras*, but it was rarely worn in practice. This drawing was one of a series printed to accompany the official dress regulations.

Above: The dead of Starke's Louisiana Brigade lie where they fell along the Hagerstown Pike, 500 yards north of the Dunker Church, at the Battle of Sharpsburg. The trousers of the man in the left foreground are darker than his jacket; the man in the right foreground has a cartridge box whose tool pouch is exposed. (Library of Congress)

Left: This photograph of stragglers, apparently from a group of prisoners being transferred from Gettysburg to northern prison camps on 16 July 1863, gives a good idea of the overall appearance of the men of Lee's Army in 1863. All are wearing slouch hats; the man on the left is lacking a jacket; the jackets and trousers of the other two are of different shades. The canteens appear to be of US Army issue, as is the haversack borne by the right-hand man, but his otherwise odd rig is unexplained. (Library of Congress)

Above: Dead men of Jenkins' South Carolina Brigade lying in a cornfield near Sherrick's House at the Battle of Sharpsburg.

The Officer Corps

Below left: Colonel John Gregg, who commanded the Texas Brigade until he was killed on 7 October 1864. Many officers, especially early in the war, tended to wear a single-breasted coat rather than the regulation double-breasted pattern. (Herb Peck, Jr. collection)

Below right: Captain James F. Tucker, Co. D, 6th Florida Infantry Battalion, photographed in 1893. He is wearing the regulation officer's coat that he wore while serving in Virginia, and at his marriage in 1864. The hat which he is holding was, he noted, struck by three bullets during the battle of Cold Harbor. (Fritz Kirsch)

Above left: The plain sack coat with turn-down collar, made much like a businessman's day coat, was popular in the field. This one is worn by Colonel James Kemper, 7th Virginia Infantry, who was promoted to the rank of brigadier general on 3 June 1863. (Library of Congress)

Above: Brigadier General William Mahone wearing a version of the jacket made with a pleated front which latter also featured on the frock-coat with straight skirts. His trousers appear to be dark-blue which was regulation for generals and staff officers, but his slouch hat has a non-regulation badge to pin up one side of the brim. (National Archives)

Left: Brigadier General Richard Taylor wearing his frock-coat with the standing collar turned down. (US Army Military History Institute)

Left: First Lieutenant W. H. Young, a North Carolina officer, wearing the waist-length jacket most preferred by officers in the field. He has an Austrian knot on each sleeve as well as the two bars of his rank on the collar. His trousers have a wide stripe down each leg. His apparently dark-blue forage cap is piped around the crown and band with a lighter colour, probably light-blue or white for infantry, and is probably a pre-war militia cap. (US Army Military History Institute)

Non-Commissioned Officers
Right: These two non-commissioned officers were probably photographed early in the war before the wearing of chevrons became unpopular and the wearing of different coloured facings became unlikely. The caps took like those issued to Florida's troops. (Michael Welch)

Left: The regulation double-breasted frock-coat was rarely worn by enlisted personnel, but this sergeant has managed to acquire one. He was possibly an ordnance sergeant, stationed at some permanent post such as at Charleston, South Carolina. But some colour sergeants also wore the regulation ordnance sergeant chevrons which this man is wearing. (US Army Military History Institute)

Training

Below: These are officers of the pre-war volunteer unit, the Washington Light Infantry, which became Co. A, 25th South Carolina Infantry Regiment. Center, facing left, is the company commander, Captain Simmonton, while facing him are Lieutenants Wilkie, Choper and Lloyd. Private Gibbs Blackwood, extreme right, is saluting as he reports. Note the extensive camp equipage seen in 1861. (US Army Military History Institute)

Training

Above left: This private is wearing a belt plate bearing the letters 'SC' for 'South Carolina'. A rope slung from his left shoulder to his right hip supports the belt. The image, as is typical of all Ambrotypes or tintypes, has been reversed so the cap box and cartridge box seen actually on his right side appear on his left. (Michael Welch)

Above right: This soldier from Georgia is wearing the rectangular belt plate bearing the letters 'CSA' that is more associated with the Army of Tennessee than the Army of Northern Virginia. (Michael Welch)

Below: Camps of Instruction usually offered better living facilities than the Confederate soldier would ever have again during his tour of duty. These men are members of a pre-war volunteer militia unit, the Washington service as Co. A, 25th South Carolina Infantry. Not only do they have wall tents, which would thereafter only be seen in headquarters, but extensive camp furniture as well, including a leather fire bucket with a company designation painted on it. Corporal W A Courtney, extreme left, and Sergeant R A Blum, extreme right, both also carry foot officers' swords. (US Army Military History Institute)

Uniforms

Left: Pre-war volunteer uniforms, as worn by this typical private of an unknown company, were usually highly decorated and elaborate, but impracticable for field service. Although in many instances they were being worn as late as the First Manassas, by the end of 1861 they had largely disappeared from the army in northern Virginia. (Author's collection)

Below left: The single-breasted frock-coat, as worn by this soldier, was typical of the first uniform issued to recruits. (Author's collection)

Below: This apparently early war image, found in a mid-Georgia attic depicts a soldier wearing what appears to be a dark-blue jacket typical of 1861 Georgia enlisted men, and a star on his slouch hat. His longarm is a converted flintlock rifle, and he has two revolvers and a knife stuffed into his belt, weapons soon abandoned in the field. The circular belt plate would appear to be a US Army cross-belt plate that has been converted to a waist-belt plate. (Michael Welch)

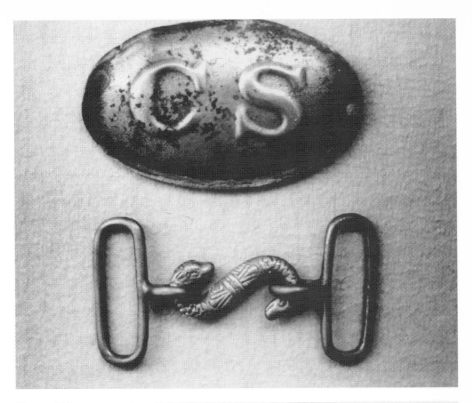

Above: This copper oval belt plate, produced as an imitation of the US Army's issue plate, is lead-backed. It was found in the Peninsula Campaign area. The 'snake buckle' beneath it was imported from England and was widely used both by officers and enlisted men. (Author's collection)

Right: This soldier, a prisoner in Philadelphia, is wearing the typical issue dark-grey uniform jacket with standing collar, and nine buttons, in this case apparently of wood, down the front. (Michael D. Jones)

Left: The first two styles of issue jacket, made by the Richmond Clothing Manufactory, came with an epaulette on each shoulder and nine buttons down the front. The second model, seen here, came without coloured branch-of-service colour. (Author's collection)

Right: Apparently a soldier from Lee's Army, this man, who was photographed in Virginia, is wearing a plain grey uniform jacket. (Michael Welch)

Above: Wood was used for the soles of these issued shoes, more commonly worn by cavalrymen than infantrymen. (Smithsonian Institution)

Rations

Above right: This young infantryman is wearing a roughly woven cloth jacket and matching trousers, apparently of jeans material, with a two-piece state belt plate. He appears to be wearing an infantry-type kepi with a blue band and grey sides and top, of the type made by the Richmond Clothing Manufactory. (Author's collection)

Morale

Below: One of the famous snowball fights during the winter encampments in 1862/3, as done from memory in I884 by a Confederate veteran, A. C. Redwood. (*Battles and Leaders of the Civil War*)

Above: Private Carlton McCarthy of the Richmond Howitzers noted that Confederate soldiers preferred to bivouack in the woods. Although this image is dim, it shows a typical early war encampment with an odd mix of tents placed apparently randomly instead of in the company 'streets' called for in regulations. The men in the left foreground are wearing grey or darker trousers, and have a mix of dark kepis and light slouch hats, possibly of straw (David Scheinmann collection)

Below: The instruments held by members of the Washington Light Infantry, a pre-war volunteer militia unit from Charleston, South Carolina, include a violin and a bugle. Sergeant R W Greer, seated, extreme right, carries a foot officers sword. The unit was extensively photographed in 1861 when it mustered into Confederate service as Co. A, 25th South Carolina Infantry Regiment. (US Army Military History Institute)

jackets had branch-of-service coloured collars and pointed cuffs which were sewn only on the front of each sleeve rather than all round the cuff. These jackets all dated from the last two years of the war.

One item of clothing was in short supply during most of the war – the common shoe. Marching wears out shoes, and hard marching wears out shoes quickly. The need of shoes was so pressing that it triggered the Battle of Gettysburg: Confederate troops were drawn there because of the shoe factories located nearby.

At one point, during the winter of 1862/3, the barefoot soldiers were given moccasins rudely cobbled from the raw skin of cows slaughtered for meats 'They were made from the green hide of cattle killed for food, sewed up with thongs or strips cut from the hide, the hair-side being inside, next to the foot. These moccasons, or whatever you may call them, were about 16 inches long, and the beef was on them. The men put them on while green, and in a few days they dried, and there was no getting them off without cutting them. It was lucky that there were no dogs in camp or they would have given us trouble,' one Virginia officer later recalled.'[16]

The main problem was the lack of leather. To make up for this, canvas shoes with leather soles were produced. 'When the quartermaster-general issued canvas shoes', the Richmond hospital matron wrote, 'there was a loud dissatisfaction expressed in constant grumbling, till some original genius dyed the whitish tops by the liberal application of pokeberries. He was the Brummel of the day, and for many months crimson shoes were the rage, and long rows of unshod men would sit under the eves of the wards, all diligently employed in the same labor and up to their elbows in red juice.'[17] But no matter how beautiful they may have been, canvas shoes failed to stand up to hard marching.

Shoes with wooden soles were also manufactured. These were, for the most part, issued to cavalrymen, but some saw infantry use. Some of them had iron horseshoe-shaped plates on toes and heels, others had an elaborately hinged instep.

Britain was another source of shoe supply. As early as August 1861, Confederate Quartermaster agents had been sent to Europe to buy military shoes for the army. But imported British shoes were criticized by their wearers. 'They were lined and filled with stiff paper, and after fording a few times they usually came to pieces,' recalled one of Lee's veterans.[18]

Not that shoes produced by Confederate Quartermaster Shoe Manufactories were much better. 'The Chief Quartermaster of the Army brought me this morning a sample of shoes recently sent from Richmond,' Lee wrote to the Army's Quartermaster General on 30 January 1864. 'One pair was of Richmond manufacture and another from Columbus, Georgia. They were intended to be fair samples of each lot and were selected with that view. Neither could compare with the shoes made in this army. In the Richmond shoe the face of the skin next the animal was turned out, which is contrary to the practice of the best makers and contrary to the arrangement of nature. Without knowing the result of experiment in this matter, I should therefore think it wrong. The leather of the Columbus shoe was not half tanned and the shoe was badly made. The soles of both slight and would not stand a week's march in mud and water.'[19]

One of his privates agreed. 'Our shoes, especially made by the Confederate department, were pitiable specimens indeed,' he wrote. 'Generally made of green or at best half-cured leather, they soon took to roaming; after a week's wear the heel would be on the side, at an angle to the foot, and the vamp, in turn, would try to do duty as a sole. It was impossible to keep them straight, and to judge by your tracks you could hardly tell whether you were going or coming. They conformed to the weather also. While hot and dry they would shrink like parchment, and when wet they just "slopped" all over your feet.'[20]

What Lee wanted to do was to get leather sent in hides to his army and shoemakers serving in the ranks would turn them into shoes. As early as the winter of 1862/3 each unit had to send a list of any men in its ranks who were skilled in shoemaking. These men were detached and given no duties but shoemaking; others were sent back to Richmond to procure tanned leather for this endeavour.

By late 1864, once Lee's Army was tied up in trench warfare, the wear on shoes had lessened considerably. In January 1865 the Quartermaster General was able to report that sufficient shoes for Lee's entire force had been issued, 167,862 pairs in all, and that there remained 'a moderate supply of shoes on hand'.[21]

REGULATION CLOTHING ISSUES
According to Confederate Army Regulations the following was to be issued to every enlisted man.

Clothing	1st Year	2nd Year	3rd Year
Cap, complete	2	1	1
Cover	1	1	1
Coat	2	1	1
Trowsers	3	2	2
Flannel shirts	3	3	3
Flannel drawers	3	2	2
Bootees,* pairs	4	4	4
Stockings, pairs	4	4	4
Leather stock	1		
Great coat	1		
Stable frock (for mounted men)	1		

Clothing	1st Year	2nd Year	3rd Year
Fatigue overall (for engineers and ordnance)	1	1	1
Blanket	1		1

*Mounted men may receive one pair of boots and two pairs of 'bootees', instead of four pair of bootees.

Rations

There was probably an even greater discrepancy between regulations and practice in the area of Confederate rations than there was in that of Confederate uniforms.

The regulations stipulated that each soldier should receive daily: ¾-pound pork or bacon (reduced by 1863 to ½-pound) or 1¼-pounds fresh or salted beef (reduced by 1863 to 1 pound); 1¼-pounds corn meal (reduced by 1863 to 1 pound); 18 ounces bread or flour, which was also reduced to a pound and a half, tops, of either flour or meal. For every hundred rations, one company's worth, the Quartermaster was also to supply eight quarts peas or beans (or ten pounds rice in lieu); six pounds coffee; twelve pounds sugar; four quarts vinegar; 1½-pounds tallow or 1¼-pounds Amandine (the albumen in sweet almonds), or one pound sperm candles; four pounds soap; two quarts of salt.

In the field, this complete issue was rarely if ever made. In fact, Lee told the Confederacy's chief commissary officer — one of the most hated figures in Confederate officialdom — on 5 August 1863 that he was forced to reduce soldiers' rations to levels well under regulation because of shortages. But the shortages were uneven, depending on a soldier's particular location and when the rations were issued. 'Sometimes there was an abundant issue of bread, and no meat,' wrote Richmond Howitzers Private Carlton McCarthy, 'then meat in quantity, and no flour or meal; sugar in abundance, and no coffee to be had for "love or money"; and then coffee in plenty, without a grain of sugar; for months nothing but flour for bread, and then nothing but meal (till all hands longed for a biscuit); or fresh meat until it was nauseating, then salt-pork without intermission.'[1]

Most food came from the resources of the agrarian South. But much of its farmland had initially been planted in cotton and tobacco rather than less profitable foodstuffs. While the government encouraged the growing of grain and vegetables instead of cotton or tobacco during the war, the demand was always greater than supply. So the commissary was forced to buy some food, especially tinned meats, overseas.

'At times the soldier's rations were execrable, really unfit,' wrote staff officer Moxley Sorrel. 'Some bacon from Nassau was coming through the blockade, and it would not be incredible for the blockading fleet to allow it to come through in hope of poisoning us. A third of a pound of this stuff and some corn-meal was then the full extent of the daily ration.'[2]

So most soldiers foraged for what they had not received. Virtually no civilian henhouse near Confederate troops was safe, nor were pigs on nearby farms. Often, citizens would invite soldiers into their houses for a meal or two, and sometimes would sell food to soldiers marching through or encamped in the neighbourhood simply to prevent looting. Small fruit pies are among the most mentioned of this road-side food. 'We fared on picket pretty well,' wrote North Carolina Private Rufus Carson on 25 November 1863. 'There was waggons going along with apples, cakes, eggs, turkeys, chestnuts etc. Chestnuts $1.00 per pt. Apples from $1.50 to $3.00 per Doz, Eggs two dollars per Doz. and so on. We get plenty to eat now. We draw some potatoes some times.'[3]

Given the generally empty wallets of many Confederate soldiers and the relatively empty pantries of Confederate civilians, more food was acquired by less than legal means than was sold. 'We thought we all could get to catch som yankeys,' wrote Private Jesse Hill, Co. K, 21st North Carolina Infantry, on 16 March 1864. 'But we did not get to see any and our men just robed the poor wimen and children. It was a site. Tha went to the houses and takeing any thing tha wanted.' But this food supply didn't last. On 26 August 1864 he wrote: 'Dear and Beloved Wife I will inform you that we dont git but verry little to eat. We only git one pint of corn meal a day and 2 onces of meat a day and with all we are very near all of us broke down and sor.'[4]

The folk back home often replied to such letters positively, sending non-perishable food in boxes if the Army was halted long enough to allow them to reach their destinations. This was so common that many states set up depots in Richmond to receive and forward boxes from home. Mississippi, Alabama, North Carolina, South Carolina and Georgia all had depots on Main Street, while both the 4th and 5th Texas Infantry Regiments had their own regimental depots in the city.

The Union Army was a major supplier of rations to Lee's men. Since the hardtack that comprised a major part of Union rations was not produced to any great extent in the South, virtually all of it and, indeed, much of the salt pork that Lee's men consumed came from Northern manufacturers. Occasionally, such as at the Second Manassas, these Northern supplies were captured in their depots and then issued through more or less official channels. At other times, soldiers obtained Union Army supplies by their own initiative.

'Rations were now scarce, and something to eat would go good. Without saying a word to anyone except Jim Diamond, we walked off in the direction of the front, where the Georgians were now skirmishing,' wrote 1st South Carolina Private Frank Mixson. 'The skirmishing had about this time ceased. We continued to go on to the front and pass the skirmish line. The battlefield of the days before was just ahead of us, and we knew if we could get to where the dead were we would get something sure. We at last came upon the ground where the dead of several days were lying. We had three or four haversacks pretty well filled, and it was not long before Jim Diamond had a fire and had on it in tin cans sliced bacon and rice, making a pillau.'[5]

In this instance Jim Diamond was the cook for this group of soldiers. His building a fire on the field and cooking what they found was not unusual. As rations were issued uncooked, the usual way of preparing them when the war began was for small groups of friends within each company to form a 'mess'. Often the cooking job was rotated; at times, the best cook took the job full-time.

Most units, including Mixson's own regiment, took advantage of a Congressional Act of 21 April 1862 which authorized the enlisting of four cooks per company. These might be whites but were more often blacks, even slaves if the owner's permission were obtained. They were responsible not only for cooking, but caring for utensils. They were issued with the same clothing as the other men; a chief cook was paid $20 a month, an assistant $15.

It seems that these cooks generally made a dedicated effort, even when the unit was in action, to keep their men fed. After Sharpsburg, for example, Mixson recalled, 'While we were holding our ground on the battlefield about midnight the cooks came up with some cooked rations.'[6]

Army rations were not much like the food the men had been used to as civilians, and new dishes were soon devised. 'The meat is too little to cook alone, and the flour will scarcely make six biscuits,' McCarthy wrote. 'The result is that "slosh" or "coosh" must do. So the bacon is fried out till the pan is half full of boiling grease. The flour is mixed with water until it flows like milk, poured into the grease and rapidly stirred till the whole is a dirty brown mixture. It is now ready to be served. Perhaps some dainty fellow prefers the more imposing "slapjack". If so, the flour is mixed with less water, the grease reduced, and the paste poured in till it covers the bottom of the pan, and, when brown on the underside, is, by a nimble twist of the pan, turned and browned again. If there is any sugar in camp it makes a delicious addition.'[7]

Once used to this concoction, soldiers actually preferred it to better food. At Petersburg, while in fairly permanent lines and suddenly getting sufficient supplies of wheat flour, the Army set up ovens and began producing good loaves of bread. 'But the men would have none of such food, it was too light and wholesome. Their stomachs wanted the flour stirred with grease in a skillet and cooked solid and hard.

When a chuck was eaten it stayed with the soldier and kept his appetite partly appeased. But these new-fangled loaves — so easily digested! Hunger came again, almost before finishing one.'[8] One night a gang of soldiers destroyed the ovens so that they could get their favoured 'slosh' again.

At first officers were not issued rations. They could purchase such rations as were available at cost from the commissary, or they were on their own. This system worked well while Confederate money still had purchasing power and foodstuffs were available, but by April 1864 neither of these conditions obtained in Lee's Army. 'A petition from officers in the field had gone to the War Department, asking that rations might be issued to them as private soldiers. It had attached a scale of prices charged the officers by the army commissaries, presumably the average cost price, and not the price of retail market. The officers paid for bacon, $2.20 per pound; beef, 75 cents; lard, $2.20 per pound; molasses, $6 per gallon; sugar, $1.50 per pound. A coat cost $350; boots, $250; trousers, $125; hat, $80 to $125; socks, $10 per pair.'[9]

These prices were a bit steep for an infantry second lieutenant who was paid $80 a month. Indeed, they were steep for his colonel who received only $195 a month, less than the cost of a pair of boots. By mid-1864, any officer who had to send money home to support a family found himself hard put to feed himself.

The petition was received favourably and implemented, but Congress at the same time rescinded the right of officers to purchase provisions at cost from the commissary. The result was that officers with servants, who had previously been allowed to buy rations for them as well as for themselves, had to share already small amounts of issued rations, which in effect put them on half rations. Their only recourse was to bid on the civilian market for their servants' food which was supplemented by food sent from home.

Artilleryman E. Porter Alexander's mess found a novel way out of this problem. 'When a commissary issued beef to a command the head was left as a perquisite to the soldier who acted as butcher, & we discovered that the butcher generally did not seem to value it highly. Possibly he had liver or some other perquisite he liked better. At any rate we rarely had any difficulty in cheating a butcher out of a whole beef's head for a little old Confederate dollar. And when a beef's head is skinned & chopped up & boiled up all day, if one is in camp, or all night if he is on the march, it makes a big camp kettle nearly full of one of the most delightful & richest stews in the world. And if any of it is left, by merely fishing out the big bones, all the meat jellies together solid when it is cold — much resembling a forced meat dish, which, in my young days, we knew as a "Pompey's head" & it at once becomes one of those questions upon which a man can never exactly make up his mind. Whether he likes it best hot for breakfast or supper, or cold, & cut into slices, & carried in the haversack for lunch along the road. But one thing about it seems to me strange enough to be recorded. I have never wanted any more since the war.'[10]

It is doubtful if any survivors of Lee's Army had any desire to replicate the meals they ate while in the service of the Confederacy.

Morale

'When Pope got into his fortified lines Gen. Lee turned his troops toward Leesburg. His army had acquired that magnificent morale which made them equal to twice their numbers, & which they never lost even to the surrender at Appomattox,' wrote E. Porter Alexander.[1]

Obviously it was not elaborate uniforms or rich rations that made the morale in Lee's Army seem so high throughout the entire war, apparently through to the final surrender. What was it?

Part of it was Lee himself and the victories through his leadership, and his personality which was at once noble but not aloof. As Alexander wrote: 'Like the rest of the army generally, nothing gave me much concern so long as I knew that Gen. Lee was in command. I am sure there can never have been an army with more supreme confidence in its commander than that army had in Gen. Lee. We looked forward to victory under him as confidently as to successive sunrises.'[2]

There was more than just Lee and victories to sustain his soldiers' morale, however. The average soldier went into the war with two positive psychological advantages. First, he thought he was by far the better fighting man than the city-dweller, often of foreign birth, of the North. Secondly, he was defending his own home, not trying to conquer somebody else's territory.

He brought with him an informality which definitely aided his morale, especially when rations and clothing were scarce, because he did not rely on either as much as did soldiers of some foreign armies. Many of Lee's soldiers brought their dogs with them, as if they were going on a hunting trip. One such dog stood all parades with the Richmond Howitzers. The dog that followed the Troup Artillery bore the proud name of Robert Lee, although it disgraced its namesake at Chancellorsville when it hid behind a tree throughout the battle. A black Labrador whose name is lost to history accompanied the charge of the 2nd Maryland Infantry Battalion at Gettysburg, only to stay behind, standing guard over the body of the soldier who had taken care of him. There the poor dog was killed by a stray bullet.

There were no formal recreational activities arranged to boost morale, but Lee's soldiers kept themselves occupied. Admittedly there were the inevitable visits to nearby brothels — the 21st North Carolina Infantry had a reported 59 cases of venereal infection from April 1862 to April 1864.[3] Drinking was also common. Less debilitating activities were, perhaps surprisingly, more common than these. Snowball fights, for example, formed a major part of winter camp scenes. After a heavy snowstorm, the 44th and 10th Mississippi Infantry Regiments together attacked the 41st Mississippi in full brigade formation, flags flying and drums beating. The 41st's colonel and several of his officers were captured, not to be exchanged until several barrels of whiskey had gone to the victorious regiment from the losers.

Indeed, a snowball fight during the last two days of January 1863 involved some 9,000 men of Lee's Army and the fighting grew so loud that Union cavalry pickets feared that a full Confederate assault on them was under way.

On a more serious note, Southern soldiers came from a very religious society and tended to reflect this. 'I have never seen more diligent Bible-readers than we had in the Army of Northern Virginia,' recalled Chaplain William Jones, who, it must be admitted, wanted very much to prove the point to a post-war nation.[4] None the less, many soldiers attended religious services whenever possible and a large number became Christians during the war, especially during the many revivals which swept through Lee's Army. The largest of these was recorded after the defeat at Gettysburg when, in one brigade, Jones said, at one service alone 610 men came forward and more than 200 said that they had become converted Christians. 'I spent the greater part of September in protected meetings, in concert with other ministers,' wrote the Revd J. L. Truman of a visit to Lee's Army. 'At one there were 140 converts, and seventy were baptized. There were converts in all of these meetings. A religious feeling of no ordinary character now prevails in the Army of Northern Virginia.'[5]

Strong religious convictions, bringing with them a belief that the New Covenant of Jesus still held, that if the men did their religious duties, especially bearing great sufferings, towards their Father, He would see that their side would prevail. This certainty was bound to help maintain a positive morale, even after defeats such as Gettysburg and hard-fought battles that did not bring victory, such as Sharpsburg.

Also, there was a very mid-19th Century frame of mind that kept the men from complaining to one another, thus lowering overall morale, because to do so would be unseemly. 'He marches. Dare he murmur or complain?' rhetorically asked Carlton McCarthy. 'No; the eyes of all are upon him, and endurance grows silently, till pain and weariness are familiar, and cheerfully borne. At home he would be pitied and petted; but now he must endure, or have the contempt of the strong spirits around him. If he shows the least cowardice he is undone. His courage must never fail. He must be manly and independent, or he will be told he's a baby, ridiculed, teased, and despised.'[6]

With such an attitude, even were a soldier to feel despondent, depressed, unsure of final victory, he could never admit it — something which in this day of revealing every feeling to virtually anyone who will listen is difficult to understand. But it certainly helped create an impression of high morale, even if individually, within the ranks, morale was lower than seemed apparent.

And certainly the long Siege of Petersburg, fought against an enemy who seemed to have endless quantities of men and equipment, sapped the morale of Lee's rank and file much more than the high command knew. 'Sometime ago I was in hopes tha would make pese but I see no chance of that untill the yankeys whips us out,' Private Jesse Hill, 21st North Carolina, struggling with his spelling, wrote home from the trenches. 'Our men is out of hart again and running away like everything. Tha was 5 left the Reg last night and tha is houndreds a going to the yankeys every week and as soon as warm wether coms nerly all our Brigade say tha will go home or somwhere else. Tha say it hant of any use to stay here and be kild for nothing. I am going to try to take care of nomber one as long as I can. I am still in hopes of getting home.'[7]

Most officers, however, did not share, nor in many cases were they aware of, this defeatist attitude. Indeed, their morale tended to be so high that they didn't believe that they could lose until the surrender was complete. McCarthy recalled how surprising news of the surrender was to his commanding officer: 'Lieutenant McRae, noticing a number of wagons and guns parked in a field near by, surprised at what he considered great carelessness in the immediate presence of the enemy, approached an officer on horseback and said, in his usual impressive manner, "I say there, what does this mean?" The man took his hand and quietly said, "We have surrendered." "I don't believe it, sir!" replied McRae, strutting about as mad as a hornet. "You musn't talk so, sir! you will demoralize my men!" '[8]

So it was that many officers' morale was so high that the moment of surrender at Appomattox, obvious as it should have been to virtually everyone, was a surprise to many of them. It would be difficult to have much higher morale in an army than that. On the other hand, most of the men, grieved though they were at the final result, expected it and, indeed, accepted it as the will of God.

Getting Out Of Lee's Army

Army Regulations were quite clear: 'No enlisted man shall be discharged before the expiration of his term of enlistment without authority of the War Department, except by sentence of general court-martial, or by the commander of the department, or of an army in the field, on certificate of disability, or on application of the soldier after twenty years' service.'[1] Clearly, no member of Lee's Army had twenty years' service so there was no getting out on those grounds. Most initial enlistments had been for one year only, and technically many of those enlistees had been released, but had to volunteer again or be re-conscripted for three years or the duration of the war, which just happened to be another three years.

This left physical disability as the only recognized legal ground for getting out of Lee's Army once sworn in. Many men, therefore, deserted, as previously noted. Others were captured, sometimes to be parolled in which case they could not rejoin Lee's Army as active fighters until officially exchanged for a set number of enemy parolees. This number was based on an elaborate numerical rating according to rank or grade, so that one private equalled another private, but the higher up the prisoner's grade or rank, the more privates it took for his exchange.

But from the very beginning individuals began looking for new legal ways to get themselves discharged. Some sought freedom by virtue of their civilian occupation. In November 1861 Bishop William Meade, Episcopal Bishop of Virginia, requested that all men who were candidates for the priesthood be immediately discharged. This request was immediately turned down by Jefferson Davis. As early as January 1862, workers whose particular skills were in demand at government-owned manufactories, such as the Richmond Clothing Manufactory, could be released from the army in order to work there.

Some sought discharge on the grounds that they were not native to the states making up the Confederacy. In early 1863, for example, two conscripts named Moloney and Farrell claimed the right to be discharged because they were British subjects who happened to live in Richmond. The Secretary of War rejected their claims because they had both lived in the state for eight years, on farms which they personally owned and cultivated, and they had voted in local elections which efectively made them Virginians and subject to conscription. None the less, as late as November 1864, the Confederate representative in Paris wrote to the Secretary of State saying that he had received a number of complaints from French diplomats about the 'forced service of French subjects in our armies, that it produced a bad feeling, and hoped it would be discontinued. I replied that I had reason to believe that when the facts could be ascertained it would be found that all demands of natives of France claiming to be exempted from military service were examined with impartiality, and when well-founded had been promptly accorded; that there might have occurred individual cases of hardship or injustice, but it could not be expected that in a war such as the North was waging against us the course of justice should not occasionally be interrupted; that the French subjects who chose to remain in the Confederacy for the purpose of bettering their fortunes had no right to claim that, while every citizen from the age of sixteen to sixty capable of bearing arms was enrolled for service in the field, they should not be called to take part in the defense of their own property; the option had been presented to them of leaving the Confederacy, and if they did not choose to avail themselves of it they could not be permitted to remain passive spectators of a struggle in which the property and even the lives of all within our limits were at stake.'[2]

However, as a class, Marylanders who had enlisted for a year's service in 1861 and so were entitled to be discharged in 1862, could be discharged and were not liable for conscription, since their state had not joined the Confederacy. The same applied to men from the few other states that had not joined the Confederacy who had joined Lee's Army at the outset. Also, those under or over age who had joined in 1861 could be discharged when their terms of service expired.

In late 1861 J. W. Ellis applied for discharge on the grounds that he had been elected to the legislature of North Carolina. His bid for freedom was turned down,[3] but so many others in like case followed him that regulations were revised on 2 April 1863 to allow discharge from the army of any Confederate or state senator or representative, judge, district attorney, clerk of any court of record, sheriff, ordinary, probate judge, collector of state taxes, or parish recorder.[4]

The Confederate Navy desperately needed trained seamen, many of whom had joined or been conscripted into the army. At first the Secretary of the Navy arranged to have many of these men posted to Navy jobs, but the Secretary of War put a stop to this in late 1862. But Congress did authorize the discharge of soldiers with maritime service so that they could be taken into the Navy.

Although medical disability remained the major reason for discharge from Lee's Army throughout the war, towards the end the army started to use some of these invalids who otherwise would have been lost to the war effort. An Invalid Corps was formed on 17 February 1864. Men who were no longer fit for field duty because of disease or wounds, but could still stand light duty such as guarding prisoners of war or assisting in hospitals, were simply transferred into the Invalids instead of being discharged. In all, some 1.063 officers and 5,139 enlisted men served in the Invalids.

Officers, even in good health, were free to resign their commission if there were sufficient reason, but they were then liable for conscription as enlisted men.

6
The Combat Arms

INFANTRY
Organization

The bulk of Lee's Army consisted of infantry. It is not known exactly how many infantry regiments the Confederates had, but one study suggests that there were 529 as against 127 cavalry regiments, the second largest branch of service. Another study has it that there were 642 infantry and 137 cavalry regiments. A third study gives 530 infantry and 125 cavalry regiments.[1] The point is, Lee's men were mostly infantrymen.

The Act of 6 March 1861 authorized a regular Confederate Army with six infantry regiments, each with a colonel, a lieutenant colonel, a major, an adjutant, a sergeant major, and ten companies. Each company was to have a captain, a first lieutenant, two second lieutenants, four sergeants, four corporals, two musicians, and ninety privates. It also stipulated that volunteer infantry companies be formed into battalions and those battalions into regiments. Each battalion was to have one lieutenant colonel or major in command, with a lieutenant serving as adjutant, a sergeant major, a quartermaster sergeant, and a principal musician or chief bugler. Each company was to number between 64 and 100 men, and was to have an additional second lieutenant.[2] A quartermaster sergeant, who received a sergeant major's pay, was authorized on 16 May 1861 and an additional sergeant per company was authorized on 21 August. An ordnance sergeant was authorized for each regimental staff on 19 April 1862. On 28 April the total number of rank and file was set at 125, but in Lee's Army in the field a company at this strength was virtually unknown — indeed, at times an entire brigade numbered no more than 125 men.

On active service, the battalion system was hardly ever used, even by volunteer units. One source estimates that there were only 51 organized infantry battalions as against 530 regiments that had no battalion structure.[3] The volunteer companies that had been formed were organized into full regiments using the system prescribed for the regular army.

On 4 May 1861 an additional regiment, designated 'Zouave', was authorized. This was to have the same basic organization as ordinary infantry regiments, except that each company had its own sergeant major, a quartermaster sergeant and four more corporals. An assistant surgeon was also authorized, 'in addition to those already authorized by law for the Medical Department'.[4] The Zouaves wore a uniform copied from that of the French colonial troops who were prominent during the Crimean War, and their system of deployment was unusually loose and rapid.

On 2 August 1861 an additional field officer for each battalion of at least six companies was authorized, so that there would be a lieutenant colonel and a major with each battalion.[5]

Tactics

Infantry tactics, at least on paper, were rather formal. They were governed by manuals that spelled out exactly each man's position in line of battle, as well as how to march and even how to load and fire one's weapon. Generally speaking, they all called for columns of men marching four abreast, to deploy into a line, two deep, to give battle. Non-commissioned officers would be positioned at each end of the line, while officers would stand behind the line, to direct fire and movement. An initial volley would be fired, followed by firing at will, the intention being to so weaken the enemy as to cause him to withdraw; the bayonet charge being reserved for the final assault.

Regimental commanders had a choice of a number of tactical infantry manuals. At the beginning of the war the most common of these was the one also most used by Northern forces. Written before the war, while he was commandant of cadets at the US Military Academy, William J. Hardee's *Rifle and Light Infantry Tactics* was first published in Philadelphia in 1861, the year he resigned in order to join the Confederate Army. Hardee served in the Western Theatre, and was a lieutenant general by the war's end. His book, and variants based on it, were widely advertised by Richmond booksellers at the war's outbreak.

For example, on 17 April 1861, an advertisement by West & Johnston in the Richmond *Daily Dispatch* listed for sale, *The Volunteer's Handbook*, by Captain James K. Lee of the 1st Virginia Volunteers, which contained an abridgment of Hardee's tactics, and another manual by a captain in the same regiment, R. Milton Cary's *Skirmishers' Drill and Bayonet Exercise*, translated from a French infantry manual.

After he had left the US Army Hardee made some changes to his original manual and authorized a new edition which was published in the spring of 1861 by S. H. Goetzel & Co., of Mobile, Alabama. Another edition, complete in one volume, was published in 1861 in Memphis, Tennessee. The complete, two-volume set of Hardee's manual was advertised for sale in the Richmond *Daily Dispatch* on 24 July 1861.

In 1861 West & Johnston also published a new tactical manual, by William Gilham, commandant of cadets at the Virginia Military Institute. He too had published this basic manual in Philadelphia before the war, but revised it for its Confederate publication. Gilham drew what he thought were the best elements from earlier books by Hardee and other experts. It became the most widely used infantry manual in Lee's Army, where Gilham served as colonel of the 21st Virginia Infantry until dropped from its rolls on 21 April 1862 when the army was reorganized.

The basis of all the systems was close-order drill. So most infantry training, either in camps of instruction or in the first camps of new units, consisted of nothing more than close-order drill following one tactical system or another. There was company drill in the morning, followed by drill in larger formations on most afternoons. Live firing exercises were rarely conducted. Bayonet and skirmishing tactics, according to various manuals, were practised from time to time.

'There was diligent drilling in the camps according to an old French drill manual that had been revised by Hardee, and I observed on the drill field only linear formations, wheeling out into open columns, wheeling in and marching up into a line, marching in line, open column marching, marching by sections, and marching in file,' wrote a European observer in 1863. 'The march proceeded at a slow stride from eighty to ninety paces a minute, or on the "double quick", a slow trot.'[1] In point of fact, however, the actual fighting against the deadly long-range rifled muskets was a rather different affair from that as described in the drill books. For the most part men marched up to the front and formed a line in accordance with the manual. But after the first rounds had been exchanged, formal order fell apart.

Men ducked behind cover, keeping within earshot of one another and their officers, but in a ragged line. They loaded and fired at will. Officers and non-commissioned officers roamed behind them, closing gaps, passing out ammunition, calling up Infirmary Corpsmen to tend to the wounded, and adjusting the line as ordered.

Essentially what had been designed as a tactical system for the company or two that each regiment was supposed to deploy some hundred yards in front of the main line, became the tactics for the entire regiment. Battle lines had become skirmish lines.

'For the battlefield is not a drillroom, nor is a battle an occasion for drill, and there is the merest semblance of order maintained,' recalled South Carolina infantryman Berry Benson. 'I say *semblance* of order, for there *is* an under-current of order in tried troops that surpasses that of the drillroom — it is that order that springs from the confidence comrades have in each other, from the knowledge that these messmates of yours whether they stand or lie upon the ground, close together or scattered apart, in front of you three paces, or in rear of you six, in the open or behind a tree or rock — that these, though they do not "touch elbows to the right", are nevertheless keeping dressed upon the colors in some rough fashion, and that the line will not move forward and leave them there, nor will they move back and leave the line.'[2]

There was still that final bayonet charge, but it too lacked the precision of period wood-cut illustrations. 'With a burst of yells, a long, wavering, loose jointed line sweeps rapidly forward, only now and then one or two stopping to fire, while here and there drop the killed and the wounded; the slightly wounded, some of them, giving no heed but rushing on, while others run hurriedly, half-bent to the rear,' Benson wrote. 'The colors drop, are seized again — again drop, and are again lifted, no man in reach daring to pass them by on the ground. Colors, not bright and whole and clean as when they came fresh from the white embroidering fingers, but since clutched in the storm of battle with grimy, bloody hands, and torn into shreds by shot and shell.'[3]

Weapons

The basic infantryman's weapon was the rifled musket, so called because it had the long barrel of a musket, usually distinguishable from the three bands that claamped it to the stock, but with rifling for better accuracy. At the beginning of the war, the US Army's standard infantry longarm was the Model 1855 rifled musket, an 0.58-calibre weapon which had all-iron furniture and an oiled American walnut stock. It fired the conical lead bullet invented by a French Army officer, Captain Minié, hence its best-known name, the 'minnie ball'. Using black powder set off by a percussion cap fitted over the cone during the loading process, it had a muzzle velocity of 950 feet per second, At a thousand yards it could penetrate 3¼ inches of pine boards, although its accuracy was minimal at that range. In most engagements the forces were well over 200 yards from each other, where the weapon, accurately fired, was deadly, the large slow-moving bullets shattering flesh and bone.

In 1861 the Harper's Ferry Armory was captured by the Confederates and the production machinery for the M1855 rifled musket was sent to an armoury at Richmond to produce copies of the weapon. The Confederate copy looked very similar to and had the same qualities as the US model, but had a simplified three-bladed leaf sight instead of the elaborately machined ladder sight, and was produced without the covered patch box in the stock and the Maynard self-priming cap system in the lock. The nosecap and buttplate were of brass instead of steel.

The Richmond Armory was capable of producing 25,000 of these weapons annually,[1] but from October 1861, when the first one was turned out, to 30 November 1863 the Armory produced only 23,381 rifled muskets. Production continued to increase, but the Armory was never able to supply Lee's infantry, let alone all the Confederate infantry in the field.

The US Army retained the 1855 rifle musket as its standard, although it, too, simplified the weapon by changing the ladder sight to a blade model and eliminating the patch box. Also, the elaborate Maynard primer system, which fed paper caps in a roll out of the lock with each shot, was eliminated. Since most of the war's early battles in northern Virginia were Southern victories, in which battered Union troops fled the field, thousands of US infantry longarms were captured. Many were in fine condition and were re-issued by ordnance officers in the field to replace the old smooth-bored muskets that many early volunteers had brought with them. Others were repaired at the Richmond Armory and issued to Lee's Army. Some 323,231 infantry weapons, chiefly repaired battlefield pickups, were issued through the Richmond Armory from 1 July 1861 to 1 January 1865.[2] Also, after Chancellorsville alone, 10,000 Confederate infantrymen apparently dropped their issued longarms and replaced them with superior Union weapons, either Northern-made or imported. In all, 19,500 rifles and muskets were turned in to the Ordnance Department from that battlefield, 9,500 of which were good Union Army weapons and 10,000 inferior Confederate-issued weapons.[3]

From the very beginning the Confederates imported British-made copies of the British Army's 1853 Pattern rifled musket. This weapon was very similar in general appearance to the Richmond-made rifled musket, although it was an inch shorter and the butt was cut less dramatically for the shoulder. It used the more elaborate ladder sight, no longer made for Richmond's rifled muskets, and had brass furniture. The barrel was generally blued or even browned, which was preferred by the troops who had to keep the bright barrels of the Northern-made and Richmond weapons polished. The British longarms, referred to generically as 'Enfields', although none was made by the British Army's Royal Small Arms Factory at Enfield, had a slightly smaller bore, at 0.577 calibre. They also fired a slightly different bullet, made with a wooden plug in the back instead of the conical space, and without the grooves of the Southern-made bullets which cleaned out fouling from the barrel after repeated firing.

So many more Enfields were imported than Richmonds were made or US rifled muskets captured, that the 0.577 calibre bullet became the standard Confederate issue.

However, there was never a total standardization of longarm calibres in Lee's Army. The 0.54 calibre Austrian Lorenz rifled musket was imported in large quantities and was known to have been carried by members of the Stonewall Brigade. Rifled muskets of 0.70 calibre bore used by Confederate infantrymen included both Belgian and Brunswick models, and 0.69 US Army-issued M1842 and earlier smooth-bore muskets also saw service, especially early in the war before the Ordnance Department had a chance to replace them all through capture, import and manufacture. Some infantrymen actually preferred the smooth-bored musket, especially for fighting at close range, since each shot contained one full-sized ball and three buckshot. While it had extremely poor accuracy, it was a deadly weapon at close range.

The US Army had also produced its 1855 model in a shorter version, called simply a 'rifle'. This differed from the rifled musket in that it had a 33-inch barrel, as opposed to the 40-inch rifled musket barrel, and took a sword bayonet with a brass grip rather than the all-iron spike bayonet of the rifled musket. The Confederate Ordnance Department prohibited the manufacture of these expensive bayonets on 14 January 1864. The production machinery for the M1855 rifle at Harper's Ferry was sent to Fayetteville, North Carolina, to turn out Confederate copies of the weapon. As with Richmond's copies of the US rifled musket, there were some slight differences. Again, brass was used for nosecap and buttplate and the patch box was eliminated from the stock. The final version of the Fayetteville rifle used an unusually shaped hammer, rather like a sideways letter 'S', which gave it greater strength.

Rifles were popular with Confederate troops. Their accuracy, especially at battle ranges, was not significantly poorer than that of the rifled muskets with their longer barrels. And their manufacture needed slightly less raw material, always at a premium in the South, than did rifled muskets.

M1841 'Mississippi' rifles, which had a slightly smaller, 0.54 calibre, bore, had been left over in state arsenals when the war began and saw a great deal of use. South Carolina had made a thousand copies of these rifles in the state's own armoury in 1851. After the war began, Georgia set up its own armoury to make copies of them as well. In early 1862 its production rate was some 125 per month complete with bayonets. The same lockplate, but with the smaller nosecap of the M1855 rifle, was used by other Confederate longarms manufacturers, including the Asheville, North Carolina, Armory; C. Chapman; Dickson, Nelson & Co. of Alabama; H.C. Lamb & Co. of North Carolina; J.P. Murray/Greenwood & Gray of Alabama; Davis & Bozeman of Alabama; and Mendenhall, Jones, and Gardner of North Carolina.

The Confederacy imported large numbers of copies of the British Army's Pattern 1856 Short Rifle, which looked like nothing so much as a shortened Enfield rifled musket. This weapon, which was 49 inches long, with a 33-inch barrel, also took a sword bayonet.

Copies of the P1856 rifle were made by several Confederate gun-makers, but most of those that would have been seen in Lee's Army would have come from Cook & Brother, which set up a plant at Athens, Georgia, after their factory in New Orleans was captured. In all, the plant at Athens produced some 6,000 rifles, some of which could well have ended up in the hands of Lee's infantry.

In the British Army P1856 rifles were carried by all sergeants in line infantry regiments. The Confederates probably made no such distinction, but infantry sergeants were distinguished by wearing a sword of unique design. Versions of this sword made by W. Walsoneid, of Solingen, Germany, had a 32-inch long straight blade with all-brass hilt and the letters 'CSA' cast on the counterguard; Southern-made versions were similar but generally had an unstopped fuller in the blade and a crudely cast hilt. Since many of Lee's sergeants didn't even want to wear chevrons, obviously fewer would bother with a sword, and such items were fairly rare.

Officers, on the other hand, almost always carried a sword, although Lee rarely did so in the field. Confederate swords were generally modelled on the US Army system, having a field officers' version carried by majors and above, including generals, and a line officers' version. Generally the two swords were similar, having a slightly curved, engraved blade, an elaborately cast and gilded hilt with black leather grips wound with twisted wire, and a black leather scabbard with gilt mountings. The field officers' version had the letters 'CS' cast in the hilt.

Southern-made officers' swords, like those for non-commissioned officers, were often more crudely made than those of Northern manufacturers. Hilts were of much simpler design and often crudely cast. Grips were often wrapped in black oilcloth instead of leather and wound around with plain, untwisted wire. Scabbards were more crudely sewn and had plainer mountings than were seen on Northern swords.

Again, Northern manufacturers came through for many of Lee's soldiers, as officers were able to arm themselves with swords captured on the battlefield. The common US Army cavalry sabre, with possibly some Southern-made versions as well, seems to have been about the most popular company-grade officers' sword. Whenever possible, Confederate officers, stuffed with romantic notions derived from the works of Sir Walter Scott, brought heirloom swords from home that had been carried in the Revolution and War of 1812. Finally, infantry officers' swords were widely imported from Britain, France and Germany.

The other basic officer's arm was the pistol. Six-shot percussion revolvers came in two patterns, the 0.36 calibre Navy model and the 0.44 calibre Army model. The Army pistol was heavier, but had considerably more stopping power, and was generally preferred by company-grade officers who actually used them in combat.

The versions of these pistols made by Samuel Colt in Connecticut were the standard by which all other pistols were judged and most Confederate officers procured one if possible. As the Navy models had been made as early as 1851 and many had been purchased by civilians in the South for personal protection before the war, there were many such weapons available. Other Northern-made pistols, by Remington, Whitney, Starr and others, were also quite popular.

But pre-war purchases and captures were not enough to supply all the Confederate officers, so Southern manufacturers set up plants to fill the gap. Their revolvers were generally copies of the Colt Navy revolver, differing, however, in that the barrels were usually turned rather than octagonal as were Colt's Navy barrels. Georgia manufacturers Leech & Rigdon (later Rigdon-Ansley) produced 1,500 of these revolvers; Griswold & Gunnison turned out 3,606, but with brass rather than iron frames; Spiller & Burr produced just under a thousand copies of the Northern-made Whitney revolver, again with brass rather than steel frames. Double-action 0.44 calibre revolvers made by Adams & Deane and by Kerr were imported from Britain.

Grenades were only issued from time to time, usually in situations such as the Siege of Petersburg. Earlier, during the retreat from Yorktown in 1862, Confederate infantrymen improvised primitive land mines in the form of artillery shells with sensitive fuze-primers planted underground. Several of these exploded, slowing the enemy advance greatly, but public opinion against such 'inhuman' weapons was so great that their use was largely discontinued by Lee's men.

Equipment

The infantryman is a self-contained fighting unit and therefore must carry everything he needs to sustain life and fight in the field.

To sustain life, a man needs food, water and shelter. The Confederate infantryman's food was carried in a haversack, essentially a sack suspended from a shoulder-strap over the right shoulder to the left hip. Usually it was made of cotton duck, and buttoned at the flap. Occasionally there was a separate food bag buttoned inside the outer sack.

Since cotton duck wouldn't keep provisions dry, a waterproof bag was more desirable than the average issue haversack. Some Southern-made tarred versions were available, and officers often carried either a tarred or all-leather haversack, depending on what was available. The well-made and waterproof US Army haversacks were always in great demand. The 1st South Carolina Infantry veteran Berry Benson, after the fighting at the Seven Days wrote that 'the whole Confederate army refitted itself with blankets, rubber clothes [i.e., groundsheets, talmas and ponchos], tent flies, haversacks and canteens. So that in the middle of the war and later, to see equipment of Southern make was somewhat of a curiosity.'[1]

A canteen was also slung from the right shoulder to the left hip by a cotton or leather strap, and rested on top of the haversack. Everyone agreed that the Union Army canteens, covered with woollen cloth to keep the contents cool, were better than the plain tin and wood drum style of canteen issued to the Confederate Army, but relic seekers and archaeologists working late-war sites find that parts of the Southern-made canteen are among the most common of all discoveries.

The last piece of life-sustaining equipment was the knapsack or blanket roll. 'The knapsack vanished early in the struggle,' wrote artilleryman Carlton McCarthy. 'It was inconvenient to "change" the underwear too often, and the disposition not to change grew, as the knapsack was found to gall the back and shoulders, and weary the man before half the march was accomplished. The better way was to dress out and out, and wear that outfit until the enemy's knapsacks, or the folks at home supplied a change.'[2]

McCarthy was exaggerating slightly for effect. Certainly, a great many Confederate infantrymen abandoned the overstuffed knapsacks with which they had left their first camps. 'In our knapsacks we carried a fatigue jacket, several pairs of white gloves, several pairs of drawers, several white shirts, undershirts, linen collars, neckties, white vest, socks, etc. — filling our knapsack to overflowing. Strapped on the outside were one or two blankets, an oilcloth, and extra shoes. Most of the knapsacks weighed between thirty and forty pounds, but some were so full that they weighed fifty pounds!'[3] In such cases, obviously the wearer would abandon something, and it would probably have been the knapsack, possibly laid aside in favour of a Union bag. Some 11,500 Union knapsacks were picked up from the field at Chancellorsville alone.[4]

If the knapsack were abandoned, and it was the most common thing to go, the remaining extra clothing such as a spare shirt or pair of drawers, was rolled into a blanket which was worn bandolier-fashion over the left shoulder, the ends tied together at the right hip. The blanket was either an issued one or, often as not, privately purchased or sent from home or 'found' in a civilian house.

But many infantrymen clung to their knapsack throughout the war, especially if it were waterproof and fitted square to the back by means of leather straps that passed over and under the shoulders. Some had wooden frames to keep them neat, others were little more than large cloth bags. British Army issue knapsacks were manufactured by a London firm, S. Isaac, Campbell & Co., and imported by the Confederacy.

The Confederate infantryman carried forty rounds of longarm ammunition in a cartridge box. Many of those who received Enfield rifled muskets or rifles received copies of British Army cartridge boxes. The rest received cartridge boxes that were copies of the Union Army black box, which had straps on the back so that it could be carried either on a strap from the left shoulder to the right hip or on a waistbelt at the centre of the back. The Union Army model held forty of the paper-wrapped cartridges in two 20-round tin containers. The box had a small pocket beneath the flap which held musket tools and cleaning equipment. The outside of the flap was decorated with a brass oval plate bearing the letters 'US'. Many of these boxes were used by Confederate soldiers, who found 8,000 of them on the Chancellorsville battlefield alone.[5]

Southern-made copies of this box usually simplified the design, the tin container often being made in one piece. Some boxes had a waistbelt strap only, some only a shoulder-strap. Some eliminated the tool pouch. Finials were often of lead or wood instead of brass. Southern-made cartridge-box flaps rarely had a brass badge, although some made in Richmond did have this bit of luxury; M. H. Richmond and Sons, for example, stamped the letters 'CS' in an oval on the flap of their boxes.

Finally, because of shortage of leather, the sling and even the outer flap of some boxes were of painted cloth. Plain cotton webbing box slings, and even rifle slings, were made.

The cartridge box was carried either on the waistbelt or on the crossbelt tucked under the waistbelt. The waistbelt was supposed to be of black leather, although undyed leather and even cotton webbing waistbelts are known to have been issued. Officially the Union Army practice of having a brass beltplate was to be followed, and indeed, an oval beltplate, the brass more red than yellow owing to a high percentage of copper, bearing the letters 'CS' was widely worn in Lee's Army. Pre-war State plates, such as the oval brass plates bearing the seals of Georgia or Texas or the letters 'NC' or 'SC', were also worn if obtainable.

But photographs of Confederate soldiers in the field indicate that most of Lee's infantrymen wore a plain frame buckle of one sort or another. The majority had a brass frame and were of the styles known as 'wishbone', from the split-tongue design, and 'Georgia', from its source. Iron buckles, often with rollers, were also common.

The infantryman had two more accoutrements on his waistbelt: a thin iron pick used to clear a fouled musket nipple, and his cap box. The latter was a small leather pouch holding his copper percussion caps, and was worn on the front right hip, next to the belt buckle. The Union model was of black leather with a sheepskin wrapper inside to prevent the caps from falling out when the flap was opened; a double flap gave extra security. Many of these Union cap boxes saw Confederate use, 4,000 of them being found on the Chancellorsville battlefield alone.[6]

Southern-made cap boxes tended to be of simpler construction, with only one strap instead of two at the rear, and lead or wood finials instead of brass. British-made cap boxes were supplied, being copies of the Conferate box and of the British Army white buff box which was secured to the cartridge-box sling instead of the waistbelt, At times, however, Confederate infantrymen wore this box on the waistbelt, possibly because they lacked a cartridge-box sling, or possibly because the practice was alien to them.

Southern-made bayonet scabbards, worn on the left hip, beneath the haversack, were plainer than those of the North. The scabbards produced for the iron spike bayonets to be used with the Richmond copies of the M1855 rifled musket were black, the frog sewn rather than riveted. The tip was a small white metal finial instead of the large brass finial of the US Army scabbard. British Enfields came complete with scabbard, these being copies of standard British Army issue.

'The infantry found out that bayonets were not of much use, and did not hesitate to throw them, with the scabbard, away,' McCarthy wrote.[7] Again, an oversimplification, but there was some truth in it; very little fighting was done with the bayonet, and the soldiers would probably have soon decided that there was little or no reason to lug an additional couple of pounds about.

Officially, musicians' drums were to be painted blue, with the company letter and regimental number on a scroll under the 'arms of the Confederate States'. A drum carried in the 13th Virginia Infantry had a dark-blue front with a shield bearing the blue Saint Andrew's cross, edged in white, on a red field, with white stars on the bars, on the front. The numeral '13' appeared in the top left of the shield, the abbreviation 'Va' in the right. But this was a rarity, most drums being of plain wood, often with red hoops. Musicians in rifle and some infantry regiments such as the 2nd Kentucky, carried bugles.

Insignia

Infantrymen wore the standard uniform of their rank or grade. The branch-of-service colour, officially used on coat trim, caps, trouser stripes, and chevrons, was sky-blue. Officers' sashes were red, as were sergeants', and their buttons were to be gilt with an embossed letter 'I', for infantry, in the centre. Originally, enlisted men were to have worn their regimental number on their brass buttons, but this never came about. Indeed, in June 1862 they were authorized to wear the 'I' on their buttons too, but a large number of Southern-made uniforms came with plain wooden buttons instead of proper brass buttons. Many men replaced regulation buttons with buttons bearing the seal of their native states.

There were some unique Confederate insignia systems that were used mainly in infantry units, that branch being by far the most numerous. In late 1863, for example, the Maryland Line were to have worn a red cloth version of the Maryland symbol, the cross *botonee*, on fields coloured according to the wearer's unit, but there was insufficient cloth available for this scheme; many individuals in Maryland units wore the symbol on their right breast, usually in the form of an engraved silver version of the badge.[11] Similarly, Lee's Texans sometimes wore a five-pointed star, the symbol of their state, on hat or jacket breast. Louisianians sometimes wore a silver crescent embracing a five-pointed star.

Although the Confederate Army had no regulation cap badges, infantry officers sometimes wore old US Army badges, presumably found in military supply stores. These gold embroidered cap badges were in the form of a bugle-horn, sometimes having an embroidered regimental number in silver within the horn's loop.

Scattered evidence suggests that cap badges of one sort or another were far from uncommon in Lee's Army. For example, a photograph of Confederate prisoners, dated mid-May 1864, shows a man with a piece of white cloth bearing the legend 'Al 4' in black on his turned-up hat brim, possibly for 4th Alabama Infantry, who were engaged in the area.[2]

'Numbers of unburied Confederates still lay about, notably, as recognized by the insignia on their uniforms, of the 11th North Carolina and the 18th Georgia,' wrote a Union soldier of the Second Manassas battlefield, a year after the battle.[3] It is not known what form of insignia this may have been, but presumably it was sufficiently common as to warrant no description. Possibly it included regimental numbers on cap tops or fronts and state seals on buttons; perhaps it was simply printed as in the case of the 4th Alabamian photographed two years later. But so far as insignia were concerned, the majority of Confederate infantrymen must have been like the prisoners seen by a Union soldier on 4 May 1865 to whom he had to explain the significance of his cap badge. 'What's that on your cap, that horn and letters, they look so nice?' they asked him. He noted that, 'The rebs has old Hats, Caps and no marks on them.'[4]

Early in the war, when both sides wore a mix of blue and grey uniform, Confederate infantrymen were issued with various unit designations, a temporary measure to aid identification on the battlefield. Just prior to the First Manassas, a system that featured reversible wings, epaulettes or coloured arm-bands was ordered — only to be abandoned when it was discovered that Union troops had very similar field designations. But as late as 31 May 1862, Major General D. H. Hill issued orders for every man to be 'supplied with a strip of white cloth. This is to be worn on the cap in battle, but do not let even your colonels know where it is to be worn until a few moments before you start.'[5]

Flags

It seems to be natural for some men to wish to distinguish themselves by flying a flag. So it was that in 1861 most volunteer companies brought their own company flags with them when they were formed into the Confederate Army in northern Virginia. Many of these flags were fairly elaborate, featuring allegorical scenes representing ideas such as the overthrow of tyranny or defence of the home. Few of these flags survived much active campaigning; soldiers needed to carry rifled muskets, not flags.

In their place each regiment had one regimental Colour, often confusingly referred to as a 'stand of Colours'.[1] The bearer was a sergeant, referred to by the unofficial title of 'Colour Sergeant', until 17 February 1864 when Congress authorized a new commissioned officer, an ensign, to carry the Colour. Although having no command, he wore the uniform of a first lieutenant. This rank did not endure, however.

Many regimental Colours, such as those carried by the 1st Texas, 2nd and 36th Virginia, and 38th and 47th North Carolina Infantry Regiments, were state flags. Indeed, in Lee's Army North Carolina and Virginia regiments were more apt to carry state flags than regiments from other states. Sometimes, but not always, the regimental designation was applied to the state flag.

On 4 March 1861 Congress approved a national flag. This was similar to the US national flag, having a dark-blue canton on which was featured a circle of five-pointed white stars, one for each state. Otherwise, it had three horizontal stripes, one white between two red, on the field. This became essentially the standard regimental Colour for the infantry units in the army in northern Virginia in 1861, except a handful of mostly Virginia regiments which still carried a state Colour.

Any number of Confederate commanders, however, complained bitterly that at the First Manassas, in the smoke of battle, at a distance, especially when the flags were hanging limp with no wind, it was impossible to distinguish the flags of the opposing forces. Precious time was lost waiting for a puff of wind to show whether a force approaching one's position were friend or foe, especially since both sides wore a mix of pre-war uniforms in a variety of colours.

The initial solution was to forbid units to carry any but state flags into combat, but this gave rise to two difficulties. Most units couldn't obtain their state flags; indeed, some states didn't have an official flag. Second, many state flags had a dark-blue field with the state seal painted on it. In the field these tended to look quite like US Army infantry regimental Colours, which also featured a dark-blue field with a painted seal. So, this would not eliminate the confusion.

Notice of the problem reached the ears of Congressman William Porcher Miles, who had sat on the first committee that had approved the national flag design. He suggested to the army's commander, General P. G. T. Beauregard, an alternate design based on one that his committee had considered. It had a red field with a blue Saint Andrew's cross, edged in white, and a five-pointed white star for each state placed on the bars of the cross.

Beauregard liked the basic design, although the army quartermaster suggested making the flag square to save material. Three samples, one for each Confederate army commander, were made in September 1861. They were approved and this flag, in a 48-inch-square size, became the official infantry regimental battle flag of what became the Army of Northern Virginia.

In all 120 such flags were made by ladies' sewing circles in Richmond from dress silks bought on the open market. The fields of these flags were actually rather pink, rather than the stipulated brilliant scarlet. The edges were hemmed in yellow silk, save for the sleeve which was of blue silk. When the 20th Georgia Infantry received their first battle flag, Colonel W. D. Smith was concerned that the pale colour might look like a white flag of surrender. 'Dye it red, sir!' Beauregard told the colonel. 'Dye it with blood, sir!'[1]

When the Navy Yard at Norfolk, Virginia, was captured, large supplies of the type of bunting used for flags was found among the stores. This was sent on to the Richmond Clothing Manufactory which used it, and bunting imported from Britain, to make additional battle flags. These differed from the first ones in that they had a true scarlet field, were machine sewn, and were edged with orange flannel. Also, they featured a thirteenth star at the point where the bars of the cross met; the first silk flags had only three stars on each bar with no centre star. These first bunting flags were issued as early as May 1862 to regiments under Longstreet's command.

In the second pattern of bunting flag issued by the Manufactory from the spring of 1862, the blue bars were narrowed from eight to 5½ inches, with proportionally smaller stars — this in a bid to conserve material. From July 1862, a so-called third bunting pattern replaced the orange edges with white 2-inch-wide bunting, and this was produced until the end of May 1864, becoming largely the standard infantry regimental battle flag of Lee's Army.

The Clothing Manufactory produced yet another pattern of bunting battle flag for Lee's Army. It was large, almost 51 inches square, with 7-inch-wide blue crosses and equally large stars. It first appeared in the spring of 1864 and production lasted until November 1864 when it was made smaller, with 5-inch-wide crosses. Slight changes in the spacing of the stars were made during that winter, and again in March 1865.

In keeping with past American military practice, battle honours were authorized to be placed on battle flags indicating honourable participation in particular battles. The first of these were printed in black block letters on white stripes of cotton and sewn to battle flags in Longstreet's Corps in June 1862. The honours were for Williamsburg and Seven Pines. It was not until 23 July 1862, however, that battle honours were officially authorized by the War Department.

The method of applying battle honours varied among brigades since commanding officers were responsible for their placement on the flag. Some were printed on strips of cotton; some were painted in gold, others in white. After April 1863 honours were applied with blue paint only on one side of the flag.

Despite there being a single standard design of flag for the whole of Lee's Army, other, non-regulation designs were carried by some infantry units throughout the war. Captain S. A. Ashe, a North Carolina infantryman, was captured at the Second Manassas and accused of carrying Union flags to fool the enemy. He admitted that 'some of our flags were company flags presented by ladies and were irregular design'.[2] Virginia and possibly North Carolina infantry regiments apparently carried blue state flags at Pickett's Charge.

Pay

On 6 March 1861 pay rates were set at: colonel, $195; lieutenant colonel, $170; major, $150; captain, $140; first lieutenant, $90; second lieutenant, $90; adjutant, $10 in addition to his lieutenant's pay; sergeant major, $21; first sergeant, $20; sergeant, $17; corporal, $13; musician, $12; private, $11.[1] On 9 June 1864, all enlisted men received a pay rise of $7 a month, so that a private then drew $18 a month. But inflation robbed this increase of much of its value; J. B. Jones reported

---

ARMY OF NORTHERN VIRGINIA BATTLE FLAGS

Most combat units of Lee's army carried some version of the famous square red colour with a blue St Andrew's cross and twelve or thirteen stars on the arms of the cross. Most of these were made by the Richmond Clothing Manufactory, which produced eight distinct patterns of the battle flag during their three years of production.

Model	Date first appeared	Cross width	Star diameter	Distance between stars	Outer edge	Infantry size	No of stars	Material used
1st	Late 1861	8in	4½in	8in	2in yellow	48in	12	Silk
2nd	Early 1862	8in	3in	6in	1½in orange	48in	13	Bunting
3rd	Mid-1862	5½in	3½–3¼in	6in	1½in orange	48in	13	Bunting
4th	Autumn 1862	5½in	3½–3¼in	8in	2in white	51in	13	Bunting
5th	Spring 1864	7in	5½in	8in	2in white	48in	13	Bunting
6th	Nov 1864	5in	4½in	9in	2in white	48in	13	Bunting
7th	Winter 1864	5in	4½in	8in	2in white	48in	13	Bunting
8th	March 1865	5in	4½in	7in	2in white	48in	13	Bunting

on 11 June that new potatoes were selling in Richmond for $5 a quart or $160 a bushel.[2]

SHARPSHOOTERS

Organization

On 21 April 1862 Congress authorized the raising of a battalion of sharpshooters for each infantry brigade. Each of these battalions was to have from three to six companies, organized in the same manner as normal infantry battalions, but armed with 'long-range muskets or rifles'. On 22 May it was further ordered that each sharpshooter battalion consist of men from the same state.[1]

Lee's Army had only a handful of battalions which actually bore the designation 'sharpshooters', however, and these were state-raised, rather than organized by brigades on the suggested *ad hoc* lines. The state sharpshooter units in Lee's Army included the 3rd Georgia Battalion of Sharpshooters, raised in the spring of 1863; the 23rd Alabama Battalion of Sharpshooters, raised in the autumn of 1863; the 30th Virginia Battalion of Sharpshooters, raised in the spring of 1861; and South Carolina's Palmetto Sharpshooters, raised in the spring of 1862. However, according to Jefferson Davis's message to Congress of 3 January 1863, 'The battalion of sharpshooters attached to each brigade has done much to restore our superiority as marksmen, which had begun to be endangered by the guns of long range and constant practice therewith by our less skillful adversaries. On many occasions, the efficiency as well as the valor of these battalions has been strikingly exhibited, and they are now felt as almost a necessity to a proper organization.'[2]

None the less, it seems as if in Lee's Army the full implementation of the Congressional Act did not come about until at least 1864 when additional sharpshooter battalions were raised. A sharpshooter battalion of three companies for McGowan's Brigade, for example, was raised on 1 March 1864 by taking several of the supposedly best shots from each company within the brigade and forming them into the battalion.[3] But these battalions do not appear on official army orders of battle, and so it is difficult to say when and how many brigades had full and dedicated sharpshooter battalions attached to them.

Tactics

Sharpshooters were generally trained in skirmish drill. In the battalion attached to McGowan's Brigade, according to its commander, 'a unique and concise system of tactics was prepared and compiled from the American skirmish and French Zouave drills and introduced by the commander for the government of the battalion on the field, while a "manual of arms" in the form of a brochure upon the subject of rifle training was furnished by Maj. Gen. Wilcox.'[1] There had been a number of manuals published before the war from which such material could have been drawn, most notably two by Chicago's Elmer Ellsworth, who made the 'Zouave' craze popular just prior to the war. They were *Light Infantry Drill Arranged for the U.S. Zouave Cadets* (his demonstration drill team) and *Zouave Drill Book*. Also, the US 7th Infantry's Lieutenant C. M. Wilcox's *Rifles and Rifle Practice* was most likely available, having been published in New York in 1859. In fact, the 'Lieutenant Wilcox' who published this book was the same 'General Wilcox' who provided the brochure used for training in 1864, and it is likely that the two publications were essentially one and the same. *An Elementary Treatise on Advanced-Guard, Out-Post and Detachment Service* by US Military Academy professor D. H. Mahan first appeared in 1847 and went through many printings before the war. It was an ideal manual for practical use by sharpshooters, dealing with such subjects as estimating distances and serving in small detachments before an enemy force.

Indeed, training in just such subjects as Mahan covered was given extensively in the sharpshooter battalion in McGowan's Brigade, as well as a great deal of target practice, practice in fighting cavalry, and bayonet drill.

Weapons
'In target drill, the Minié rifle, the Enfield, the Austrian, Belgian, Springfield and Mississippi rifles were put to the test. And while each and all of them proved accurate and effective at short range, the superiority of the Enfield rifle for service at long range, from 600 to 900 yards, was clearly demonstrated, both as to force and accuracy of fire. The ulterior range of the Enfields proved reliable and effective to a surprising degree to a distance of 900 yards, while the other rifles named could only be relied on at a distance of 500 yards.'[1]

While the sharpshooters of McGowan's Brigade's may have been equipped with ordinary issue Enfield rifled muskets, others used weapons specially designed for their work. Some used civilian target rifles, which had extremely heavy barrels, suitable only for firing from a resting position, with scopes or finely adjusted peep sights, and triggers which fired on a very light pressure. These target rifles weighed from 9 to 35 pounds, but had tremendous accuracy at ranges up to 1,000 yards.

The British Whitworth Rifle Co., of Manchester, produced a sharpshooter's weapon which the Confederacy imported in small numbers and placed in the hands of a number of sharpshooters in Lee's Army. In external appearance it was like the ordinary Enfield rifled muskets, save for the iron nosecap which was closer to the muzzle, although it did accept a socket bayonet. But it had a special, hexagonal 0.45 calibre bore, with fitting ammunition, that produced a high degree of accuracy at extremely long range; it had a killing range of some 1,500 yards.

Southern sharpshooters received standard infantry uniform and equipment, those with civilian target rifles carried rests for the weapons. No special insignia were authorized, but on 2 April 1865 a Union private noted that while following Lee's Army to Appomattox: 'We took the road and lots of prisoners. The sharp shooters had a red cross on their arms.'[1] A piece of 1½-inch, eight-sided black cloth bearing a scarlet felt cross was worn by Henry A. Wise, Co. B, 2nd Maryland Infantry and was presented as a 'Sharp Shooter's Badge' to the Maryland Historical Society. It is possible that this insignia was commonly worn by sharpshooters; certainly it would have been sensible to be able to identify men whose duties were independent of the battle line, if only to prevent their being mistaken for shirkers. But any such insignia would have been authorized at brigade level and would probably have been improvised from anything the brigade quartermaster could find. Although theirs were more skillful and demanding duties than those of ordinary infantrymen, sharpshooters received the standard infantry pay of their rank.

ARTILLERY
Organization
The Congressional Act that set up the Confederate Army on 6 March 1861 specified that the artillery personnel of the regular army should consist of a colonel, a lieutenant colonel, ten majors, who would mostly be involved with ordnance duties, an adjutant holding the rank of first lieutenant, a sergeant major, and ten companies. Each company would have a captain, two first lieutenants, one second lieutenant, four sergeants, four corporals, two musicians and 70 privates. As many light batteries as were needed were also authorized, each battery to consist of six cannon.[1]

On 21 August Congress increased the corps by adding a lieutenant colonel, two majors and one sergeant per company or battery.[2] On 19 April 1862 an ordnance sergeant was added to each regimental staff.

The army had too few officers of sufficiently high rank to command all the artillery it would require, so on 22 January 1862 Congress authorized the appointment of one brigadier general for every 80 guns within a command, a colonel for every 40, a lieutenant colonel for every 24 and a major for every 16 guns.[3]

On 3 March 1862 General Samuel Cooper, the Army's Adjutant and Inspector General, submitted a memorandum to the Secretary of War, Judah P. Benjamin, in which he complained of the heavy artillery's organization, which was limited by the act of 6 March, while the light artillery could muster as many officers and men as was thought necessary. He felt that each gun should have a sergeant and a corporal on its crew, whereas under the law an 8-gun company had only four sergeants and four corporals.[4] On 3 April the law was changed to correct this error, adding non-commissioned officers as required,[5] and on 28 April the total personnel of a company of field artillery was set at 150.[6]

On 1 November 1862 the Adjutant and Inspector General's Office issued the organizational tables for the light artillery. A 6-gun battery was to have a captain, two first lieutenants, two second lieutenants, either a sergeant major or a first sergeant, a quartermaster sergeant, six sergeants, twelve corporals, two buglers or trumpeters, a guidon-bearer, two artificers, and no more than 125 or fewer than 64 privates. A 4-gun battery was to have a captain, a first lieutenant, two second lieutenants, a sergeant major or first sergeant, a quartermaster sergeant, four sergeants, eight corporals, two buglers, a guidon-bearer, two artificers, and from 64 to 125 privates.[7]

The basic component of artillery was the cannon, or piece, with attached caisson carrying ammunition. This combination was called a platoon, two platoons, a section. Two sections made up a 4-gun battery, three sections, a 6-gun battery. On the outbreak of war there were some 8-gun batteries, but these were soon pared down to a more manageable size.

Initially batteries were assigned to infantry brigades, and came under command of the brigadier general. 'Besides these,' artilleryman E. Porter Alexander later wrote, 'a few batteries were held in reserve under old Gen. Pendleton. Naturally our guns & ammunition were far inferior to the enemy's, & this scattering of the commands made it impossible ever to mass our guns in effective numbers. For artillery fire loses effect if scattered.

'Later, we organized our artillery into battalions, of 4 to 6 batteries each, & we put about 5 battalions to each corps of 3 divisions. One battalion would usually march with each division of infantry, to be near it in case of need, & the other two battns. were in reserve, under a chief of arty. for the corps, who had command of it all.'[8]

Pendleton's reserve corps had been organized as three battalions on 4 June 1862, when the Army's General Order No. 69 distributed the artillery to the corps, save for a general reserve. Corps commanders were free to distribute their guns even more widely, so that the bulk of Confederate artillery in northern Virginia fought at a battery level from the First Manassas until 16 April 1863 when the army-wide battalion organization Alexander mentioned went into effect.

This was the basic organization obtaining that year when a European observer visited Lee's Army: 'The artillery is organized into battalions; five battalions in a corps of three divisions, one to each division, and two in reserve. They always mass the artillery now, and the commanders of battalions say they lose no more men in a battalion than they formerly did in a single battery. Each battalion is complete in itself, with quartermaster, adjutant, ordnance officer, surgeon, &c. The whole is under the control of the chief of artillery of the army, but assigned at convenience to the corps commanders, one of whose staff-officers is chief of artillery to the corps, and another chief of ordnance.

'The duty of the chief of ordnance is to supply the guns and everything for their equipment, with ammunition and stores of every description, excepting horses and provisions.

'The chief of artillery places them in action, and controls them there.

'The chief of ordnance to an army is usually a lieutenant-colonel, and has two captains as assistants; to a corps a major, with a lieutenant as assistant; and the divisional ordnance officer is a captain. The ordnance officers of brigades and artillery battalions are generally majors, but some are lieutenant-colonels.

'The chief of artillery to an army is a brigadier- general; to a corps, a colonel; and to a division, a major.'[9]

On 8 June 1864, Lee's artillery chief, William Pendleton, submitted a suggested reorganization of the army's artillery in a memorandum which was passed on for Congressional approval. Under his plan, each battery was to have only four guns, with a captain, two first lieutenants, a second lieutenant, a sergeant major, a guidon-bearer, four sergeants, eight corporals, and from 100 to 125 privates. Four batteries would make up one battalion, which would also have a lieutenant colonel, a major, an adjutant ranking as a first lieutenant, an assistant quartermaster ranking as a captain, a chaplain, a surgeon and an assistant surgeon. Two or three battalions would make up a regimental group commanded by a colonel, assisted by an adjutant ranking as a captain and an aide ranking as a first lieutenant. Two regimental groups would form a brigade, commanded by a brigadier general whose staff would include a chief surgeon, a commissary ranking as a major, a quartermaster ranking as a major, an adjutant general ranking as a captain, an ordnance officer ranking as a captain, an inspector general ranking as a captain, and an aide-de-camp ranking as a first lieutenant. Lee's endorsement of the plan noted that the army's artillery should be commanded by a major general, while each corps' artillery should be commanded by a brigadier general.'[11]

The result of these suggestions would have been to add commissioned officers for better artillery control. Although it was an excellent plan, it fell into the quagmire of government. And, in the meantime, in April 1864 Ordnance Bureau Chief Josiah Gorgas reported that: 'The number of pieces is as follows: General Lee's army (not including the battalion of Washington Artillery at Petersburg), 197, of which about one-half are rifles, including eight 20-pounder Parrotts and one 2-pounder Whitworth; General Longstreet's corps, 27, of which fourteen are rifles, including two 20-pounder Parrotts...

'I respectfully submit that a maximum be fixed for the artillery, not to exceed five pieces for each brigade of infantry...

'By the rule suggested, allowing twenty pieces to the division of cavalry, as at present (quite too much), the artillery of General Lee would be reduced to about 170, including Eshleman at Petersburg, instead of 213. Besides, an increase of thirty pieces has been asked and is preparing under the requisition of General Pendleton, approved by General Lee.'[12]

Not until September 1864, with seven months of life left for Lee's Army, was Pendleton's plan to reorganize Lee's artillery even referred to the Congressional Committee of Military Affairs. None the less, within Lee's Army, as horses and harness became scarce and fodder even more so, Gorgas's suggestion was implemented unofficially and batteries were reduced to four guns. In fact, by December 1864 there were no 6-gun batteries left in Lee's Army, although there were a number of batteries with only two guns.[13] At the end, on 9 April 1865, Lee's artillery consisted of only 61 guns and 13 caissons.[14]

Tactics

When the war began, the manual with which artillerymen were most familiar was *Instruction for Field Artillery*, which had been compiled by a 'board of artillery officers', and published in Philadelphia in 1860. But leading Confederate artilleryman R. Snowden Andrews said that he found the work 'complex and confusing',[1] and drilled his battery with the aid of a captured copy of George Patten's *Artillery Drill*, which had been published in New York in 1861. Finally, while recovering from a near-fatal wound, he produced his own book, *Andrews' Mounted Artillery Drill*, which was published in Charleston, South Carolina, in 1863, and which became a standard Confederate drill manual.

Whichever manual the battery or battalion commander preferred, it formed the basis of virtually all the training that artillerymen received. Even after having been in action, gunner Edward Moore of the Rockbridge Artillery recalled when in camp, 'An hour or two each day was spent in going through the artillery manual.'[2]

Tactically, artillery generally had two targets, infantry and artillery, and initially Confederate artillery was ineffectual compared to Union artillery. Commanders blamed inferior ammunition or badly trained gun crews, and while these were factors, the root cause was the assignment of fire at battery level instead of *en masse*. It was not until eighteen guns under S. D. Lee tore into Union infantry attacking Jackson's right and broke up the potential assault within a half hour at the

Second Manassas that the Confederate artillery truly came into its own.

In preparation for Pickett's Charge at Gettysburg on 3 July 1863, the artillery's chief mission was counter-battery fire in an endeavour to silence Union's guns on Cemetery Ridge so that Confederate infantry could advance.

Lee's artillery was also used to aid infantry in its assault on the Darbytown Road in the autumn of 1864, when Union forces occupied a line of entrenchments that Lee wanted taken. 'There was a considerable stretch of open & level ground & it gave me the only opportunity I ever had, in action, to use that beautiful manoeuvre in artillery drill of "Fire advancing by half battery". One half of a battery stands & fires, while the second half advances a short distance, when it also halts & opens fire. At its first shot, the first half stops firing, limbers up, & then at a gallop itself passes the second & takes a still more advanced position & opens. So they go, alternately, one half always firing & the other advancing.'[3]

In defence, at Fredericksburg, Lee's artillery concentrated on the Union infantry who were assaulting prepared positions on the heights beyond the town — they were unsuccessful, largely thanks to Lee's gunners.

Weapons
THE BATTERY: ITS REGULATION EQUIPMENT

The following is the list of regulation equipment according to *The Field Manual For The Use of the Officers on Ordnance Duty* which was published in Richmond in 1862.

Type of Battery	12-pdr	6-pdr
Guns		
12-pounder, mounted	4	
6-pounder, mounted		4
Howitzers		
24-pounders	2	
12-pounders		2
Total Guns	6	6
Travelling Forge	1	1
Battery Waggon	1	1
Whole number of carriages with a battery	20	14
Ammunition		
For 4 Guns		
Shot	448	400
Spherical case	358	320
Canisters	90	80
Total rounds	896	800
For 2 howitzers		
Shells	168	120
Spherical case	112	160
Canisters	42	32
Total rounds	322	312
Total number of rounds with a battery	1,218	1,112
Draught horses 6 to each carriage	120	84
Spare horses, one-twelfth	10	7
Total	130	91

Note: For two 32-pdr. howitzer carriages and four cassons the number of rounds is: Shells, 112; spherical case, 84; canisters, 14; total rounds, 210.

THE RANGES OF CONFEDERATE CANNON

Drawn from data published in the 1862 *Field Manual for Officers on Ordnance Duty*, the following are the effective ranges of the various cannon in use in Lee's Army.

Cannon	Type of Round	Range (yards)
6-pounder	Shot	318–1,523
M1841 12-pounder	Shot	909–1,663
Napoleon	Shot	325–1,680
	Shell	300–1,135
12-pounder howitzer	Shell	195–1,072
24-pounder howitzer	Shell	295–1,322
24-pounder Coehorn mortar	Shell	25 –1,200

ARTILLERY AMMUNITION AVAILABLE

This report of ammunition in the ordnance trains of the artillery of Lee's Army, dated 18 May 1864, gives a good idea of the types of gun available and the variety of ammunition used.

Rounds of	First Corps	Second Corps	Third Corps	Total
Napoleon shell	170	72	176	418
Napoleon shot	208		136	344
Napoleon case	960	104	1,000	2,064
Napoleon canister		8	16	24
3-inch rifle shell	920	140	580	1,640
3-inch rifle canister			54	54
10-pdr Parrott shell	982	432	572	1,986
10-pdr Parrott canister			18	18
20-pdr Parrott shell	272	288	72	632
20-pdr Parrott canister		8		8
24-pdr howitzer case	72		24	96
24-pdr howitzer shell	72			72
12-pdr howitzer shell	170			170
Total ammunition	3,834	1,044	2,588	7,466*

*OR, 1, XXXVI, part 2, p. 1020.

'It was extremely rare at any period of the war to find a battery with uniform equipment. There was at no time in the Army of Northern Virginia more than six or eight batteries of Napoleon guns, and a less number of 3-inch rifles. It seems to have been thought desirable to have a section of rifles and a section of smoothbores. But it was not unusual to find in the same section rifles of different caliber, or a

Napoleon with a 6-pounder, or perhaps a howitzer; and in a battery of four guns, there was not infrequently at least three different calibers which required different ammunition. This made the supply of ammunition more difficult and impaired the effectiveness of the battery.'[1]

Initially, most Confederate batteries were armed with 6-pounder brass or iron cannon of pre-war manufacture. These smoothbores could fire a solid round shot to 300-1,500 yards, or spherical case to 600-1,200 yards (maximum).

The standard Union battery had larger guns, usually 12-pound smoothbore Napoleons, or 3-inch rifles, or 10-pound Parrott rifles. So the Ordnance Department began boring out 6-pound guns to 12-pound size and making its own 12-pound Napoleon guns. Also, of course, it added to its supplies through captures, starting with the first major battle, the First Manassas, where 28 pieces of artillery and 64 artillery horses complete with harness were taken.[2]

By 1862, the Confederate Ordnance Department had listed the following types of artillery as being in use in its service: the 12-pound Napoleon gun, some late-war Southern-made versions of which were iron as well as bronze; the 10-pound Parrott gun and the 3-inch iron rifle, both made in Rome, Georgia, and captured; and 27 purchased bronze Austrian-made guns including seven 24-pound howitzers and sixteen 6-pound guns. Also 12-pound bronze howitzers saw a great deal of field use. These were shorter and lighter than normal guns, and were designed for use at shorter ranges.

The Ordnance Department imported several types of British-made guns, including the 12-pound rifled Blakely gun, the breech-loading Clay rifled gun, and a few of the technically advanced Whitworth breech-loading rifled guns which were superior to anything used by either side throughout the war. Lee's artillery included four 3-inch Whitworths in 1863, and the Army had four 6-inch Whitworths at Gettysburg.

The Clay gun, which was based on the Armstrong rifle, totally failed its initial testing and none of these weapons saw action. The Blakely guns did not operate well with the poor quality ammunition from the Confederate arsenals, and their trails tended to crack after relatively light use. The Whitworths were found superior, although their complicated breech mechanisms often required repair, and their carriages were rather heavier than those of American weapons, which made them rather less mobile. The Whitworth had a maximum range of some 10,000 yards at 30 degrees elevation, 2,600 yards' range at 5 degrees. Several British-made Armstrong breech-loading rifled cannon reached the South at the very end of the war, too late to see field service with Lee's Army.

'The field-piece most generally employed is the smooth-bored 12-pound "Napoleon" (*canon obusier*), which fires solid shot, shell, case, and cannister,' noted a European observer in 1863, adding, 'Opinions are divided as to the merits of Napoleons, Parrotts, and 3-inch rifled guns; but for general use, almost all consider the Napoleon most serviceable.'[3]

In June 1863, Lee's artillery consisted of 107 Napoleons, 103 iron rifled guns, which were both 3-inch rifles and 10-pound Parrotts, thirty 12-pound howitzers, and four 6-inch Whitworths, which were assigned one to a battalion.[4] As of 1 January 1865, it consisted of 192 Napoleons and howitzers and 90 rifled field pieces.[5] By that time, during the Siege at Petersburg, the artillery were also using a variety of mortars and fixed siege guns.

Confederate artillery was almost always at a disadvantage because the quality of the Union artillery, especially their ammunition, was vastly superior. On 8 October 1861, for example, Brigadier General John Magruder complained to the Chief of Ordnance: 'There is a great defect about our shells and spherical-case shot for field pieces. They explode (about one-half of them) at the muzzle of the piece. The friction tubes also are worthless; not those made of brass, but those of lead or mixed metal. I think they came from the Virginia Armory. I tried many, and not one would explode. We shall be ruined unless you can send me good shell and spherical-case shot and good friction primers.'[6] This problem was not wholly resolved throughout the war.

As late as May 1864, the defences of Richmond, which were largely manned by heavy artillerymen, included James 12-pound rifles and even some old 6-pound smooth-bore cannon. The gun crews had infantry longarms as their personal weapons. At that time the artillery stores included 1,125 obsolete 0.69 calibre smooth-bore muskets, 28 rifled 0.69 calibre muskets, 215 0.58 rifle muskets, and 260 Mississippi rifles. 'In no case were the arms in as good order as is required of troops in garrison,' reported an inspector of the heavy artillery troops. 'Many were rusty.'[7]

In the stores there were none of those novel swords that were unique to heavy artillerymen, although the Confederacy did produce such weapons. These swords, derived from the ancient Roman sword, had a heavy two-edged blade some 19 inches long, with an all-brass hilt into which the letters 'CS' were sometimes cast. The idea was that could be thrust into the bellies of enemy horses attempting to storm the barricades. Examples of these swords have been dug up at Confederate artillery sites, so they must have seen some use, but they were rare in the extreme.

The only weapon allocated officially to light artillerymen was a brass-hilted sabre. This had a deeply curved blade, much more so than the cavalry sabre, some 30 inches long, and only a single branch on the hilt. 'The artillerymen, who started out with heavy sabres hanging to their belts,' recalled Richmond Howitzers veteran Carlton McCarthy, 'stuck them up in the mud as they marched, and left them for the ordnance officers to pick up and turn over to the cavalry.'[8] Certainly a sabre would be an embarrassment while serving a gun, and of little use when defending a battery. A handgun would have been more practicable, and many gunners managed to obtain revolvers, although they were not officially issued.

Equipment

Artillerymen required various items of equipment peculiar to their trade. Each crew member was identified by number. Number One, who stood on the right side of the muzzle as it faced the enemy, had a long staff with a piece of carpet or similar material, of a size to fit the bore, tacked around one end and a solid block on the other end. His job was to dip the carpet end into a bucket of water beneath the muzzle after a round had been fired and sponge out the bore so as to extinguish any smouldering matter that could prematurely fire the next round.

After Number Two, standing on the other side of the muzzle, had received a round from Number Five and placed it in the muzzle, Number One used the solid end of the rammer to push the round and powder snugly against the chamber.

Number Three stood at the rear of the gun in line with Number One. He wore a leather thumb-stall on his left thumb. After a round had been fired, he covered the vent with the thumbstall so that no air would pass into the bore while Number One was swabbing it out. While the gun was being aimed Number Three positioned himself at the rear of the carriage, to adjust its position with the trail handspike.

Number Four also stood at the rear of the gun, in line with Number Two. He wore a waistbelt with a leather pouch, usually brown, on its front. Inside this were friction primers, lanyard and vent picks. His job was to fire the gun which he did by sticking the thin iron vent pick through the vent to open up the powder bag, inserting a friction primer in the vent and hooking the end of the lanyard through a loop in the friction primer. When the order to fire was given, he stood away and yanked hard on the lanyard, pulling the pin out of the friction primer to ignite it and send a spark through the vent to set off the charge.

Number Five stood some five yards behind the left-hand wheel. He had a large brown leather sack, the 'gunner's haversack', slung from his left shoulder to his right side. His job was to take a cartridge from Numbers Six or Seven back at the ammunition chest, place it in this haversack, and carry it up to Number Two.

Number Six had a fuze gauge to adjust the shell and spherical case shot fuzes to the correct range as ordered by the gunner.

The gunner, who aimed the piece, decided what type of ammunition was to be used, and ordered the firing and reloading, had some specialized aiming equipment that included a gunner's level, a breech sight which was not permanently mounted on the tube, a gunner's quadrant, and pendulum hausses, which were sights with a weight at one end so that they would always hang perfectly vertically when placed on the rear of the tube.

Heavy artillery musicians carried drums, officially painted red with the 'arms of the Confederate States', the letter of the company and the regimental number on a scroll beneath the arms. Light or horse artillery musicians carried bugles.

Insignia

The branch-of-service colour for artillerymen was red, which was to be used on collars, cuffs, trouser stripes, caps and sashes. The regulation button for all ranks was to bear the letter 'A' on its otherwise plain face.

It appears to have been a fairly common practice for light artillery officers, all of whom were mounted, to substitute a more comfortable and convenient waist-length, single-breasted jacket for the regulation frock-coat. Unlike the ordinary soldier's jacket which many infantry officers wore in the field, however, the typical artillery officer had his jacket piped with red and wore the regulation Austrian knot on each sleeve. At times the red braid used to pipe the collar, front and breast-pocket flap was substituted for the gold lace of the Austrian knot.

Heavy artillery officers, who had the luxury of living in static garrisons, often chose to wear a frock-coat with a turned-down collar such as found on civilian frock-coats. They had this coat piped with red, rather than have full red collar and cuffs, and wore their rank insignia on the front top of each collar. Enlisted men in the heavy artillery also seem to have benefited from their distance from the front and obtained regulation double-breasted frock-coats, trimmed with red collars and cuffs.

Heavy and light artillery officers tended, more than officers of any other branch, to wear the regulation cap with dark-blue band and red crown and sides. It was usually trimmed with the usual regulation gold lace on front, back, sides and top. Artillery officers called it their 'woodpecker caps'. Many officers added the regulation US Army artillery crossed cannon badge to the cap front. Many of these cap badges came from pre-war militia artillery organizations, others were obtained from pre-war stores or captures.

Enlisted men, too, were especially proud of their branch of service. 'Through the war I used to think the artillerymen were the bravest people on earth,' admitted 4th Texas Infantry Private Val Giles. 'They could pull through deeper mud, ford deeper springs, shoot faster, swear louder, and stand more hard pounding than any other class of men in the service.'[1]

Artillerymen felt that way about themselves, and liked to show off their branch of service by flaunting the red colour whenever possible. When they could obtain the material they added red trimmings to their otherwise plain issue jacket, and tried to get forage caps trimmed red. Grey jeans material caps with a red band were actually produced by Confederate clothing manufactories, and many of those produced by the Richmond Manufactory also had red tops.

Flags

Initially most artillery batteries carried a guidon, and heavy artillery regiments carried the first national flag or a state flag. When the Army of Northern Virginia battle flag became standardized, however, they were ordered to carry this 36-inch square flag.

One of these, apparently not made by the Richmond Clothing Manufactory since the stars are placed evenly on its bars, was carried by Company C, 1st North Carolina Artillery Regiment. It was marked '10 NC' in yellow roman letters around the centre star, the regiment being officially the 10th North Carolina, and 'ARTILLERY CO C' in dark-blue letters at the top of the field and 'CAPT. JOSEPH GRAHAM' at the bottom.

Graham's battery flag, as was the Army of Northern Virginia battle flag carried by the King William Artillery Battery of Virginia, was actually infantry-sized, four feet square. The King William Battery flag was of the third bunting pattern made by the Richmond Clothing Manufactory and bore battle honours in blue roman lettering on the obverse of the Colour only. It is typical of battery flags, as the infantry sized flag was the norm for artillery batteries in Lee's Army.

ARTILLERY STRENGTHS

Designation	Date	Total Strength
Reserve Artillery	21 May 1862	907
Pendleton's & Rhett's	20 July 1862	3,252
Reserve Artillery	30 Sept 1862	766
Reserve Artillery	20 Oct 1862	910
Reserve Artillery	20 Dec 1862	721
Artillery	31 Jan 1863	2,874
Artillery	31 May 1863	4,460
Artillery Corps	31 July 1863	4,736
Artillery Corps	31 Aug 1863	4,929
Artillery Corps	31 Oct 1863	4,067
Artillery Corps	31 Dec 1863	4,138
Artillery Corps	31 Jan 1864	3,842
Artillery Corps	10 April 1864	4,720
Artillery Corps	30 June 1864	5,520
Artillery Corps	10 July 1864	5,569

Designation	Date	Total Strength
Artillery Corps	31 Aug 1864	3,631
Artillery Corps	10 Sept 1864	4,735
Artillery Corps	31 Oct 1864	5,654
Artillery Corps	30 Nov 1864	6,144
Artillery Corps	10 Jan 1865	5,376
Artillery Corps	31 Jan 1865	4,881
Artillery Corps	28 Feb 1865	5,399

Pay

On 6 March 1861, pay rates were set at: colonel, $210; lieutenant colonel, $185; major, $150 ($162 when serving on ordnance duties); captain, $130; first lieutenant, $90; second lieutenant, $80; adjutant, $10 in addition to his lieutenant's pay; sergeant major, $21; first sergeant, $20; sergeant, $17; corporal or artificer, $13; musician, $12; private, $11. Light artillery enlisted men received the same pay as cavalrymen, which gave corporals, musicians, farriers and blacksmiths $13, and privates $12.[1] On 19 April 1862, the pay of master armourers was set at $2,000 a year.[2] On 9 June 1864, all enlisted men received an increase of $7 a month, so that a heavy artillery private then drew $18 a month and a light artilleryman, $19.

CAVALRY
Organization

The Regular Confederate Army, as authorized on 6 March 1861, was to include one cavalry regiment consisting of a colonel, a lieutenant colonel, a major, an adjutant, and a sergeant major and ten companies. A quartermaster sergeant was added to each regimental staff as of 16 May 1861, and was joined by an ordnance sergeant on 19 April 1862. Each company was to include a captain, a first lieutenant, two second lieutenants, four sergeants, four corporals, two musicians, one farrier, one blacksmith and 60 privates.[1] A commissary was authorized on 23 May 1864. The number of privates in a company was raised to 80 on 16 April 1862.[2] This was the basic establishment to which volunteer cavalry regiments would conform.

Unlike his artillery, Lee's cavalry was organized into large fighting groups from the very start. On 24 September 1861, Colonel J. E. B. Stuart was promoted to the rank of brigadier general and given command of a newly formed Cavalry Brigade, which included the 1st, 2nd, 4th and 6th Virginia Cavalry Regiments, the 1st North Carolina Cavalry, and the Jeff Davis Legion which included two companies from Alabama, one from Georgia and three from Mississippi, virtually all the Southern cavalry in northern Virginia.

On 28 May 1862, Stuart's command was expanded to include the Wise Legion Cavalry, the Hampton Legion Cavalry and the Cobb

Legion Cavalry, as well as odd cavalry units that had been serving in the Aquia District of Virginia. As of 23 July he was commanding all of these plus a battery of horse artillery under an outstanding gunner, Captain John Pelham, and Critcher's Virginia Battalion as an independent fighting unit.

On 25 July 1862, the brigade was enlarged to a division and Stuart was promoted to major general to command it; it was then divided into two brigades. In August a third brigade, comprising troops who had served under Turner Ashby in the Valley of Virginia, was added, and on 10 November a fourth. Stuart's horse artillery at this time, under Pelham who was promoted to the rank of major, included five batteries. All told, Stuart's division numbered 603 officers and 8,551 enlisted men as of 20 November 1862.

Two more brigades were formed from troopers serving farther south, so that by the time of Gettysburg the Cavalry Division numbered six brigades. At this point the division was the strength of a small corps and, indeed, Stuart and his officers began calling it the 'Cavalry Corps'. It was not until the army's reorganization of 9 September 1863, however, that the brigades were officially formed into two divisions and Wade Hampton and Fitzhugh Lee were promoted to major general to command them. But Stuart, much to his displeasure, was never promoted to the rank of lieutenant general as befitting a corps commander. Nor, after his death, were his successors in command of the corps, Wade Hampton and Fitzhugh Lee, given this rank, although this was perhaps not unreasonable given that the corps was never much larger than an infantry division.

Tactics

'The duty of cavalry after battle is joined', wrote one of Stuart's staff officers after the war, 'is to cover the flanks to prevent the enemy from turning them. If victorious, it improves the victory by rapid pursuit. If defeated, it covers the rear and makes vigorous charges to delay the advance of the enemy — or in the supreme moment, in the crisis of battle, when victory is hovering over the field, uncertain upon which standard to alight — when the reserves are brought into action and the death struggle has come, *then* the cavalry comes down like an avalanche, upon the flanks of troops already engaged, with splendid effect.'[1]

The basic cavalry tactical system for achieving all this had been in use before the war. Long-established, it was carried on when the new Confederate cavalry were organized. The system was essentially a translation of a French cavalry tactical system, which was first ordered to be published by US Secretary of War J. R. Poinsett on 10 February 1841, and thereafter became known as the 'Poinsett tactics' or the '41 tactics'.

The system was published as *Cavalry Tactics* in three volumes, the first covering dismounted drill; the second, mounted drill; the third, the evolution of a regiment. A manual on the Colt revolver was included in some editions. The system that the manual espoused was complicated enough, involving deployment of the mounted unit in two ranks. What was worse was that there were references to types of cavalry such as cuirassiers, lancers and hussars — common enough in the Europe of the 1830s, but scarcely relevant, apart from some fanciful company titles, in the South of 1861.

So simplified versions of cavalry manuals soon began to appear, most notably the *Trooper's Manual* by J. Lucius Davis, which was the most important cavalry manual published in the Confederacy. Davis himself served as a colonel of the 10th Virginia Cavalry until he was wounded and captured near Hagerstown on 6 July 1863.

A simplification of Poinsett tactics written by a Northern officer, George Patten, entitled *Patten's Cavalry Drill and Saber Exercise*, originally published in New York in 1861, was reprinted by West & Johnston in Richmond in 1862.

The emphasis in all cavalry manuals of the time was on fighting mounted, especially the mounted charge with sabres flashing. Indeed, this is what most Southern volunteer cavalrymen expected to do. The reality of most cavalry fighting was rather different, however. Much of the cavalry's work entailed the screening of the army's infantry from the prying eyes of enemy cavalry along picket lines, and the gathering of intelligence as to the whereabouts and strength of the enemy forces. Southern cavalry carried out a number of raids against wagon trains and rear echelons, but it was not until near the end that they found themselves attacking or defending against equal numbers of opposing cavalry.

British observer Fremantle noted: 'Stuart's men, though excellent at making raids, capturing waggons and stores, and cutting off communications, seem to have no idea of charging infantry under any circumstances.'[2] And, he noted, engagements between opposing cavalry units fared little better. 'These cavalry fights are miserable affairs. Neither party has any idea of serious fighting with the sabre. They approach one another with considerable boldness, until they get to within about forty yards, and then, at the very moment when a dash is necessary, and the sword alone should be used, they hesitate, halt, and commence a desultory fire with carbines and revolvers.'[3] Often this latter tactic was performed while dismounted, one man holding the horses of three of his fellows in rear of the firing line.

One of the reasons for the emphasis on dismounted combat was certainly the improved accuracy of infantry longarms which could break up a charge before it reached most lines, but there was another factor to be considered. Confederate troopers had to provide their own horses. According to General Order No. 67, dated 25 May 1863, 'Whenever a cavalryman fails and refuses to keep himself provided with a serviceable horse, he may, upon the order of the corps commander, be transferred into any company of infantry or artillery in the same army that he may select.'[4] Indeed, even conscripts could not get into the cavalry unless they provided their own horses.

Since a horse cost many times a private's monthly wage – the army was paying $600 for a horse in Virginia in 1863 – and since cavalry service was esteemed as being vastly superior to that in the other branches, it was natural that the troopers should wish to protect their investments — even at the cost of a glorious sabre charge.

Finally, the traditional cavalry drill, including the sabre charge, took a great deal of training and discipline, something that critics of Confederate cavalry said was sadly lacking. 'The difficulty of converting raw men into soldiers is enhanced manifold when they are mounted. Both men and horses require training, and facilities for rambling, with temptation so to do, are increased. There was but little time, and it may be said less disposition, to establish camps of instruction,' Richard Taylor wrote. 'Cavalry officers naturally desired to have as large commands as possible, and were too much indulged in this desire. Brigades and regiments were permitted to do the work of squadrons and companies, and the cattle were unnecessarily broken down. Assuredly, our cavalry rendered much excellent service, especially when dismounted and fighting as infantry,' he went on, 'but their achievements, however distinguished, fell far below the standard that would have been reached had not the want of discipline impaired their efforts and those of their men.'[5]

Weapons

'Much of the Southern cavalry was ridiculously equipped,' wrote a civilian who had seen both Northern and Southern armies in the field. 'In one regiment I have seen four or five different kinds of rifles and shot-guns, all sorts of saddles, some with rope stirrups, many of the saddles without blankets; all sorts of bridles, and in fact a conglomerate get-up fairly laughable.'[1]

In theory, and in practice in the Union Army, there was no more completely armed man than the cavalryman. He carried a sabre, a revolver and a carbine.

The basic Confederate sabre was a copy of the M1840 US Army cavalry sabre, a nicely made, heavy weapon copied from the 1822 French sabre. It featured a brass hilt with three branches, a leather grip wrapped with twisted wire, and a slightly curved blade, almost 36 inches long, with two fullers. Southern-made copies of this weapon were similar but crude, with reddish brass used, grips wrapped in oil-skin with untwisted wire wound around them, and with an unstopped single fuller — or even without a fuller at all. Scabbards were often of brass or leather rather than iron.

Since, however, the cavalry charge was largely a thing of the imagination among Lee's cavalry, the obvious question arises, why carry a sabre at all? John Mosby, later a noted partisan ranger, decided early on that there was no purpose in it. 'We had been furnished with sabres before we left Abingdon, but the only real use I ever heard of their being put to was to hold a piece of meat over a fire for frying. I dragged one through the first year of the war, but when I became a commander, I discarded it. The sabre and lance may have been very good weapons in the days of chivalry, and my suspicion is that the combats of the hero of Cervantes were more realistic and not such burlesques as they are supposed to be. But certainly the sabre is of no use against gunpowder.'[2]

Not every cavalryman was as extreme in his condemnation of the sabre as was Mosby. Sabres were carried in Lee's cavalry. British observer Fremantle noted: 'Unlike the cavalry with Bragg's army, they wear swords, but seem to have little idea of using them — they hanker after their carbines and revolvers. They constantly ride with their swords between their left leg and the saddle, which has a very funny appearance; but their horses are generally good, and they ride well.'[3]

The revolvers they 'hankered after', were Colt revolvers, in both Army (0.44) and Navy (0.36) calibres, some of which were available from the pre-war South. Several factories, all private concerns since the Ordnance Department did not attempt to produce their own revolvers, were set up and supplied copies of the Colt Navy revolver.

A novel pistol was acquired in small numbers for Confederate cavalry use, and, indeed, Stuart himself carried one. 'This pistol is manufactured by M. Le Mat of Paris. It has a cylinder which revolves, containing nine chambers, a rifled barrel and a smooth-bored barrel. The latter receives a charge of eleven buckshot, and is fired by a slight change of the hammer. Some are in our service.'[4] This weapon, which would seem ideal for cavalry use, with its buckshot for close-in fighting, had been invented by a New Orleans man who then moved to Paris to make them. They were not terribly successful, being largely of poor quality.

Union cavalrymen carried breech-loading carbines, some having brass cartridge cases and some, such as the Spencer, being magazine-fed weapons. The Confederacy was hard pressed to duplicate these weapons, so there was a much greater variety of weapons carried by Lee's cavalry.

There were a number of Maynard carbines whose brass-cased cartridge was inserted into a breakaway breech. Northern-made, they had been imported in relatively small numbers by Georgia, Florida and Mississippi before the war. The brass cartridge case used by this carbine, and by the Morse carbine made for South Carolina troops at the Greenville Military Works, were extremely difficult to manufacture in the South. Less than a thousand Morse carbines, which were of very high quality although of complicated design, were manufactured.

Otherwise, paper-wrapped cartridges were used in the relatively small number of 0.54 carbines made by Bilharz, Hall & Co., Pittsylvania Courthouse, Virginia, and the 0.52 calibre carbines made by Keen, Walker & Co., Danville, Virginia. Paper-wrapped cartridges were also used in a Southern-made version of the Sharps, the standard Union carbine during the early part of the war. This 0.52 calibre breech-loader was produced by S. C. Robinson, whose Richmond factory was later taken over by the central government to keep carbine production going. Unfortunately, the weapons got a bad reputation for gas leakage early in the war, and many Confederate cavalrymen disliked them and replaced them with captured Union weapons whenever possible.

Most of Lee's cavalrymen used single-shot, muzzle-loading carbines, however. These were little more than cut-down rifle muskets in an 0.58 calibre version of the M1855 rifle musket from the Richmond Arsenal and an 0.577 calibre version of the M1853 British Army carbine made by Cook & Brothers Armory, Athens, Georgia.

The latter, and imported versions of it, were so popular that in July 1863, when Lee demanded that a standard carbine be produced, this model was chosen and a plant to make it was set up in Tallassee, Alabama. The first set of 500 were completed and ready for shipment on 3 April 1865 — a bit too late for Lee's troopers who were then only days from their final surrender. Some cavalrymen eschewed any true military weapons, instead using shotguns whose wide spread of shot was most effective at close quarters. These were usually double-barrelled and the barrels were often cut down for easier handling and wider shot patterns.

Equipment

Each cavalryman had the same haversack and canteen as the infantryman. On his waistbelt he had a cap box on the right front hip, a holster on the right side, a revolver cartridge box on his back, and the straps for his sabre on his left side. There was no regulation plate for this belt, but the standard horseman's plate seems to have been the circular two-piece brass plate, bearing the letters 'CS' on one side and the encircling wreath on the other. State plates and the usual variety of frame buckles were also used.

Carbines were carried on a wide strap slung from the left shoulder to the right-hand side, an iron hook on the strap engaging the slide on the side of the carbine opposite the lockplate. A brass frame buckle was usually worn square on the centre of the back or chest to adjust the carbine sling. The cartridge box was usually attached to the strap and was worn on the trooper's back. Sometimes the ammunition box was worn on the waistbelt, but it would have been a tight fit and would have made for an uncomfortably heavy load on the belt.

According to the Confederate Ordnance Department's Field Manual: 'A complete set of horse equipments for cavalry troops consists of 1 bridle, 1 watering bridle, 1 halter, 1 saddle, 1 pair of saddle bags, 1 surcingle, 1 pair of spurs, 1 curry comb, 1 horse brush, 1 picket pin, and 1 lariat (1 link and 1 nose bag, when specially required).'[1]

Since Confederate cavalrymen owned their own horses they initially supplied their own saddles. These were generally light saddles of the 'English round tree' model. Suitable for a pleasant ride, they lacked durability and there was nowhere to hang such items as fodder bags, camp kettles and other impedimenta of campaign life.

The Ordnance Department chose a saddle that had been patented by Walter H. Jenifer, a veteran of US cavalry service before the war, and colonel of the 8th Virginia Cavalry until its reorganization in May 1862. His saddle featured a flat English seat combined with military-style pommel and cantle to which equipment could be attached. It also took a girth and surcingle. It came with a valise which fitted closely to the cantle and had an opening in its centre. Stirrups were wooden, the seat was of rawhide. The ride was similar to that of the pre-war riding saddle and was therefore initially popular, but soon cavalry officers began to complain that its use 'ruined the horses' backs,' Lee wrote to the Chief of Ordnance on 8 June 1863. 'The English saddles which you import are said to be good. It is the tree of the Richmond saddle that is complained of.'[2] The Ordnance Department selected the Union Army's McClellan saddle for its next model. This was apparently acceptable, but the Southern-made version was less durable under field conditions than the genuine, Northern-made article.

Other horse equipment, such as bits, pads and housings, picket pins and ropes, saddle bags and valises, stirrups, draft harness and carbine thimbles, were also copies of US Army cavalry equipment.

The official 75-inch by 67-inch saddle blanket was dark-grey and bore the legend 'CS' in orange letters, six inches high, in the centre, and had a 3-inch wide red stripe three inches in from the blanket's edge. But most observers noted a wide variety of saddle blankets in use.

STRENGTH OF THE CAVALRY

Designation	Date	Total Strength
Cavalry Brigade	21 May 1862	1,289
Cavalry Division	10 Oct 1862	5,733
Cavalry Division	20 Nov 1862	9,154
Cavalry Division	31 Dec 1862	8,814
Cavalry Division	31 Mar 1863	6,509
Cavalry Corps	31 May 1863	9,536
Cavalry Corps	10 Aug 1863	8,999

Designation	Date	Total Strength
Cavalry Corps	20 Sept 1863	8,107
Cavalry Corps	31 Oct 1863	7,917
Cavalry Corps	10 Dec 1863	8,033
Cavalry Corps	10 Jan 1863	8,071
Cavalry Corps	20 Mar 1864	4,770
Cavalry Corps	10 April 1864	7,928
Cavalry Corps	30 June 1864	7,421
Cavalry Corps	31 Aug 1864	6,739
Cavalry Corps	10 Sept 1864	10,919
Cavalry Corps	31 Oct 1864	5,654
Cavalry Corps	10 Nov 1864	6,045
Cavalry Corps	10 Jan 1865	5,759
Cavalry Corps	10 Feb 1865	3,967
Cavalry Corps	28 Feb 1865	6,041

Insignia

The official branch-of-service colour of collar, cuffs, trouser stripes and sashes worn by officers and sergeants was yellow. Officers' buttons were to bear the letter 'C' on the face, enlisted men's buttons, their regimental number. But no numbered buttons were ever produced, and in June 1862 all ranks were authorized the 'C' button.

'One of our boys managed to get a splendid suit with Virginia buttons on it,' wrote 12th Virginia Cavalry Private William Wilson on 17 April 1863, a month later adding that, 'Common Virginia buttons sell at 18 dollars per doz.'[1] Obviously, state buttons were often preferred to the regulation 'C' button.

A short jacket being more comfortable when in the saddle than the regulation frock-coat, all ranks also adopted waist-length jackets. Many officers had these made double-breasted, so that they looked like the regulation frock-coat but without the tails. Some officers also wore US Army cavalry officers' buttons, which featured a spread eagle with the letter 'C' on a shield in the centre of its chest.

Cavalrymen also preferred the broad-brimmed slouch hat, inspired no doubt by the plumed hat that Stuart himself wore. Tall boots and leather gauntlets were also preferred for riding, but these were not issued and became quite expensive as the war went on and tanned leather became scarce.

'I re'cd four letters from you — up to May 1st,' wrote Private Wilson on 24 May 1864, 'also the Laurel badge which Miss E sent. It is much admired.'[1] The badge Wilson mentioned was something unusual among Confederate units — a special brigade insignia. The brigade had been formed out of the 7th, 11th and 12th Virginia Cavalry Regiments and the 35th Virginia Cavalry Battalion which had served under Turner Ashby in the Valley of Virginia until his death. Thereafter it was formed into a regular cavalry brigade which, in January-February 1864, had raided into West Virginia, capturing a supply train of 95 wagons. In honour of this exploit, brigade commander Thomas L. Rosser proclaimed that the unit would take the name 'Laurel Brigade' and wear laurel leaves on their hats. Since the wearing of real leaves was not always practicable, most officers and men had their women embroider a sprig of five or so leaves on a heart-shaped badge trimmed with metallic thread or tape, and wore this on the hat front.

Flags

Most volunteer cavalry companies arrived at their first camps with, or received there, unique company flags. These were usually versions of state flags or the first national Confederate flag, made smaller for ease of carrying while mounted. The first national flag, with a state seal in its canton, carried by Co. E, 1st Maryland Cavalry, for example, measured 27½ inches by 46½ inches. But when the Army of Northern Virginia's battle flag became official, cavalry regiments were to carry a version of that flag but only 30 inches square. During the last year of his life, Stuart's headquarters flew a second national flag measuring four feet by six feet, made at the Richmond Clothing Manufactory.

Pay

On 6 March 1861, pay rates were set at: colonel, $210; lieutenant colonel, $185; major, $162; captain, $140; first lieutenant, $100; second lieutenant, $90; adjutant, $10 in addition to his lieutenant's pay; sergeant major, $21; first sergeant, $20; sergeant, $17; corporal, farrier and blacksmith, $13; musician, $13; private, $11.[1] On 9 June 1864, all enlisted men received an increase of $7 a month.

PARTISAN RANGERS
Organization

Since much of the South began to fall into Federal hands almost immediately, the Confederate Congress authorized bands of partisan rangers to operate behind enemy lines fairly early in the war. Officially only a handful of these units were on the establishment of Lee's Army, although several were operating in his theatre and reported to his cavalry chief.

On 27 March 1862, Virginia alone authorized ten to 20 companies of rangers, each to include 100 men who lived in districts 'overrun by the public enemy', and who would serve for a year. Each company would number a captain, a first and second lieutenant and not less than 75 men, including four sergeants and four corporals. Four companies operating together would be commanded by a major, six by a lieutenant colonel, ten, by a full colonel.[1] Confederate Army regulations of 31 July 1862 called for each man to be not less than 35 years old.

The War Department officials made it clear to would-be partisan ranger company commanders that they had to provide their own arms and equipment.[2] Mosby recalled that his men carried a pair of Colt revolvers captured from Union Army sources. Others also carried shotguns from home and captured carbines.

Usually cavalry insignia, with yellow trim and regulation Confederate Army rank badges were worn whenever formal uniforms were worn. Generally the men wore a mix of versions of Confederate Army uniforms, captured Union dress, and civilian clothing.

The type of ambush tactics employed by the rangers could scarcely be conducted with flags flying, but Mosby, whose battalion was probably the best disciplined and most formal of all the partisan bands, had a headquarters flag which he flew whenever he was far enough away from Union forces. It was a first national flag measuring some 51 inches by 114 inches — large enough to attract serious attention — hand-made from unbleached cotton, with red bunting for the stripes, and the blue wool fatigue blouse of a Union soldier for the canton.

Pay was to be the same as for regular Confederate infantry, even though rangers were almost always mounted.

Such ranger infantry or cavalry units were authorized by the Confederate Congress on 21 April 1862, but on 21 August Lee requested the Secretary of War to restrict these ranger units to their home states; he preferred regular cavalry in his army.[3] Moreover, by 12 September 1862, according to War Department records, the partisan ranger units were well short of regulation strength. The 62nd Virginia Regiment, for example, had but one company, the 24th Virginia Battalion had three, and the strongest Virginia unit, the 27th Battalion, still had only five organized companies. All told, however, there were 96 partisan ranger companies operating throughout the Confederacy at that time.[4]

Too many of these companies were operating on their own hook, reporting to nobody and in fact were little better than bands of brigands — often not even better, at that. Therefore, on 12 June 1863, the Adjutant and Inspector General's Office issued its General Order No. 82 which called for all such companies to be organized into regular battalions and regiments by the generals commanding their districts. Companies operating behind enemy lines were obviously exempted from the order.[5]

'The act authorizing bands of partisan rangers has been carried into execution,' reported Secretary of War George Randolph on 12 August 1862. 'Apprehending that the novelty of the organization, and the supposed freedom from control, would attract great numbers in the partisan corps, the Department adopted a rule requiring a recommendation from a general commanding a department before granting authority to raise partisans. Notwithstanding this restriction, there is reason to fear that the number of partisan corps greatly exceed the requirements of the service, and that they seriously impede recruiting for regiments of the line.'[6]

Indeed, who wouldn't rather serve in a unit which would always be stationed near his home, so that he could go home and do his regular work during most days, and where discipline was often slight and booty was promised? Also, while regulations called for all captured military equipment to be turned over to proper military authorities, rangers were authorized, unlike other soldiers, to be 'paid their full value in such manner as the Secretary of War may prescribe'.[7] Small wonder then that on 26 November 1863 Secretary of War James Seddon reported that partisan rangers companies were, on the whole, a failure. Indeed, he wrote, they were 'more formidable and destructive to our own people than to the enemy'. He suggested that they should 'either be merged in the troops of the line or be disbanded and conscribed.'[8]

The Adjutant and Inspector General, Samuel Cooper, then queried all commanders in the field as to the value of these rangers. Lee replied on 1 April 1864: 'The organizations of Partisan Rangers serving with this army are the 4th & 5th North Carolina Cavalry (59th & 63rd Regiments), now absent in North Carolina; Lt Col Mosby's battalion, serving in Faquier County (Virginia); Capt Kincheloe's company, serving in Prince William County (Virginia); Capt McNeill's company & Maj Gilmor's battalion & Maj O'Ferrall's battalion, serving in the Valley Department.'

Lee suggested making the two North Carolina units regular cavalry regiments; retaining Mosby's battalion as partisans since they were well disciplined and served well; and disbanding all the others. 'Experience has convinced me that it is almost impossible, under the best officers even, to have discipline in these bands of Partisan Rangers, or to prevent them from becoming an injury instead of a benefit to the service, and even where this is accomplished the system gives licence to many deserters & marauders, who assume to belong to these authorized companies & commit depreciations on friend & foe alike. Another great objection to them is the bad effect upon the discipline of the army from the constant desire of the men to leave their commands & enjoy the great licence allowed in these bands.'[9]

All partisan ranger units were officially disbanded by an act of Congress approved on 21 April 1864, and the men were ordered to be re-formed as regular cavalry units.[10] But some partisan ranger units remained in service throughout the war. Mosby's 43rd Battalion of Virginia Cavalry was not disbanded until 20 April 1865.

7
The Support Arms

CORPS OF ENGINEERS
Organization
The Corps of Engineers was authorized on 6 March 1861, its establishment to consist of a colonel, four majors, five captains, plus a company of sappers, miners and pontoniers with a captain, as many lieutenants as necessary, ten sergeants or master workmen, ten corporals or overseers, 39 privates of the first class, or artificers, 39 privates of the second class, or labourers, and two musicians.[1] While one company conforming to this establishment was actually raised at Knoxville, Tennessee, there appear to have been no others in the regular army, and certainly none such ever served in Lee's Army.

Given the fortifications that would feature prominently in the defensive war envisaged by the Confederacy, it was apparent that more engineers would be needed, so on 16 May 1861 an additional lieutenant colonel (who would receive a cavalry officer's pay) and not more than five captains were authorized for the Corps.[2] The next day a company of sappers and bombardiers to consist of a captain, two first lieutenants, a second lieutenant, ten sergeants or master workmen, ten corporals or overseers, 39 privates of the first class, or artificers, 39 privates of the second class, or labourers, and two musicians was authorized.[3] This company was raised in New Orleans and served in that area, so was never part of Lee's Army.

Also, officers who had been trained in engineering were needed to design fortifications which local troops would construct, so on 31 December 1861 the President was authorized to appoint no more than 50 officers, ranking no higher than captain, into the Corps for the duration of the war.[4] Finally, on 21 April 1862 a total of no more than 100 engineer captains was authorized.[5]

The building of fortifications and bridges and the laying of roads was carried out by groups of slaves hired or impressed from nearby owners, or by enlisted men temporarily transferred into a 'Pioneer Corps' which came under the command of the army's chief engineer. This was not a formal, permanent organization, but consisted of *ad hoc* groups of as many men as were needed for a specific task.

Free African Americans living near specific job sites were liable to be called up for labour as well as the slaves of nearby owners, at first under authority of the Secretary of War, then later under a Congres-

147

sional Act of February 1864. At first, each area commander simply impressed slaves from nearby owners according to his needs. He was authorized to pay each owner 50 cents a day, and had to feed the slaves. Each slave had to bring an entrenching tool, such as a spade, shovel, grubbing-hoe or axe, with him.

Eventually these men were formed into organized units when General Order No. 86, dated 5 December 1864, was issued. According to that order, when 50 slaves were gathered together they were to be sent to the Chief Engineer of the Army. He 'will organize them into gangs of 100 men each (selecting four of the number as foremen), over whom will be placed a manager and two overseers. Every eight gangs will constitute a section, for which a superintendent will be selected. Three sections will compose a force, over which will be placed a director. Two clerks will be employed or detailed for each director, and one for each superintendent.' Also there was to be a purveyor for each force and an assistant purveyor for each section who had to obtain food, clothing and other necessities. A medical officer was also assigned to each section.[6]

John Casler, an infantryman assigned to the Pioneer Corps, later recalled that in his brigade pioneers drawn from fighting regiments were organized into messes of twelve, one from each mess remaining in camp to cook, while the others went out to work. In May 1864 the men detailed to the corps in his brigade were re-assigned to their regular infantry duties to fill gaps in the battle line, their place being taken by regular engineering troops.

Indeed, experience showed that an untrained work force was an undependable work force. Owners were loath to let their slaves join an army work force, fearing that they might be mistreated, injured, or might run off to the nearby Union Army. Indeed, many slaves, who were not particularly motivated to serve the Confederacy, did escape, while others did a lackadasical job at best. Infantrymen grumbled about having to work with a pick and shovel instead of fire a musket which they had enlisted to do. There were still too few qualified commissioned engineers to perform all the tasks required.

On 26 December 1862, J. F. Gilmer, the chief of engineers, suggested forming a full regiment of engineers to be assigned to the Army of Northern Virginia. Therefore, on 23 May 1863, in response to authorization of 20 March, the Adjutant and Inspector General's Office issued General Order No. 66 which called for one company of engineers to be drawn from every division in the army. Each company was to consist of a captain, a first lieutenant, two second lieutenants, eight sergeants, seven corporals, 40 artificers, and 45 labourers. These companies were to be organized into regiments of ten companies each, with two companies assigned as pontoniers. Each regiment would also have a colonel, a lieutenant colonel, a major, an adjutant ranking as a first lieutenant, a sergeant major, and a quartermaster sergeant.[7] An additional quartermaster sergeant and two musicians per company were added to each engineer regiment on 20 March 1864. Mounted engineers, drawn from the cavalry, were also authorized on that date.[8]

As a result, the 1st Engineers Regiment was organized and had begun work at an instruction camp in Richmond by that autumn. The regiment joined Lee's Army at the end of April 1864. It could have been ready for action sooner, but Lee wanted it split up and assigned to various divisions, and insisted that its ranks be largely filled with conscripts not volunteers. The Secretary of War overruled Lee, and ordered that it stay intact as a regiment. Its personnel, however, consisted of men who volunteered to join the regiment while they were still at conscript camps of instruction, rather than troops transferred from line units.

A 2nd Engineers Regiment was organized, with Companies C, G, H and K being assigned under the 1st Engineers to Lee's Army, so that by 16 February 1865 there were twelve companies of Engineers serving in Lee's Army. Other companies of this regiment served elsewhere in the South.

The regiments reported to Lee's Chief of Engineers, as did all the officers of that branch assigned to staffs of general officers below Lee. The Chief of Engineers reported not only to Lee, but also to the Chief of the Engineer Bureau in Richmond.

Leaders

Lee's staff was so informally organized, and engineer officers so scarce and badly needed in the field rather than at headquarters, that often the army had to do without a Chief Engineer.

Major Walter Husted Stevens, a US Military Academy graduate and US Corps of Engineers officer until his dismissal for submitting his resignation on 2 May 1861, was the Army's first Chief Engineer. Commissioned a captain of engineers in the Provisional Army of the Confederate States (PACS), he served as engineer officer on General Beauregard's staff at the First Manassas. He was then promoted to major and given the job of Chief Engineer to the army around Richmond, serving under General Joseph E. Johnston. He received a further promotion to colonel and, when Lee was given command of the Army, was placed in charge of the defences ringing Richmond, as Chief of Construction, Department of Northern Virginia.

Colonel, later major general, Jeremy Francis Gilmer, a brilliant engineer, served as Chief Engineer, Department of Northern Virginia, from 2 August 1862 until 4 October 1862, when he was named Chief of the Engineer Bureau. Prior to the war, Gilmer had been an officer of the US Army Corps of Engineers until he resigned on 29 June 1861. He was wounded at the Battle of Shiloh, in the Western Theatre, when serving as Chief Engineer to General Albert Sidney Johnston. Duties kept him in Richmond for much of the time when he was technically on Lee's staff, so his direct involvement with Lee's Army was less than it could have been.

Lieutenant Colonel William Proctor Smith, who had been a captain in the regular Confederate Army, served as the Army's Chief Engineer for much of the summer of 1863. During the Gettysburg campaign, however, the Army's Chief Engineer post was filled by his assistant, Captain Samuel R. Johnston.

Major General Martin Luther Smith, who had served as engineer officer at the unsuccessful defence of Vicksburg, Mississippi, was appointed Chief Engineer to the Army of Northern Virginia on 16 April 1864. An officer in the US Army's Corps of Topographical Engineers until his resignation on 1 April 1861, he had been brevetted for meritorious service in mapping the valley below Mexico City during the war there in 1848. He served in Lee's Army until 20 July 1864 when he was assigned to the Army of Tennessee, and later to the defences of Mobile, Alabama.

After Smith left, the post of Chief Engineer was filled, once again, by Walter Stevens, who had been the first to hold that position. He took the post as a colonel, but was promoted to the rank of brigadier general on 28 August 1864. Stevens was supposedly the last Confederate soldier to cross Mayo's Bridge when Richmond was evacuated, and served until the surrender at Appomattox.

Actual field command of the 1st Regiment and the four companies of the 2nd Regiment fell to the son of an old friend of Lee's, Thomas Mann Randolph Talcott. He had been appointed a captain of engineers in the PACS in 1861 and joined Lee's staff on 26 April 1862. There he served in various duties, such as field reconnaissance and carrying orders, receiving promotions to major (26 April 1862) and lieutenant colonel (25 July 1863). He was appointed colonel and given command of the 1st Engineers Regiment on 1 April 1864, in which post he served until Appomattox.

Tactics

The Richmond *Daily Dispatch* of 24 July 1861 advertised an edition of '*Capt. Buckholtz's Infantry Camp Duty, Field Fortifications And Coast Defence*, with plates. Books like this one, which was said to have been produced by a European officer as a condensation of previous engineering works, were just about all the would-be Confederate military engineer found available. Pre-war US Army engineering manuals that Confederate engineers often consulted included *Tables and Formulae*, by Captain T. J. Lee, which had been first published in 1849 for the Corps of Topographical Engineers; *An Elementary Course In Civil Engineering for the Use of Cadets of the United States Military Academy*, by D.

H. Mahan, published in 1857; *A Treatise on Field Fortifications*, published in 1836; and *Papers on Practical Engineering*, by the US Army Engineer Department, published in 1841. According to Confederate Army regulations, each engineer officer was to carry not only a bound copy of the regulations of the corps, but also Vauban's *Fortifications* and Bousmard's *Fortifications*. An American edition of Vauban, *Vauban's First System, The Modern System, and Field-Works*, by Kimber, first appeared in 1852. Captain James K. Boswell, topographical engineer on Stonewall Jackson's staff, noted in his diary that he was in Richmond on 14 April 1863: 'Rec'd from the Bureau a copy of Mahan's *Permanent & Field Fortifications* and two maps of Va.'[1] Also, Colonel Stevens produced a work, *Notes on Sapping and Mining*, which, in February 1864, he wished to have printed by the War Department. Unfortunately this project was never completed because of funding problems, but individuals may well have seen and used his manuscript. In September 1864 the Richmond Pontoon Yard had a series of plates engraved for a work on military bridges.

Despite the specialist nature of the branch, there were no training schools for personnel commissioned as engineer officers. Enlisted men recruited to the two regiments as artificers or higher grades had already received some training, at least in theory, while those taken on as labourers were unskilled and learned their duties in the field.

Even so, when first organized the engineers who went into Lee's Army received training in a camp of instruction near Richmond. There they were taught the basics of their duties which were, according to General Order No. 104, dated 28 July 1863, to serve as pioneers in making and repairing roads and bridges on the march and in delaying an enemy advance by destroying bridges and breaking up roads. 'They will also be employed in making rapid reconnaissances and surveys of the country occupied or marched over by the army; preparing sketches and maps of the roads and topographical features; laying out camps, and entrenching military positions. During battle they will be held in reserve, and used as circumstances may demand, either in their special duties, or as infantry, under the command of their officers. They may be employed in the construction of ovens for baking bread, and other works requiring mechanical skill, but not on mere police duty, or the like, unless connected immediately with their own organization; nor are they to be employed altogether on mere fatigue service — but, once instructed in the duties of the engineer soldier, they will be frequently employed in laying out works, and also in aiding and directing the labors of other troops detailed for their construction.'[2] Officers and men learned to use the special equipment of their trade in the camps of instruction. For example, Sergeant J. W. Reid wrote that when in the camp his company, Co K, which was a pontoon company, 'went every day to a millpond not far off and put in a pontoon bridge and would then take it out again. In this way we soon learned to understand the business well.'[3]

Despite this training, Lee, himself an engineer, failed to use the technical skills of his engineers in the way as his opponent. Although they did build one redoubt at Cold Harbor after the battle, it was never used and they did not perform this type of duty at any other time.

Weapons

It had been suggested that the enlisted men be armed with revolvers and sabres since they would not be involved in infantry-style combat, but the Ordnance Department always had difficulty in obtaining sufficient revolvers for front-line troops and sabres were useless for men building bridges and laying roads, so neither of these weapons was issued except to commissioned and non-commissioned officers. Sergeant Reid wrote that: 'A sergeant in the engineers is about equal in rank to a lieutenant in the infantry. They carry a sword and do the same duties as a lieutenant and receive about the same pay.'[1]

General Order No. 104 specified that enlisted men were to be issued 'light arms', presumably short rifles such as produced by the Fayetteville, North Carolina, Arsenal and the Cook & Brothers factory in Athens, Georgia. But apparently insufficient short-arms were available by July 1863, when the men were in their camp of instruction, so they received infantry rifle muskets — Lieutenant Colonel W. W. Blackford of the 1st Regiment said the unit was armed and drilled as infantry — with which they were armed when guarding a supply depot at Guiney's Station, and later in actual combat when in support of a cavalry brigade defending the Telegraph Road on the right of Lee's position in Spotsylvania during the early 1864 campaign. Men of the 1st and 2nd Engineers also manned the trenches of Petersburg in March 1865 to cover a Union probe there when infantry had had to be withdrawn farther west. Ten of Lee's engineer companies were pressed into infantry service defending the Deep Bottom line as well. Finally, engineer troops served as infantry at Saylor's Creek and in defence of a line along the Appomattox River at High Bridge only days before the final surrender. The 1st Engineers had two men killed and 28 wounded during these actions; 38 officers and 272 enlisted men in both regiments surrendered with Lee at Appomattox.

Engineers were supplied with the tools of their trade, picks, shovels and axes. Most of the men carried one or other of these tools. They were also issued with the equipment for the laying of pontoon bridges, consisting of the framework for flat-bottomed boats, covered with canvas lashed to the frame timbers, which were hooked together so that planks could be laid over them. Special wagons were built to carry each boat. Although two companies per regiment were pontoon bridge specialists, all the companies did some bridging work.

The Corps of Engineers were responsible for supplying Lee's maps, so a number of officers and men were provided with surveying and drafting equipment such as T-squares, Indian ink, water-colours, horn protractors, pantographs, triangles, steel rules, pens and pencils, and tracing linen or paper. In many instances civilian mapmakers were employed if the commissioned engineers hadn't the necessary training or knowledge of the local terrain. By the end of 1862, the Corps was able to provide field commanders in Virginia with lithographed, rather than traced, maps. Photographically reproduced maps were produced at the Photographic Establishment at Richmond. These were made by laying well-inked maps on photographically sensitive paper and exposing them to sunlight. By September 1864 the Corps had issued some 146 photographic prints of maps of the Petersburg vicinity.

Each Engineer company was issued a minimum of two wagons, each drawn by four horses or mules, to carry building and entrenching equipment, and a light ambulance drawn by two horses in which was stored surveying instruments, stationery, maps, drawing-boards, etc. Each company was also assigned twelve horses, because the officers were mounted and enlisted men needed horses when deployed on reconnaissance duties.

Insignia

Only the officers wore regulation uniform, enlisted men having come late into the Corps. It featured buff collar, cuffs and trouser stripes, and their buttons were to bear the Old English letter 'E'. Sashes were red. For dress uniform officers were to wear a *chapeau*, or cocked hat, with elaborate gold trim and black ostrich feathers. The undress kepi was all dark-blue with gold lace indicating rank as in other branches. Buff was difficult to keep clean, so the majority of officers of engineers wore either an all grey uniform or one with narrow buff or white edging on collar and cuffs. Often the turn-down collar was worn instead of the standing collar; such a double-breasted grey frock-coat trimmed with buff was worn by Captain Charles Dimmock who laid out the outer line of the defences of Petersburg. A blouse, cut like a civilian day coat, with four patch pockets outside, a turn-down collar and a single row of four or five brass buttons, were highly popular among officers of Engineers.

A dark-blue forage cap was commonly worn. Colonel Talcott had the regulation three gold stripes up the sides and front, although not on the top, of his cap. He also had a black velvet square, with clipped corners, edged with gold binding, and the silver Old English letter 'E' on the cap's front. Captain William D. Echols wore the insignia of an officer of the US Army's Corps of Topographical Engineers, a shield within a wreath, on the front of his dark-blue cap (his coat was of regulation cut but trimmed in buff rather than made with all buff collar and cuffs). In the field, a slouch hat was more practical and hence often worn; Captain Dimmock was photographed holding his slouch hat rather than a cap.

Most buttons worn by officers of engineers bore the regulation letter 'E', but an interesting variant produced by Charles Jennens, a London manufacturer, had the US Army Corps of Engineers' symbol, a turretted castle, on the face surrounded by the legend 'CONFEDERATE STATES ENGINEERS'.[1]

Enlisted men of the corps had no distinctive regulation uniform. By the time that the two regiments were formed, the standard issue through the quartermaster at Richmond included the plain grey jacket with a single row of nine buttons, some of which may have been the general service CSA design made in England and worn in Lee's Army as early as July 1863. Trousers were grey, and the slouch hat was commonly worn. Chevrons, as with infantry non-commissioned officers, would probably have been rarely worn, but might have been of a buff or white tape to match the officers' coat trim or the readily available black.

Flags

Although no Corps regimental flags are known today, the headquarters flag of the Corps in Lee's Army has survived. Not an ANV battle flag or a national flag, but a plain red bunting flag measuring 3 feet 8½ inches by 5 feet 9 inches on the fly. It bears a unit designation in rather crude yellow bunting letters 11 inches high. The first line reads 'Chief Engineer', the second, 'A.N.V.'.

Pay

Pay was set at: a colonel, $210; a major, $162; a captain, $140; and lieutenants serving with enlisted men, the equivalent pay of cavalry officers.[1] On 17 May 1861 the pay for the Company of Sappers and Bombardiers was set at $140 for a captain; $100 for first lieutenant; $90 for second lieutenant. Enlisted men's pay for all engineer troops was; $34 for sergeants; $20 for corporals; $17 for first-class privates; $13 for second-class privates and musicians.[2] On 22 May 1863 pay for engineer troops was set as above, save that a lieutenant colonel would receive $185 a month and the adjutant would receive an additional ten dollars monthly. A sergeant major and a quartermaster would each receive $21.[3] On 20 March 1864 sergeant majors and quartermaster sergeants were to receive $34 a month.[4] On 9 June 1864, all enlisted men received an increase of $7 a month.

THE SIGNAL CORPS
Organization

While serving out west in the 1850s, a US Army assistant surgeon, Albert James Myer, noted how the Indians passed information over many miles using smoke signals. The clear air and great distances between high points, with little brush and few trees intervening, were ideal for the system. Myer developed a signalling system that used a flag by day and a torch by night, waved to left or right, to indicate Bain Code symbols. These were similar to the Morse Code but employed only two elements instead of the four that Morse required for letters sent over telegraph lines. He quickly enlisted the help of a newly commissioned second lieutenant of engineers, Edward Porter Alexander of Georgia. In the winter of 1860/1 the two men went to Washington to demonstrate the system to the Senate's military committee which included the then Senator Jefferson Davis.

When the war broke out, Alexander resigned his commission to accept a Confederate commission as a captain of engineers. Davis, who recalled his performance in Washington, ordered him to have equipment made for a signal detachment to be formed of troops serving in Northern Virginia. This was quickly done and Alexander had ten or twelve 'intelligent young privates who would be suitable for promotion afterwards' assigned to him from Longstreet's Virginia Brigade and Jones's Mississippi Brigade.[1]

'Captain E. P. Alexander, Confederate States Engineers, fortunately joined my headquarters in time to introduce the system of new field signals, which under his skillful management rendered me the most important service preceding and during the engagement,' wrote General Beauregard of the First Manassas.[2] This was the first time in American military history that an official signals unit had transmitted information in the midst of a battle. During that battle, signallers spotted a Union column threatening the Confederate position and were able to alert Beauregard in time.

After the battle Alexander was appointed the army's Chief of Ordnance. 'I remained in charge of the signals also but could not give it a great deal of personal attention. I instructed my brother J. H. in the system & soon afterwards lieutenantcies were given to most of the men I had trained, & they were distributed about in our army & sent to other armies to introduce the system everywhere. A general signal officer for the Confederacy was wanted & I was offered the position with the rank of colonel, but I declined being unwilling to leave the field. It was accordingly given to a Col. Norris, who had been signal officer at Norfolk & was an excellent man.'[3]

Indeed, Alexander's experimental unit proved so successful at the First Manassas that the army set up signal stations at a number of threatened posts. On 19 April 1862, Congress authorized the President to appoint ten PACS lieutenants or captains and ten infantry sergeants to a signal corps that could be attached either to the Engineer Corps or to the Adjutant and Inspector General's Department, as he thought best.

As a result, Army Headquarters in Richmond issued General Order No. 40 on 29 May 1862. This declared that: 'A signals officer will be attached to the staff of each general or major general in command of a corps, and of a major general in command of a division. These signals officers will each be assisted by as many signals sergeants, and instructed non-commissioned officers and privates, selected from the ranks for their intelligence and reliability, as circumstances may require; and as many lance sergeants as are required may be appointed.'[4] On 27 September 1862, Congress authorized an increase in the Corps to include one major, ten first and ten second lieutenants, and 20 more sergeants.[5]

By 3 January 1863 the Secretary of War was able to report that: 'The Signal Corps has been filled and organized and is now in effective operation. It justifies the expectations entertained of its utility and contributes materially to the dispatch of orders, the transmission of intelligence, and the general safety of the Army.'[6]

That year a foreign observer with Lee's Army reported that: 'The signal corps is an institution peculiar to the American armies. On marches and during battles, high and commanding positions are occupied by squadrons of this corps, who communicate with each other, by flags, on the old semaphore system, and report all important communications to their generals. The corps was found very useful last year, and has been very much increased since.'[7]

All told, 61 officers were commissioned as signals officers, and some 1,500 men were detached from other branches to serve in the Corps. In the field they were formed into squads of three to five mounted men commanded by a lieutenant or sergeant, and assigned to an infantry division, cavalry brigade or corps headquarters.

In addition to the Signal Corps, which provided officers and men for each of Lee's command headquarters, there was an independent unit designated the Signal Corps and Scouts which was originally stationed in the Norfolk, Virginia, area until that city was captured, and later expanded its coverage from Petersburg all the way down to the North Carolina coast. This unit specialized in a nautical system of signalling using coloured balls on lines, to and from ships, although it did also adopt the Myer/Alexander system when in support of the army in that area. The unit's two companies were commanded by Major James F. Milligan; they were not directly involved in any of the operations of Lee's Army.

The Signal Corps also handled military intelligence (though Lee and his Army were not directly involved with this), organizing and running the so-called 'Secret Line,' a chain of 'safe houses' between Richmond and Washington, along which spies and government couriers passed. Many US government documents, as well as newspapers and new Union army manuals, went South along this line as well.

Leaders

Captain, later brigadier general, Edward Porter Alexander, Corps of Engineers, first organized the signals operations in the army in Northern Virginia. Born in Washington, Georgia, on 26 May 1835, he graduated from the US Military Academy in 1857. He resigned his US Army commission on 1 May 1861 and quickly received a Confederate commission. Alexander was apparently one of the most intelligent officers on either side during the war. After launching the Signal Corps, he transferred to the artillery, first as a chief of ordnance then as chief of artillery of Longstreet's Corps. He was severely wounded at Petersburg, but returned to duty in time to surrender at Appomattox.

Major William Norris, who was named the army's chief signals officer after Alexander had declined the position, came from Baltimore. Educated at Yale, he had been a lawyer before the war. He had been judge advocate in the US Navy's Pacific Squadron at San Francisco during the gold rush in the early 1850s but had returned to his family's estates near Reistertown, Maryland, to raise a family. When the war broke out, family ties had brought him to Virginia where he was commissioned a captain and named signals officer of the Army of the Peninsula in the autumn of 1862.

Norris was more interested in the intelligence-gathering and secret service aspect of the Signal Bureau than in field communications, and he soon established his headquarters in Richmond where he directed all the activities of the Corps, until he was named commissioner of exchange (of prisoners of war) and promoted to the rank of colonel by the war's end.

In fact, there was no individual who filled the position of 'Chief of Signals' at Lee's headquarters. Certainly there was a signal detachment there, but it did not regulate operations of the corps in the field, and only passed signals to and from other signal detachments commanded by their headquarters commandant.

Tactics

According to General Order No. 40, each divisional signals officer was to instruct each regimental adjutant in the system of signals then in use so that a trained signalman would be available in each regiment in the field. Verbal instruction was inadequate if a uniform training were to be achieved, so a confidential instructional pamphlet was prepared by a corps member in early 1862. According to the Secretary of War in August 1862, the pamphlet contained 'the principles of the art merely, and does not disclose the key to any signal or cipher' so that if it fell into enemy hands it would not do the Corps great harm.[1]

As a further safeguard against Union signalmen learning the Confederate codes, they were changed periodically. Brass decoders consisting of letters engraved around an outer ring and a removable inner ring with another alphabet on it were also issued. These allowed letters of the alphabet being signalled to be switched with other letters to confuse any one trying to read flagged messages in the field.

In action signalmen had first to find high ground close enough to their headquarters to be of use. 'To establish a line of communication for temporary use in the field was short and easy work for those who had experience,' wrote a Signal Corps veteran. 'Of course this was more difficult in a flat than a hilly country. The stations were not far apart and glasses were not always necessary. Whenever possible, some elevated central point was chosen as a station to and from which, as a medial point, messages could be sent from the field.'[2]

Equipment

Each Signal Corps detachment needed a flag for daytime signalling, a torch, which was filled with turpentine, for night-time signalling, and field glasses. Turpentine for the torches was carried in drum-shaped tin canteens, two inches thick and 9½ inches in diameter. They had two spouts, a small one from which to pour the turpentine into the torch, and a wide one with which to fill the canteen. A Signal Corps Manufactory was set up in Richmond under E. Pliny Bryan to make flags and torches for the Corps. Field glasses were not manufactured in the South, and had to be acquired from civilian sources or be imported.

'The flags were about four feet by two and a half feet in size and contained in their centres squares of another color than that of the body of the flag,' wrote Signalman Charles E. Taylor after the war. 'For use against a dark background like a forest or hillside, the white flag was used; against the sky, a dark blue flag; and against a field of snow a scarlet flag.'[1] A requisition for signal flags dated 31 August 1863 shows that larger flags, some eight feet by twelve feet, were also on issue. Surviving examples of these flags, however, are not rectangular or square but pennons. One white one bears a red Latin cross as the contrasting design, while a dark-blue one, a second repeater, bears a white square.

Insignia

There was no official Signal Corps uniform designated. As the officers were staff officers, presumably the buff collar, cuffs and trouser stripes would have been authorized, together with red sash and French *chapeau* for dress and dark-blue cap for undress. Buttons would have been the staff button, which bore an eagle surrounded by thirteen stars in its centre. Some staff buttons had a shield on the eagle's chest with the letters 'CS' at the top of the shield. Major Norris was photographed in a coat of regulation cut, but plain grey, apparently even lacking the Austrian knots on each sleeve, and with a single gold star on a standing grey collar.

Enlisted men would have received the plain grey jacket and trousers, a slouch hat and, when possible, the general service, British-made CSA button on the jacket. Chevrons might have been made of white tape, to match the buff colour used on officers' facings, or the typical black used by non-commissioned officers in all branches of service.

Signalman Taylor, then a private, wrote home on 2 October 1863 requesting 'a pair of silver plated cross flags w'h can be gotten on Wall St., or near the Columbian Hotel' (in Richmond). This was near the district where Francis La Barre, a silversmith who made metal cipher discs for the Signal Corps, had his shop. On 1 May 1864 Taylor also referred to 'the signal badge'. Specimens of insignia consisting of a pair of crossed rectangular signal flags in silver, a square in the centre of each, attached to a spear-pointed pole, have been discovered at military sites in Virginia. It is possible that these were cap badges, and the only insignia unique to the officers and enlisted men of the Signal Corps.[1]

Pay

Officers in the Signal Corps were to receive the same pay as their equivalent ranks in the infantry, according to the Congressional Act signed on 19 April 1862. However, General Order No. 40, dated 29 May 1862, authorized them to receive the equivalent forage and allowances as officers of similar rank of cavalry. Enlisted men received infantry pay, with an additional forty cents a day.[1]

MEDICAL DEPARTMENT

Organization

The Medical Department was one of the first elements of the Confederate Army to be raised. On 26 February 1861, Congress authorized an Army Medical Department consisting of a surgeon general ranking as a colonel, four surgeons as majors, six assistant surgeons as captains, and 'as many assistant surgeons as the service may require', each to receive captain's pay.[1] Each regiment was also to have its own medical officers, both a surgeon and an assistant surgeon whenever possible.

On 16 May 1861, as many hospital stewards, who were to receive the pay and allowance of sergeant majors, as needed were also authorized.[2] According to Confederate Army Regulations, a hospital steward was to be intelligent, sober, honest and skilled in pharmacy. A hospital steward was authorized to each command whose senior medical officer requested one; by this, a regimental surgeon could have a hospital steward assigned to the regiment. Generally speaking, regimental surgeons chose their hospital stewards from among the enlisted men in their units with an eye towards a man who was not only literate and trustworthy, especially since he controlled the issue whisky, but also had some medical or pharmaceutical education or experience. In fact, most did, and Hospital Steward George E. Waller, 24th Virginia Infantry, for example, was so trustworthy that he ended up in charge of a field hospital for the winter of 1863/4.

Enlisted men also served as clerks to the regimental surgeon. On 9 December 1862, Private John A. Gholson of the 14th Tennessee Infantry was given the odd, non-regulation title of 'Regimental Prescriptionist', perhaps as a temporary measure, since he was promoted to the grade of hospital steward the following month.

Dentists were also given the grade of hospital steward. In addition to their normal work of filling or extracting teeth and removing tartar, they dealt with fractures of bones of the mouth. Indeed, they staffed a special dental ward in a Richmond hospital devoted to maxillo-facial surgery.

On 26 March 1862, the Secretary of War issued an organizational scheme for the Medical Department in the field:

'1. An army corps or military department will have a medical officer assigned as medical director, who will have the general control of the medical officers and hospital.

'2. A division will have a medical officer assigned, on the recommendation of the medical director, as chief surgeon; or the senior medical officer of the division, on the same recommendation, will be relieved from regimental duty, and placed in general charge as chief surgeon of the division.

'3. A brigade will be under the general medical charge of the senior surgeon of brigade, who will not be relieved from regimental duty.

'4. Medical directors, chief surgeons of divisions, and senior surgeons of brigades, will inspect the hospitals of their commands, and see that the rules and regulations are enforced, and the duties of the surgeons and assistant surgeons are properly performed.'[3]

In 1863, a foreign observer in Lee's Army described this organization as it was practised by that force: 'The medical department is organized thus: — Medical director of the army; medical director of the army corps; chief surgeon of division; senior surgeon of brigade. Each regiment has a surgeon, an assistant-surgeon, two ambulances, and a medical waggon, belonging to it. Two men from each company are detailed to act as litter-bearers and attendants upon the wounded; these follow the troops on the field of battle, and convey men to the hospitals in the rear.'[4]

During the first year of war, members of each regiment's band — and almost every regiment had a band — had the job of acting as stretcher-bearers during combat. 'We had considerable experience in giving first aid to the wounded, and I, for one, got myself to believe that I could amputate a man's leg as well as some of the doctors,' wrote

Bandsman Julius Leinbach of the 26th North Carolina Infantry's band.[5] This policy proved a failure in the long run. Bandsmen were not directly under the control of the regimental surgeon so they were often unavailable for training — practising their music instead of medicine. Nor were they the most steady of troops when under fire. Therefore, Lee's Army adopted a system of assigned litter-bearers during the war's second year. As James Nisbet, a veteran of the 21st Georgia Infantry, later recalled: 'Then, each company had two men detailed as litter-bearers who were excused from all company duty and the regimental drill. Their principal duty was to pick up wounded men and carry them back to the surgeon and assist the surgeons after the battle. The captains selected the strongest and bravest men for this duty. Often each litter-bearer had to carry a man on his back or in his arms, which called for greater strength, and to return to the firing line was more trying than to stay and shoot.'[6]

These litter-bearers formed the Ambulance Corps, which did not have a formal organization at any beyond regimental level. In the field, the twenty Ambulance Corpsmen from each regiment were directed by the regiment's assistant surgeon, the spread-out group following the front line to aid wounded soldiers on the spot, then bring them back to a regimental hospital set up by the surgeon and the hospital steward.

During active campaigning seasons there were too few surgeons in the army for all the patients, so early in 1864 the Medical Department organized the Reserve Surgical Corps from surgeons at fixed hospitals. One doctor for every five hundred beds was appointed to the Corps. These doctors were to be sent to help out in field hospitals as needed. In point of fact, their performance was, on the whole, not wholly successful; it being thought that were rather too anxious to get back to their comfortable hospitals in the rear.

Leaders
Surgeon Thomas H. Williams, who had previously held a US Army commission as surgeon, was the first medical director of the army in northern Virginia. He had been medical director of the US Army forces that marched into Utah in 1859. Resigning his commission in April 1861, he was appointed medical director of the Virginia army on 24 June 1861. He held that position until Lee assumed command of the army, Lee's medical director outranking him. He was then named medical director and inspector of hospitals in Virginia, where he served for several months before being transferred to Richmond to become director of the Medical Purveyors' Department, a post he held until the war's end.

Lee's man had the distinguished name of Lafayette Guild. Guild, who had also been a US Army surgeon until resigning at the war's outbreak, was commissioned a surgeon in the regular Confederate Army. He served with Lee's Army as its medical director until its surrender.

Practice

While senior medical officials were often veterans of US Army service, the majority of new surgeons had little or no experience in the types of wound they now found themselves dealing with, ranging from bones shattered by musket-balls to the rare sucking chest wound caused by a bayonet. There were two ways of learning how to handle such wounds, on-the-job training and books.

By Army Regulations, each surgeon was to be supplied with five reference books: a book on anatomy, a book on medical practice, a copy of medical department regulations, a book on practical surgery and Thompson's *Conspectus*.[1]

Books, however, were rare. Surgeon Deering J. Roberts recalled how he obtained a copy of Erichsen's *Surgery* by trading with a civilian doctor near his camp for an ounce of sulphate of quinine which, for some odd reason, he happened to have more than enough of at the time. He also carried an 1857 book on anatomy, Wilson's *Dissector*, which he had brought from home. Otherwise, from time to time he carried copies of, as he later wrote, Druitt's *Surgery*, Bartlett's *On Fevers*, Wood's *Practice*, Watson's *Practice*, Tanner's *Practice* and a copy of *United States Dispensatory* by Wood & Bache.

'Occasional copies of *The Confederate States Medical and Surgical Journal*, reached field and hospital surgeons. It was published in Richmond by Ayres & Wade, with the approval and under the supervision of the Surgeon-General, monthly from January, 1864, until February 1865...

'Dr. J. J. Chisolm, who entered the army as a surgeon from Charleston, South Carolina, wrote an excellent little "Manual of Military Surgery" of about four or five hundred 12mo pages; another manual, about the same size, was prepared by surgeons detailed for that purpose by Surgeon-General (Preston) Moore, and published in Richmond, in 1862 or 1863. These were supplied to many field and hospital surgeons by the Government.

'Another work published at Richmond ... was entitled *Resources of the Southern Fields and Forests, Medical, Economical, and Agricultural*, being also a Medical Botany of the Southern States, with Practical Information of the Useful Properties of the Trees, Plants, and Shrubs. A large number of copies was printed, and the book supplied to the medical officers and all others who applied.'[2]

The book by G. B. Wood and F. Bache, *The Dispensatory of the United States of America*, which Roberts mentioned, was first published in Philadelphia in 1854. According to its first edition's preface, 'The

162

objects of a Dispensatory are to present an account of medicinal substances in the state in which they are brought into the shops, and to teach the modes in which they are prepared for use.' The book was commonly in the field libraries of surgeons, both north and south.

The book by J. Julian Chisolm, *A Manual of Military Surgery for the use of Surgeons in the Confederate Army*, which Surgeon Roberts mentioned, a second edition of which appeared in Richmond in 1862, was important because it contained the rules and regulations of the medical department as well as medical information. It was, however, only one of several such books available to Confederate surgeons. The book he mentioned as having been published under authority of the Surgeon General, *A Manual of Military Surgery*, was published in Richmond in 1863. Edward Warren wrote *An Epitome of Practical Surgery for Field and Hospital* which was published at the same place and time as the Surgeon General's manual. And, although Felix Formento's *Notes and Observations on Army Surgery* was published in New Orleans in 1863, while that city was occupied by Federal troops, it was widely available for Southern surgeons. Formento was a surgeon in Richmond's Louisiana Hospital.

It should be noted that these basic military medicine texts covered only two types of treatment, chemical and surgical. These were the two basic approaches that doctors of the period took towards helping patients to recover.

The first, the use of drugs, was the most popular for virtually every ailment unless it was obvious that the patient had something grievously physically wrong such as a bullet wound. The great majority of cases that Confederate doctors had to deal with were of the type that appeared to them to be best treated with one drug or another. This was because there were too many men — many of them rather too old for active field service as the conscription age began to creep up — from rural backgrounds who had never before been exposed to such common diseases such as mumps, chicken pox, or measles. Added to this was the fact that man for man, the average soldier in Lee's Army was generally less healthy than the average soldier in the opposing army. The climate of the South encouraged mosquitoes, worm eggs and larvae, and waterborne protozoa and bacteria to flourish, infecting Southerners of all ranks more constantly than Northerners. Hookworm, imported by slaves from Africa, affected as much as 40 per cent of the South's population, according to some estimates, leaving its victims weak, anemic, listless, short of breath, subject to bowel complaints and susceptible to other illnesses.

Impure water, bad sanitary arrangements and bad rations poorly prepared, eaten by men with inadequate shelter from weather and insects and sometimes badly clothed, led to a large number of diseases of the intestinal tract, including diarrhoea and severe constipation. The lack of interesting activities, the monotony of day-to-day existence in the average camp, coupled with often severe homesickness among boys and men who had never been more than several miles from the spot where they had been born, also led to depression and caused the development of physical ailments.

Diarrhoea was the most common complaint problem and it was sometimes fatal. Officially it was treated with doses of calomel, strychnia, opium and acetate of lead, administered under the names of 'blue mass', lastrgt pills' and 'diarrhoea mixture'. Many doctors had their own remedies, often using local plants known for their medicinal qualities.

Besides childhood diseases and diarrhoea, soldiers were in danger from malaria, typhoid fever, scarlet fever, pneumonia, tuberculosis, rheumatism and venereal and mental diseases. These, too, were largely treated with various drugs, although many physicians recognized that rest and good diet were also major treatments for them all. When possible, especially for depression caused by homesickness or 'nostalgia', many doctors attempted to arrange furloughs as the best of all treatments.

A number of soldiers, affected both by nostalgia and the pressures of battle, succumbed to what today is known as Post Traumatic Stress Disorder. Many of them in Lee's Army were sent to the Louisiana Hospital in Richmond which was, as of 27 March 1865, set aside strictly for the treatment of such cases of mental illnesses.

Clinical complaints, such as diarrhoea before it became chronic, were treated by the regimental surgeon during the daily sick call held at his tent every morning. The surgeon made generally only a cursory examination, then issued a prescription for a drug to the regimental hospital steward who was responsible for the unit's pharmacy, mostly opium and 'blue mass', a mixture of mercury and chalk, hardly conducive to good health.

If the trouble persisted or became severe, the soldier was sent to a hospital in the rear. There were 34 hospitals in Richmond, ranging from small private concerns and hospitals set aside for various states' troops (Alabama had three such hospitals, Georgia had four), to the giant Chimborazo which could care for 3,000 patients, although at one time 3,500 patients were there. In all, 77,889 soldiers spent some time at the Chimborazo; 16,000 of them are buried at the nearby Oakwood Cemetery.

Not all patients could be treated with drugs; Lee's Army was a fighting army, and in 1863 alone 27,206 soldiers had to be treated in hospital for gunshot wounds.

When action seemed imminent, the medical department went to work. Each brigade's chief medical officer selected a site for a brigade field infirmary which would be close enough to the front line for men to brought there quickly, yet out of range of most missiles. Houses, churches and barns were preferred for such field infirmaries. Cooks were assigned to prepare food for the expected casualties; dressings, blankets and clothing were made ready.

At times, chief medical officers of divisions even massed their brigade medical personnel into a larger, divisional hospital, but this was not common. These field hospitals were marked with distinctive flags so that wounded men and Ambulance Corpsmen could see them from most points on the nearby battlefield.

At times a brigade field hospital would be staffed by regimental surgeons, but if it were too far away a regimental field hospital would be set up near the regiment's front line. Stewards accompanied the regimental surgeons to assist at the field hospitals. The assistant regimental surgeons checked the equipment of the the regimental Ambulance Corpsmen who then followed the infantry into action. When battle was joined the assistant surgeon found a spot for a relatively safe first aid station. Ambulance Corpsmen brought the wounded men back to the assistant surgeon who performed just enough work to keep the man in one piece before being sent on to the field hospital. Some casualties would have their wounds treated there and would then return to their comrades at the front rather than go back to the field hospital.

'Our command then took position in the woods near the cut of an unfinished railroad and sent out skirmishers, who soon retreated and fell back on the main line,' wrote Surgeon Spencer Glasgow Welch, 13th South Carolina Infantry of Second Manassas. 'I remained some distance in rear of our line and saw Mike Bowers, Dave Suber, and two other men bringing someone back on a litter, and I said: "Mike, who is that?" and he said: "Goggans," just as they tumbled him down. I looked at him as he was gasping his last, and he died at once. Then the wounded who could walk began to come back, and those who could not were brought to me on litters. I did all I could for them until the ambulances could carry them to the field infirmary, and this continued until late in the afternoon...

'Our brigade was not relieved until about four o'clock ... and I then went back to the field infirmary, where I saw large numbers of wounded lying on the ground as thick as a drove of hogs in a lot. They were groaning and crying out with pain, and those shot in the bowels were crying for water. Jack Fellers had his arm amputated without chloroform. I held the artery and Dr. Huot cut it off by candle light.'[2]

Most of the medical work performed on soldiers wounded in action involved some surgery. The large, slow-moving bullets splintered bones and mangled flesh, and amputation was thought to be the best way of treating such wounds. 'The shattering, splintering, and splitting of a long bone by the impact of the minié or Enfield ball were, in many instances, both remarkable and frightful, and early experience taught surgeons that amputation was the only means of saving life,' Surgeon Roberts wrote, adding, 'Conservative surgery was, I might say, almost, if not entirely, a universal principle with the Confederate surgeon; conservatism, first as to the life of the wounded soldier, secondly, as to his future comfort and usefulness.'[3]

According to the current medical theory, the operation should be performed as soon as possible after the wound had been received, certainly within 24 hours before it had a chance to become septic. And, indeed, statistics kept by Southern hospitals tend to confirm that such operations performed within the 24-hour period were more successful than those done some time later.

The preferred anaesthetic for major surgery was chloroform poured on to a sponge or cloth placed over the patient's nose and mouth until he was unconscious. But chloroform was often unavailable so patients were given whisky or brandy or, often, nothing at all.

And nothing at all was used to sterilize instruments or protect the wound from infection, the existence of bacteria having as yet scarcely been guessed at by the world's best medical minds. Surgeons simply dipped their instruments into bloody water after one operation, wiped their hands off on their bloody aprons, and began work on the next patient. From time to time the operating-table, often nothing more than a bench or a door taken from its hinges, would be splashed clean of blood.

In one way, as it turned out, the blockade of Southern ports which made proper medical equipment so rare, actually helped the wounded. Sponges, which were dipped in water after use, were virtually unobtainable so cotton rags were used and these could be washed cleaner than sponges, thus in a small way helping prevent infection. Certain specifics used to kill maggots were often unavailable, but the surgeons found that maggots actually destroyed gangrenous tissue, then dropped away, leaving healthy tissue. Some surgeons treated wounds with turpentine, chlorides or powdered charcoal to speed healing; some of these actually worked as disinfectants and did, indeed, promote healing.

After treatment in the field hospital, badly wounded men were sent back to a permanent hospital, of which there were 44 in Richmond in 1862 alone, where the recovery process continued if not arrested by any of the four so-called surgical fevers, tetanus, erysipelas, hospital gangrene and pyaemia, certainly the most fatal of the four. Essentially, save for surgical removal of gangrenous tissue, there were no treatments for these diseases except rest and adequate food and ventilation, which was thought to be quite important for healing. Drugs, which did little good, were sometimes prescribed.

If the patient managed to avoid these diseases, and was found fit for service after his stay in the hospital, he was returned to his unit.

If not, he was discharged, at least until the formation of the Invalid Corps into which many disabled men were transferred.

There were many discharged veterans whose wounds failed to heal properly. In February 1865, Surgeon James B. Read was ordered to set up an orthopedic hospital to treat these old injuries. Another similar hospital was to have been set up for western Confederate troops at Lauderdale Springs, Mississippi, but the end of the war intervened.

Equipment

Each regimental medical staff of surgeons and enlisted personnel could be considered to comprise a small hospital, and so Army Regulations allocated to it a wide range of equipment including 68 specifics for the medicine chest, ranging from alcohol and ammonia to potassium chlorate aand quinine.

Unfortunately, rather few of these medicines were domestically produced, most supplies of them coming either from the North or from abroad. Therefore, on 2 April 1862 the Surgeon General issued a directive to all medical officers to be on the lookout for local plants which could have the same medical effects as the prescribed drugs. On 22 July the office in Richmond instructed surgeons to use dogwood, tulip-bearing poplar, willow, boneset and centaury for malaria; crane's-bill, marsh rosemary, blackberry and sweet gum for 'bowel complaints of the warm season'; and the calico bush for intermittent fever.[1] Scurvy was to be treated with wild mustard, watercress, wild garlic or onion, sassafras, lamb's-quarters, sorrel, shoots of the pokeweed, artichoke, plume of the dandelion, garden parsley, peppergrass or wild yam.[2] The common elder was used to expel maggots from wounds.[3] A substitute for quinine, used against malaria, was to be made from 30 parts dried dogwood bark, 30 parts dried poplar bark and 40 parts dried willow bark, two pounds of this mixture in one gallon of 45 proof whisky.[4] Whisky itself was made from sorghum seed rather than grain.[5]

Each surgeon was supposed to have two sets of amputating knives, two ball forceps, a dozen fougies, a case of nine catheters, a dozen cupping glasses and tines, five lancets, a dozen surgeon's needles in a case, two sets of pocket knives, six probangs, two scarificators, a set of assorted splints, twenty types of syringe, a set of dental implements, a tongue depressor, fourteen tourniquets, a trepanning set, two trocars, and a hernia truss. Also, quantities of arrow root, farina, ginger, nutmeg, tea and three dozen bottles of whisky.

The regimental medical stores were to include fourteen dozen roller bandages and a dozen suspensory bandages, eighteen binders boards, a couple of hatchets, four lanterns, ten litters and hand stretchers, two bed pans, a 'washed' sponge, four scissors, two coffee mills, and two mortars and pestles, plus a wide range of materials needed to maintain a hospital.

'I kept with me my regimental medicine chest, amputating and pocket-case instruments, and the assistant surgeons had their own pocket instruments,' wrote Surgeon Roberts of the equipment he carried in the field. Moreover, 'Instruments were procured by the medical bureau in the earlier part of the war from stock in the hands of dealers in the larger cities, later by blockade-runners, and by the handiwork of a few skilled workers in the Southern States. Some were somewhat crude and clumsy, and lacked the beautiful polish and finish given by the experienced and well-equipped instrument maker. Occasionally a fortunate surgeon would acquire a good case of instruments by capture; but quite a number of our surgeons brought from their homes both amputating- and pocket-cases, their private property purchased before the coming on of hostilities.'[6]

Some of the medical issue items were to be carried in the two regimental hospital knapsacks. According to Army Regulations, this knapsack was 'of same dimensions with ordinary knapsacks, of light material; and to be covered with canvas. It is to be carried on a march or in battle, by a hospital orderly, who is habitually to follow the medical officer. The purpose of this knapsack is to carry such instruments, dressings, and medicines, as may be needed in an emergency on the march or in the field.'[7] What exactly was to be carried in each knapsack was apparently left up to the medical officer in the field.

Every Ambulance Corpsman was to carry a canteen, a tin cup, and a haversack filled with four bandages, two long and two short wood splints, a variety of tourniquets and sponges, ⅛-pound of lint, and a pint bottle of 'alcoholic stimulant', according to orders issued in the Departments of South Carolina, Georgia, and Florida in early 1863. Ambulance Corpsmen in Lee's Army were probably similarly equipped. Non-commissioned officers in the Ambulance Corps were armed so as to be able to protect their men from 'stragglers and marauders'; the privates were unarmed.

Insignia

Surgeons ranked as commissioned officers and therefore wore the regulation uniform. There were, however, certain differences in dress. Their facings — collar and cuffs — were black. Indeed, a number of surviving surgeons' coats have the regulation black collar and cuffs, but lack the gold Austrian knot on each sleeve.

Surgeons were to wear staff officers' buttons, with the spread eagle within the circle of stars. Their dark-blue trousers were to have a black velvet stripe 1¼ inches wide, edged on each side with gold cord. Sashes were of green silk net.

According to Surgeon Roberts, 'on the front of the cap or hat were the letters 'M.S.' embroidered in gold, embraced in two olive branches. On the coat sleeve of the assistant surgeon were two rows of gold braid, with three gold bars on the ends of the coat collar extending back about one and a half inches; while the surgeon had three rows of braid on the coat sleeves, and a single star on each side of the coat collar about an inch and a half from the end. The chevrons on the coat sleeves of the hospital steward were similar to those worn by an orderly or first sergeant, but were black in color.'[1] But no regulation insignia or uniform was prescribed for hospital stewards. Indeed, surviving jackets lack any insignia at all.

Photographs of surgeons, however, confirm not only regulation dress, but Roberts' suggestion of a cap badge worn by surgeons. A photograph of Surgeon William Philpot, 4th Georgia, for example, shows a regulation double-breasted coat, although plain grey throughout, and a dark-blue forage cap with two rows of gold lace up the front, sides and back, and the Old English letter 'M' on the left of the front two rows of lace and the letter 'S' on the right of them. Surgeon William F. Steuart, however, wore the wreath that Roberts mentioned around the letters 'M.S.' on his forage cap front. And William Stevenson was seen in Richmond in 1862 'in the dress of an assistant surgeon, with the M.S. upon my cap'.[2]

On the other hand, Surgeon Thomas Williams, first head of the Virginia army's medical department, simply wore the regulation four rows of lace around the base and up the sides of his otherwise plain cap. Indeed, he wore a totally regulation Confederate surgeon's uniform and carried a US Army Medical Department officer's sword. And Surgeon William B. Wise simply wore a plain dark-blue copy of the French kepi.

In 1863, a British observer with Lee's Army noted 'a certain number of unarmed men carrying stretchers and wearing in their hats the red badges of the ambulance corps'.[3] No regulations specifying a design for this badge are known. There is, however, at least one physical example of a rectangle of red wool on top of which has been sewn a smaller rectangle of white cotton, the top made with a convex curve, bearing the black letters 'AMBULANCE/CORPS'. The word 'AMBULANCE' is slightly curved to fit the curve of the top of the rectangle, while 'CORPS' runs straight along the bottom.

Flags
In battle, hospitals had to be easily identifiable by walking wounded and Ambulance Corpsmen. A readily recognizable flag was the easiest way to achieve this, and therefore Army Regulation 714 specified that: 'The ambulance depot to which the wounded are carried or directed for immediate treatment, is generally established at the most convenient building nearest the field of battle. A red flag marks its place, or the way to it, to the conductors of the ambulances and to the wounded who can walk.' Such a plain red flag, with a white bunting hoist and a

rope tie at each end of the hoist, was captured by Union troops and became a US War Department trophy.

Union forces, however, flew yellow flags over their hospitals and this practice may have spread to some of Lee's Army at least. According to Private J. O. Casler, a Stonewall Brigade veteran, hospital tents in Lee's Army were marked by yellow rather than red flags.

Pay

On 6 March 1861 pay for medical officers was set at $3,000 a year for the surgeon general. A surgeon with ten years of service in that grade was to receive $200 a month, while one with fewer years of service earned $162. An assistant surgeon of ten years service in that grade earned $150 a month; an assistant surgeon with between five and ten years earned $130; and an assistant surgeon with fewer than five years in the grade earned $110.[1]

Hospital Tents

According to the 1863 Confederate Army Regulations, 'Hospital tents, having on one end a lapel, so as to admit of two or more tents being joined and thrown into one with a continuous covering or roof, will be made of these dimensions:

'Length, 14 feet; width, 15 feet; height (centre), 11 feet, with a wall 4½ feet, and a "fly" of appropriate size. The ridge pole will be made in two sections, measuring 14 feet when joined.

'This tent will accommodate from eight to ten patients comfortably.

'The following allowance of tents for the sick, their attendants, and hospital supplies, will be issued on requisitions on the Quartermaster Department:

Command	Hospital Tents	Sibley Tents	Common Tents
For a company	–	1	1
For three companies	1	1	1
For five companies	2	1	1
For seven companies	2	1	1
For ten companies	3	1	1*

*Official, *Army Regulations*, p. 282.

BANDS

Initially, each regiment brought, or wanted to bring, a band into the field. According to Army Regulations, each regiment was authorized sixteen musicians. On 10 December 1861, a principal musician, or chief bugler, was appointed to each regiment to run its band or at least its field music corps, which consisted of fifers and drummers. The sixteen musicians were to muster as a separate squad under the principal musician, although they were also to be trained in the regiment's combat duties and were liable to serve in the ranks if needed. The band was to be kept at regimental headquarters. In fact, many regimental bands had served together before the war as local bands. Smith's Armory Band of Richmond, for example, became the regimental band of the 1st Virginia Infantry Regiment in April 1860. The Mountain Saxhorn Band of Staunton, Virginia, became the band of the 5th Virginia Infantry Regiment, later gaining fame as the Stonewall Brigade Band. The Salisbury Brass Band became the 4th North Carolina Infantry Regiment's band. The 48th Virginia Infantry's band had been the Valley Brass Band before the war. The Americus Brass Band became the band of the 4th Georgia Infantry Regiment, with twelve members originally and men drawn from the ranks to bring it up to the full eighteen allowed.

Field musicians, however, differed from bandsmen in that they were assigned at company level where they served, being only massed for special regimental occasions such as reviews and grand parades.[1]

'Almost every regiment had a small band with brass instruments,' wrote a British observer in 1863.[2] In fact it would appear that not every regiment was able to recruit enough musicians for a band. Only seventeen bands were reported as being present at a review of the Army's III Corps in September 1863; there was another band in the corps apparently, but it was not present at the review.

Bands were unique among Confederate military formations in that African Americans were allowed to serve in them. Indeed, according to an Act of 15 April 1862, Confederate black musicians were to receive the same pay as white musicians.[3]

Confederate units had to cast their nets wide to acquire their bandsmen, for in the South musical training on instruments other than the guitar and the banjo was rare. 'Many of the regiments had little bands of three or four musicians, who played rather discordantly. The Southerners are said to be extremely fond of music, though they seldom take the trouble to learn to play themselves, and seem not very particular as to whether the instruments they hear are in tune or not. The bandsmen are almost all Germans,' wrote a European professional military man who was accustomed to the fine martial bands of European armies.[4]

Most Confederate would have disagreed, perhaps strongly, with the European's view of their music. Stonewall Jackson supposedly told his wife Anna about the 'sweet music' of the 5th Virginia's band in an effort to get her to visit him in late 1861. 'There is music on the Square in Richmond every Tuesday and Friday afternoon by the Band now, and I understand the place is crowded every afternoon by ladies and gents,' wrote Hospital Steward Luther Swank, 15th Virginia Infantry, in August 1864. 'The Band of the 30th Regiment of our Brigade performed there yesterday afternoon and [I] have no doubt [that they made] some very sweet music as [the] men composing it are splendid performers.'[5]

Many of the performers in North Carolina's bands were of German ancestry, drawn from the Moravian community in the Winston-Salem area which had a strong instrumental tradition. Regimental bands of the 21st and 26th North Carolina Infantry Regiments came from this area. In fact, the band of the 26th had, before the war, been the eight-strong Moravian Salem Brass Band, which joined the regiment as a single group in March 1862, led by bandmaster Samuel Mickey who played the cornet.

Indeed band music was quite popular and Confederate bands were often used to boost the men's morale. 'When the cannonade was at its height,' wrote a British observer of the time just before the launching of Pickett's Charge at Gettysburg, 'a Confederate band of music, between the cemetery and ourselves, began to play polkas and waltzes, which sounded very curious, accompanied by the hissing and bursting of shells.'[6]

The morale-boosting quality of band music was recognized at the highest level. 'I don't believe we can have an army without music,' Lee himself said in 1864 after being serenaded by one of the army's bands.[7]

The music they played varied in range according to pre-war training and what music was available. Polkas and waltzes were civilian music; the ones played included such anonymous works as the Slumber Polka and the Louisa Polka. Bands in Lee's Army were known to have played more then just these types of musical composition. The outbreak of war produced a number of patriotic songs such as 'The Bonny Blue Flag', 'Strike For The South', 'The Southern Marseillaise', 'Stonewall Jackson's Way', 'Riding A Raid', 'God Save The South', 'The Southern Girl' and 'Maryland, My Maryland' which was never quite as popular after Sharpsburg. Ironically, the song that became the most popular, almost an unofficial national anthem for the South, was written in 1859 by a Northerner, a native of Ohio named Daniel Emmett: 'I Wish I Was In Dixie's Land', better known as 'Dixie'.

After a period in the field, patriotic songs lost their sheen. Other types of song, played by the bands and sung by the soldiers, became more standard. They varied in type considerably. The 1st Virginia Infantry, wrote the adjutant of Louisiana's Washington Artillery in 1861, 'had an excellent band, better, I think, than ours, and each gave excellent music at guard-mounting and dress parade. "Listen to the Mocking-bird" was the favorite air of the Virginians.'[8] The men of the 1st Maryland Infantry were known to prefer 'Gay And Happy Still'. 'There is a brass band and they are playing "Shells of Ocean", wrote a Confederate from the Wilderness in 1864, 'and as the familiar notes of this sweet air are gently wafted in delightful cadences over the woody hills and dewy fields, numberless visions of home in happier hours and sweet reminiscences of the past crowd thick and fast upon my soul.'[9]

Some songs, such as 'Come In Out Of The Draft' and 'Grafted Into The Army' mocked the conscripts. Some like 'Goober Peas' kidded the militia and the army itself. So did the lugubrious 'Somebody's Darling' which began, 'Into the ward of the whitewashed hall, wounded by bayonets, sabres and ball, somebody's darling was borne one day.' Yet, while sarcastic in its intent, it also touched a vein of real grief about the war and its results.

Songs like 'Tenting Tonight On The Old Camp Ground', 'Just Before The Battle, Mother', 'When Upon The Field Of Glory' (the Southern version of 'Weeping, Sad And Lonely'), and 'Lorena', the most popular song among Southern soldiers, allowed the singers to show their true emotions about the war within socially accepted forms. Finally, Lee's bands always included hymns in their repertoires. One evening after a day's fighting at Spotsylvania, a Confederate band was heard to play 'Nearer, My God, to Thee'.

Band instrument included cornets, French horns, tubas, trombones (both with and without slides), clarinets, flutes, oboes and piccolos. Side, tenor and bass drums were often added as well. But reed instruments, which had been the mainstay of military bands until the 1850s, were dying out. Most Southern bands were based on civilian 'brass bands', which used a family of instruments invented by a Belgian, Adolphe Antoine-Joseph Sax. Known as 'Saxhorns', these horns came in seven bell-over-the-shoulder types: E flat soprano, B flat soprano, E flat alto, B flat baritone, B flat bass, E flat bass, and double B flat bass.

Uniform

Unlike their counterparts in the US Army, Confederate musicians had no special uniform or insignia, according to Army Regulations. None the less, a single-breasted frock-coat with horizontal bars of tape around the buttons on the front, in an apparent copy of the US Army musicians' coat, was known.

THE PROVOST MARSHAL

There was no mention of a Provost Marshal nor troops assigned to the duties performed by such an individual in the Congressional Acts that set up the army. But such troops were obviously needed to maintain order within such a large body of men who quite often lacked personal discipline, and committed such military offences as straggling and being absent without leave and civilian offences such as theft, pillage and even rape.

On 5 June 1862, orders issued by the Headquarters of the Department of Northern Virginia stipulated that a provost guard for each division be formed. Each would consist of an officer, a non-commissioned officer, and ten men from each regiment in the division, each guard member to be selected on the basis of reliability and efficiency.[1] In point of fact, it seems as if commanders took advantage of this draft on their units to send off men who had been wounded or were chronically ill and unfit for active field service.

Even so, on 4 September similar provost units were ordered to be formed at brigade level and at army headquarters so they must have proved successful enough, but they were not ordered for the Cavalry Corps until after Gettysburg.

Then too, units of varying size were sometimes temporarily assigned to provost guard duty. Jones's Brigade was sent as provost guard to Frederick, Maryland, in early September 1862 during the Maryland campaign.[2] The 12th Georgia spent 3 May 1863 as provost guard for Doles's Brigade near Chancellorsville. The 6th Alabama Infantry Regiment formed the provost guard in Martinsburg, Virginia, on 16 June 1863.[3] On 14 November 1863, Lieutenant G. M. Ryals, Provost Marshal of the cavalry corps, directed Major General Wade Hampton to assign temporary provost guards at Spotsylvania Court House, Guiney's Station and Bowling Green.[4] Men of the 1st Regiment of Engineer Troops served as provost guards around Richmond at various times, while the 60th Alabama Infantry Regiment was assigned to provost marshal duty in Richmond for the month of May 1864. During the last years of the war, at various times, both the 9th and 41st Virginia Infantry Regiments were sent as provost guards to capture deserters heading south along the Blackwater River just south of Richmond.

There were also several units permanently assigned to provost marshal duty. II Corps assigned a 2-company unit designated 1st North Carolina Infantry Battalion, Sharpshooters, in June 1863 as its provost guard. The battalion's commander was Major Rufus W. Wharton. He was captured near Port Royal, Virginia, on 11 January 1863, not being exchanged until 6 April 1863. He went on to act as an aide-de-camp to Brigadier General Robert Hoke from early 1864.

The 5th Alabama Infantry Regiment served as provost marshal guard to III Corps on a temporary basis at Harper's Ferry in September 1862 while the rest of the corps went on to Sharpsburg. At Harper's Ferry they were assigned the important provost marshal job of guarding captured Union weapons and equipment. They were permanently assigned to this duty in July 1863, although they did see some action — some of it rather heroic, such as the successful defence of the Confederate line during the Wilderness on 5 May 1864. They were serving as the Corps' provost guard when it surrendered at Appomattox. The 5th was commanded by Major Albert S. Van de Graaff.

On 4 June 1863 Lee assigned the 1st Virginia Battalion (the 'Irish Battalion'), commanded by Major David B. Bridgford, to provost marshal duty at army headquarters. Although this was was meant to have been temporary, the unit was officially assigned to Second Corps as provost guard on 12 December 1862 and continued in this duty for the duration of the war. It served not only as the army's police force, but also provided guards for Headquarters, and prisoners of war at reception points behind the line.

Bridgford, a 30-year-old merchant in Richmond at the war's outbreak, had been assigned with his unit as provost marshal of II Corps early on. Son of a Canadian militia officer of the War of 1812, he was also involved in intelligence-gathering activities. He was said to have attracted the notice of his superiors, but failed to measure up to expectations aand was later replaced as battalion commander by Major James Seddon.

Strangely, there appears to have been no regularly assigned provost guard in First Corps. In March 1865 Co. B, 44th Virginia Battalion, which had been part of the Reserve Forces of Virginia, was assigned as provost guard of Lee's Army. The company by now consisted largely of under-aged boys, and was only eight-strong when it surrendered little more than a month later at Appomattox.

In February 1865, the 2nd Maryland Battalion, which was not plagued by desertions since it was so difficult for its men to get across Union lines, was employed as a provost guard against desertions from Lee's Army. The battalion was set up in picket posts around its brigade to try to stop the flow of deserters until the final Appomattox campaign. That month, too, the 7th North Carolina was sent back to its home state to arrest deserters who had fled back there, although a Union thrust on the Danville Railroad which had to be turned back prevented the unit from reaching its destination.

The duties of the provost marshal's troops were summed up by General Arthur Manigault: 'The Provost Guard, as its name would imply, was strictly a police force, in no manner charged with the protection of the camp, but responsible for the safe keeping of all culprits, carrying out the sentences of Courts-Martial, or the infliction of such punishment as the brigade commander authorized, and correcting all breaches of camp orders, a detachment of them being nearly always on duty, scouting around the neighbourhood, arresting all stragglers, marauders, or men absent from their commands without leave. In battle they are most often used, deployed in the rear of the line, to prevent any skulking or passing to the rear without proper authority, although on several such occasions they were attached to some regiment and took part in the fight, or were used to prolong a line, when the space allotted us was rather greater than we could fill with safety, without making use of them. All prisoners captured were turned over to them for safe keeping. On the march they brought up the rear, allowing no one to drop behind without authority, or to straggle on the flanks of the column, into farm houses, orchards, or fields of corn, sugar-cane, or the like.'[5]

Major Bridgford reported how he deployed his 1st Virginia Battalion as the Second Corps provost guard at the Battle of Fredericksburg. He placed the unit in a line about a half mile behind the two-mile Corps front line. The men were ordered to arrest any soldiers found without passes. Indeed, they were authorized to shoot such stragglers who would not stop for them. A provost surgeon was to examine any claiming to be sick or wounded. Any apparently well soldier lacking a pass was to be escorted to the nearest division commander with orders to have the offender placed in the most exposed position possible. In all, the command returned only some 526 men to the fight.

In much the same way, the 5th Alabama Battalion formed a straggler line behind Third Corps during the Wilderness fighting in April and May 1864.

Posts manned by provost guards were set up along likely straggler lines, and surgeons would examine suspected malingerers. Men fit enough to fight would be escorted back to the battle line. Mounted provost men patrolled the fixed straggler line.

The posts were also used as collecting points for prisoners of war: from 29 September to 1 October 1864 the 1st Virginia Battalion collected 1,663 prisoners whom they sent back to Richmond prison camps.

The provost marshal's troops also monitored the passage of African Americans within the army's areas. Many of them were apparently runaways attempting to reach Union lines and freedom. These, the provost marshal's men returned south. During the invasion of Pennsylvania they picked up hundreds of African Americans living in that state whom they claimed were runaways from Virginia. They were sent into slavery in the South, regardless of their legal status. And many men who had been serving in the Union forces, once the recruiting of black troops had been authorized, were also considered to be runaways rather than prisoners of war and they too were sent into slavery in the South. The provost marshal's men were also responsible for African Americans who had been released into army work gangs by their owners.

Finally, the whole business of capturing and holding spies, potential spies and Union Army deserters fell to the men of the provost marshal. Until the end of 1862 Union deserters were treated as prisoners of war, but Confederate officials soon realized that this fate would not encourage enemy troops to desert. Thereafter, Union deserters who swore an allegiance to the Confederacy were treated as Southern civilians, often put to work at industrial plants in Virginia and North Carolina. Finally, in August 1864, a system was authorized to get Union deserters to some point on the lines where they would be able to return to their homes, a task again undertaken by the provost marshal.

Brigadier General John B. Gordon used his brigade's provost guard as an advanced unit when going into York, Pennsylvania, during the Gettysburg campaign. There they were ordered to remove the US flag flying over the York courthouse and occupy the city.

All these varied duties were demanding and certainly lacked glory, that mainstay of 19th-century military life. So it is not surprising that most officers and men assigned to provost duty were unhappy and wished to return to line units.

Although provost guardsmen must have had some kind of insignia indicating their status, no official orders specifying such, or any insignia that might seem to be unique to the provost corps exist. It is possible that, like the Ambulance Corpsmen whose activities they monitored during battle, the provost men wore a simply printed badge with black letters on a white ground, perhaps on the hat front or side.

ANV PROVOST MARSHAL OFFICERS

Name	Unit	Service Dates
Blount, Lt Col R. P.	Longstreet's Corps	1862–3
Bond, Capt F. A.	Gettysburg Town	1863
Boyle, Maj Cornelius	ANV HQ	1861–5
Bridgford, Maj D. B.	1st Va Bn	1863–5
Brooke, Lt F.	Pickett's Division	
Capers, 1st Lt J. H.	ANV HQ (Adj)	1865
Clifton, 2nd Lt W. E.	Heth's Division	1864–5
Cockrill, 2nd Lt D. H.	Gordon's Corps	1865
Davidson, Maj C.A.	13th Va Bn	1864–5
De Butts, Surgeon J.	1st Va Bn	1865
Goff, 1st Lt J. M.	Rodes' Division	1864
Haslett, Capt S. D.	Second Corps	1864–5
Hawes, Lt N. B.	ANV	1865
Hinton, Capt W. E.	Dearing's Brigade	1864
Lamb, Lt W. G.	Hoke's Division	1864
Litty, 2nd Lt P. B.	Second Corps	1865
Macfie, Capt J. P.	Hampton's Brigade	1863
Moore, 2nd Lt Cleon	Second Corps	1865
Pritchard, Lt Hoskiner	Second Corps	1865
Randolph, Lt Peyton	Armistead's Brigade	1862
Reese, Lt George	Law's Brigade	1864
Ritter, Capt Wade	5th Alabama Bn	1865
Rives, Lt G. S.	Beale's Brigade	1865
Ryals, Maj G. M.	Cavalry Corps HQ	1863–5
Scott, Capt	Jackson's Corps	1863
Sherrard, Maj J. B.	Jackson's Division	1862

Name	Unit	Service Dates
Simpson, Lt S. J.	W. E. Jones's Brigade	1863
Stone, Lt W. R.	ANV HQ	1863
Van De Graaff, Maj A. S.	5th Alabama Bn	1862–5
Wharton, Maj R. W.	1st NC Bn	1862–4
Whiting, Maj H. A.	Rodes' Division	1864
Willis, Col Edward	Greencastle, Penna.	1863
Wilson, Lt L. J.	42nd Mississippi	1862

Chaplains

As of 3 May 1864, one chaplain was authorized for every volunteer regiment and brigade as the President saw fit.[1] Battalions, as smaller units, were not allowed their own chaplains until 31 May 1864.[2]

While the President was the individual appointed by law to nominate chaplains, it was usually commanding officers who recommended men for the posts. When newly ordained Episcopal Minister Randolph H. McKim, for example, joined the army in June 1864, he thought he was to be the chaplain of Chew's Artillery Battalion. 'But I was to be disappointed,' he later recalled. I learned on investigation that formal application for my appointment as chaplain of the battalion had never been made, and Major Chew informed me that until I received the appointment, I could not draw rations or forage. He proceeded at once to make the formal application to the Department, but, pending its action, I had no status in the army, and was obliged with great chagrin to leave camp and await my commission as chaplain.'[3] In fact, McKim was later nominated chaplain of the 2nd Virginia Cavalry on 23 August 1864.

A charge often made by the authorities when rejecting suggested mominees was that some commanding officers tended to prefer a good companion in their mess rather than an individual who would primarily concern himself with the spiritual welfare of the men. But in most cases, chaplains seem to have met with the men's approval. More commonly, units didn't have a chaplain. In March 1864 more than half the regiments in Gordon's Brigade had no chaplain; in September 1863 Hampton's Brigade of Cavalry had only two. Often clergymen were over-aged and generally unfit to keep up with a combat unit, and the first chaplains did well to last through the first winter.

One regiment, the 14th Tennessee Infantry, which may have found it more difficult to get a chaplain than units from nearer states, seldom had a chaplain throughout its entire field service. Their first, J. M. Pirtle, came with the regiment when it was organized in 1861 but resigned in February 1862. Then Chaplain John E. King was assigned on 23 September 1863 and promptly fell foul of Surgeon John B. Newton of the Medical Director's Office in Richmond who had King arrested on 14 December 1863. He was not seen again. Finally, Chaplain Luther H. Wilson joined the regiment at Petersburg in September 1864. He was captured at Hatcher's Run and was not released until after the war. So the 14th Tennessee did not have a chaplain from February 1862 to September 1863, from December 1863 to September 1864, and from February to April 1865. Indeed, some 50 regiments and battalions were reported as lacking chaplains during the winter of 1863/4.

The various denominations had different approachs to the question of releasing clergy to the army. The Protestant Episcopal Church of the Confederate States of America, although its Virginia Diocesan Missionary Society did publish a special edition of *The Army and Navy Prayer Book* at Richmond in 1864, attempted to maintain its activities along the same lines as they had before the war. For example, the report of the Rt Revd Stephen Elliott, Bishop of Georgia, in 1861, although detailing the numbers of individuals he had confirmed at each church in his diocese, did not mention the war at all, save to state that prayers for Jefferson Davis had been substituted for prayers for Abraham Lincoln. Indeed, the Southern bishops in 1862 issued a pastoral letter in which they noted a special trust owed to slaves.

None the less, many Southern leaders were members of the Protestant Episcopal Church, which had been the established church in several Southern states such as Virginia before the war. Lee, Stuart and Pendleton, of the top command in the Army of Northern Virginia, were all dedicated members of the denomination. So there were a number of chaplains, such as Revd McKim, from that denomination in the field, even if there were fewer from other denominations. The Virginia Diocesian Missionary Committee sent tracts to the army while the Revds Gatewood and Kepler were in charge of its activities in the area of the Army of Northern Virginia.

The General Assembly of the Presbyterian Church voted to nominate a chaplain or missionary — who performed the same functions as a chaplain but without an official government commission — in each brigade at the Church's expense. The Church also produced a monthly paper, *The Soldier's Visitor*, which was circulated within the army.

The Methodist Episcopal, South, Church organized its Soldier's Tract Association in March 1862. Its semi–monthly, *The Soldier's Paper*, was produced in Richmond and distributed throughout the army by its colporters, or travelling missionaries, who were not necessarily ordained ministers. In 1863 alone its report indicated that some 50,000 copies of the newspaper had been produced and distributed. Also its Missionary Society Board of Managers set up a branch called the Army Mission in 1863 to supply missionary ministers to the army.

The Baptists, who had a strong dedication to the separation of church and state and felt therefore that the military should not include its ministers as commissioned chaplains, sent a large number of colporters with a variety of tracts and Bibles among the men of Lee's Army. In 1864, the Domestic Mission Board of the Southern Baptist Convention reported that it had 78 missionaries in the field and was supplementing the salaries of eleven Baptist army chaplains. The Virginia Baptist Publication Board had more than 100 colporters and army evangelists in the field as well.

According to a chaplain in Lee's Army in 1864, there were 36 Methodist, 20 Baptist, 20 Presbyterian, six Episcopalian, one Lutheran and three Roman Catholic (who served largely with Louisiana troops) chaplains in Second and Third Corps.[4]

Regulations did not spell out exactly what a chaplain was supposed to do in the field. They were free to spend all their time in the officers' mess if they preferred, although liquor was so scarce that few might wish to do so. Chaplain McKim says that he 'established the rule of having prayers in the regiment daily, both morning and evening, and that I generally made a short address'. His first act when joining his regiment was to produce a list of all church communicants in the unit. Then he organized a choir and held practices as often as possible. He organized a branch of the Young Men's Christian Association within his regiment, and many units had some such Christian organization. He obtained Bibles and reading material and distributed them as needed. He spent a great deal of time talking to individuals, attempting to make converts and strengthen the faith of the converted. He ministered to those in hospitals.

There was a great deal of debate as to the proper place for a chaplain in battle. Many stayed with their men in the front line, some even joining in the fighting. The chaplains of II and III Corps wrestled with this problem and decided in May 1863 that, 'No absolute rule can be laid down. A chaplain shall be wherever duty calls him, irrespective of danger. but ordinarily it is thought wrong from him to take a musket. Some shall be in charge of the ambulances, some at the field infirmaries, and some at the point where the litter-bearers meet the ambulances, and where many die. The chaplain should ascertain the opinion of his regiment on this subject.'[5]

Indeed, at Spotsylvania, Chaplain William B. Owen, 17th Mississippi Regiment, while helping the wounded, had his elbow shattered and died of his wound. Chaplain John C. Granberry, 11th Virginia Infantry, was badly wounded in the head at Malvern Hill while in the front line with his regiment; he lost the sight of one eye. Chaplain W. G. Curry, 5th Alabama Infantry, picked up a wounded man of his regiment under fire at Chancellorsville — which so impressed the Union soldiers that they stopped firing to let him reach safety. Chaplain James Sinclair actually acted as lieutenant colonel of his 5th North Carolina Infantry at Manassas, leading several charges.

Uniforms

There was no regulation uniform for Confederate chaplains. Most of them wore black civilian priest or minister's attire, although some feared that the dark dress too closely resembled that of the enemy and preferred plain versions of the officer's regulation frock-coat.

Chaplain Nicholas A. Davis of the 4th Texas Infantry was described in 1862 as wearing a plain black, single-breasted frock-coat with brass buttons and an olive branch about six inches long embroidered on each cuff. His trousers were also plain black.

Some chaplains took their assumed ranks very seriously, and indicated as much by their dress. Father Darius Hubert, chaplain of the 1st Louisiana, wore 'gold-braid festooned upon his blue kepi and embroidered upon the sleeves of his high-collared frock-coat; the golden buttons of his waistcoat emblazoned with the Louisiana pelican; his gold–filleted trousers falling neatly into a pair of comely boots,' Father Louis-Hippolyte Gache, 10th Louisiana chaplain, wrote home in November 1861. Also, 'According to Father de Carriere, Father Prachensky (3rd Alabama) has already informed you of his assumed title of "major". I had heard rumors about this nonsense myself, but knowing that Confederate chaplains are chaplains and nothing else, and that they enjoy no legal title to any rank whatsoever, I regarded the whole business as a joke. But I was wrong. Father Prachensky is dead serious when he puts on that he is a major, and the proof of it is that he wears a uniform with all of the accessories ... He is so set on wearing this uniform that no amount of reasoning will make him give it up.' However, Father Gache was pleased to add that 'to my knowledge they are the first and only Catholic chaplains to wear a military uniform.'[6] Gache himself wore the Jesuit's cassock, with rosary beads attached to the cincture, and a biretta.

Some Protestant chaplains were described as wearing a variety of insignia, including brass or silver emblems of the Bible on their collar and large braid crosses on their shoulders.

Chaplains in Second and Third Corps formed an association in May 1863 and promptly appointed a Committee to come up with some form of insignia for them all to wear. In June they announced that they had decided to adopt a letter 'C', probably in Old English script as was the style with other letters representing branches of service, within a half–wreath of olive leaves worked in gold bullion on a black velvet background, the whole about 2½ inches wide.

Pay

According to the Congressional Act of 3 May 1861, chaplains were to receive $85 a month, but Congress quickly decided that it had been too generous and on 16 May reduced the monthly pay to $50.[1] Because this placed chaplains at a disadvantage, since they had to live on their pay alone, on 31 August 1861 Congress authorized them to receive the same rations as privates.[2] But life as a chaplain was too hard to attract good men, so on 19 April 1862 Congress increased their pay to $80 a month.[3] In fact, most denominations supplemented the pay of their clergy in the field.

Chaplains of The Army of Northern Virginia

Each of the following has been identified as having been an officially assigned chaplain. In many instances the period of service is not known; the dates given indicate a period in which the individual was known to have been serving. Denominations are rarely mentioned in references to chaplains, and more often than not are unknown.

Unit	Name	Denomination	Date
HEADQUARTERS			
First Corps	Theodore Pryor	Presbyterian	1863
Second Corps	B. T. Lacy		1863
	L. Rosser		1865
	E. J. Willis	Baptist	1865
Third Corps	George D. Armstrong	Presbyterian	1864–5
	J. William Jones	Baptist	1865
SECOND CORPS			
Artillery	George Gilmer	Presbyterian	
BRIGADE HEADQUARTERS			
Benning's	T. B. Harden		
Blanchard's	Michael O'Keefe	Roman Catholic	1862
Conner's	William P. DuBose	Episcopalian	1864
Dibrell's	Austin W. Smith		
Gordon's	A. C. Hopkins	Presbyterian	
Pegram's	Adam C. Bledsoe	Methodist	1864
Sorrel's	J. O. A. Cook	Methodist	
ARTILLERY BATTALION HEADQUARTERS			
Braxton's	A. B. Brown		
	James Nelson		
Cutshaw's	Timon Page		
Hardaway's	Henry M. White		1863–4
	T. M. Niven	Presbyterian	
Haskell's	J. A. Chambliss		
Nelson's	T. Walker Gilmer	Presbyterian	1863
Pegram's	Erskine M. Rodman	Episcopalian	1864
Poague's	James M. Wheary	Presbyterian	
Rockbridge's	James P. Smith		1861–2
ALABAMA CAVALRY			
1st Regiment	Telfair Hidgson	Episcopalian	
ALABAMA INFANTRY			

1st Regiment	E. M. McNair	Presbyterian	
3rd Regiment	Joseph Prachensky	Roman Catholic	1862
	W. G. Curry	Baptist	1863
	Thomas J. Rutledge	Methodist	1865
4th Regiment	W. D. Chadick		
	Robert Frazier		
5th Regiment	W. G. Curry	Baptist	1863
6th Regiment	James G. Barbee		
	G. R. Talley		1865
8th Regiment	W. E. Massey		
9th Regiment	H. L. Whitten	Methodist	1863
10th Regiment	J. J. D Renfroe	Baptist	1863
	James M. B. Roach		1865
11th Regiment	James B. Sheeran	Roman Catholic	1862
	W. G. Johnson		1863
12th Regiment	H.G. Moore		
13th Regiment	T. H. Howell (F. H. Howle)		1863
	J. S. Lane		
14th Regiment	A. G. Raines (Rains)		
26th Regiment	William E. Cameron		1863
43rd Regiment	N. G. Phillips		
44th Regiment	W. G. Perry		
	F. S. Petaway		
48th Regiment	R. J. Price		

ARKANSAS INFANTRY

3rd Regiment	George E. Butler		

FLORIDA INFANTRY

2nd Regiment	John W. Timberlake		1861–3
8th Regiment	J. W. Mills		1862
11th Regiment	Little		

GEORGIA INFANTRY

1st Regiment	W. H. Fleming	Methodist	
	Henry Sneed		
2nd Battalion	J. O. A. Cook		1863
2nd Regiment	J. H. DeVotie	Baptist	
3nd Regiment	J. M. Stokes		1863
	William Flinn	Presbyterian	
4th Regiment	James O.A Sparks		1863
	C. D. Campbell		
	W. M. Cunningham	Presbyterian	
	Robert F. Evans	Methodist	
	James Lowery		
6th Regiment	Alex M. Thigpen	Methodist	1863
7th Regiment	John G. Fry		
	David C. Stokes	Methodist	

8th Regiment	W. C. Dunlap	Methodist	
9th Regiment	A. B. Campbell		1862
	Joel. C. Burnham (Bennus/Burnshaw)		1863
	H. A. Tupper	Baptist	1865
10th Regiment	J. C. Camp	Baptist	
11th Regiment	W. A. Simmons	Methodist	
12th Regiment	A. Mathias Marshall	Baptist	1862–3
	W. P. Pledger		
	P. G. Powledge (Pouledge)		
13th Regiment	T. P. Cleveland	Presbyterian	
14th Regiment	Alex W. Moore	Methodist	1863
	Robert Mickle	Presbyterian	
15th Regiment	W. T. Robinson (W.F Robertson)		
17th Regiment	John N. Hudson		
19th Regiment	W. H. C.Cone		1861–2
	A. J. Jarrell		
20th Regiment	James A.Garrison		
21st Regiment	William Haslett		
22nd Regiment	W. E. Jones		1863
	N. H. McAfee (W. H. McAfee)		
23nd Regiment	William A. Dodge		
27th Regiment	George Emory		
28th Regiment	A. D. McVoy		
31st Regiment	J. L. Pettigrew		
35th Regiment	John H. Taylor		
	E. W. Yarborough		
38th Regiment	J. M. Brittain		
44th Regiment	Thomas Beck		
	H. T. Brooks		
	(H. E. Brookes)		1863
45th Regiment	Edward B. Barrett		1863
	W. H. Stuart		
48th Regiment	Hilliam Hauser		1863
	J. A. Lowry		1865
50th Regiment	W. L. Curry	Baptist	1862–5
51st Regiment	George Macawlay		
	Crawford H. Toy	Baptist	
60th Regiment	Samuel H. Smith		1863
61st Regiment	A. B. Woodfin	Baptist	1864
Phillips Legion	George Smith		1862
	Flinn		
LOUISIANA INFANTRY			
1st Regiment	Darius Hubert	Roman Catholic	1861
	Anthony Carius	Roman Catholic	
	B. S. Dunn	Episcopalian	

184

	James B. Sheeran	Roman Catholic	1865
2nd Regiment	Robert Hardee		
	Peter G. Roberts		
5th Regiment	Livias H. Baldwin	Not ordained	1861–62
	William M.Strickler		1863
7th Regiment	Darius Hubert	Roman Catholic	1865
8th Regiment	Egidius Schmulders	Roman Catholic	
9th Regiment	R.McCarthy		
10th Regiment	Louis–Hippolyte		
	Gache	Roman Catholic	
14th Regiment	J. A. Godfrey	Methodist	
	James B. Sheeran	Roman Catholic	1862
	G. W. Stickney	Episcopalian	

MARYLAND INFANTRY

1st Regiment	Stephen F. Cameron		1861–5
(2nd Battalion)			

MISSISSIPPI INFANTRY

2nd Regiment	F. D. Witherspoon	Presbyterian	
11th Regiment	E. C. Davidson	Presbyterian	
12th Regiment	William B. Owen	Methodist	1863
	Charles H. Dobbs	Presbyterian	1863–4
13th Regiment	L. S. West		1863
16th Regiment	A. A. Lomax		
17th Regiment	William B. Owen	Methodist	1862
18th Regiment	Ely Foster		
	J. A. Hackett		
19th Regiment	Hugh M. Morrison	Presbyterian	
	Thomas L. Duke		
21st Regiment	Claiborne McDonald		
26th Regiment	M. B. Chapman		
42nd Regiment	Thomas Witherspoon	Presbyterian	
48th Regiment	A. E. Garrison		

NORTH CAROLINA INFANTRY

1st Regiment	William R. Gwaltney		1863
	David Kerr		
	E. A. Yates		
2nd Battalion	Tennant		
2nd Regiment	H. E. Brooks		
	Frederick Fitzgerald	Episcopalian	
	A. A. Watson	Episcopalian	
	A. N. Wells	Methodist	
3rd Regiment	John N. Andrews		
	George Patterson	Episcopalian	1863
	Robert E. Terry	Episcopalian	1863
	Maurice Vaughan	Episcopalian	

4th Regiment	Robert B. Anderson	Presbyterian	1863–4
	T. M. Boyd	Episcopalian	
	W. A. Wood	Presbyterian	
5th Regiment	James Sinclair		1861–2
	Bennett Smedes	Episcopalian	
6th Regiment	Kensey J. Stewart	Episcopalian	
8th Regiment	H. C. Cheatham		
11th Regiment	James P. Moore	Episcopalian	1863
12th Regiment	J. H. Robbins		
13th Regiment	William Vann		
14th Regiment	N. B. Cobb		
	W. C. Power	Methodist	1863
	Alexander D. Betts		1865
15th Regiment	S. W. Howerton		1863
	A.W. Mangum		
16th Regiment	J. F. Watson		
17th Regiment	G. W. Phelps	Episcopalian	
18th Regiment	William Jordan	Roman Catholic	
	Colin Shaw	Presbyterian	
20th Regiment	James M.Sprunt		1863
	Louis A. Bihle (Binkle)		1865
22nd Regiment	F. H. Wood		
23rd Regiment	T. S. W. Moore	Episcopalian	1863
24th Regiment	Evander McNair	Presbyterian	
	Thomas B. Neill		
26th Regiment	James Sprunt		
	A. N. Wells		
27th Regiment	W. B. Lacy	Presbyterian	
28th Regiment	Francis M. Kennedy	Methodist	1863
	D. S. Henkel		
30th Regiment	Alexander D.Betts	Methodist	1863
	W. C. Power		1865
31st Regiment	Orvin Churchill		
32nd Regiment	Joseph Murphey	Episcopalian	
	John Tennent	Episcopalian	
	W. B. Richardson		1865
33rd Regiment	Thomas J. Eatman		
34th Regiment	A. R. Benick		
37th Regiment	A. L. Stough		1863
38th Regiment	McDairmid		
42nd Regiment	J. M. Cline		
	Sam I. Hill		
43rd Regiment	Eugene Thompson		
44th Regiment	John Tillinghast	Episcopalian	
	R. S. Webb		1865

45th Regiment	Ephrain H. Harding	Presbyterian	
46th Regiment	A. D. Cohen	Baptist	
47th Regiment	W. S. Lacey	Presbyterian	1865
48th Regiment	C. Plyler (Tyler)		
49th Regiment	P. Nicholson		
51st Regiment	J. R. Alford		
52nd Regiment	J. M. Cline		1863
	W. F. Landford (Sanford)		
53nd Regiment	J. H. Colton	Presbyterian	1863–4
	James Bolton		
54th Regiment	John Paris	Methodist	1863
55th Regiment	William Royall		
	John Paris		1865
61st Regiment	W. B. Jones		
SOUTH CAROLINA CAVALRY			
1st Regiment	George Williams	Episcopalian	
2nd Regiment	Manning Brown		
SOUTH CAROLINA INFANTRY			
1st Regiments	George T. T. Williams	1863	
	T. D. Gwin		
	W. H. King		
	Robert L. Smythe	Presbyterian	
	A. H. Stevens		
	(Stephens)	Methodist	
1st Rifles	Francis Mullally	Presbyterian	
2nd Regiment	Elias Meynardie	Methodist	
	Pickens Smith		
	W. E. Walters		
4th Regiment	William Walters		
5th Regiment	J. A. Craig		1863
	H. H. DuRant		
6th Regiment	W. E. Boggs	Presbyterian	
	James McDowell	Presbyterian	
7th Regiment	J. M. Carlisle		1861–2
8th Regiment	Martin Barley		
	G. W. Boggs	Presbyterian	
	H. M. Brearley		
	John T. James		
11 th Regiment	A. B. Stevens	Methodist	1863
	(Stephens)		
12th Regiment	J. Monroe Anderson		1863
	Dixon		1865
13th Regiment	J. N. Bouchelle		
	Wallace W. Duncan		
14th Regiment	W. B. Carson	Baptist	1863

	W. C. Power	Methodist	1863
15th Regiment	A. R. McCallaine		
	(H. B. McCallum)		
17th Regiment	A. A. Morse		
18th Regiment	A. A .James	Presbyterian	
20th Regiment	E. J. Meynardie		1862
	Wallace W. Duncan	Methodist	
21st Regiment	W. A. Hemmingway	Methodist	
22nd Regiment	Edward D. Dill		
23rd Regiment	J. L. Girardeau	Presbyterian	
25th Regiment	C. T. Winkler	Baptist	
26th Regiment	W. L. Black		1863
	J. L. Girdeau		1865
Holcombe Legion	A. W. Morse		
Palmetto Sharp-shooters	James McDowell	Presbyterian	1862–5
TENNESSEE INFANTRY			
1st Regiment	Collins D. Elliott	Methodist	
	Charles T. Quintard	Episcopalian	
	J. K. Stringfield	Presbyterian	
	W. T. Helm		1865
2nd Regiment	Joseph Cross	Methodist	
	Green Henderson		
	Joseph Jarboe	Roman Catholic	
	John McFerrin	Methodist	
3rd Regiment	T. H. Davenport		
7th Regiment	W. H. Armstrong	James R.Harris	
14th Regiment	J. M. Pirtle		1861–2
	John E. King		1863
	Luther H. Wilson	Presbyterian	1863–4
17th Regiment	A. B. Moore		
23rd Regiment	E. C. McElyea		
	B. M. Taylor		
25th Regiment	David P. Richie		
	A. S. Smith (A. W. Smith)		1864
35th Regiment	David Ritchey	Presbyterian	
44th Regiment	A. T. Brooks		
63d Regiment	Joseph Flora		
	E. C. Godby		
TEXAS INFANTRY			
1st Regiment	J. R. Vick		
4th Regiment	Nicholas A. Davis	Presbyterian	1861–3
5th Regiment	P. Swan		
VIRGINIA CAVALRY			
1st Regiment	Dabney Ball		

	John Landstreet		
2nd Regiment	W. W. Berry		
	Randolph H. McKim	Episcopalian	1863–65
3rd Regiment	Thomas N. Conrad		
5th Regiment	William Meredith	Episcopalian	
6th Regiment	B. F. Ellison		
	Richard Davis	Episcopalian	
	George T. Wilmer	Episcopalian	1862
7th Regiment	James B. Avirett	Episcopalian	1861–5
	T. M. Carson		
8th Regiment	J. T. Johnson		
9th Regiment	H. B. Richards		
	W. H. Wheelwright		
10th Regiment	J. B. Tyler		
12th Regiment	G. H. Zimmerman		
13th Regiment	B. C. Spiller	Methodist	
15th Regiment	Adam Bledsoe	Methodist	
17th Regiment	S. Sheppard		
	Edward Vertigan		
18th Regiment	J. D. Blackwell	Methodist	
19th Regiment	Thomas T. Wade		
20th Regiment	J. D. Leachman		
22nd Regiment	P.J. Lockhart		

VIRGINIA INFANTRY

1st Regiment	William A. Aldrich	Not ordained	1864–5
	J. A. Harrold	Episcopalian	
2nd Regiment	McVeigh		1861–2
	A. C. Hopkins	Presbyterian	1862–3
3rd Regiment	W. Hammond	Methodist	
	Thomas Hume	Baptist	
	J. W. Ward		1863
4th Regiment	F. C. Tebbs	Methodist	1862–3
	William R. McNeer	1863	
	Peter Roberts	Episcopalian	
5th Regiment	E. Payson Walton	Baptist	1862–3
	C. S. M. See (CLM Lee)	1863	
6th Regiment	Maurice Longhorn		
	John C. Granbury	Methodist	1864
7th Regiment	James B. Averitt	Episcopalian	1861
	Florence McCarthy	1863	
	John H. Bocock		1865
	Frayser		1865
8th Regiment	Thomas A. Ware	Methodist	1864
9th Regiment	George W. Easter	Episcopalian	
	Robert Taylor		

	J. W. Walkup	Presbyterian	1863
10th Regiment	M. G. Balthis (L. M. Y. Bolthis)		
	S. S. Lambeth	Methodist	
	J.P. Hyde		
11th Regiment	John C. Granbury	Methodist	1862
	Thomas Jennings	Methodist	1863
12th Regiment	Sam V. Hoyle		
13th Regiment	J. William Jones	Baptist	1863
	William S. Ryland		1865
14th Regiment	William A. Crocker	Methodist	
17th Regiment	Robert M. Baker	Episcopalian	
	John L. Johnson (Johnston)		
18th Regiment	Robert L. Dabney		1861–2
	E. J. Willis	Baptist	
	J. D. Blackwell		1865
19th Regiment	John W. Griffin	Episcopalian	
	Philip Slaughter	Episcopalian	1862
21st Regiment	J. Harvie Gilmore		
	Robert Nelson		
22nd Regiment	Charles Fisher		
	Sam Rodgers		
	Thompson Smith	Episcopalian	
23rd Regiment	George R. Edwards		
	Paul C. Morton (Norton)	Episcopalian	1863
24th Regiment	William F. Gardner	Episcopalian	
25th Regiment	George B. Taylor		
	John W. Jones		
26th Regiment	W. E. Wiatt	Baptist	1863–4
27th Regiment	L. C. Vass	Presbyterian	1863–5
28th Regiment	Peter Tinsley	Episcopalian	1862
29th Regiment	Alex Phillips		
30th Regiment	James Carmichael	Episcopalian	
	Walter R. D. Moncure		
	N. G. Robinson		
31st Regiment	A. D. Lepps		
32nd Regiment	John McCabe	Episcopalian	
	R. W. Ridgood		
33rd Regiment	J. M. Grundin	Methodist	1862
38th Regiment	James Cosby	Episcopalian	1861–2
	Colton	Methodist	1862–3
	R. W. Cridlin	Baptist	1863
40th Regiment	George F. Bagby	Baptist	1861–2
	James M. Anderson		1862–3

Regiment	Chaplain	Denomination	Year
41st Regiment	John W. Pugh	Presbyterian	
42nd Regiment	Thomas N. Williams		
44th Regiment	Richard I. McIlwaine		
	James Nelson	Baptist	1863
46th Regiment	W. Gaines Miller		1863
47th Regiment	J. M. Meredith		1863
	S. B. Barber	Roman Catholic	1865
48th Regiment	George E. Brooker	Methodist	1863
	George Slaughter		
49th Regiment	J. Powel Garland	Methodist	1863
	J. W. McMarron		
50th Regiment	George H. Denny	Presbyterian	1863–4
51st Regiment	Burton S. Highley		
52rd Regiment	John McGill (Magell)	Episcopalian	1863
53rd Regiment	W. S. Penick		1863
	P. H. Fontaine		1864
	Colton		1865
55th Regiment	R. B. Beadles		
	H. H. Jones		
	Robbins		
57th Regiment	James E. Joyner	Methodist	1863
58th Regiment	P. Frank August	Episcopalian	1861
	George Slaughter		1863
	L. B. Madison		
59th Regiment	Lyman B.Wharton	Episcopalian	1863
60th Regiment	M. Bibb		1863
	J. C Brown	Presbyterian	
61 st Regiment	John F. Deans		
	Hilary E. Hatcher		

THE INVALID CORPS

Although not directly under Lee as part of his field army, many Invalid Corps members were stationed in the Richmond area where they supported his efforts during the last years of the war. Moreover, a fair number of his officers and men ended up in the organization.

The Corps was authorized by Congress on 17 February 1864. It was to be staffed by Confederate army, navy or marine corps personnel of all ranks who were no longer able to perform active field duty because of wounds or disease contracted in the field. They were to report directly to the office of the Secretary of War who would assign them tasks they were physically able to perform.[1]

Eventually, 1,063 officers and 5,139 enlisted men were assigned to the Corps. They garrisoned a number of posts in Richmond. For example, Co. H, 1st Invalid Battalion was assigned to the Confederate

States Barracks in that city, which was a transit camp for troops en route to the front from hospital or recruiting duties.

There were no special insignia, uniforms or flags for the Invalid Corps.

TRANSFERS TO THE INVALID CORPS
The following field–grade officers transferred to the Invalid Corps from Lee's Army.

Individual	Date Transferred	Cause
Barbee, Lt Col A. R.	Aug 1863	Wounds to right elbow and left hip
Holliday, Col F. W. M.	21 Mar 1864	Lost arm, Cedar Mt
Harrison, Col. F. E.	8 Apr 1864	Wounded, Gaines' Mill
Weems, Col. J. B.	9 May 1864	Wounded, Savage Station, Gettysburg
Hoke, Col. W. J.	18 June 1864	Wounded, Mechanics-ville, Gettysburg
Lowe, CoI S. D.	8 July 1864	Wounded, Gettysburg
Pyles, Col. L. G.	12 July 1864	Wounded, Seven Pines
Jones, Maj. J. F.	4 Aug 1864	Lost arm, Chancellorsville
Gholston, Lt Col J. S.	24 Aug 1864	No reason given
Means, Lt Col R. S.	29 Aug 1864	Wounded, South Mountain
Fletcher, Maj Richard	7 Sept 1864	Lost leg, Gettysburg
Tilghman, Lt Col W. F.	17 Sept 1864	Wounded, Gettysburg
Read, Maj. J. H., jnr.	10 Oct 1864	No reason given
Coffee, Capt. J. A.	14 Oct 1864	Wounded, Chickamauga
Peyton, Lt Col C. S.	24 Oct 1864	Lost arm, 2nd Manassas, Wounded, Gettysburg
Graves, Capt. G. A.	2 Nov 1864	Wounded, Gettysburg
Gordon, Lt Col G. T.	25 Nov 1864	Wounded July and September 1863, June 1864

SUTLERS

In the pre–war US Army, whose practices shaped so much of the thinking of Confederate officials, it was assumed that the army would only provide the soldier's necessities at a bare subsistence level. Because so many of its posts were far from civilization, the army set up a system whereby each post or independent command would be authorized a civilian sutler.

The sutler stocked and sold a wide variety of items much like a general store. In a permanent post, or even a fixed camp such as winter quarters, sutlers occupied the same type of buildings as did the troops, who often helped build their quarters. In the field, sutlers followed the

Infantry

Right: A completely equipped infantryman of 1861, with a pre-war cap rather like those worn at the time of the Mexican War. His frame buckle, however, is of typical Confederate issue. His jacket has piping around the top and front of the collar. (Michael Welch)

Far right: Most of Lee's infantrymen wore their cartridge box on their waist-belt, as does Alabama Private John T. Davis seen here. His weapon is a Pattern 1853 Enfield rifled musket. (US Army Military History Institute)

Below: The infantryman's equipment, in this instance all of Southern make. The copy of the US M1855 cartridge box is marked 'SEMA [Alabama] ARSENAL' on its flap; its sling is of of natural canvas with leather tips to buckle to the box. Inside is a single tin to hold the cartridges (US-made boxes had two tins). The haversack is a plain white canvas bag. The small black percussion cap box was

made of black-painted cotton, and is typical of cap boxes made in Columbus, Georgia. The Union canteen was universally preferred to the tin drum-style canteen seen here, which is probably the reason why this latter is the most common Confederate artefact to be found on battle sites —

dumped when something better became available. The waist-belt has a 'Georgia frame buckle' typical of those produced by McElroy & Hunt of Macon, Georgia. The bayonet scabbard's frog has a tin tip, and is sewn rather than riveted as in US Army examples. (Author's collection)

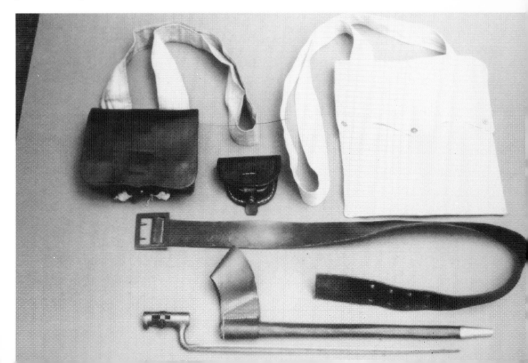

Left: The first weapons produced by the Richmond Armory had a tall 'hump' in the lock which matched the M1855 US rifle musket's automatic percussion cap system. (Russ Pritchard)

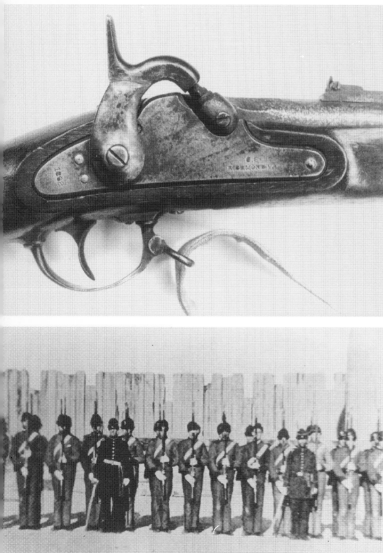

Left: The lockplate of the second version of the Richmond Armory's copy of the M1855 US Army rifled musket was distinguished by a smaller 'hump' lock, and the letters 'C.S.' over 'RICHMOND VA' on the lock plate; the date of manufacture was placed behind the hammer.(Russ Pritchard)

Below: The Charleston Zouave Cadets (McClellan Zouaves), photographed in that South Carolina city in 1861, wore a grey chasseur uniform with red facings and white gaiters with leather greaves. Their forage cap was red. Officers wore the dark-blue state uniform. Armed with the M1841 'Mississippi' Rifle, the Company saw Confederate service for three months in 1861 as part of the 1st South Carolina Regiment of Rifles; many of its officers and men then joined other serving units. (Library of Congress)

Above: This First National Flag, judging from the written description of how it was captured that obscures one star, was flown during the Peninsula Campaign. It measures 31 by 57 inches and is made entirely of cotton. (Mike Miner)

Right: This first bunting-pattern flag was carried by the 6th South Carolina Infantry. The battle honours for WILLIAMSBURG and SEVEN PINES! are in black printed on white strips that were issued to Longstreet's troops as the first type of battle honour in the army. (South Carolina Confederate Relic Room and Museum)

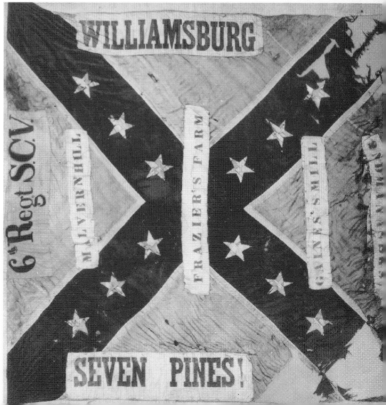

Artillery
Left: A Confederate-made Napoleon 12-pound cannon from the Columbus, Georgia, foundry. (Gettysburg National Battlefield Park)

Left: A gun crew of the Washington Artillery at Marye's Hill, Fredericksburg, December 1862. The gunner is sighting the gun, while Number Five rushes up another round, without using the regulation haversack in which the round should behave carried. (*Battles and Leaders of the Civil War*)

Left: One of the 27 bronze Austrian M1857 field pieces in the army's inventory. The handles over the tube's centre of gravity were used on older US Army Napoleons, but were out of date by this time. (Gettysburg National Battlefield Park)

Right: A 10-pound Parrott rifled cannon. (Gettysburg National Battlefield Park)

Right: A 20-pound Parrott rifled cannon. (Gettysburg National Battlefield Park)

Right: A 3-inch rifle. (Gettysburg National Battlefield Park)

Cavalry
Above: These sky-blue trousers were worn by Colonel Thomas Ruffin, 1st North Carolina Cavalry Regiment. They lack the extra piece of cloth placed between the leg and the horse that was typical of US Army cavalry trousers. (North Carolina Museum of History Collection)
Below left: Private John P. Sellman, Co. K, 1st Virginia Cavalry Regiment, wearing a typical uniform of Lee's cavalry, with a second-pattern Richmond Clothing Manufactory jacket, matching trousers, and a US Army sword belt with pistol and cap box, but lacking his sabre. (Charles T. Jacobs/US Army Military History Institute)
Below right: This cavalryman is clearly distinguished as a Virginian by both the belt plate which bears the state's seal and his antique Virginia Manufactory sabre. (Herb Peck, Jr.)

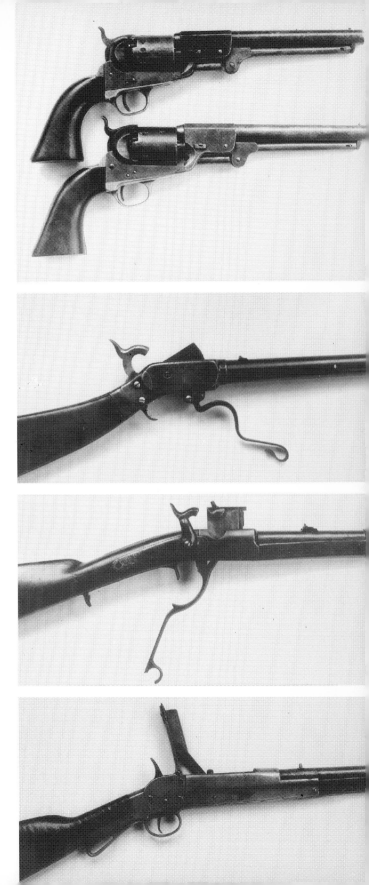

Right: These copies of the Colt M1851 0.36 calibre revolver were made by the Southern firm of Leech & Rigdon (bottom), the second largest Southern producer of revolvers, and Rigdon & Ansley, which began production in Augusta, Georgia, in January 1864. (Russ Pritchard)

Right: A total of 282 of these 0.52 calibre breech-loading carbines, here shown with the breech open, were made by Keen, Walker & Company, Danville, Virginia. (Russ Pritchard collection)

Right: Only a handful of these 'rising block' breech-loading 0.54 calibre carbines was made by Bilharz, Hall & Company, Pittsylvania Courthouse, Virginia. The carbine is shown with the breech open, ready to accept a paper cartridge. (Russ Pritchard collection)

Below right: The most technologically advanced carbine produced in the South was this Morse carbine, made by the Greenville Military Works for the South Carolina state militia. The 0.50 calibre carbine used a metallic centre-fire cartridge which was inserted into the breech, here shown open. Fewer than 1,000 of these brass-framed weapons were produced. (Russ Pritchard collection)

Partisan Rangers

Above left: Major John S. Mosby was the best partisan ranger commander in the Confederate Army, the only one of whom Lee wholly approved. He is wearing a single-breasted coat, cut like a civilian day coat, with the single star of his rank on his collar and the regulation Austrian knot on each sleeve. (Library of Congress)

Left: Mosby wore this jacket after he had been promoted to the rank of colonel. It is faced with yellow cuffs, collar and piping down the front, and has the three stars of a colonel on the collar. The buttons are regulation US Army cavalry officers' buttons, bearing an American eagle with the letter 'C' on a shield on its chest. The slash pocket on the lower breast was typical. (Smithsonian Institution)

Above: This engraving was made from a photograph of Mosby, taken late in the war, wearing the short jacket (the facings photographed black, but they were yellow) and the complete belt and sword which he rarely wore in action. (*Battles and Leaders of the Civil War*)

The Engineer Corps

Right: Captain David Stewart Hessey spent most of his time in Company 1, 1st Regiment of Engineers, after its formation in 1863. He had been an assistant right-of-way engineer in Delaware before the war, and joined the 13th Virginia Infantry Regiment in 1861. Badly wounded during the Seven Days, he joined the Corps on his recovery. Here he is holding binoculars, apparently given to him by General Lee in appreciation of his Company's prowess in bridge-bulilding. He was then given command of the regiment's Company A. His two-piece belt plate appears to bear the Virginia state seal; his coat is plain grey with buff piping but no Austrian knots on the sleeves, although his dark-blue kepi is decorated with gold lace. His captain's bars are embroidered on a white backing sewn to the collar. His trousers are a slightly lighter shade than his coat; perhaps they are the old infantry officer's sky-blue trousers. (Delaware State Archives)

Medical Department

Right: This astonishing photograph of Confederate troops in the field was taken by a Northern photographer from the other side of the Rappahannock River. The man standing fifth from the right is wearing a large white cap badge, rather like surviving examples of the Ambulance Corps' badges which were printed in black letters on white backgrounds edged by red. The man second from the left in the double-breasted frock-coat is apparently an officer. (National Archives)

Above left: A Rosenstock family member photographed the men of Lee's Army passing in front of his store on Patrick Street, in Fredericksburg, Maryland, on 10 September 1862. A close scrutiny reveals a wide variety of head-dress, mostly slouch hats, as well as an assortment of blanket rolls and even the odd knapsack. One man, probably a sergeant, is standing beside the column, with a knapsack and rifled musket; another, apparently armed with a pistol, who is probably an officer, stands on the sidewalk opposite, presumably dealing with stragglers — a problem that was to dog the Confederacy throughout the war. The photograph repays study for such details as how the blanket roll vs. the knapsack was worn. (Courtesy of The Historical Society of Frederick County, Maryland)

Local Defence Corps
Left: These troops, assigned to guard Union officers at Libby Prison in Richmond, were available to back up Lee's defences of the city, as were hundreds of other troops in the city's garrison. Unlike line infantry units, they have good walled tents as billets. Their commander, Major Thomas P. Turner, stands in front of their encampment in this summer of 1863 photograph. (Author's collection)

Above right: This image came from an Atlanta estate sale and apparently shows a Georgia soldier wearing a home-made frock-coat. The waist-belt plate clearly reads 'US', which is not surprising because a large percentage of Confederate soldiers appear to have worn US Army-issue equipment, captured or obtained locally. (Michael Welch)

Above: From left to right: Privates Columbus C. Taylor, James D. Jackson and James H. Porter, Co. D, 3rd Georgia Infantry Regiment, photographed during the winter of 1861/2. Taylor and Jackson were killed in the regiment's first major battle, Malvern Hill, on I July 1862. Note that Jackson is wearing the legend '3 G V' in brass on his slouch hat, which was perhaps a common type of badge at the time. Porter, who appears to be wearing an officer's cap, was transferred to detached service, apparently in January 1862, so this photograph must have been taken before then. (Museum of the Confederacy)

Left: Sergeant Joseph C. LeBleu, Co. K, 10th Louisiana Infantry Regiment, saw service in the Peninsula Campaign, but later served in the 7th Louisiana Cavalry in the western theatre, so this photograph dates from 1861-2. He is wearing sergeant's chevrons, and has a frame-type buckle on his waist-belt. (Michael Dan Jones)

Opposite page, top left: Ensign Emanuel Rudisill, Co. M, 16th North Carolina Infantry Regiment, wearing the state-issue uniform of grey tunic with black epaulettes, grey trousers with a black stripe down each leg, and a grey kepi. In this post-war photograph he is standing in front of the regiment's Colour, one of the Army of Northern Virginia's battle flags, and appears to be holding a non-commissioned officer's regulation sword. (North Carolina Department of Archives and History)

Opposite page, top right: This battle flag was produced by the Richmond Clothing Manufactory who apparently marked the unit designation in yellow around the centre star, as this type of designation appears on a great many of these flags. The battle honours were also applied by the Manufactory, but in blue. (North Carolina Museum of History)

Above left: This photograph of an unidentified cavalryman was found at a Baltimore estate sale. He is wearing a US Army mounted man's belt plate, which was probably the most common sword belt plate worn by Confederate troops. (John Sickles)

Above right: This photograph, which came from Tennessee, is of a private who is wearing a frock-coat of a type commonlystate. (Michael Welch)

Opposite page: top left: Private J. J. Dodd, Co. C, 4th South Carolina Cavalry Regiment, holding an M1833 dragoon sabre and a revolver. His frock-coat suggests an early date, although the regiment was not formed until January 1863. (Library of Congress)

Opposite page, top right: Private J. O. Sheppard, Co. F, 6th South Carolina Cavalry Regiment, belonged to the regiment's 'Cadet Company'. His grey jacket is trimmed, apparently with yellow tape, in the same manner as the regulation US Army cavalry dress jacket, and he is wearing a US Army cavalry sword belt. He was killed at Trevilian Station on 12 June 1864. (US Army Military History Institute)

Opposite page, bottom left: William C. Smith, colour sergeant of the 12th Virginia Infantry Regiment, holding his regimental Colour, an Army of Northern Virginia battle flag. He has an officer's kepi although his three sergeant's chevrons have been clearly tinted light-blue on the photograph. His gaiters were on issue as late as 1862, and the second pattern jacket made by the Richmond Clothing Manufactory appeared fairly late in the war. (Lee A. Wallace, Jr.)

Opposite page, bottom right: John Booker, Co. D., 21st Virginia Infantry Regiment, had himself photographed as he thought he would look at the front, complete with revolver and Bowie knife, but such items were soon sent home. His pre-war unit, the Cumberland Grays, which became Co. D, was apparently equipped with this single-breasted frock-coat and dark kepi with the Company designation in brass letters on the front. (Richard Carlile)

Right: Taken from a photograph of artillerymen in the defences of Charleston, South Carolina, this etching made for a period artillery manual shows frock-coats and forage caps worn by South Carolina light artillerymen.

Right: These two men of the 6th Virginia Cavalry Regiment were photographed when their unit was formed in 1861, judging from the overshirts they are wearing as jackets. These garments did not last into 1862, being soon replaced by jackets. The man on the left has a Colt M1851 Navy revolver in his belt, his companion has a 0.31 calibre M1849 5-shot Colt revolver. Note, too, the US Army cavalry cap badge. (Library of Congress)

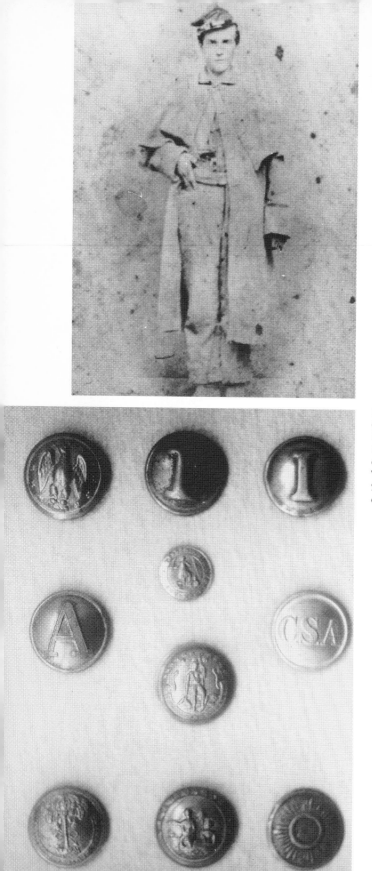

Left: Private Andrew G. Walton, Co. A, 23rd Virginia Infantry Regiment, is wearing a foot-soldier's issue greatcoat and an unusual Confederate forage cap which resembles that issued by the US Army. Walton enlisted on 1 March 1862 and died of pneumonia on 10 July of that year. (Michael Dan Jones)

Left: A representative group of Confederate Army buttons. From top, left to right: general and staff officer's, infantry, artillery, Virginia, North Carolina, and South Carolina. (Author's collection)

troops with heavily laiden wagons, skillets hanging from ropes over the top, banging against the wagon sides.

The troops could buy food such as tinned oysters to supplement their otherwise dull diet. They could buy items of clothing such as shirts and boots, stationery, tobacco, toothbrushes, combs, pipes, knives and forks, boot blacking and button boards for polishing their brass buttons. Alcohol was forbidden, but many sutlers did manage to sell it under one guise or another.

Therefore, when the Confederate Army published its regulations, ten of them applied specifically to sutlers. The Secretary of War was to appoint one sutler to every post, and unit commanders would appoint one sutler to every regiment, corps or separate detachment. These sutlers were to sell the same sort of items as had pre-war sutlers, under a fixed price system. They were allowed to sell to soldiers on credit, collecting what they were due on pay-days, although the monthly sum was not to exceed one–third of a month's pay without the commanding officer's permission, or half a month's pay if permission were given.

However, when the Confederate regiments took the field and posts were established, sutlers were noticeably missing. A Congressional committee looking into various army departments reported in January 1862 that: 'The comfort of the volunteer would be consulted by a definite number of sutlers, judiciously selected, properly restricted, and a tariff of prices with moderate profits adopted.'[1]

A Maryland officer, McHenry Howard, for example, noted that in the winter of 1863/4 he was often hungry. 'Officers', he wrote, 'drew one ration each, the same as the men, were prohibited from purchasing from the commissary, there were no sutlers, and as nothing could be had in the thinly settled neighborhood for love or money, we could only occasionally buy a few articles, such as apple butter, sorghum molasses, half a dozen eggs, etc., when our wagons went over to the Valley or other remote regions for supplies.'[2] Indeed, when the memoirs of most Confederate veterans refer to sutlers at all, they mention the Northern sutlers' wagons which fell into their hands.

There were several reasons for this lack of sutlers in Lee's Army. One was that in the South before the war, comparatively few individuals had been involved in retailing of this kind; the wagon peddler was a Northerner. Secondly, a high percentage of Southern men of an age to follow a sutler's trade were already in the army. Finally, the blockade had halted the supply of many of the delicacies that sutlers traditionally stocked and sold. The sort of stock that retailers could purchase, such as candles, pins, writing materials, utensils, etc., that had got through the blockade, could be more easily and profitably sold to civilians than to poorly paid soldiers — and without the expense and even danger of following the army in a wagon.

None the less, there were a handful of sutlers who served Lee's men from time to time. Some of the regiments known to have had sutlers, at least at one point in their histories, are listed below.

SUTLERS TO LEE'S ARMY

Regiment	Sutler
17th Georgia Infantry	M. Ezekiel
63rd Tennessee Infantry	G. C. Sawtell
1st Virginia Infantry	Asher and Kahn
2nd Virginia Cavalry	J. L. O'Neal
3rd Virginia Infantry	G. G. Sawtell, W. W. Sherwood
4th Virginia Infantry	W. S. Deupre
5th Virginia Infantry	K. Kahn, ? Rice
8th Virginia Infantry	unknown
9th Virginia Infantry	unknown
10th Virginia Infantry	M. Hartman
13th Virginia Infantry	I. T. Guthrie
15th Virginia Infantry	unknown
23rd Virginia Infantry	A. Kohn

CIVILIAN SUPPORT ORGANIZATIONS

Since the Army of Northern Virginia operated so frequently close to Richmond, the Confederacy's largest city, it was able to take advantage of civilian organizations for its support. One of the first of these to function was the Richmond Ambulance Committee. Organized in the spring of 1862 by men exempt from military service, its goal was to help attend wounded soldiers and transport them between field hospitals or collection points and permanent hospitals set up in Richmond. By 5 May 1862, the Battle of Williamsburg, the Committee had 39 ambulances in operation.

Committee members sent their ambulances far and wide to help the men of Lee's Army. During the Gettysburg campaign, for example, many of its members went to Winchester where they spent three weeks caring for Lee's wounded men. 'The "Richmond Ambulance Committee" has been near the army for over three weeks, rendering invaluable assistance to the wounded of every State. They are thoroughly organized, and a set of real working men who do not mind taking off their coats and pitching right into anything which can promote the comfort of our poor wounded fellows,' a chaplain wrote home during the 1864 spring campaign.[1] When the wounded flooded the city, such as during the Peninsula Campaign, civilians of both sexes and all ages also turned out to help wherever they could, and empty buildings were turned into makeshift hospitals.

With so many men packed into Richmond's hospitals, it became difficult for visitors to find their loved ones. So in May 1863,

Chaplain William A. Crocker, 14th Virginia Infantry, formed the Army Intelligence Office in the city to keep track of them all. The Secretary of War assigned him a staff of disabled veterans and volunteers who listed on a daily basis the names and stations of some 30,000 men who passed through the city's hospitals. Eventually they also maintained the army's casualty lists and compiled lists of locations of army units for the public. They also corresponded with foreign governments about any nationals wounded in Confederate service, and provided Union officials with records of their dead.

The large number of employees at the various manufacturing plants and government offices, who were exempt from field service, were available for Home Defence units. They were formed into a brigade, known as the 'Local Brigade', under Lee's eldest son, Major General G. W. C. Lee, organized by places of employment. They were called out during special emergencies to man the city's defensive lines when regular troops were unavailable, which freed Lee from having to man every foot of the line.

For example, during the March 1864 Union cavalry raid on the city, War Department clerk J. B. Jones reported: 'The Department Clerks were in action in the evening in five minutes after they were formed in line. Capt. Ellery, Chief Clerk of 2nd Auditor, was killed, and several were wounded. It rained fast all the time, and it was very dark. The enemy's cavalry charged up on them, firing as they came; they were ordered to lie flat on the ground. This they did, until the enemy came within fifteen yards of them, when they rose and fired, sending the assailants to the right and left, helter-skelter. How many fell is not yet known.'[2]

Finally, Richmond boosted the morale of the soldiers, acting as a magnet for those who were able to get away from the front line for a while. It offered every type of entertainment possible, from high–brow theatre to a large number of bars and a well-established red light district.

8
Combined Arms in Action

CHANCELLORSVILLE: COMBINED ARMS IN THE FIELD

The final test of how well any army comprising a variety of branches — from engineers to cavalry — works together is in battle. Here the record of Lee's men was outstanding.

Possibly Lee's most perfect battle, if a battle can said to be perfect, was Chancellorsville. There Lee's Army was greatly outnumbered, with one entire corps too far away to be of assistance. It was placed in the position of having to defend a long river line, from Fredericksburg where it had easily turned back a badly advised assault in December 1862, east along the Rappahannock with its many fords. Since the Fredericksburg fiasco, the Union Army of the Potomac, under a new general, Major General Joseph Hooker, had been largely rebuilt and its morale greatly restored. Hooker was a capable planner and known to be a 'fighting general', hence the nickname, which he disliked, of 'Fighting Joe'.

Hooker's plan of attack was an excellent one. He would leave a large force to threaten Lee's lines at Fredericksburg, while the bulk of his army — a larger force than Lee's entire army — would move west along the river, then turn and flank Lee's forces. The Army of Northern Virginia would be forced to come out from behind those entrenchments which had proved so deadly at Fredericksburg and meet a much larger force in the open. In the end, Lee met and defeated this force, partly through a loss of nerve on Hooker's part, but more importantly because his force functioned so well as a team.

Most of the activity during the days before the battle was performed by the various staff engineer officers, who reconnoitred all potential battle terrain and weak spots, while combat troops cleaned their weapons and equipment and support troops stock-piled supplies. In early April, for example, Captain James K. Boswell, an engineer officer on Jackson's staff, noted in his diary: 'April 6, Yerby's. Rode with Williamson to examine Banks' and U. S. Fords and the crossing between the two; I don't think there is any probability of the enemy's attempting to cross at Banks as we have great advantage over them at that point...

'Tuesday, April 7, Yerby's. Examined all the works about U. S. Ford; they are pretty well constructed, though some of them are very badly located as they can be taken in reverse, and some of the rifle pits can be.

'Wednesday, April 8. Made sketches of U. S. and Banks, Fords for Gen'l Jackson.'[1]

Signal Corps officers involved in intelligence work meanwhile combed enemy newspapers and agents' reports for any ideas of what the enemy's next move would be. And Signal Corps stations along the river would be the first to spot any enemy movements, while cavalry patrols scouted along the river's edge, also watching for enemy movement.

It was the cavalry who first made contact with enemy forces when, on 14 April, Union cavalry forces attempted to cross the river and were beaten off by Fitzhugh Lee's cavalry brigade and two of W. H. F. Lee's regiments. The enemy force was reinforced, cavalry pickets reporting enemy infantry and artillery crossing on pontoon bridges which their engineers had laid on 28 April. The information that these troops came from two different enemy corps was forwarded to Lee on 1 May. He then ordered his own infantry towards the crossroads hamlet of Chancellorsville, one of the few open spots in what was otherwise a tangled wilderness.

Major General Richard Anderson, commanding the First Corps division that was given the assignment on 29 April, was told to have his men dig in along a strong line there. They should have two days' rations in their haversacks, and camp equipage was to be sent to the rear.

Therefore, before the men left, regimental commissary officers and non-commissioned officers had to make sure there was enough food available for two days' issue, or get it from the central stores. The men had to check their ammunition and percussion cap supplies and replenish their cartridge boxes before the regimental quartermaster packed up his ammunition wagon.

Reserve ammunition trains were to be supervised by the army's chief of ordnance; regimental ordnance wagons, ambulances and medical wagons were packed up and followed the infantry to their new positions. In many cases, especially since the army had been in relatively permanent quarters for some time, this packing would be an involved affair. Most of the supplies would have been kept in tents or huts built for their storage, and they would have to be moved from the huts into the wagons and the wagons secured for transport before the infantry could march. Although there were no formal methods of 'combat loading' wagons, those who had used them during battle would know that the stores would have to be so arranged that vital items would be to hand.

Having no enlisted engineer troops, Anderson's units would have sent their temporarily organized pioneer units in front to lay out lines and start digging entrenchments. These men built most of the defensive works themselves, using bayonets, tin cups and plates.

The Army's Chief Engineer, Colonel W. P. Smith, and an assistant engineer officer, Captain Johnston, from headquarters, had gone ahead of Anderson's infantry to examine the position to be defended and stake out an entrenchment line. Anderson met them when they arrived at the intersection of the two main roads through the area, and the two engineers told the general what his troops should do. Anderson's infantry were joined at about dawn by the 3rd Virginia Cavalry. Anderson used this unit in the traditional way, sending out pickets on each flank and along his front line.

At the same time, Lee telegraphed such intelligence as he had to Brigadier General William N. Pendleton, his chief of artillery, at Chesterfield Depot, on the Richmond and Fredericksburg Railroad Line, where artillery units were concentrated, the better to care for their horses and equipment. Some 1,621 artillerymen of all ranks were located there. Pendleton got his units moving towards Chancellorsville and Fredericksburg within a couple of days, although mud slowed them down somewhat.

Pendleton himself was ordered to join Lee's headquarters, which he did by 1 May. He was then ordered to stop sending guns towards Chancellorsville, but concentrate what remained of his reserve artillery around Fredericksburg. He was ordered to take personal responsibility for the artillery defence of that position. This made a great deal of sense, for the underbrush in the Chancellorsville area limited the use of artillery for all but close-quarters defence — and Lee was already thinking offensively rather than defensively — while the field below the slopes above Fredericksburg were ideal for defence by artillery.

Indeed, Lee telegraphed the War Department on 30 April 1863: 'Learning yesterday afternoon that the enemy's right wing had crossed the Rapidan, and its head had reached the position assumed on our extreme left to arrest their progress, I determined to hold our lines in rear of Fredericksburg with part of the force and endeavor with the rest to drive the enemy back to the Rapidan. Troops were put in motion last night and will soon be in position.'[2]

Infantry left to defend Fredericksburg were ordered to man previously constructed rifle pits along the heights above the town, while sharpshooters were to remain in the ruins of the town to slow up any enemy advance. All troops were to have one day's rations in their haversacks.

Infantry action began between enemy skirmishers and the defending Confederates just after noon on 1 May. Enemy artillery joined the battle and the enemy made several direct attacks on McLaws' Division which had joined that of Anderson. Together they had some 15,649 men of all ranks. Cavalry reported a further enemy approach along the Mine Road, so McLaws sent Captain Johnston, the engineer from Lee's headquarters, to guide an infantry brigade with artillery support to protect his right. The line picked out by the engineers held successfully throughout 1 May.

Once battle lines had been formed, men of the provost guards formed their lines behind the main forces, to intercept any men fleeing the front and take charge of captured Union troops. By this time Bridgford's 1st Virginia Battalion, although still officially Second Corps provost guard, was serving with army headquarters. It numbered some 200 officers and men, who set themselves up in small picket posts and lines.

Jackson had earlier reported himself pleased with the performance of Bridgford and his men at Fredericksburg in reducing the number of stragglers from the firing line. The 9th Alabama Infantry Regiment set up posts to collect prisoners of war whom they turned over to the Army's Provost Marshal to be forwarded to Richmond.

Regimental and higher medical staffs also set up their field hospitals, Ambulance Corpsmen following the battle lines to remove the wounded to the rear as quickly as possible. This was difficult in the tangled underbrush of the Chancellorsville battlefield, reported John Casler, a Virginia private: 'The dead and badly wounded from both sides were lying where they fell. The woods, taking fire that night from the shells, burnt rapidly and roasted the wounded men alive. As we went to bury them we could see where they had tried to keep the fire from them by scratching the leaves away as far as they could reach. But it availed not; they were burnt to a crisp.'[3]

On the evening of 1 May, Lee met his brilliant subordinate, Lieutenant General T. J. 'Stonewall' Jackson, to discuss ideas for repelling the enemy advance, having already telegraphed the War Department that he was keen to do this. Jackson had already been attempting to study the road network in the area. He had sent his topographical engineer, Jed Hotchkiss, to find a possible way around the enemy. Hotchkiss soon returned with a sketch map of a possible route. Also, cavalry commander Major General J. E. B. Stuart found a local man who guided some of his cavalrymen along roads that turned the enemy's flank.

Other than picket and scouting duty, however, Stuart's cavalry would contribute fairly little to the overall battle. In part this was due to the terrain. But, as one of his brigade commanders, Fitzhugh Lee, was later to say: 'The Confederate cavalry operations, from smallness of numbers, were very much circumscribed. Stuart only had five regiments at Chancellorsville, three of them being on Lee's left and two on his right, while two more had been left to contend as best they could with Stoneman's ten thousand troopers.[4] This latter Union force was sent around Lee's Army in what amounted to little more than an abortive raid. Stuart had available some 6,509 all ranks in his cavalry units.

Nor, in fact, would either side's artillery be used as effectively as it might have been. 'These forest conditions naturally had their effect upon the military features of the Chancellorsville position,' wrote artilleryman E. P. Alexander. 'There was no room for a large artillery force — of which force the Federals had an excess. But, on the other hand, defensive lines were quick & easy to make, & to hold, &, by cutting a little abattis in front of them, an entanglement would result which only rabbits could get through.'[5]

None the less, the artillery did see action, and proved most useful as single pieces or in sections. Alexander protected one road with only a single gun which was pulled by prolonge ropes, the horses having been left in rear. He had an infantry squad deployed on each side of the gun for its protection. His was only one of a number of similar single pieces in operation during the battle.

In the meantime Jackson had been given approval for his force of 33,333 officers and men to take off on their flank march. The general orders covering the manner of this march were quite clear. Each division was given a specified time to start. The rate of march was not to be over 25 minutes' marching followed by a break of ten minutes. Batteries and wagon trains were not allowed to halt to water their horses; if they had to fall out for some reason, they were not to pass other units in order to regain their original places. Ambulances from each brigade were to move together.

Jackson sent R. E. Rode's Division in the front of his corps, with Fitzhugh Lee's cavalrymen covering the rear and flanks. Skirmishers would have led the way, followed by detailed pioneers, commanded by engineer or infantry officers as available, who would ensure that the roads were clear.

During the afternoon of 2 May, Jackson's troops encountered Union troops in their defensive positions near Melzi Chancellor's house, which was also called Dowdall's Tavern, and called for an immediate attack. The Union troops were seen to be resting, cook-pots on the fire and arms stacked. It took some two hours — during which time the Union troops did not discover their danger — for Rode's Division, the lead division, to deploy into line of battle. While this might seem to be very slow, in fact by the standards of the time it was fairly quickly done since the infantry had to deploy from columns, four abreast, into two lines with everyone in correct position. The difficult undergrowth certainly did not make things easier.

Shortly after this, at about 5.15 by Confederate watches, the order to attack was given. The sharpshooter battalions were deployed about 400 yards in advance of the main line, and their fire completely surprised the enemy troops who fled, leaving behind quantities of weapons, clothing and equipment. Many of the men took advantage of this to refill their cartridge boxes, and surgeons re-equipped their medicine chests.

Despite the limited ranges possible, guns of Stuart's horse artillery were present, as noted by Brigadier General R. E. Colston, who was in command of Trimble's Division that day. Indeed, Colonel S. Crutchfield, Second Corps' chief of artillery, was able to mass batteries on the final Union position around the heights of Chancellorsville by the end of the assault.

The attack was halted; the Union troops generally withdrew although a minor counter-attack at about midnight was easily repelled. Jackson and his staff, including topographical engineer Boswell, Signal Corps Captain Wilbourn, and, it was especially noted, several Signal Corps sergeants, went off to reconnoitre the enemy's new positions. Unfortunately, in the underbrush and dark and generally uncertain conditions, troops of Lane's North Carolina Brigade took this mounted party for Union cavalry. The volley which the North Carolinians fired into them killed Boswell outright and mortally wounded Jackson. A little later, A. P. Hill, who took over command after Jackson's wounding, and his staff were also mistaken for Union cavalry and fired upon. Hill was wounded, and cavalry commander Stuart took command of the Corps.

Wishing to carry on the fine work of the previous day, Stuart sent E. P. Alexander to select artillery positions to support a continued attack. He, accompanied by a courier, rode all over the field by the light of a full moon, from about nine until three the next morning. From time to time the enemy could be clearly heard working on entrenchments. Eventually Alexander selected five positions for the corps artillery.

On his return he briefed Colonel Lindsay Walker, who was in command of A. P. Hill's divisional artillery, so that Walker could select the batteries to be placed in Alexander's positions. Rapidly Walker gave orders for this to be done; the weary gunners were woken, the complicated business of harnessing horses to guns and caissons, all by moonlight, was achieved so efficiently by the well-trained and experienced gunners that most of the division's artillery was on the road by about four in the morning.

It should be noted that from this moment on, the master plan having been created by Lee, his activities were little evident — and purposely so. According to Captain Justus Scheibert, a Prussian observer of the Army during this time, Lee told him that he did 'my duty insofar as my powers and capabilities will permit, until the moment when the battle begins: I then leave the matter to God and the ... subordinate officers. My supervision during the battle does more harm than good.

It would be unfortunate if ... I could not rely upon my division and brigade commanders. I think and work with all my powers to bring my troops to the right place at the right time; then I have done my duty.'[6] Even so, Lee's staff were busy throughout the battle. According to his final report, 'General Chilton, chief of staff, Lieutenant-Colonel (E.) Murray, Major (Henry E.) Peyton, and Captain (H. E.) Young, of the Adjutant and Inspector General's Department, were active in seeing to the execution of orders; Lieutenant-Colonel (William P.) Smith and Captain (Samuel R.) Johnston, of the Engineers, in reconnoitring the enemy and constructing batteries; Colonel (Armistead L.) Long in posting troops and artillery.

'Majors (Walter H.) Taylor, (T. M. R.) Talcott, (Charles) Marshall, and (Charles S.) Venable were engaged night and day in watching the operations, carrying orders, &c.'[7] Lee accompanied his troops on their final assault on enemy positions at Chancellorsville on the morning of 3 May.

Regimental quartermasters and commissaries also worked throughout the night bringing up food and ammunition. Lee also said that: 'Lieutenant-Colonel (Robert G.) Cole, chief commissary of subsistence, and Lieutenant-Colonel (Briscoe G.) Baldwin, chief of ordnance, were everywhere on the field attending to the wants of their departments.'[8] Chief Quartermaster Lieutenant Colonel J. L. Corley spent his time in charge of the disposition and safety of the army's wagon trains.

None the less, by dawn Stuart saw that the men of Rode's Division had not received rations, save those they found in the haversacks of the slain. He therefore delayed the renewal of the attack so that food could be distributed. At About eight in the morning his troops stormed the enemy's hastily constructed entrenchments. Sunrise signalled the moment for other Confederate forces to advance: Early moved along the Telegraph Road and recaptured Marye's and adjacent hills.

The attacks were successful, the Union troops withdrawing to the river to regain the safety of the northern bank. The tangled underbrush slowed the retreat, but equally it slowed the Confederate pursuit. By six that evening Anderson's Division, which had been in defence from the beginning, moved forward at the same time as Early to drive some of the last Union troops from the southern side of the Rappahannock.

The battle was over, but the army's work was not. To begin with, there was the debris, human and *matériel*, to clean up. Medical Director Surgeon Lafayette Guild reported that 1,581 officers and 8,700 enlisted men had been killed and wounded in the battle. Also, fleeing Union troops left many of their dead and wounded behind. Some were in Union field hospitals manned by that Army's medical personnel; others lay where they fell and had to be brought to Confederate aid stations. This was done; Union medical officers lauded the attention paid to their men by Confederate medical personnel after the battle, much though they lamented the loss of their own medical equipment which made their own treatment of their men difficult.

The dead were carried to central sites for burial by members of the Pioneer Corps. The wounded of both sides had to be found and brought to hospitals for treatment. A number of Union medical officers came into the Confederate lines after the battle and were allowed to remove their wounded to shelter.

Confederate wounded suffered from the general shortage of ambulances in the Army; Surgeon Guild had complained as recently as the month before the battle that transportation within the army was one of its two most serious problems. It was at this point that the civilian Richmond Ambulance Committee was of great use. A large number of its members arrived at the battlefield as soon as the last shot had been fired and began gathering wounded to take back to the hospitals in Richmond. In all, Committee members brought some 7,000 wounded officers and men from Chancellorsville to Richmond.

There was less urgency about gathering up the *matériel*. After a victory such as Chancellorsville, where the bulk of the enemy army had had to leave the field quickly, this amounted to a great deal of booty. The job of collecting, repairing and reissuing equipment was the responsibility of the Ordnance Department whose officers and sergeants at regimental level supervised its dispatch to depots. On 20 May 1863, the Army's Chief of Ordnance, Lieutenant Colonel Briscoe G. Baldwin, wrote:

'I have the honor to report the following as the principal captures in the recent engagements near Fredericksburg [officially, the Army considered the holding action at Fredericksburg as being separate from the attack at Chancellorsville]:

'Artillery — Five 12-pounder Napoleons, seven 3-inch rifles, one 10-pounder Parrott, nine caissons, four rear parts of caissons, three battery wagons, two forges, 1,500 rounds artillery ammunition, a large lot of artillery harness, and a large lot of wheels, axles, ammunition chests, &c.

'Infantry — Nineteen thousand five hundred muskets and rifles (29,500 collected, 10,000 admitted dropped by our men, leaving 19,500 captured), 8,000 cartridge boxes, 4,000 cap- pouches, 11,500 knapsacks, 300,000 rounds infantry ammunition.

'I have carefully confined myself to what has been reported as collected and counted. This, of course, is considerably less than the amount actually captured, as a number of unarmed men supplied themselves with arms, accoutrements, &c., and the army generally helped themselves from the cartridge-boxes of the enemy. Also every day small lots of muskets and rifles are brought in, and without doubt quite a number of arms &c., are retained in regimental ordnance wagons for future contingencies and not reported.

'A large quantity of lead has been and is now being collected from the battle-fields.'[9]

That much in the way of abandoned equipment was still uncollected a month later is evidenced by a note from a British observer on 20 June: 'Near this place [Gordonsville, Virginia] I observed an enormous pile of excellent rifles rotting in the open air. These had been captured at Chancellorsville; but the Confederates have already such a superabundant stock of rifles that apparently they can afford to let them spoil.'[10]

Finally, unit commanders had to prepare their official reports of the battle, while topographical engineers — the first and last soldiers on the field — surveyed the area to prepare maps to accompany these reports. Also, elections were held in a number of infantry companies to select men who had been especially heroic during the battle to be awarded a 'badge of distinction'. Some companies decided that it would be unfair to single out individuals, and did not select any of their number for such honours.

Although no medals were produced or awarded, a 'Roll of Honor' listed each of the 23 officers, 102 non-commissioned officers and 167 privates considered by their peers to be most deserving. Yet, it was the teamwork of all 57,112 officers and men in Lee's Army that gave Lee such a magnificent victory.

PETERSBURG: COMBINED ARMS IN DEFENCE

In a technical sense, Lee's Army was never involved in a siege. At no time was it unable to retreat or entirely cut off from re-supply. But the so-called Siege of Petersburg in 1864–5 was a siege in the sense that entrenched troops fought to defend a fixed point, using all the siege techniques of the period. As a result, it clearly demonstrates how the different branches of service in Lee's Army operated in a static defensive situation.

Much of the work of the different branches of the army was the same in siege warfare as it was in the open field. Cavalrymen secured the flanks and protected supply lines, as well as raiding enemy supply lines, although by this time they were badly hampered by a lack of forage and horses. 'My command is suffering for forage and many of my horses are broken down,' cavalry commander Wade Hampton reported on 20 June 1864.'[1]

Infantrymen manned the main defensive lines. Artillerymen supported the infantry by tearing apart enemy artillery and infantry concentrations. Signal corpsmen passed messages over long distances and gathered intelligence. Medical personnel maintained field and general hospitals for the sick and wounded. The one branch whose importance increased during defensive operations, was the Corps of Engineers.

As in a field action such as Chancellorsville, troops of the Engineers and Signal Corps were first on the scene. Before Grant and the Army of the Potomac came south, below Richmond, across the James and Appomattox Rivers, engineer officers had already constructed a series of lunettes and redoubts that commanded the approaches to the City of Petersburg. These positions were manned by infantry and artillery under General Beauregard, who was the first to realize what the Union forces were up to. He and his chief engineer, Colonel Harris, staked out a line of fortifications for a shorter, inner line. These were built by Pioneer Corps troops and slave labour under engineer supervision. The combat troops were in position manning these fortifications just in time to beat off Grant's initial assault on the Petersburg lines on 18 June 1864.

Earlier, too, according to the 1st Regiment's Colonel Talcott: 'One company of engineer troops was detached with a pontoon train and sent to Petersburg, where a bridge was needed to facilitate crossing the Appomattox River at that point. Of the eleven companies of engineer troops which remained north of the James during General Grant's first operations against Petersburg, one company was in charge of the pontoon bridge at Chaffin's Bluff and ten served as infantry on what was known as the Deep Bottom line.'[2]

The engineer officers with Beauregard and, later, Lee's engineers, then had to draw up a series of defensive lines to keep the Union troops out of Petersburg, a vital link in the rail line that fed Richmond. They built conventional fortifications, essentially a series of redoubts and forts with raised earthen walls, reinforced on their rear by logs held in place by standing logs, and gabions, which were cylindrical woven wicker baskets about three feet high, and filled with earth. The gabions were topped with logs about six feet long and nine inches in diameter called 'trench fascines'. These fortifications had loopholes in the walls, called 'embrasures', through which poked the muzzles of the cannon planted behind the earthen walls. The cannon, consisting of field guns and larger, less mobile guns that fired a much larger shell, were mounted on carriages that rested on wooden floors to prevent them from digging in. A dug-in magazine, its entrance facing rearwards, was built near each fort or redoubt.

The redoubts were connected by a trench-line, known as the 'rifle pits', whose like would be seen during the First World War. These were often wood lined and had fire steps; in places fascines were fitted across the top of the trench to give head protection for sharpshooters. Magazines and living quarters were often dug into the earth on the side of the trench facing the enemy. Sandbags were widely used to shore up walls, top fortifications, and line embrasures for sharpshooters.

Listening-posts for detection of enemy mining or movements were established in small dug-outs beyond the front trench line. Sharpened poles were planted in the walls of the fortifications, and *chevaux-de-frise*, sharpened stakes driven about a foot apart at right angles to one another through logs about twelve feet long and ten inches thick, were scattered about in front of fortifications, both devices to break up enemy attacks.

Engineers laid out, and pioneers and infantry built, trench lines running parallel to each other so that if one line were captured, it would be almost surrounded by other defensive lines.

Artillery was also more important in defensive line warfare than in the field, not only the field and more static guns previously mentioned, but also the mortar, which was generally not used in the field. The mortar, a squat tube resting on a wooden base, threw its shell in a high, arcing trajectory rather than directly at the target.

Confederate mortars were the bronze 12-pound and 24-pound models, called 'Coehorns' after the Dutch inventor, Baron van Menno Coehoorn. According to one Federal observer, 'For practice against troops, the 12-pounder Coehorn is decidedly more deadly than the 24-pounder as its shell, when the fuse burns too slowly, does not bury itself on striking and the fragments thus scatter widely.'[3] Alexander reported: 'I received my first installment of mortars, 12 of them, on June 24th & had them in action on the 25th,' adding that he went right to work 'firing at the big forts we could see going up everywhere and at the strong rifle pits in front of the Elliott Salient'.[4]

To make life for an attacker even worse, Alexander 'also sent to Richmond to have a large lot of hand grenades made, of a pattern which Gen. Rains had recently devised. They were thin iron shells, about the size of a goose egg, filled with powder & with a sensitive paper percussion fuze in the front end, & a two foot strap, or strong cord, to the rear end. A man could swing one of these & throw it 60 yards, & they would burst wherever they struck.'[5]

The result of all these measures was to make an entrenched defensive line, manned by soldiers determined not to be overrun, virtually impossible to take unless the defenders were vastly outnumbered. While there were more Union soldiers available than Confederate defenders, it was almost impossible to mass enough attackers in any given area to overwhelm the defending lines. Since there was no way to launch an airborne assault, the Union forces had to be content to: 1. nibble away at the flanks, 2. wear out Lee's Army with slow, constant losses to the point where the line would be too thin to be defended, and 3. try other methods of breaking through. It was largely the cavalry's job to attempt the first method, while infantry and artillery took on the second. As to the third, Federal forces did attempt to explode a mine under a section of Confederate trench line. The engineers were responsible for countering the enemy's mining activities. 'Two pits were sunk in the trenches, from the bottom of which drifts or tunnels were extended some distance beyond the entrenchments, and a circumvallating gallery was in progress, which, if it had been completed in time, might have discovered the exact location of the underground approach of the foe,' Colonel Talcott later wrote.[6]

As the colonel indicated, countermining was not effective. On 30 July 1864 the Union forces exploded a huge mine containing some 8,000 pounds of gunpowder directly under the Confederate line, at a point defended by the 19th and 22nd South Carolina Infantry Regiments, killing almost 300 men. The resulting crater was some 170 feet long, about 70 feet wide and 30 feet deep.

Inept Union leadership versus the quick reactions of General William Mahone, caused the ensuing attack to fail, but Confederate troops thereafter were always wary of mining. Lee ordered eight companies from north of the James into the Petersburg lines solely for countermining measures, and a number of infantry units were also assigned to this job.

Still, Confederate combat soldiers, who feared nobody they could see, were constantly terrified about the dangers under their feet. One of Lee's men, however, devised a mine-detection technique which put their minds at ease. It consisted of digging bore-holes to any desired depth and filling them with water. According to 1st Engineers Lieutenant Colonel W. W. Blackford:

'These holes, kept full of water, would of course indicate with certainty whether the enemy was underneath, for if he tapped the hole with his mine the water would run out and as long as the hole remained full of water the men knew that there was no danger. The contrivance was as simple as it was effective, working perfectly in that tenacious red clay, though in other soils it might not have answered. It consisted of a sheet of iron about one-sixteenth of an inch thick, bent into a truncated cone, about one foot long and about two and a half inches in diameter at one end and three and a half at the other, with the lap brazed together. Halfway there was cut a hole, and the lower edge was sharpened on the inside, with a chisel edge outward, and into the smaller end was inserted a pole (securely fastened with nails) five or six feet long. The implement was used as follows: two men held it vertically and rammed it down by raising it a few feet and letting it fall. The clay would be cut by the edges and slightly compressed, so that to the depth it had gone the clay remained in the tool, another blow cut another depth and pushed the first cut higher up the cylinder, and so on until it reached the hole in the cylinder. The clay in the tool was then punched out by running a stick though the hole, and the ramming was then continued until the tool was again full and so on.

'When the handle of the tool had sunk so deep that it could not be reached without stooping too low, a cord was tied to it and the blow given by jerking the tool up and letting it fall. In this way a hole twenty feet deep could be sunk in half a day or less. The movement of the cutting edge shaved off the inside of the hole until it became about half an inch larger than the diameter of the cutter, thus freeing it and making it work easily as it rose and fell. The contrivance took like wildfire.'[7]

Meanwhile, Lee kept his engineers busy elsewhere. 'Anticipating the necessity for the abandonment of Richmond and Petersburg, General Lee, during the winter of 1864/5, required the engineer troops to rebuild Bevill's Bridge over the Appomattox River west of Petersburg, and to send a pontoon bridge to the Staunton River in Charlotte County,' Talcott wrote.

'The engineer troops also prepared a map showing the routes to the different crossings of the Appomattox River, to be used whenever the army should be withdrawn from Richmond and Petersburg.'[8]

Of course, in April 1865 that was just what happened, and the end came only days later.

9
The Units of Lee's Army

ALABAMA: ARTILLERY
Jeff Davis Battery Formed: Selma, May 1861. ANV service: January 1862–April 1865. Assigned: Early's Brigade (until end of March 1862), D. H. Hill's Division, Rodes' Division, Carter's/Page's Battalion, Page's Battalion, Cutshaw's Battalion. Commanders: Captains Joseph T. Montgomery, James W. Bondurant, William J. Reese. Notes: September 1862 armed with two 3-inch rifles and two 12-pound howitzers.

ALABAMA: INFANTRY
3rd Regiment Formed: Montgomery, April 1861. ANV Service: May 1861–April 1865. Brigades assigned: Withers', Mahonel's, Rodes', O'Neal's, Battle's. Commanders: Colonels Tennent Lomax (July 1861–May 1862), Cullan A. Battle (May 1862–August 1863), Charles Forsythe (August 1863–April 1865). Notes: 1861–2 uniform was grey cap with black band, single–breasted grey jacket with shoulder–straps and pointed cuffs, grey trousers with black stripes. M1855 rifled muskets. Suffered 56. 4 per cent losses at Malvern Hill.

4th Regiment Formed: Dallas, Georgia, 2 May 1861. ANV Service: May 1861–September 1863, April 1864–April 1865. Brigades

assigned: Bee's, Whiting's, Law's, Perry's. Commanders: Colonels Egbert J. Jones (May–September 1861), Evander McIvor Law (November 1861–October 1862), Pickney D. Bowles (October 1862–April 1865). Notes: Late 1861 uniform was grey frock coat with black trim, grey cap and trousers. M1855 rifled muskets.

5th Battalion Formed: Dumfries, Virginia, December 1861. ANV Service: December 1861–April 1865. Brigades assigned: Wigfall's, Archer's, Provost Guard. Commanders: Major Albert S. Van de Graaff, Lieutenant Colonel Henry H. Walker.

5th Regiment Formed: Montgomery, June 1861. ANV service: June 1861–April 1865. Brigades assigned: Ewell's, Rodes', Battle's. Commanders: Colonels Robert E. Rode (June–October 1861), Allen C. Jones (November 1861–April 1862), Christopher C. Pegues (April–July 1862), Josephus M. Hall (July 1862–November 1864), Edwin L. Hobson (November 1864–April 1865). Notes: Suffered 40. 8 per cent losses at Malvern Hill.

6th Regiment Formed: Montgomery, May 1861. ANV service: May 1861–April 1865. Brigades assigned: Ewell's, Rodes', Battle's. Commanders: Colonels John J.

Seibels (May 1861–April 1862), John B. Gordon (April 1862–November 1862), James N. Lightfoot (May 1863–May 1865). Notes: First officers' uniform was bottle green double-breasted frock coat with US Army buttons. Suffered 59 per cent losses at Seven Pines.

8th Regiment Formed: Richmond, Virginia, June 1861. ANV service: June 1861–April 1865. Brigades assigned: Winston's, McLaws', Pryor's, Wilcox's, Perrin's, Sanders', Forney's. Commanders: Colonels John A. Winston (June 1861–June 1862), Young L. Royston (June 1862–June 1864), Hilary A. Herbert (June 1864–November 1864). Notes: Co I wore dark-green frock coat; Co A wore Sicilian cap in 1861. Co. A had Mississippi rifles in 1861.

9th Regiment Formed: Richmond, Virginia, June 1861. ANV service: June 1861–April 1865. Brigades assigned: E. K. Smith's, Wilcox's, Perrin's, Sanders', Forney's. Commanders: Colonels Cadmus M. Wilcox (June–October 1861), Samuel Henry (October 1861–March 1863), Joseph H. King (March 1863–April 1865).

10th Regiment Formed: Montgomery, June 1861. ANV service: July 1861–April 1865. Brigades assigned: E. K. Smith's, Wilcox's, Perrin's, Sanders', Forney's. Commanders: Colonels John H. Forney (June 1861–March 1862), John J. Woodward (March 1862–June 1862), William H. Forney (September 1862–February 1865).

11th Regiment Formed: Lynchburg, Virginia, June 1861. ANV

service: July 1861–April 1865. Brigades asigned: E. K. Smith's, Wilcox's, Perrin's, Sanders', Forney's. Commanders: Colonels Sydenham Moore (June 1861–August 1862), John C. C. Sanders, George E. Taylor (August 1864–April 1865). Notes: Suffered 50. 7 per cent losses at Glendale.

12th Regiment Formed: Richmond, Virginia, July 1861. ANV service: July 1861–April 1865. Brigades assigned: Ewell's, Rodes', O'Neal's, Battle's. Commanders: Colonels Robert T. Jones (July 1861–May 1862), Bristow B. Gayle (June 1862–September 1862), Samuel B. Pickens (September 1862–April 1865). Notes: Suffered 52. 6 per cent losses at Fair Oaks.

13th Regiment Formed: Montgomery, July 1861. ANV service: September 1861–April 1865. Brigades assigned: Rains', Colquitt's, Archer's, Fry's, Sanders', Forney's. Commanders: Colonels Birkett D. Fry (July 1861–May 1864), James Aiken (May 1864–April 1865).

14th Regiment Formed: Alburn, July 1861. ANV service: September 1861–April 1865. Brigades assigned: Walker's, Pryor's, Wilcox's, Perrin's, Sanders', Forney's. Commanders: Colonels Thomas J. Judge (July 1861–July 1862), Alfred C. Wood (July–October 1862), Lucius Pinckard (October 1863–April 1865).

15th Regiment Formed: Fort Mitchell, July 1861. ANV service: August 1861–September 1863, April 1864–April 1865. Brigades assigned: Trimble's, Law's, Perry's. Commanders: Colonels James

Cantey (July 1861–January 1863), John F. Treutlen (January–April 1863), William C. Oates (April 1863 but not confirmed), Alexander A. Lowther (April 1863–April 1865). Notes: November 1861 issued grey frock coat, grey trousers, grey cap 'that fell over in front' with brass letters on top, grey greatcoat.

26th Regiment Formed: Richmond, through enlarging of 3rd Battalion, March 1862. ANV service: March 1862–February 1864 (sent to Richmond to garrison until June 1864 when sent to Army of Mississippi). Brigade assignments: Rain's, Rodes', O'Neal's, Battle's. Commander: Colonel Edward A. O'Neal (March 1862–February 1864). Notes: Suffered 40 per cent losses at Malvern Hill.

41st Regiment Formed: Tuscaloosa, May 1862. ANV service: May 1864–April 1865. Brigades assigned: Gracie's, Moody's. Commanders: Henry Talbird (May 1862–June 1863), Martin L. Stansel (June 1863–April 1865).

43rd Regiment Formed: Mobile, May 1862. ANV service: May 1864–April 1865. Brigades assigned: Gracie's, Moody's. Commanders: Colonels Archibald Gracie, Jr. , Young M. Moody.

44th Regiment Formed: Selma, May 1862. ANV service: June 1862–September 1863, April 1864–April 1865. Brigades assigned: Wright's, Law's, Perry's. Commanders: Colonels James Kent (May–September 1862), Charles A. Derby (September

1862), William F. Perry.

47th Regiment Formed: Loachapoka, May 1862. ANV service: July 1862–September 1863, April 1864–April 1865. Brigades assigned: Taliaferro's, Law's, Perry's. Commanders: Colonels James M. Oliver (May–August 1862), James W. Jackson (August 1862–July 1863), Michael J. Bugler (July 1863–February 1865). Notes: Issued Austrian rifles, July 1862.

48th Regiment Formed: Auburn, May 1862. ANV service: July 1862–September 1863, April 1864–April 1865. Brigades assigned: Taliaferro's, Law's, Perry's. Commanders: Colonel James L. Sheffield (May 1862–May 1864), Major John W. Wigginton (May 1864–April 1865).

59th Regiment Formed: consolidation of 2nd Infantry Battalion, Hilliard's Legion, 4th Artillery Battalion of Hilliard's Legion at Charleston, November 1863. ANV service: May 1864–April 1865. Brigade assigned: Gracie's. Commander: Colonel Bolling Hall, Jr. (November 1863–May 1864).

60th Regiment Formed: Charleston, November 1863, by consolidation of 3rd Infantry and four companies of Hilliard's Legion. ANV service: May 1864–April 1865. Brigade assigned: Gracie's. Commander: Colonel John W. A. Sanford (November 1863–April 1865).

61st Regiment Formed: Pollard, May 1863. ANV service: February 1864–April 1865. Brigade assigned: Battle's. Commander: Colonel William G. Swanson (April 1864–May 1865).

ARKANSAS: INFANTRY

1st Regiment Formed: Little Rock, May 1861. ANV service: May 1861–January 1862. Brigade assigned: Walker's. Commander: Colonel James F. Fagan (May 1861–September 1862).

2nd Battalion Formed: Aquia District, Department of Northern Virginia, October 1861. ANV service: October 1861–July 1862 (merged into 3rd Infantry). Commander: Major William N. Bronaugh.

3rd Regiment Formed: North–west Virginia, July 1861. ANV service: July 1861–April 1865. Commanders: Colonels Albert Rust (July 1861–March 1862), Vannoy H. Manning (March 1862–April 1865).

CONFEDERATE UNITS

1st Engineers Regiment Formed: Richmond, autumn 1863. ANV service: April 1864–April 1865. Assigned: Headquarters. Commander: Colonel Thomas M. R. Talcott (April 1864–April 1865).

1st Infantry Battalion Formed: From three companies of the 2nd Alabama, and one each from Florida, Georgia and Tennessee in the Western theatre, spring 1862. ANV service: spring 1864–April 1865. Brigade assigned: J. R. Davis's. Commanders: Lieutenant Colonels George H. Forney and Francis B. McClung.

2nd Engineers Regiment Formed: Richmond, summer 1863. ANV service: spring 1864–April 1865. Did not serve as a single regiment. Commander: Major D. Wintter.

7th Cavalry Regiment Formed: Through the consolidation of the 4th North Carolina Battalion Partisan Rangers and seven independent companies from Georgia, October 1862. ANV service: spring 1864–July 1864 (disbanded). Brigades assigned: James Dearing's. Commanders: Colonels William C. Claiborne and V. H. Taliaferro.

8th Cavalry Regiment (Dearing's) Formed: Richmond, winter 1863/4. ANV service: spring 1864–July 1864 (disbanded). Brigade assigned: Dearing's. Commander: Colonel James Dearing (April 1864).

FLORIDA: INFANTRY

2nd Regiment Formed: Jacksonville, July 1861. ANV service: September 1861–April 1865. Brigades assigned: Garland's, Pryor's, Perry's, Finegan's. Commanders: Colonel George T. Ward (July 1861–May 1862), Edward A. Perry (May–August 1862), Lewis G. Pyles (August 1862–July 1864), Walter R. Moore (July 1864–April 1865). Notes: Arms issued by state, including Maynard carbines; lost its Colour at Gettysburg to the 13th Vermont.

5th Regiment Formed: Camp Leon, April 1862. ANV service: August 1862–April 1865. Brigades assigned: Pryor's, Perry's, Finegan's. Commander: Colonel John C. Hateley (April 1862–July 1863).

8th Regiment Formed: By companies, May–July 1862. ANV service: August 1862–April 1865. Brigades assigned: Pryor's, Perry's, Finegan's. Commanders: Colonels Richard F. Floyd (July–October 1862), David Lang (October

1862–April 1865).

9th Regiment Formed: By merger of 6th Battalion and three independent companies, April 1864. ANV service: April 1864–April 1865. Brigades assigned: Perry's, Finegan's. Commanders: Colonels John M. Martin (April 1864–late 1864), Robert B. Thomas (acting).

10th Regiment Formed: By merger of 1st Special Battalion and four companies of the 2nd Battalion, June 1864. ANV service: June 1864–April 1865. Brigades assigned: Perry's, Finegan's. Commander: Colonel Charles R. F. Hopkins (June 1864–April 1865).

11th Regiment Formed: By merger of 4th Battalion, two companies of the 2nd Battalion, and an independent company, June 1864. ANV service: June 1864–April 1865. Brigades assigned: Perry's, Finegan's. Commander: Colonel Theodore W. Brevard.

GEORGIA: ARTILLERY

Macon Light Artillery Formed: Macon, summer 1862. ANV service: 1862–3, 1864–5. Assigned: Moseley's Battalion, Blount's Battalion. Commanders: Captains N. H. Ells, C. W. Slaten. Notes: Armed with two 30-pound Parrotts in December 1862; four Napoleons in December 1864.

Milledge's Battery Formed: spring 1861. ANV service: September 1862–April 1865. Assigned: Richardson's Battalion, Nelson's Battalion. Commander: Captain John Milledge, Jr. Notes: September 1862 armed with one 10-pound Parrott, three 3-inch rifles, one Hotchkiss rifle, and one James rifle; in December 1864 with three 3-inch rifles.

Pulaski Light Artillery Formed: Pulaski County, autumn 1861. ANV service: winter 1861/2–April 1865. Assigned: 1st Regiment Virginia Artillery, Cabell's Battalion. Commanders: Captains John C. Fraser, John P. W. Read. Notes: September 1862 armed with one 10-pound Parrott, one 12-pound howitzer, and two 6-pound smoothbore guns; in December 1864 with four Napoleons.

Troup Light Artillery Formed: La Grange County, autumn 1861. ANV service: autumn 1861–April 1865. Assigned: Cabell's Battalion. Commanders: Captains H. H. Carlton, M. Stanley. Notes: First uniform green with red trim; armed in September 1862 with two 10–pound Parrotts, one 12-pound howitzer, two 6-pound smoothbores; in December 1864 with four 10-pound Parrotts.

GEORGIA: CAVALRY

7th Regiment Formed: By merger of the 21st and 24th Battalions and the Hardwick Mounted Rifles, Rome, spring 1864. ANV service: spring 1864–April 1865. Brigades assigned: Young's, Gary's. Commander: Colonel William P. White (January–April 1864).

8th Regiment Formed: By merger of seven companies, 62nd Regiment, and three companies, 20th Battalion Partisan Rangers, July 1864. ANV service: July 1864–April 1865. Brigade assigned: Dearing's. Commander: Colonel Joel R. Griffin (July 1864–April 1865).

10th Regiment Formed: By merger of seven companies, 7th Confederate Cavalry Regiment, and three companies, 20th Battalion Partisan Rangers, Petersburg, Virginia, July 1864. ANV service: July–winter 1864. Commander: Colonel V. H. Taliaferro.

20th Battalion Partisan Rangers Formed: Liberty County, summer 1862. ANV service: spring 1864–April 1865. Brigade assigned: Young's. Commander: Lieutenant Colonel John M. Millen (September 1863–May 1864).

GEORGIA INFANTRY

1st Regiment Regulars Formed: Macon, April 1861. ANV service: spring 1861–spring 1863. Brigades assigned: Toombs', Anderson's. Commanders: Colonels Charles J. Williams (March 1861–February 1862), William J. Magill (February 1862–August 1864). Notes: Initially varied militia uniform; July 1861 mostly grey frock coats and trousers with black trim. Regimental Colour: first national flag.

2nd Independent Battalion Formed: Norfolk, Virginia, April 1861. ANV service: June 1862–April 1865. Brigades assigned: Walker's, Wright's. Commanders: Majors Thomas Hardeman, Jr. , C. J. Moffett, George W. Ross.

2nd Regiment Formed: Brunswick, June 1861. ANV service: July 1861–September 1863, April 1864–April 1865. Brigades assigned: Toombs', Benning's. Commanders: Colonels Paul J. Semmes (June 1861–March 1862), Edgar M. Butt (April 1862–April 1865).

3rd Battalion Sharpshooters Formed: Richmond, April 1863. ANV service: April–September 1863, April 1864–April 1865. Brigades assigned: Wofford's, DuBose's. Commanders: Lieutenant Colonel Nathan L. Hutchins, Jr. (April–August 1863), Majors Phillip E. Davant (August–September 1863), William E. Simmons (September 1863–August 1864).

3rd Regiment Formed: Augusta, April 1861. ANV service: June 1862–April 1865. Brigades assigned: Wright's, Sorrell's. Commanders: Colonels Ambrose R. Wright (May 1861–July 1862), Edward J. Walker (July 1862–August 1864). Notes: 1861 uniform grey with green trim in Co. A, red trim in Co. B, black trim in most other companies.

4th Regiment Formed: Augusta, April 1861. ANV service: June 1861–April 1865). Brigades assigned: Wright's, Ripley's, Doles', Cook's. Commanders: Colonels George P. Doles (May–November 1862), Philip Cook (September 1862–August 1864), William H. Willis (August 1864–April 1865). Notes: Several companies wore pre-war blue uniform in 1861, carried smooth-bore muskets; 1862 uniform grey cap and jacket, light-blue trousers. Had a regimental band.

6th Regiment Formed: Macon, April 1861. ANV service: spring 1861–May 1863, spring–winter 1864. Brigades assigned: Rains', Colquitt's. Commanders: Colonels Alfred H. Colquitt (May 1861–September 1862), John T. Lofton (Sep-

tember 1862–January 1865).
Notes: First issued M1842 muskets.
7th Regiment Formed: Atlanta,
May 1861. ANV service: June
1861–September 1863, April
1864–April 1865. Brigades
assigned: Bartow's, Anderson's.
Commanders: Colonels Lucius J.
Gartrell (May 1861–January 1862),
William T. Wilson (February–
August 1862), William W. White
(August 1862–July 1864), George
H. Carmical (July 1864–April
1865). Notes: First issued M1842
muskets.
8th Regiment Formed: Georgia,
spring 1861. ANV service: June
1861–September 1863, April
1864–April 1865). Brigades assigned: Bartow's, Anderson's. Commanders: Colonels Fancis S.
Bartow (April–July 1861), William
M. Gardner (never served with the
regiment), Lucius M. Lamar (never
served with the regiment), John R.
Towers (December 1862–April
1865). Notes: Grey uniform, July
1861.
9th Regiment Formed: Georgia,
June 1861. ANV service: late
spring 1861–September 1863,
April 1864–April 1865. Brigade
assigned: Anderson's. Commanders: Colonels Edwin R. Goulding
(June 1861–April 1862), Richard A.
Turnispeed (April–July 1862), Benjamin Beck (August 1862–March
1864), Edward F. Hoge (March
1864–April 1865). Notes: 1861
uniform was: Co. A, cadet grey
trimmed with green; Co. H, tan
trimmed with black velvet. Suffered 55 per cent losses at Gettysburg.
10th Battalion Formed: Americus,

summer 1862. ANV service: spring
1864–April 1865. Brigades
assigned: Wright's, Sorrell's. Commander: Major James D. Frederick
(June 1864–April 1865).
10th Regiment Formed: Jones-
boro, June 1861. ANV service: July
1861–September 1863, April
1864–April 1865. Brigades
assigned: Semmes', Bryan's,
Simms'. Commanders: Colonels
Alfred Cumming (June 1861–October 1862), John B. Weems (October 1862–May 1864), Willis C.
Holt (May–October 1864), Andrew
Jackson McBride (February–April
1865). Notes: Issued both M1855
and Enfield rifled muskets and
Enfield rifles. Suffered 56. 7 per
cent losses at Sharpsburg.
11th Regiment Formed: North
Georgia, late spring 1861. ANV
service: July 1861–September
1863, April 1864–April 1865.
Brigade assigned: Anderson's.
Commanders: George T. Anderson
(from formation –November
1862), Francis H. Little (November
1862–April 1865). Notes: Wore
grey uniform, at times with black
trim, from 1861.
12th Regiment Formed: Richmond, Virginia, June 1861. ANV
service: June 1861–April 1865.
Brigades assigned: E. Johnson's,
Elzey's, Trimble's, Doles', Cook's.
Commanders: Edward Johnson
(June–December 1861), Zephanier
T. Conner (December 1861–May
1862), Edward Willis (January
1863–April 1865). Notes: Initially
issued M1816 muskets.
13th Regiment Formed: Griffin,
June 1861. ANV service: spring
1862–April 1865. Brigades

assigned: Lawton's, Gordon's, Evans'. Commanders: Colonels Walton Ector (July 1861–February 1862), Marcellus Douglass (February–September 1862), James M. Smith (September 1862–December 1863), John H. Baker (December 1863–April 1865, but captured July 1863 and thereafter absent), Lieutenant Colonels Samuel W. Jones (March–May 1864), Richard Maltbie (May 1864–April 1865). Notes: Armed with Enfield rifled muskets, 1862.

14th Regiment Formed: Georgia, July 1861. ANV service: spring 1861–April 1865. Brigades assigned: Hampton's, Anderson's, Thomas's. Commanders: Colonels Arnoldus V. Brumby (July–November 1861), Felix L. Price (December 1861–October 1862), Robert W. Folsom (October 1862–May 1864), Lieutenant Colonel William Lester (June 1864–April 1865).

15th Regiment Formed: Athens, July 1861. ANV service: July 1861–September 1863, April 1864–April 1865. Brigades assigned: Toombs', Benning's. Commanders: Colonels Thomas W. Thomas (July 1861–March 1862), William MacPherson McIntosh (March–June 1862), William T. Millican (July–September 1862), Dudley McIver DuBose (January 1863–November 1864). Notes: Suffered 51 per cent losses at Gettysburg.

16th Regiment Formed: Georgia, early summer 1861. ANV service: spring 1862–September 1863, April 1864–April 1865. Brigades assigned: H. Cobb's, T. R. R. Cobb's, Wofford's, DuBose's.

Commanders: Colonels Howell Cobb (from formation–February 1862), Goode Byran (February 1862–August 1863), Henry P. Thomas (August–November 1863), Lieutenant Colonel James Gholston (November 1863–August 1864). Notes: Issued both M1855 and Enfield rifled muskets and Enfield rifles.

17th Regiment Formed: Steward County, summer 1861. ANV service: spring 1862–September 1863, April 1864–April 1865. Brigades assigned: Toombs', Benning's. Commanders: Colonels Henry L. Benning (from formation–January 1863), Wesley C. Hodges (January 1863–April 1865).

18th Battalion (Savannah Guards, Savannah Volunteer Guards) Formed: Savannah, spring 1862. ANV service: May 1864–April 1865. Brigades assigned: Barton's, C. A. Evans'. Commander: Major William S. Basinger (May 1863–April 1865).

18th Regiment Formed: Georgia, June 1861. ANV service: spring 1861–September 1863, April 1864–April 1865. Brigades assigned: Wigfall's, Hood's, T. R. R. Cobb's, Wofford's Dubose's. Commanders: Colonels William T. Wofford (June 1861–January 1863), Solon Z. Ruff (January–November 1863), Joseph Armstrong (January 1864–April 1865). Notes: 1861 issued M1842 muskets and M1841 rifles, later replaced with Enfield rifles. Suffered 57. 3 per cent losses at Sharpsburg.

19th Regiment Formed: Georgia, June 1861. ANV service: April

1862–May 1863, April 1864–April 1865. Brigades assigned: W. Hampton's, Archer's, Colquitt's. Commanders: Colonels William W. Boyd (June 1861–January 1862), Andrew Jackson Hutchins (January–August 1863), James H. Neal (August 1863–April 1865). Notes: 1861, issued M1842 muskets.

20th Regiment Formed: Columbus, May 1861. ANV service: spring 1862–September 1863, April 1864–April 1865. Brigades assigned: Early's, Toombs', Benning's. Commanders: Colonels William D. Smith (July 1861–March 1862), John B. Cumming (March 1862–1864), John Augustus Jones (May–July 1863), James D. Waddell (July 1863–April 1865).

21st Infantry Formed: Richmond, Virginia, July 1861. ANV service: July 1861–April 1865. Brigades assigned: Trimble's, Hoke's, Doles', Cook's. Commanders: Colonels John T. Mercer (September 1861–April 1864), Thomas W. Hooper (April–September 1864). Notes: Suffered 76 per cent losses at Manassas.

22nd Infantry Formed: Big Shanty, August 1861. ANV service: spring 1862–April 1865. Brigades assigned: A. R. Wright's, Sorrel's. Commanders: Colonels Robert H. Jones (August 1861–April 1863), Joseph Wasden (April–July 1863), George H. Jones (November 1863–April 1865). Notes: Issued M1855 rifles, sabre bayonets, and rifle accoutrements.

23rd Infantry Formed: Big Shanty, September 1861. ANV service: spring 1862–May 1863. Brigades assigned: Rains', Colquitt's. Commanders: Colonels Thomas Hutcherson (August 1861–June 1862), William P. Barclay (June–September 1862), Emory F. Best (November 1862–December 1863).

24th Infantry Formed: Georgia, summer 1861. ANV service: spring 1862–September 1863, April 1864–April 1865. Brigades assigned: H. Cobb's, T. R. R. Cobb's, Wofford's, DuBose's. Commanders: Colonels Robert McMillan (August 1861–January 1864), Christopher Columbus Sanders (January 1864–April 1865). Notes: Issued both M1855 and Enfield rifled muskets.

26th Infantry Formed: Brunswick, August 1861. ANV service: spring 1862–April 1865. Brigades assigned: Lawton's, Gordon's, Evans'. Commanders: Carey W. Styles (August 1861–May 1862), Edmund N. Atkinson (May 1862–April 1865). Notes: 1861–2 armed with Enfield rifled muskets.

27th Regiment Formed: Camp Stevens, summer 1861. ANV service: April 1862–May 1863, spring–winter 1864. Brigades assigned: Featherston's, Colquitt's. Commanders: Colonels Levi B. Smith (September 1861–September 1862), Charles T. Zachry (September 1862–April 1865).

28th Regiment Formed: Big Shanty, August 1861. ANV service: spring 1862–May 1863, spring–winter 1864. Brigades assigned: Featherston's, Colquitt's. Commanders: Colonels Thomas Jefferson Warthen (September

1861–July 1862), Tully Graybill (November 1862–April 1865). **31st Regiment** Formed: Cusseta, November 1861. ANV service: spring 1862–April 1865). Brigades assigned: Lawton's, J. B. Gordon's, C. A. Evans'. Commanders: Colonels Pleasant J. Phillips (November 1861–May 1862), Clement A. Evans (May 1862–May 1864), John H. Lowe (May 1864–April 1865). Notes: Initially poorly armed but refused to accept pikes. Had a regimental band. **35th Regiment** Formed: Atlanta, October 1861. ANV service: October 1861–April 1865. Brigades assigned: French's, Pettigrew's, J. R. Anderson's, E. L. Thomas's. Commanders: Colonels Edward L. Thomas (October 1861–November 1862), Bolling H. Holt (November 1862–April 1865). Notes: Initially armed with converted flintlock muskets. **38th Regiment** Formed: Decatur, summer 1861. ANV service: May 1862–April 1865. Brigades assigned: Lawton's, J. B. Gordon's, C. A. Evans'. Commanders: Colonels Augustus R. Wright (August 1861–February 1862), George Washington Lee (February–July 1862), James D. Mathews (December 1862–October 1864). Notes: Issued Enfield rifled muskets in 1861 to replace 0. 69 calibre muskets. **44th Regiment** Formed: Camp Stevens, Georgia, March 1862. ANV service: June 1862–April 1865. Brigades assigned: Ripley's, Doles', Cook's. Commanders: Colonels Robert A. Smith (March–June 1862), John B. Estes

(June 1862–May 1863), Samuel P. Lumpkin (May–September 1863), William H. Peebles (September 1863–April 1865). Notes: Suffered 65. 1 per cent losses at Mechanicsville and 45. 7 per cent losses at Malvern Hill. **45th Regiment** Formed: Georgia, winter 1861/2. ANV service: May 1862–April 1865. Brigades assigned: J. R. Anderson's, E. L. Thomas's. Commanders: Colonels Thomas Hardeman, Jr. (March–October 1862), Thomas Jefferson Simmons (October 1862–April 1865). **48th Regiment** Formed: Macon, March 1862. ANV service: spring 1862–April 1865. Brigades assigned: Ripley's, A. R. Wright's, Sorrel's. Commanders: Colonels William Gibson (March 1862–November 1864), Matthew R. Hall (November 1864–April 1865). **49th Regiment** Formed: Georgia, November 1861. ANV service: spring 1862–April 1865. Brigades assigned: J. R. Anderson's, E. L. Thomas's. Commanders: Colonels Andrew Jackson Lane (March 1862–May 1863), Samuel T. Player (June 1863–March 1864), John T. Jordon (March 1864–April 1865). **50th Regiment** Formed: Savannah, spring 1862. ANV service: August 1862–July 1863, April 1864–April 1865. Brigades assigned: Drayton's, Semmes', Brayan's, Simms'. Commanders: Colonels William R. Manning (March 1862–July 1863), Peter A. S. McGlashan (July 1863–April 1865). Notes: Issued both M1855 and Enfield rifled muskets.

51st Regiment Formed: Georgia, February 1862. ANV service: August 1862–July 1863, April 1864–April 1865. Brigades assigned: Defayton's, Semmes', Bryan's, Simms'. Commanders: Colonels William M. Slaughter (March 1862–May 1863), Edward Ball (May 1863–November 1864), James Dickey (November 1864–April 1865). Notes: Issued short Enfield rifles.

53rd Regiment Formed: Georgia, spring 1862. ANV service: spring 1862–September 1863, April 1864–April 1865. Brigades assigned: Semmes', Bryan's, Simms'. Commanders: Colonels Leonard T. Doyal (May–October 1862), James P. Simms (October 1862–December 1864). Notes: Issued both M1855 and Enfield rifled muskets.

59th Regiment Formed: Georgia, spring 1862. ANV service: spring 1863–September 1863, April 1864–April 1865. Brigade assigned: G. T. Anderson's. Commander: Colonel William A. J. 'Jack' Brown (May 1862–April 1865).

60th Regiment Formed: Savannah, spring 1862. ANV service: spring 1862–April 1865. Brigades assigned: Lawton's, J. B. Gordon's, C. A. Evans'. Commanders: Colonels William H. Stiles (July 1862–August 1864), Waters B. Jones (August 1864–April 1865).

61st Regiment Formed: Charleston, South Carolina, May 1862. ANV service: spring 1862–April 1865. Brigades assigned: Lawton's, J. B. Gordon's, C. A. Evans'. Commander: Colonel John H. Lamar (June 1862–April 1865).

64th Regiment Formed: Georgia, spring 1863. ANV service: May 1864–April 1865. Brigades assigned: Wise's, A. R. Wright's, Sorrell's. Commanders: Colonels John W. Evans (May 1863–July 1864), Walter H. Weems (July 1864–April 1865). Notes: Served as provost guards under Wise.

Cobb's Legion Formed: Georgia, spring 1861. ANV service: spring 1862–September 1863, April 1864–April 1865. Brigades assigned: H. Cobb's, T. R. R. Cobb's, Wofford's, DuBose's. Commanders: Colonels Thomas R. R. Cobb, Lieutenant Colonels Richard B. Garnett, Luther J. Glenn, G. B. Knight, Jefferson M. Lamar. Notes: Infantry battalion served apart from the Troup Light Artillery and cavalry battalion; carried both M1855 and Enfield rifled muskets.

Phillips Legion Formed: Georgia, June 1861. ANV service: autumn 1862–September 1863, April 1864–April 1865. Brigades assigned: Dayton's, T. R. R. Cobb's, Wofford's, DuBose's. Commanders: Colonel William Phillips, Lieutenant Colonels E. Sandy Barclay, Robert T. Cook, Joseph Hamilton, Seaborn Johns, Jr. Note: Infantry battalion served independently from cavalry battalion; issued both M1855 and Enfield rifled muskets.

KENTUCKY : INFANTRY

1st Regiment Formed: summer, 1861. ANV service: summer 1861–spring 1862 (disbanded). Brigades assigned: Stuart's, D. R. Jones's. Commander: Colonel

Thomas H. Taylor. Notes: Provost duty at Orange Court House, considered one of the two best dressed regiments in the army.

LOUISIANA: ARTILLERY

Donaldson Artillery Formed: Donaldsonville, 1837. ANV service: September 1861–April 1865. Assignments: Anderson's Division, Third Corps artillery. Commanders: Captains Victor Maurin (August 1861–July 1864), R. Prosper Landry (July 1864–April 1865). Notes: Armed with two 10-pound Parrotts, one 3-inch rifle, and three 6-pound smoothbores in September 1862; with two Napoleons and two 10-pound Parrotts in December 1864.

Louisiana Guard Battery Formed: Virginia, July 1861. ANV service: July 1861–April 1865. Assignments: Jackson's Corps, Wade Hampton's Division. Commanders: Captains Camille E. Girardey (July 1861–July 1862), Louis D'Aquin (July–December 1862), Charles Thompson (December 1862–June 1863), Charles A. Green (June 1863–April 1865). Notes: Armed with one 10-pound Parrott and two 3-inch rifles in September 1862 and with four Napoleons in December 1864.

Madison Light Artillery (Madison Tips) Formed: New Carthage, May 1861. ANV service: May 1861–April 1865. Assignments: Longstreet's Corps. Commanders: Captain George V. Moody, Lieutenant Jordan C. Parkinson. Notes: Armed with two 3-inch rifles and two 24-pound howitzers in September 1862; with two 12-pounders and four 24-pound howitzers in December 1864.

Washington Battalion Formed: New Orleans, 1838. ANV service: June 1861–April 1865. Assignments: Longstreet's Division. Commanders: Lieutenant Colonels James B. Walton (May 1861–February 1864), Benjamin F. Eshleman (February 1864–April 1865). Notes: 1861 uniform included dark-blue frock coat and sky–blue trousers with red trim, red kepi and white canvas gaiters; 1st Company armed with one 10-pound Parrott and three 3-inch rifles, 2nd Company with four Napoleons, 3rd Company with four Napoleons, and 4th Company with three Napoleons and a 10-pound Parrott in December 1864.

LOUISIANA: INFANTRY

1st Battalion Formed: New Orleans, February 1861. ANV service: June 1861–May 1862 (disbanded). Brigade assignment: Griffith's. Commanders: Lieutenant Colonels Charles D. Dreux (February–July 1861), N. H. Rightor (July 1861–May 1862). Notes: First dress varied by company, later grey jacket and trousers trimmed with blue, and blue vest and cap. M1855 rifled muskets issued.

1st Special Battalion Formed: Camp Walker, New Orleans, June 1861. ANV service: June 1861–August 1862 (disbanded). Brigade assigned: First Louisiana. Commander: Major Chatham R. Wheat (June 1861–July 1862). Notes: Zouave dress with striped trousers, red shirt, dark-blue jackets trimmed with red, red caps and straw hats, white gaiters. M1841 rifles issued.

1st Zouave Battalion Formed: Pensacola, Florida, April 1861. ANV service: June 1861–December 1864 (disbanded). Brigades assigned: Pryor's, Starke's. Commanders: Lieutenant Colonel George A. G. Coppens (April 1861–September 1862), Marie A. Coppens (September 1862–November 1864), Major Fulgence De Bordenave (November–December 1864). Notes: Zouave uniform with dark-blue jacket trimmed with gold cords or yellow tape, red full trousers, blue sash, red fez, russet leather greaves, white canvas gaiters. Converted flintlock muskets issued.

1st Regiment Formed: New Orleans, April 1861. ANV service: May 1862–April 1865. Brigade assignment: 2nd Louisiana. Commanders: Colonels Albert G. Blanchard (April–September 1861), William G. Vincent (September 1861–April 1862), Samuel R. Harrison (April–June 1862), William R. Shievers (June 1862), Lieutenant Colonel James Nelligan (July 1863–April 1865). Notes: 1861 companies wore different volunteer uniforms.

2nd Regiment Formed: Camp Walker, New Orleans, May 1861. ANV service: spring 1862–April 1865. Brigade assignments: Cobb's, 2nd Louisiana. Commanders: Colonels Lewis G. DeRussy (May–July 1861), William M. Levy (July 1861–April 1862), Isiah T.

Norwood (April–July 1862), Jesse M. Williams (July 1862–May 1864), Ross E. Burke (May 1864–April 1865). Notes: 1861 companies wore different volunteer uniforms until state clothing issued about September 1861.

3rd Battalion Formed: Camp Pulaski, June 1861. ANV service: May–August 1862 (merged into 15th Regiment). Brigade assigned: Anderson's. Commanders: Lieutenant Colonels Charles M. Bradford (June 1861–July 1862), Edmund Pendleton (June–August 1862).

5th Regiment Formed: Camp Moore, Louisiana, June 1861. ANV service: spring 1862–April 1865. Brigades assigned: McLaws', Semmes', Hays', York's. Commanders: Colonels Theodore G. Hunt (June 1861–July 1862), Henry Forno (July 1862–April 1864), Lieutenant Colonel Bruce Menger (April–May 1864), Major Alexander Hart (May 1864–March 1865). Notes: Had a *vivandière* who wore a black alpaca uniform in May 1861; had brass band.

6th Regiment Formed: Camp Moore, June 1861. ANV service: spring 1861–April 1865. Brigade assigned: First Louisiana. Commanders: Colonels Isaac G. Seymour (June 1861–July 1862), Henry B. Strong (July September 1862), Nathaniel C. Offutt (September–November 1862), William Monaghan (November 1862–August 1864), Lieutenant Colonel Joseph Hanlon (August 1864–April 1865).

7th Battalion (St. Paul Foot Rifles, *Chasseurs–à-pied*, Washington Battalion) Formed: Manassas, Virginia, October 1861. ANV service: October 1861–August 1862 (merged into 15th Regiment). Brigade assigned: Attached to 1st Zouave Battalion May 1861. Commanders: Majors Henry St. Paul, McGavock Goodwyn (acting).

7th Regiment Formed: Camp Moore, June 1861. ANV service: July 1861–April 1865. Brigade assigned: First Louisiana. Commanders: Colonels Harry T. Hays (June 1861–July 1862), Davidson B. Penn (July 1862–April 1865).

8th Regiment Formed: Camp Moore, June 1861. ANV service: July 1861–April 1865. Brigade assigned: First Louisiana. Commanders: Colonels Henry B. Kelly (June 1861–April 1863), Trevanian D. Lewis (April–July 1863), Alcibiades DeBlanc (July 1863–August 1864). Notes: 1861 uniform included brown jacket and trousers, grey caps and drab felt hats. Issued with Enfield rifled muskets and British–type accoutrements.

9th Regiment Formed: Camp Moore, July 1861. ANV service: July 1861–April 1865. Brigade assigned: First Louisiana. Commanders: Colonels Richard Taylor (July–October 1861), Edward G. Randolph (October 1861–April 1862), Leroy A. Stafford (April 1862–October 1863), William R. Peck (October 1863–February 1865), Lieutenant Colonel John J. Hodges (February–April 1865). Notes: Had a band.

10th Regiment Formed: Camp Moore, July 1861. ANV service: summer 1861–April 1865. Brigades assigned: McLaws', Semmes', Starke's, Nicholl's, Iverson's, Stafford's, York's. Commanders: Colonels Mandeville Marigny (July 1861–July 1863), Eugene Waggaman (July 1863–April 1865).

14th Regiment (Sulakowski's 1st Regiment, Polish Brigade) Formed: Camp Pulaski, Louisiana, August 1861. ANV service: September 1861–April 1865. Brigades assigned: Pryor's, Hay's, Starke's, Nicholl's, Iverson's, Stafford's, York's. Commanders: Colonels Valery Sulakowski (August 1861–February 1862), Richard W. Jones (February–August 1862), Zebulon York (August 1862–May 1864), David Zable (May 1864–April 1865).

15th Regiment Formed: Richmond, Virginia, July 1862. ANV service: September 1862–April 1865. Brigades assigned: First, Second Louisiana. Commanders: Colonel Edmund Pendleton (July 1862–April 1865).

MARYLAND: ARTILLERY

1st Company (Maryland Flying Battery) Formed: Richmond, July 1861. ANV service: July 1861–April 1865. Assigned: R. S. Andrews', J. W. Latimer's, C. M. Braxton's Battalions, The Maryland Line, D. G. McIntosh's Battalion. Commanders: Captains Richard Snowden Andrews (July 1861–June 1862), William F. Dement (June 1862–April 1865). Notes: Armed with four 6-pound smoothbores in September 1862; with four Napoleons in December 1864.

2nd Company (Baltimore Light Artillery) Formed: Richmond, Sep-

tember 1861. ANV service: September 1861–April 1865. Assigned: Jackson's Command, The Maryland Line. P. M. B. Young's and B. T. Johnson's Brigades. Commanders: Captains John B. Brockenborough, William H. Griffin. Notes: Armed with one 3-inch rifle, one 12-pound howitzer and two Blakely guns in September 1862.
4th Company (Chesapeake Battery) Formed: Richmond, spring 1861. ANV service: spring 1861–April 1865. Assigned: J. W. Latimer's, R. S. Andrews', C. M. Braxton's Battalions. Commanders: Captains William D. Brown, Walter S. Chew. Notes: Presented with four 10-pound Parrotts for distinguished service, August 1862, but had two 10-pound Parrotts and one 3-inch rifle that September; December 1864 had one 10-pound Parrott and two 3-inch rifles.

MARYLAND: CAVALRY

1st Regiment Formed: Winchester, Virginia, May 1862. ANV service: May 1862–April 1865. Brigades assigned: W. E. Jones's, F. Lee's, Lomax's, The Maryland Line. Commanders: Lieutenant Colonels Ridgely Brown (November 1862–June 1864), Gustavus W. Dorsey (June 1864–April 1865).
2nd Battalion (Partisan Rangers) Formed: Staunton, Virginia, September 1863. ANV service: September 1863–late 1864. Assigned: The Maryland Line (never actually joined). Commander: Lieutenant Colonel Harry W. Gilmor. Notes: After leaving the Valley, served with McNeill's Rangers in West Virginia.

MARYLAND: INFANTRY

1st Regiment Formed: Winchester, Virginia, summer 1861. ANV service: summer 1861–August 1862 (disbanded). Brigade assigned: Elzey's. Commanders: Colonels Arnold Elzey (May–July 1861), George H. Steuart (July 1861–March 1862), Bradley T. Johnson (March–June 1862), Lieutenant Colonel Edward R. Dorsey (June–August 1862). Notes: Initially armed with Hall carbines, converted flintlock muskets, M1842 muskets, M1841 rifles without bayonets.
2nd Battalion Formed: Winchester, Virginia, September 1862. ANV service: September 1862–April 1865. Brigades assigned: Steuart's, The Maryland Line, H. H. Walker's, McComb's. Commander: Lieutenant Colonel James R. Herbert (October 1862–April 1865). Notes: Both field officers taken prisoner at Gettysburg and senior captains commanded for much of the rest of the war; armed with captured US Army longarms, including Enfield and M1855 rifled muskets. Suffered 48 per cent losses at Gettysburg.

MISSISSIPPI: ARTILLERY
Confederate Guards Light Artillery Formed: Pontotoc, summer 1861. ANV service: June 1864– April 1865. Assigned: J. C. Coit's Battalion. Commander: Captain William D. Bradford. Notes: In the defences of Richmond and Petersburg; not present at Appomattox.
Madison Light Artillery Formed: Canton, spring 1863. ANV service:

summer 1863–April 1865. Assigned: W. T. Poague's Battalion. Commanders: Thomas J. Richards, George Ward, John W. Yeargain, Thomas J. Kirkpatrick. Notes: Armed with four Napoleons in December 1864.

MISSISSIPPI: CAVALRY

2nd Battalion Formed: Manassas, Virginia, October 1861. ANV service: October 1861–January 1862 (merged into Jeff Davis Cavalry Legion). Commander: Major William T. Martin.

Jeff Davis Cavalry Legion Formed: Richmond, January 1862. ANV service: January 1862–summer 1864 (surrendered with Army of Tennessee). Commander: Colonel William T. Martin.

INFANTRY

2nd Battalion Formed: Jackson, summer 1861. ANV service: summer 1861–November 1862 (enlarged to form 48th Regiment). Brigades assigned: Garland's, Featherston's. Commanders: Lieutenant Colonels John G. Taylor (November 1861–June 1862), William S. Wilson (June–November 1862), Thomas B. Manlove (November 1862).

2nd Regiment Formed: Corinth, April 1861. ANV service: summer 1861–April 1865. Brigades assigned: Whiting's, Law's, J. R. Davis'. Commanders: Colonels William C. Falkner (May 1861–April 1862), John M. Stone (April 1862–April 1865). Initially armed with converted flintlock muskets.

11th Regiment Formed: Corinth, May 1861. ANV service: June

1861–April 1865. Brigades assigned: Bee's, Whiting's, Law's, J. R. Davis'. Commanders: Colonels William H. Moore (May 1861–April 1862), Philip F. Liddell (April–September 1862), Francis Marion Green (September 1862–May 1864), Lieutenant Colonel George W. Shannon (May–December 1864), Colonel Reuben 0. Reynolds (December 1864–April 1865). Notes: Each company initially differently uniformed; arms included 'US long range rifles', converted percussion rifles, percussion rifles and apparently some Colt revolving rifles.

12th Regiment Formed: Corinth, May 1861. ANV service: spring 1861–April 1865. Brigades assigned: Rodes', Featherston's, Posey's, Harris'. Commanders: Colonels Richard Griffith (May–November 1861), Henry Hughes (November 1861–October 1862), William H. Taylor (April 1862–March 1864, but left mid 1863), Merrie B. Harris (mid 1863–June 1864). Notes: Initially some men had percussion rifles and others had M1842 muskets; had a regimental band.

13th Regiment Formed: Corinth, May 1861. ANV service: spring 1861–April 1865. Brigades assigned: Griffith's, Barksdale's, Humphreys'. Commanders: Colonels William Barksdale (May 1861–August 1862), James W. Carter (August 1862–July 1863), Kennon McElroy (July–November 1863), Major George L. Donald (November 1863–April 1865). Notes: Initially armed with M1842 muskets, issued 0. 54 calibre rifles in 1862, eventually all had Enfield rifles with sword bayonets.

16th Regiment Formed: Corinth, June 1861. ANV service: summer 1861–April 1865. Brigades assigned: Trimble's, Featherston's, Posey's, Harris'. Commanders: Colonels Carnot Posey (June 1861–November 1862), Samuel E. Baker (December 1862–May 1864), Edward C. Councell (May–August 1864), Lieutenant Colonel Seneca M. Bain (October 1864–April 1865). Notes: Companies initially differently dressed; had a regimental band. Suffered 63. 1 per cent losses at Sharpsburg.

17th Regiment Formed: Corinth, June 1861. ANV service: summer 1861–April 1865. Brigades assigned: D. R. Jones's, H. Cobb's, Griffith's, Barksdale's, Humphreys'. Commanders: Colonels Winfield Scott Featherston (summer 1861–March 1862), William D. Holder (April 1862–February 1864), John Calvin Fizer (February–June 1864). Notes: Issued converted flintlocks initially, then both Enfield and Austrian rifled muskets in 1862, eventually all had Enfield rifles with sword bayonets.

18th Regiment Formed: Corinth, June 1861. ANV service: June 1861–April 1865. Brigades assigned: Griffith's, Barksdale's, Humphreys'. Commanders: Colonel Erasmus R. Burt (June–October 1861), Lieutenant Colonels Walter G. Kearney (November 1861–April 1862), William H. Luse (April–November 1862), Colonel Thomas M. Griffin (November 1862–November

1864), Major George B. Gerald (November 1864–April 1865). Notes: Armed with converted flintlock muskets and some M1841 rifles in 1862, eventually all had Enfield rifles with sword bayonets. Suffered 44. 6 per cent losses at Sharpsburg.

19th Regiment Formed: Oxford, May 1861. ANV service: June 1861–April 1865. Brigades assigned: Wilcox's, Featherston's, Posey's, Harris'. Commanders: Colonels Christopher H. Mott (June 1861–May 1862), Lucius Quintus Cincinnatus Lamar (May–November 1862), John B. Mullins (November 1862–May 1864, but absent with wounds from Seven Days on), Nathaniel H. Harris (1862–3–January 1864), Thomas J. Hardin (January–May 1864), Richard W. Phipps (May 1864–April 1865).

21st Regiment Formed: Manassas, Virginia, October 1861. ANV service: October 1861–September 1863, April 1864–April 1865). Brigades assigned: Griffith's, Barksdale's, Humphreys'. Commanders: Colonels Benjamin G. Humphreys (November 1861–August 1863), William L. Brandon (August 1863–June 1864), Daniel Moody (October 1863–April 1865). Notes: Two companies in 1861 had Enfield rifles with sword bayonets, others M1841 rifles; eventually all had M1855 rifled muskets, some of which were Richmond copies of the US Army weapon, or an Enfield rifle with a sword bayonet.

26th Regiment Formed: Iuka, summer 1861. ANV service: February 1864–April 1865. Brigade assigned: J. R. Davis'. Commander: Colonel Arthur E. Reynolds (September 1861–April 1865).

42nd Regiment Formed: Oxford, May 1862. ANV service: June 1862–April 1865. Brigade assigned: J. R. Davis'. Commanders: Colonels Hugh R. Miller (May 1862–July 1863), William A. Feeny (December 1863–May 1864), Andrew M. Nelson (May 1864–April 1865).

48th Regiment Formed: Fredericksburg, Virginia, November 1862. ANV service: November 1862–April 1865. Brigades assigned: Featherston's, Posey's, Harris'. Commander: Colonel Joseph M. Jayne (November 1862–April 1865).

NORTH CAROLINA: ARTILLERY

1st Regiment, Co. A (Ellis Light Artillery, Ellis Flying Artillery) Formed: Raleigh, April 1861. ANV service: March 1862–April 1865. Assigned: Semmes', Griffith's Brigades, Magruder's Division, McLaws' Division, Cabell's Battalion. Commanders: Captains Stephen D. Ramseur (April 1861), Bernard B. Guion, Basil C. Manly. Notes: Armed with two 12-pound howitzers and three 6-pounder smoothbores on formation; one 3-inch rifle, two 12-pound howitzers, and three 6-pounder smoothbores in September 1862; two Napoleons and two 3-inch rifles in December 1864.

1st Regiment, Co. C (Charlotte Artillery) Formed: Charlotte, May 1861. ANV service: April–June 1862, May 1863–April 1865.

Assigned: Branch's Brigade (1862), Pickett's Division, Poague's Battalion. Commanders: Captains Thomas H. Breme, Joseph Graham, Arthur B. Williams. Notes: Armed with four 12-pound howitzers in June 1862 and with two Napoleons and one 3-inch rifle in December 1864; also manned a Whitworth gun, May–September 1864.

1st Regiment, Co. D (Rowan Artillery) Formed: Weldon, May 1861. ANV service: July 1861–April 1865. Assigned: Whiting's, Law's Brigades; Whiting's/Hood's Divisional artillery battalion, Haskell's Battalion. Commanders: Captains James Reilly, John A. Ramsay. Notes: Armed with two 10-pound Parrotts and two 24-pound Dahlgren siege guns in July 1861; with the same guns plus two 3-inch rifles in September 1862; and with one 12-pound Whitworth and two 8-pound Armstrongs in December 1864.

1st Regiment, Co. E (Wilmington Light Artillery) Formed: Camp Boylan, August 1861. ANV service: October 1864–April 1865. Assigned: Moseley's Battalion. Commander: Captain John 0. Miller. Notes: Armed with four 10-pound Parrotts in December 1864.

3rd Light Artillery Battalion, Co. A (Northampton Artillery) Formed: Camp Mangum, February 1862. ANV service: September–December 1862. Assigned: Moore's Battalion, Artillery Reserve. Commander: Captain Andrew J. Ellis. Notes: Armed with one 3-inch rifle, one

Napoleon, and two 6-pound smooth-bores.

3rd Light Artillery Battalion, Co. B (Edenton Bell Artillery) Formed: Camp Mangun, March 1862. ANV service: September–December 1862. Assigned: Moore's Battalion. Commander: Captain William Badham, Jr. Notes: Armed with two 6-pound smoothbores and two 12-pound howitzers.

3rd Regiment, Co. G Formed: Edgecombe County, spring 1862. ANV service: August–October 1862 (disbanded 8 October). Assigned: D. H. Hill's Divisional artillery battalion. Commander: Captain Whitnel P. Lloyd. Notes: Armed with two 6-pound smoothbores and two 12-pound howitzers.

3rd Regiment, Co. H (Branch Artillery, 13th Light Artillery Battalion, Co. F) Formed: New Bern, January 1862, as Branch Artillery; redesignated Co. H 9 September 1863; redesignated Co. F, 13th Light Artillery Battalion 4 November 1863. ANV service: May 1862–April 1865. Assigned: Branch's Brigade, A. P. Hill's Divisional artillery battalion, Hood's Divisional artillery battalion, Hentyls/Haskell's Battalion. Commanders: Captains Alexander C. Latham, John R. Potts, Henry G. Flanner. Notes: Armed with two Napoleons and two 6-pound smoothbores in September 1862; with four Napoleons in December 1864.

13th Light Artillery Battalion, Co. C. Formed: by redesignation of 2nd Regiment, Co. C, 4 November 1863. ANV service: October 1864–April 1865 (1st Section). Assigned: Moseley's, Blount's Battalions. Commander: Captain James D. Cumming. Notes: Section armed with two Napoleons.

NORTH CAROLINA: CAVALRY

1st Regiment (9th Regiment State Troops) Formed: Camp Beauregard, Ridgeway, August 1861. ANV service: October 1861–March 1862, August 1862–April 1865. Brigades assigned: Ransom's, Hampton's, Baker's, Gordon's, Barringer's. Commanders: Colonels Robert Ransom, Jr. (August 1861–March 1862), Laurence S. Baker (March 1862–July 1863), James B. Gordon (July–September 1863), Thomas Ruffin (September–October 1863), William H. Cheek (October 1863–April 1865). Notes: 1861 armed with sabres, rifles, carbines and percussion pistols.

2nd Regiment (19th Regiment State Troops) Formed: Camp Clark, Kittrell's Springs, June 1861. ANV service: November 1862–April 1865. Brigades assigned: W. H. F. Lee's, Baker's, Gordon's, Barringer's. Commanders: Colonels Samuel B. Spruill (June 1861–March 1862), Matthew L. Davis, Jr. (April 1862), Solomon Williams (June 1862–June 1863), William G. Robinson (September 1863–May 1864 but actually not with regiment), William P. Roberts (June 1864–February 1865), Clinton M. Andrews (February 1864), Lieutenant Colonel James L. Gaines (March–April 1865). Notes: Issued weapons included M1842 and Enfield rifled muskets, Enfield rifles with sabre bayonets, 0. 54 calibre Austrian rifles, Spencer rifles and Burnside, Sharps and Smith carbines.

3rd Regiment (41st Regiment State Troops) Formed: In the field, September 1862–August 1863. ANV service: May 1864–April 1865. Brigade assigned: Barringer's. Commanders: Colonel John A. Baker (September 1862–June 1864), Lieutenant Colonel Roger Moore (August 1864–April 1865). Notes: Armed with a variety of Colt Army and Navy revolvers, rifles and muskets.

4th Regiment (59th Regiment State Troops) Formed: Garysburg, August 1862. ANV service: May 1863–April 1864, June 1864–April 1865. Brigades assigned: Robertson's, Baker's, Gordon's, Dearing's, Roberts'. Commanders: Colonel Dennis D. Ferebee (August 1862–March 1865), Major James B. Mayo (March–April 1865).

5th Regiment (63rd Regiment State Troops) Formed: Camp Long, Garysburg, September 1862. ANV service: May 1863–April 1865. Brigades assigned: Robertson's, Baker's, Gordon's, Barringer's. Commanders: Colonels Peter G. Evans (October 1862–June 1863), Lieutenant Colonel Stephen B. Evans (June 1863–November 1864), Colonel James H. McNeil (November 1864–March 1865).

16th Battalion Formed: In the field, July 1864. ANV service: July 1864–April 1865. Brigades assigned: Dearing's, Roberts'. Commanders: Lieutenant Colonels John T. Kennedy (never present with battalion), Thomas B. Edelin (December 1864–March 1865).

NORTH CAROLINA: INFANTRY

1st Battalion Sharpshooters Formed: Gordonsville, Virginia, April 1862. ANV service: April 1862–January 1864, December 1864–April 1865. Brigades assigned: Trimble's, Hoke's, Johnston's. Commander: Major Rufus W. Wharton.

1st Regiment Formed: Warrenton, June 1861. ANV service: August 1861–April 1865. Brigades assigned: Walker's, Ripley's, Doles', Taliaferro's, Colston's, Steuart's, Ramseur's, Cox's. Commanders: Colonels Montfort S. Stokes (May 1861–June 1862), John McDowell (July–December 1862), Lieutenant Colonel Matt W. Ransom (December 1862–June 1863), Major Jarrette N. Harrell (June–December 1863), Colonel Hamilton A. Brown (December 1863–March 1865). Notes: First armed with M1842 muskets, later issued better weapons, Co. B receiving Enfield rifles with sabre bayonets.

2nd Battalion Formed: Richmond, Virginia, November 1861. ANV service: May 1863–April 1865. Brigades assigned: Daniel's, Grimes'. Commanders: Lieutenant Colonels Wharton H. Green, (December 1861–September 1862), Charles E. Shober (October 1862–June 1863) Hezekiah L. Andrews (June–July 1863), Major James J. Iredell (transferred from 53rd Regiment, August 1863–May 1864). Notes: First armed with shotguns and converted flintlock muskets.

2nd Regiment Formed: Camp Advance, Garysburg, June 1861. ANV service: July 1861–March 1862, June 1862–April 1865. Brigades assigned: Walker's, G. B. Anderson's, Ramseur's, Cox's. Commanders: Colonels Charles C. Tew (June 1861–September 1862), William P. Bynum (September 1862–March 1863), William R. Cox (March 1863–May 1864), John P. Cobb (August–September 1864), Lieutenant Colonel James T. Scales (September 1864–April 1865).

3rd Regiment Formed: Garysburg, May 1861. ANV sevice: July 1861–April 1865. Brigades assigned: Walker's, Ramseur's, Cox's. Commanders: Colonels W. Gaston Meares (May 1861–July 1862), William L. DeRosset (July 1862–October 1863), Stephen Decatur Thruston (October 1863–April 1865). Notes: First armed with M1842 muskets. Suffered 50 per cent losses at Gettysburg.

4th Regiment Formed: Camp Hill, Garysburg, May 1861. ANV service: August 1861–April 1865. Brigades assigned: Manassas Garrison, G. B. Anderson's, Winder's, Featherston's, Ramseur's, Cox's. Commanders: Colonels George B. Anderson (May 1861–June 1862), Byron Grimes (June 1862–March 1864), James H. Wood (March–July 1864), Edwin A. Osborne (July 1864–April 1865). Notes: First armed with M1842 muskets, later issued M1855 rifled muskets and one Whitworth rifle

to its best shot. Band before the war was the Salisbury Brass Band. Suffered 54. 4 per cent losses at Seven Pines.

5th Regiment Formed: Camp Winslow, June 1861. ANV service: July 1861–April 1865. Brigades assigned: Longstreet's, Early's, Garland's, Iverson's, Johnston's. Commanders: Colonel Duncan K. McRae (July 1861–November 1862), Lieutenant Colonel Peter J. Sinclair (November–December 1862), Major William J. Hill (December 1862–January 1863), Colonels Thomas M. Garrett (January 1863–May 1864), John W. Lea (May 1864–April 1865). Notes: First armed with M1842 muskets.

6th Battalion Formed: Richmond, early 1862. ANV service: June–July 1862 (disbanded). Assigned: Department of North Carolina (but was at the Seven Days and Malvern Cliff). Commander: Lieutenant Colonel John T. P. C. Cohoon. Notes: After disbanding, North Carolinians went into the 60th Infantry Regiment.

6th Regiment Formed: Charlotte, May 1861. ANV service; July 1861–April 1865. Brigades assigned: Bee's, Whiting's, Law's, Hoke's, Lewis', Godwin's. Commanders: Colonels Charles F. Fisher (May–July 1861), William D. Pender, Robert Fulton Webb (July 1861–November 1863 as needed), Lieutenant Colonel Samuel McD Tate (November 1863–April 1865). Notes: First issued weapons included M1842 muskets (four companies) and M1822 muskets (six companies), later received a variety of weapons including M1841 and Sharps rifles and Enfield rifled muskets.

7th Regiment Formed: Camp Mason, Alamance County, August 1861. ANV service: May 1862–February 1865. Brigades assigned: Branch's, Lane's. Commanders: Colonels Ruben P. Campbell (August 1861–June 1862), Edward G. Haywood (June 1862–November 1864), William L. Davidson (November 1864–April 1865). Notes: First armed with M1842 muskets (eight companies) and rifles (two companies). Suffered 56. 2 per cent casualties at the Seven Days.

8th Regiment Formed: Camp Macon, Warrenton, September 1861. ANV service: October–December 1864. Brigade assigned: Clingman's. Commander: Lieutenant Colonel Rufus A. Barrier.

11th Regiment Formed: Camp Mangum, Raleigh, March 1862. ANV service: June 1863–April 1865. Brigades assigned: Pettigrew's, Kirkland's, MacRae's. Commander: Colonel William J. Martin (June 1863–April 1865). Notes: Flag burned by unit members 9 April 1865.

12th Regiment Formed: Garysburg, May 1861, as 2nd Regiment Volunteers. ANV service: April 1862–April 1865. Brigades assigned: Mahone's, Branch's, Garland's, Iverson's, Johnston's. Commanders: Colonels Solomon Williams (May 1861–June 1862), Benjamin H. Wade (June–December 1862), Lieutenant Colonel Robert D. Johnston (December 1862–May 1863), Colonel Henry

E. Coleman (May 1863–April 1865). Notes: At first armed with M1842 muskets (eight companies), flintlocks (one company) and rifles (one company).

13th Regiment Formed: Garysburg, May 1861, as 3rd Regiment Volunteers. ANV service: April 1862–April 1865. Brigades assigned: Colston's, Garland's, Pender's, Scales'. Commanders: Colonels William Dorsey Pender (May 1861–June 1862), Alfred M. Scales (June 1862–June 1863), Joseph H. Hyman (June 1863–April 1865). Notes: First armed with M1842 muskets (nine companies) and M1841 rifles (one company).

14th Regiment Formed: Garysburg, June 1861 as 4th Regiment Volunteers. ANV service: April 1862–April 1865. Brigades assigned: Colston's, G. B. Anderson's, Ramseur's, Cox's. Commanders: Colonels Junius Daniel (June 1861–April 1862), Philetus W. Roberts (April–July 1862), Risden T. Bennett (July 1862–September 1864), Lieutenant Colonel William A. Johnston (September 1864–April 1865). Notes: First armed with M1842 muskets (nine companies) and rifles (one company).

15th Regiment Formed: Garysburg, June 1861, as 5th Regiment Volunteers. ANV service: April 1862–January 1863, September 1863–April 1865. Brigades assigned: Cobb's, Cooke's. Commanders: Colonels Robert M. McKinney (June 1861–April 1862), Henry A. Dowd (April 1862–February 1863), William MacRae (February 1863–June 1864), William H. Yarborough (June 1864–April 1865). Notes: First armed with M1822 muskets (eight companies) and M1842 muskets (two companies), later issued both M1855 and Enfield rifled muskets.

16th Regiment Formed: Raleigh, June 1861, as 6th Regiment Volunteers. ANV service: November 1861–April 1865. Brigades assigned: Hampton's, Pender's, Scales'. Commanders: Colonels Stephen Lee (June 1861–February 1862), Champion T. N. Davis (April–June 1862), John Smith McElroy (June 1862–December 1863), William A. Stowe (December 1863–April 1865). Notes: First armed with M1822 muskets (six companies), M1842 muskets (two companies) and rifles (two companies).

17th Regiment (2nd formation) Formed: Camp Mangum, May 1862. ANV service: October–December 1864. Brigade assigned: Kirkland's. Commander: Colonel William F. Martin.

18th Regiment Formed: Camp Wyatt, Washington, June 1861, as 8th Regiment Volunteers. ANV service: May 1862–April 1865. Brigades assigned: Branch's, Lane's. Commanders: Colonels James D. Radcliffe (July 1861–April 1862), Robert H. Cowan (April–November 1862), James T. Purdie (November 1862–May 1863), John D. Barry (June 1863–August 1864), Lieutenant Colonel John W. McGill (August 1864–April 1865). Notes: First armed with M1842 muskets (eight companies) and M1822 muskets

(two companies), but issued Enfield rifled muskets in September 1862. Suffered 56. 5 per cent casualties at Seven Days.

20th Regiment Formed: Fort Johnston, Southport, June 1861, as 10th Regiment Volunteers. ANV service: June 1862–April 1865. Brigades assigned: Garland's, Iverson's, Johnston's. Commanders: Colonels Alfred Iverson, Jr. (June 1861–November 1862), Lieutenant Colonel Nelson Slough (November 1862–February 1863), Colonel Thomas F. Toon (February 1863–May 1864; August 1864–March 1865). Notes: First armed with M1822 muskets (two companies), M1842 muskets (seven companies) and rifles (one company).

21st Regiment Formed: Danville, Virginia, June 1861, as 11th Regiment Volunteers. ANV service: July 1861–January 1864, May 1864–April 1865. Brigades assigned: Bonham's, Early's, Crittenden's, Trimble's, Hoke's, Lewis', Godwin's. Commanders: Colonels William W. Kirkland (June 1861–August 1863), Robert F. Hoke (commanded during recovery from wounds of Colonel Kirkland at First Winchester), Majors Alexander Miller (March–July 1863), William J. Prohl (August 1863–October 1864), James F. Beall (October 1864–April 1865). Notes: First armed with M1822 muskets (nine companies) and M1842 muskets (one company). Had a band.

22nd Regiment Formed: Raleigh, July 1861, as 12th Regiment Volunteers. ANV service: June

1862–April 1865. Brigades assigned: Pender's, Scales'. Commanders: Colonels James Johnston Pettigrew (July 1861–February 1862), James Conner (June 1862–September 1863), Thomas S. Galloway, Jr. (September 1863–April 1865). Notes: First armed with M1822 muskets (eight companies) and M1842 muskets (two companies); by May 1862 three companies had Enfields, two companies had M1841 rifles.

23rd Regiment Formed: Garysburg, July 1861, as 13th Regiment Volunteers. ANV service: July 1861–April 1865. Brigades assigned: Early's, Garland's, Iverson's, Johnston's. Commanders: Colonels John F. Hoke (July 1861–April 1862), Daniel H. Christie (April 1862–July 1863), Charles C. Blacknall (July 1863–September 1864). Notes: First armed M1822 muskets (nine companies) and M1842 muskets (two companies) until re-armed with captured rifled muskets in 1862.

24th Regiment Formed: July 1861, as 14th Regiment Volunteers. ANV service: September 1862–January 1863, October 1864–April 1865. Brigade assigned: Ransom's. Commanders: Colonel William J. Clarke (July 1861–February 1865), Lieutenant Colonel John L. Harris (February–April 1865). Notes: First armed with M1822 muskets (six companies) and M1842 muskets (four companies).

25th Regiment Formed: Camp Clingman, Asheville, August 1861. ANV service: September 1862–Jan-

uary 1863, October 1864–April 1865. Brigade assiged: Ransom's. Commanders: Colonels Thomas L. Clingman (August 1861–May 1862), Henry M. Rutledge (May 1862–April 1865). Notes: Had a band.

26th Regiment Formed: Crabtree, August 1861. ANV service: June 1863–April 1865. Brigades assigned: Pettigrew's, Kirkland's, MacRae's. Commanders: Colonels Henry K. Burgwyn, Jr. (August 1862–July 1863), John R. Lane (July 1863–April 1865). Notes: Had a band. Suffered 71. 7 per cent losses at Gettysburg.

27th Regiment Formed: In the field, September 1861. ANV service: September 1862–January 1863, September 1863–April 1865. Brigades assigned: Walker's, Cooke's. Commanders: Colonels John Rogers Cooke (April 1862–November 1862), Richard W. Singletary (November–December 1862), John A. Gilmer, Jr. (December 1862–January 1865), George F. Whitfield (January–April 1865, but had acted as commander some months earlier). Notes: Armed in October 1862 with a mix of muskets, rifled muskets, M1855 rifles, M1841 rifles and Enfield rifled muskets; had a band, described as being the best in the division. Suffered 61. 2 per cent losses at Sharpsburg.

28th Regiment (The Bethel Regiment) Formed: Camp Fisher, High Point, September 1861. ANV service: May 1862–April 1865. Brigades assigned: Branch's, Lane's. Commanders: Colonels James H. Lane (September

1861–November 1862), Samuel D. Lowe (November 1862–July 1864), William H. A. Speer (July 1864–April 1865). Notes: Captured rifled muskets replaced original converted flintlock muskets.

30th Regiment Formed: Camp Mangum, September 1861. ANV service: June 1862–April 1865. Brigades assigned: G. B. Anderson's, Ramseur's, Cox's. Commander: Colonel Francis Marion Parker.

31st Regiment Formed: Hill's Point, September 1861. ANV service: October December 1864. Brigade assigned: Clingman's. Commander: Colonel John V. Jordan.

32nd Regiment Formed: In the field, March 1862. ANV service: May 1863–April 1865. Brigades assigned: Daniel's, Grimes'. Commanders: Colonels Edmund C. Brabble (March 1862–May 1864), David G. Cowand (May 1865–April 1865). Notes: Carried a 2nd National Flag from June 1863.

33rd Regiment Formed: Raleigh, September 1861. ANV service: May 1862–April 1865. Brigades assigned: Branch's, Lane's. Commanders: Colonels Clarke M. Avery (January 1862–May 1864), Robert V. Cowan (June 1864–April 1865). Notes: Suffered 41. 4 per cent losses at Chancellorsville.

34th Regiment Formed: In the field, October 1861. ANV service: June 1862–April 1865. Brigades assigned: Pender's, Scales'. Commanders: Colonels Collett Leventhrope (October 1861–July 1863), Richard H. Riddick (April–September 1862), William L. J. Lowrance

(February 1863–April 1865).

35th Regiment Formed: Camp Mangum, November 1861. ANV service: August 1862–January 1863, October 1864–April 1865. Brigade assigned: Ransom's. Commanders: Colonels Matt W. Ransom (April 1862–June 1863), James T. Johnson (June 1863–April 1865).

37th Regiment Formed: High Point, November 1861. ANV service: May 1862–April 1865. Brigades assigned: Branch's, Lane's. Commanders: Colonels Charles C. Lee (November 1861–June 1862), William M. Barbour (July 1862–September 1864), Lieutenant Colonel William G. Morris (September 1864–April 1865).

38th Regiment Formed: Camp Mangum, January 1862. ANV service: June 1862–April 1865. Brigades assigned: Pender's, Scales'. Commanders: Colonels William J. Hoke (January 1862–June 1864), John Ashford (June 1864–April 1865). Notes: Issued M1855 rifled muskets and 0. 69 calibre muskets.

42nd Regiment Formed: Salisbury, April 1862. ANV service: October–December 1864. Brigade assigned: Kirkland's. Commander: Lieutenant Colonel John E. Brown.

43rd Regiment Formed: Camp Mangum, March 1862. ANV service: May 1863–April 1865. Brigades assigned: Daniel's, Grimes'. Commanders: Colonel Thomas S. Kenan (March 1862–July 1863), Lieutenant Colonel William G. Lewis (July

1863–May 1864), Major Walter J. Boggan (May–December 1864).

44th Regiment Formed: Camp Mangum, March 1862, ANV service: July 1863–April 1865. Brigades assigned: Kirkland's, MacRae's. Commander: Colonel Thomas C. Singletary (June 1862–April 1865). Notes: Had a band.

45th Regiment Formed: Camp Mangum, April 1862. ANV service: May 1863–April 1865. Brigades assigned: Daniel's, Grimes'. Commanders: Colonels Julius Daniel (April–September 1862), John H. Morehead (September 1862–June 1863), Samuel H. Boyd (June 1863–May 1864), John R. Winston (May 1864–April 1865).

46th Regiment Formed: Camp Mangum, April 1865. ANV service: September 1862–January 1863, September 1863–April 1865. Brigades assigned: Walker's, Cooke's. Commanders: Colonels Edward D. Hall (April 1862–December 1863), William L. Saunders (December 1863–April 1865).

47th Regiment Formed: Camp Mangum, March 1862. ANV service: June 1863–April 1865. Brigades assigned: Pettigrew's, Kirkland's, MacRae's. Commanders: Colonels Sion H. Rogers (March 1862–January 1863), George H. Fairbault (January 1863–January 1865), Major William C. Lankford (January–April 1865).

48th Regiment Formed: April 1862. ANV service: September 1863–April 1865. Brigade assigned: Cooke's. Commanders: Colonels Robert C. Hill (April 1862–December 1863), Samuel H. Walkup (December 1863–April 1865).

49th Regiment Formed: Garysburg, April 1862. ANV service: August 1862–January 1863, May 1864–April 1865. Brigade assigned: Ransom's. Commanders: Colonels Stephen D. Ramseur (April–November 1862), Leroy M. McAfee (November 1862–April 1865).

51st Regiment Formed: Wilmington, April 1862. ANV service: October–December 1864. Brigade assigned: Clingman's. Commander: Colonel Hector M. McKethan.

52nd Regiment Formed: Camp Mangum, April 1862. ANV service: June 1863–April 1865. Brigades assigned: Pettigrew's, Kirkland's, MacRae's. Commanders: Colonel James K. Marshall (April 1862–July 1863), Lieutenant Colonel Eric Erson (July 1863–March 1865), Colonel Marcus A. Parks (March–April 1865).

53rd Regiment Formed: Camp Mangum, May 1862. ANV service: May 1863–April 1865. Brigades assigned: Daniel's, Grimes'. Commanders: Colonels William A. Owens (May 1862–July 1864), James T. Morehead (July 1864–March 1865).

54th Regiment Formed: Camp Mangum, May 1862. ANV service: November 1862–January 1864, May 1864–April 1865. Brigades assigned: Hoke's, Lewis', Godwin's. Commanders: Colonels James C. S. McDowell (September 1862–May 1863), Kenneth M. Murchison (May–November 1863), Major James A. Rogers

(November 1863–April 1864), Lieutenant Colonel Anderson Ellis (April 1864–April 1865). Notes: Had a band.

55th Regiment Formed: Camp Mangum, May 1862. ANV service: June 1864–April 1865. Brigades assigned: Davis', Cooke's. Commander: Colonel John K. Connally (March 1864–April 1865). Notes: Had a band.

56th Regiment Formed: Camp Mangum, July 1862. ANV service: January–February 1863, October 1864–April 1865. Brigade assigned: Ransom's. Commanders: Colonel Paul F. Faison (July 1862–?1863), Lieutenant Colonel Granville G. Luke (?1863–April 1865).

57th Regiment Formed: Salisbury, July 1862. ANV service: November 1862–January 1864, May 1864–April 1865. Brigades assigned: Hoke's, Lewis', Godwin's. Commanders: Colonels Archibald C. Godwin (July 1862–August 1864), Hamilton C. Jones (August 1864–April 1865).

61st Regiment Formed: Wilmington, September 1862. ANV service: October–December 1864. Brigade assigned: Clingman's. Commander: Colonel William S. Devane.

66th Regiment Formed: By merger of 13th Battalion and 8th Partisan Rangers, October 1863. ANV service: October–December 1864. Brigade assigned: Kirkland's. Commander: Colonel John H. Nethercutt.

Thomas's Legion Formed: Late 1862. ANV service: June–November 1864. Brigade assigned: Smith's. Commander: Lieutenant Colonel James R. Love.

SOUTH CAROLINA: ARTILLERY

Brooks Light Artillery Formed: Charleston, spring 1862. ANV service: spring 1862–September 1863, April 1864–April 1865. Assigned: S. D. Lee's, E. P. Alexanders's, F. Huger's Battalions. Commanders: Captains A. B. Rhett, William W. Fickling. Notes: Armed with two 20-pound Parrotts and two 10-pound Parrotts in September 1862; with fourteen 12-pound howitzers in December 1864.

Chesterfield Light Artillery Formed: Columbia, November 1861. ANV service: July–August 1862, June 1864–April 1865. Assigned: J. C. Coit's Battalion. Commanders: Captains James C. Coit, James I. Kelly. Notes: Armed with two Napoleons in December 1864.

German Light Artillery (Charleston German Artillery) Formed: Charleston, before the war. ANV service: spring 1862–October 1863. Assigned: B. W. Frobel's, M. W. Henry's Battalions. Commander: Captain William K. Bachman. Notes: Armed with four Napoleons in September 1862; initially wore dark-blue coatee with three rows of buttons and worsted epaulettes, light-blue trousers, and Prussian helmets for dress; grey satinet jacket trimmed with yellow braid, kepi, and dark-grey trousers for undress.

Macbeth Light Artillery Formed: Berkeley County, summer 1861. ANV service: July–autumn 1862. Assigned: Evans' Brigade, B. W. Frobel's Battalion. Commander:

Captain Robert Boyce. Notes: Armed with smoothbore guns.

Palmetto Light Artillery Formed: Charleston, spring 1862. ANV service: spring 1862–April 1865. Assigned: B. W. Frobel's, M. W. Henry's, J. C. Haskell's Battalions. Commander: Captain Hugh R. Garden. Notes: Armed with one Napoleon and one 12-pound howitzer in September 1862; with three Napoleons and one 10-pound Parrott in December 1864.

Pee Dee Light Artillery Formed: Florence County, winter 1861. ANV service: spring 1862–September 1863, April–May 1864. Assigned: R. L. Walker's, W. J. Pegram's Battalions. Commanders: Captains Ervin B. Brunson, David G. McIntosh, First Lieutenant William E. Zimmerman. Notes: Armed with one 10-pound Parrott, one 3-inch rifle, one Napoleon, and one 12-pound howitzer in September 1862.

Washington Light Artillery Formed: As part of Hampton Legion, June 1861. ANV service: spring 1862–April 1865. Assigned: Jones's Divisional artillery, Stuart's horse artillery, R. P. Chew's Battalion. Commanders: Captain James F. Hart (June 1861–October 1864), First Lieutenant E. Lindsay Halsey (October 1864–April 1865). Notes: Armed with four 3-inch rifles in December 1864; initially wore US Army dress heavy artillery coat with grey jacket and cap with black oilcloth cover for fatigues.

SOUTH CAROLINA: CAVALRY

1st Regiment Formed: October 1861, from 1st Cavalry Battalion. ANV service: autumn 1862–winter 1864. Brigades assigned: W. Hampton's, M. C. Butler's, W. H. F. Lee's, P. M. B. Young's. Commander: Colonel John L. Black.

2nd Regiment Formed: In Virginia, August 1862 by merger of 4th Battalion and cavalry of Hampton's Legion. ANV service: August 1862–April 1865. Brigades assigned: Hampton's, Butler's, Young's, Gary's. Commanders: Colonels Matthew C. Butler (August 1862–September 1863), Thomas Jefferson Lipscomb (September 1863–April 1865).

4th Regiment Formed: December 1862, by merger of 10th and 12th Battalions. ANV service: March–August 1864. Brigade assigned: Butler's. Commander: Colonel Benjamin H Rutledge. Notes: Armed with Enfield rifles, sabres and some revolvers.

5th Regiment Formed: January 1863, by merger of 14th and 17th Battalions. ANV service: March–August 1864. Brigade assigned: Butler's. Commander: Colonel John Dunovant (January 1863–August 1864). Notes: Armed with Enfields.

6th Regiment (Dixie Rangers, 1st Regiment Partisan Rangers) Formed: January 1863, from 16th Battalion. ANV service: March–August 1864. Brigade assigned: Butler's. Commander: Colonel Hugh K. Aiken. Notes: Armed with Enfield rifles and sabres.

7th Regiment Formed: In the field, March 1864. ANV service: March 1864–April 1865. Brigade assigned: Gray's. Commander:

Colonels William P. Shingler (March–May 1864), Alexander C. Haskell (June 1864–April 1865).

SOUTH CAROLINA:
INFANTRY

1st Regiment, Provisional Army Formed: Richmond, Virginia, August 1861, from men of the 1st Volunteers. ANV service: August 1861–April 1865. Brigades assigned: Gregg's, McGowan's. Commanders: Colonels Maxey Gregg (August–December 1861), Daniel H. Hamilton, Sr. (December 1861–August 1863), C. W. McCreary (August 1863–April 1865). Notes: Initially wore grey single–breasted frock coat, trousers and forage cap all trimmed in blue, but by 1862 most men had grey jacket with blue trim. Suffered 53. 3 per cent losses at Second Manassas.

1st Regiment Rifles (Orr's Rifles) Formed: Sandy Springs, July 1861. ANV service: April 1862–April 1865. Brigades assigned: Gregg's, McGowan's. Commanders: Colonels James L. Orr (July 1861–January 1862), Jehu Foster Marshall (January–August 1862), Daniel A. Ledbetter (August 1862), James W. Livingston (September–November 1862), James Monroe Perrin (November 1862–May 1863), George McD. Miller (May 1863–April 1865). Notes: Initial uniform included single–breasted grey frock coat trimmed with green, US Army broad–brimmed slouch hat; officers wore straight bars of gold lace on each cuff to indicate rank; initially armed with M1842 muskets.

Suffered 56. 9 per cent losses at Gaines' Mills.

1st Regiment Volunteers (Hagood's) Formed: Barnwell, December 1860. ANV service: July 1862–September 1863, April 1864–April 1865. Brigades assigned: Jenkins', Bratton's. Commanders: Colonels James R. Hagood (December 1860–July 1862), Thomas J. Glover (July–August 1862), William H. Duncan (acting) (September 1862–January 1863), Franklin W. Kilpatrick (January–October 1863), James R. Hagood (November 1863–April 1865). Notes: Issued 'short gray blouses' in April 1861.

2nd Regiment (2nd Palmetto Regiment) Formed: Richmond, Virginia, May 1861. ANV service: May 1861–September 1863, April–June 1864. Brigades assigned: Bonham's, Toombs', Kershaw's Kennedy's, Conner's. Commanders: Colonels Joseph B. Kershaw (May 1861–January 1862), John D. Kennedy (January 1862–October 1864).

2nd Regiment Rifles Formed: May 1862, from 5th Battalion Rifles. ANV service: June 1862–September 1863, April 1864–April 1865. Brigades assigned: Jenkins', Bratton's. Commanders: Colonels John V. Moore (May–September 1862), Thomas Thomason (September 1862–December 1863), Robert E. Bowen (December 1863–April 1865). Notes: Armed with M1855 and Enfield rifled muskets and Enfield rifles.

3rd Battalion (Laurens Battalion) Formed: Camp Hampton, Columbia, November 1861. ANV service: July 1862–September 1863, April–June 1864. Brigades assigned: Drayton's, Kershaw's, Kennedy's, Conner's. Commanders: Lieutenant Colonels George S. James (February–September 1862), William G. Rice (September 1862–January 1865).

3rd Regiment Formed: Columbia, February 1861. ANV service: May 1861–September 1863, April–June 1864. Brigades asigned: Kershaw's, Kennedy's, Conner's. Commanders: Colonels James H. Williams (February 1861–May 1862), James D. Nance (May 1862–May 1864), William D. Rutherford (May–October 1864), Major Rutherford P. Todd (October 1864–April 1865). Notes: Armed with M1855 and Enfield rifled muskets and M1841 rifles.

4th Battalion Formed: In the field, April 1862, by reduction of 4th Regiment. ANV service: April–November 1862 (merged into Hampton's Legion). Brigades assigned: R. H. Anderson's, M. Jenkins'. Commander: Major Charles S. Mattison.

4th Regiment Formed: Anderson, March 1861. ANV service: spring 1861–April 1862 (see 4th Battalion). Brigade assigned: N. G. Evans'. Commander: Colonel John B. E. Sloan.

5th Regiment Formed: Laurens, March 1861. ANV service: spring 1861–September 1863, April 1864–April 1865. Brigades assigned: D. R. Jones's, R. H. Anderson's, M. Jenkins', Bratton's. Commanders: Colonels Micah Jenkins (March 1861–April 1862),

John R. R. Giles (April–June 1862), Asbury Coward (August 1862–April 1865).

6th Regiment Formed: Columbia, April 1861. ANV service: July 1861–September 1863, April 1864–April 1865. Brigades assigned: J. E. B. Stuart's, R. H. Anderson's, M. Jenkins', Bratton's. Commanders: Colonels Charles S. Winder (April 1861–March 1862), John Bratton (March 1862–May 1864), John M. Steedman (May 1864–April 1865). Notes: Suffered 51. 6 per cent losses at Fair Oaks.

7th Battalion (Enfield Rifles) Formed: Kershaw County, January 1862. ANV service: spring 1864–Spring 1865. Brigade assigned: Hagood's. Commanders: Lieutenant Colonels Patrick Henry Nelson (July 1862–June 1864), James H. Rion (June 1864–April 1865).

7th Regiment Formed: Columbia, April 1861. ANV service: June 1861–September 1863, April–June 1864. Brigades assigned: Kershaw's, Kennedy's, Conner's. Commanders: Colonels Thomas G. Bacon (April 1861–May 1862), David Wyatt Aiken (May 1862–August 1863), Lieutenant Colonels Elbert Bland (August–September 1863), Elijah J. Goggans (September 1863–April 1865). Notes: Suffered 52. 2 per cent losses at Sharpsburg.

8th Regiment Formed: Marion, May 1861. ANV service: May 1861–September 1863, April–June 1864. Brigades assigned: Kershaw's, Kennedy's, Conner's. Commanders: Colonels Ellerbee B. C. Cash (May 1861–May 1862),

John W. Henagan (May 1862–September 1864), Lieutenant Colonel Eli T. Stackhouse (September 1864–April 1865). Notes: Armed with both M1855 and Enfield rifled muskets and M1841 rifles.

9th Regiment Formed: Lancaster, Dillon, Kershaw, Lexington Counties, April 1861. ANV service: April 1861–April 1862 when disbanded. Brigade assigned: D. R. Jones's. Commander: Colonel James D. Blanding.

11th Regiment Formed: Beaufort, Clarendon, Colleton Counties, July 1861. ANV service: spring–winter 1864. Brigade assigned: Hagood's. Commander: Colonel Frederick H. Gantt (November 1862–May 1865).

12th Regiment Formed: Lightwoodknot Springs, July 1861. ANV service: April 1862–April 1865. Brigades assigned: Gregg's, McGowan's. Commanders: Colonels Richard G. M. Dunovant (September 1861–April 1862), Dixon Barnes (April–September 1862), Cadwallader Jones (September 1862–February 1863), John L. Miller (February 1863–May 1864), Edwin F. Bookter (May–September 1864), Lieutenant Colonel Thomas F. Clyburn (September–October 1864). Notes: By 1864 mostly armed with M1855 rifled muskets; one company had M1842 muskets, one Whitworth rifle in regiment. Suffered 54 per cent losses at Manassas.

13th Regiment Formed: Lightwoodknot Springs, July 1861. ANV service: April 1862–April 1865. Brigades assigned: Gregg's, McGowan's. Commanders:

Colonels Oliver E. Edwards (September 1862–May 1863), Benjamin T. Brockman (June 1863–May 1864), Isaac F. Hunt (June 1864–April 1865).

14th Regiment Formed: Lightwoodknot Springs, July 1861. ANV service: April 1862–April 1865. Brigades assigned: Gregg's, McGowan's. Commanders: Colonels James Jones (September 1861–April 1862), Samuel McGowan (April 1862–January 1863), Abner M. Perrin (February–September 1863), Joseph N. Brown (September 1863–May 1864, August 1864–April 1865) Lieutenant Colonel Edward Croft (May–August 1864). Notes: Had a band. Suffered 43 per cent losses at Gaines' Mill.

15th Regiment Formed: Lightwoodknot Springs, September 1861. ANV service: summer 1862–September 1863, April–June 1864. Brigades assigned: Draton's, Kershaw's, Kennedy's, Conner's. Commanders: Colonels William D. DeSaussure (September 1861–July 1863), Joseph F. Gist (July 1863–January 1864), John B. Davis (January 1864–April 1865). Notes: Armed with M1855 and Enfield rifled muskets and M1841 rifles; had a band.

17th Regiment Formed: Barnwell, York, Chester, Lancaster, Fairfield Counties, November 1861. ANV service: July–October 1862, June 1864–April 1865. Brigades assigned: Evans', Elliott's, Wallace's. Commanders: Colonels John H. Means (December 1861–August 1862), FitzWilliam

McMaster (September 1862–March 1865), Lieutenant Colonel John R. Culp (March–April 1865). Notes: Initially armed with British Brown Bess flintlocks (eight companies) and Enfield rifled muskets (two companies). Suffered 66. 9 per cent casualties at Second Manassas.

18th Regiment Formed: January 1862. ANV service: July–October 1862, June 1864–April 1865. Brigades assigned: Evans', Elliott's, Wallace's. Commanders: Colonels James M. Gadberry (January–August 1862), William H. Wallace (August 1862–September 1864), Lieutenant Colonel William B. Allison (September 1864–April 1865).

20th Regiment Formed: Orangeburg, January 1862. ANV service: April–June 1864. Brigades assigned: Kershaw's, Kennedy's, Conner's. Commanders: Colonels Laurence M. Keitt (January 1862–June 1864), Stephen M. Boykin (June–October 1864).

21st Regiment Formed: Pee Dee, January 1862. ANV service: March–June 1864. Brigade assigned: Hagood's. Commander: Colonel Robert F. Graham.

22nd Regiment Formed: December 1861. ANV service: July–October 1862, March 1864–April 1865. Brigades assigned: Evans', Elliott's, Wallace's. Commanders: Colonels Spartan D. Goodlett (May 1862–April 1864), Olin M. Dantzler (April–June 1864), David G. Fleming (June–July 1864), William Burt (July 1864–April 1865).

23rd Regiment Formed: Charleston, November 1861. ANV service: July–October 1862, June 1864–April 1865. Brigades assigned: Evans', Elliott's, Wallace's. Commanders: Colonel Henry L. Benbow (April 1862–October 1863), Lieutenant Colonel John M. Kinloch (October 1863–April 1865). Notes: Suffered 66. 2 per cent losses at Second Manassas.

25th Regiment (Eutaw Regiment) Formed: From men of the 11th Battalion, Charleston, July 1862. ANV service: March–December 1864. Brigade assigned: Hagood's. Commanders: Colonel Charles H. Simonton (March–August 1864), Lieutenant Colonel John G. Pressley (August–December 1864). Notes: Had a band.

26th Regiment Formed: By merger of 6th and 9th Battalions, Charleston, September 1862. ANV service: May 1864–April 1865. Brigades assigned: Elliott's, Wallace's. Commanders: Colonel Alexander D. Smith (September 1862–January 1864, July 1864–April 1865), Lieutenant Colonel Joshua H. Hudson (January–July 1864).

27th Regiment Formed: By merger of Charleston Infantry Battalion and 1st Battalion Sharpshooters, September 1863. ANV service: May–December 1864. Brigade assigned: Hagood's. Commander: Lieutenant Colonel Julius A. Blake (May–August 1864, October 1864–January 1865), Major Joseph Abney (August–October 1864, January–March 1865).

Hampton Legion Formed: spring 1861. ANV service: July 1861–September 1863, April–May 1864 (merged into 2nd Cavalry Regiment). Brigades assigned: Hampton's, Hood's, M. Jenkins'. Commanders: Colonels Wade Hampton (spring 1861–May 1862), Martin G. Gary (May 1862–May 1864).

Holcombe Legion Formed: November, 1861. ANV service: spring–October 1862, spring 1864–April 1865. Brigades assigned: Evans', Elliott's, Wallace's. Commanders: Colonels Peter F. Stevens (November 1861–October 1862), William P. Shingler (October 1862–early 1864), Stephen Elliott, Jr. (early–1864), William J. Crawley (September 1864–March 1865). Notes: Initially armed with M1841 rifles and percussion and flintlock rifles; by 1862 mostly with Enfield rifled muskets.

Palmetto Regiment Sharpshooters Formed: From men of the 2nd, 5th, 9th Regiments, April 1862. ANV service: spring 1862–September 1863, April 1864–April 1865. Brigades assigned: R. H. Anderson's, Jenkins', Bratton's. Commanders: Colonels Micah Jenkins (April–July 1862), Joseph Walker (July 1862–March 1864), Lieutenant Colonel John W. Goss (March 1864–April 1865). Notes: Suffered 67. 7 per cent losses at Glendale.

TENNESSEE: INFANTRY
1st Regiment, Provisional Army (1st Confederate Infantry Regiment) Formed: Winchester, April 1861. ANV service: May 1861–April 1865. Brigades assigned: S. R. Anderson's, Hat-ton's, J. J. Archer's, Walker's, Fry's, McComb's. Commanders: Colonel Peter Turney (April 1861–December 1862), Lieutenant Colonel Newton J. George (December 1862–July 1863, August 1864–April 1865), Captain William S. Daniel (July 1863–August 1864). Notes: Apparently initially armed with M1841 rifles and sabre bayonets.

1st Regiment Formed: Nashville, May 1861. ANV service: December 1861–February 1862. Brigade assigned: S. R. Anderson's. Commander: Colonel George Maney.

2nd Regiment Formed: Nashville, May 1861. ANV service: May 1861–February 1862. Brigades assigned: Holmes', J. G. Walker's. Commander: Colonel William B. Bate. Notes: Armed with muskets (mostly converted flintlocks) and some M1841 rifles.

3rd Regiment Formed: Knoxville, May 1861. ANV service: June 1861–February 1862. Brigades assigned: A. P. Hill's, Elzey's, E. K. Smith's. Commander: Colonel John C. Vaughn.

7th Regiment Formed: Camp Trousdale, Sumner County, May 1861. ANV service: July 1861–April 1865. Brigades assigned: J. B. Floyd's, T. H. Holmes', Hatton's, J. J. Archer's, H. H. Walker's, B. D. Fry's, Mayo's, McComb's. Commanders: Colonels Robert Hatton (May 1861–May 1862), John F. Goodner (May 1862–April 1863), John A. Fite (April 1863–April 1865). Notes: Initially armed with M1841 rifles, exchanged by 1863 for M1855 or Enfield rifled muskets.

14th Regiment Formed: Camp Duncan, Clarksville, June 1861. ANV service: July 1861–April 1865. Brigades assigned: as 7th Regiment. Commanders: Colonels William A. Forbes (June 1861–September 1862), William McComb (September 1862–January 1865), James W. Lookert (January–April 1865). Notes: Initially issued with converted flintlock muskets.

17th Regiment Formed: Camp Harris, May 1861. ANV service: May 1864–April 1865. Brigades assigned: Johnson's, McComb's. Commanders: Colonels Richard H. Keeble (May–August 1864), Horace Ready (August 1864–April 1865). Notes: Armed with Enfield rifled muskets; merged with 23rd Regiment as field unit November 1863.

23rd Regiment Formed: Camp Trousdale, July 1861. ANV service: May 1864–April 1865. Brigade assigned: Johnson's. Commanders: Colonels Richard H. Keeble (May–August 1864), Horace Ready (August 1864–April 1865). Notes: Suffered 54. 1 per cent losses at Chickamauga; merged with 17th Regiment as field unit November 1863.

25th Regiment Formed: Camp Zollicoffer, August 1861. ANV service: May 1864–April 1865. Brigades assigned: Johnson's, McComb's. Commanders: Colonel John M. Hughs (July 1862–March 1865), Captain Joseph E. Spencer (March–April 1865). Notes: Merged with 44th Regiment as field unit, November 1863.

44th Regiment Formed: Camp Trousdale, December 1861. ANV service: May 1864–April 1865. Brigades assigned: Johnson's, McComb's. Commanders: Colonel John M. Hughs (November 1863–March 1865), Captain Joseph E. Spencer (March–April 1865). Notes: Merged with 25th Regiment as field unit, November 1863.

63rd Regiment (74th Regiment) Formed: East Tennessee and Virginia, July 1862. ANV service: May 1864–April 1865. Brigades assigned: Johnson's, McComb's. Commanders: Major John A. Aiken (May 1864–January 1865), Captains A. A. Blair (January–February 1865), John W. Robertson (February–April 1865), Lieutenant L. L. Etter (April 1865). Notes: Lost Colours to 11th New Hampshire at Petersburg, 17 June 1864.

TEXAS: INFANTRY

1st Regiment Formed: Richmond, August 1861. ANV service: August 1861–September 1863, April 1864–April 1865. Brigades assigned: Hood's, J. B. Robertson's, J. Gregg's. Commanders: Colonels Louis T. Wigfall (August–October 1861), Hugh McLeod (October 1861–January 1862), Alexis T. Rainey (January–June 1862), Lieutenant Colonel Peter A. Work (June 1862–July 1864), Frederick S. Bass (July 1864–April 1865). Notes: Armed with Enfield rifled muskets by 1862; noted as not being 'strong on dress, drill and discipline'; suffered 82. 3 per cent losses at Sharpsburg, the largest percentage of any Confederate regiment throughout the war.

4th Infantry Formed: Richmond, September 1861. ANV service: as

1st Texas Infantry. Brigades assigned: as 1st Texas Infantry. Commanders: Colonels John B. Hood (September 1861–March 1862), John Marshall (March–June 1862), John C. G. Key (June 1862–April 1864), John Bane (April 1864–April 1865). Notes: Armed with Enfield rifled muskets by 1862; band became the brigade band. Suffered 53. 5 per cent losses at Sharpsburg.

5th Infantry Formed: Richmond, September 1861. ANV service: As 1st Texas Infantry. Brigades assigned: as 1st Texas Infantry. Commanders: Colonels James J. Archer (September 1861–June 1862), Jerome Bonaparte Robertson (June–November 1862), Robert M. Powell (November 1862–July 1863), Major Jefferson C. Rogers (July–September 1863), Colonel Powell (February–April 1865). Notes: Armed with Enfield rifled muskets by 1862.

VIRGINIA: ARTILLERY
Virginia had a full regimental artillery organization system. However, the batteries assigned to each regiment actually operated independently, so for all practical purposes, the regiments themselves are meaningless in terms of campaigns of Lee's Army. Therefore, batteries are listed by their best known titles, with regimental assigments, if any, noted in parentheses.

10th Heavy Artillery Battalion Formed: Richmond, April 1862. ANV service: April–May 1862, April 1865. Assigned: Ewell's Command, Magruder's Command, G.

W. C. Lee's Division. Commanders: Majors William Allen, (April–August 1862), James O. Hensley (August 1862–April 1865).

Albemarle Artillery (2nd Co. A, 12th Battalion, Light Artillery) Formed: Albemarle County, March 1862. ANV service: October 1864–April 1865 (as an independent battery from January 1865). Assiged: Bogg's, Sturdivant's Battalions. Commander: Captain Nathan A. Sturdivant (March 1862–January 1865). Notes: Armed with four Napoleons, two 8-inch mortars, seven 12-pound mortars, and five 24-pound Coehorn mortars in December 1864.

Albemarle Light Artillery (Everett Artillery, Co. H, 1st Regiment Artillery) Formed: Albemarle County, June 1861. ANV service: June 1861–July 1862, June 1863–April 1865. Assigned: L. M. Coleman's, R. S. Andrews', W. T. Poague's Battalions. Commanders: Captains William H. Southall, Charles F. Johnston, James W. Wyatt. Notes: Armed with a 10-pound Parrott, a 12-pound howitzer, and two 3-inch rifles in July 1863; with one Napoleon and two 10-pound Parrotts in December 1864.

Alburtis'/Wise Battery (Co. B, 1st Light Artillery) Formed: Martinsburg, November 1859. ANV service: April 1861–October 1862. Assigned: S. D. Lee's Battalion. Commanders: Captains Ephram G. Alburtis (April 1861–January 1862), James S. Brown (February–October 1862). Notes: Armed with two 10-pound Parrotts and one 3-inch rifle in September 1862.

Alexandria Light Artillery (Co. E, 18th Battalion, Heavy Artillery) Formed: Alexandria, March 1861. Assigned: Bonham's/Kershaw's Brigade, C. E. Lightfoot's Battalion, 18th Heavy Artillery Battalion (January 1864–April 1865). Commanders: Captains Delaware Kemper (March 1861–July 1862), David L. Smoot (July 1862–April 1865). Notes: Armed with four 6-pound smoothbores in May 1861; dismounted in January 1864.

Alleghany Artillery (Alleghany Roughs) Formed: Converted from Co. A, 27th Infantry, November 1861. ANV service: November 1861–April 1865. Assigned: Stonewall Brigade, Jackson's/Johnson's Divisional artillery, Andrews'/Braxton's Battalion. Commanders: Captains Joseph Carpenter (November 1861–February 1863), John C. Carpenter (February 1863–April 1865). Notes: Armed with four 3-inch rifles in May 1862; with two 3-inch rifles and two Napoleons in September 1862 and January 1863; with two Napoleons in December 1864.

Amherst Artillery Formed: Amherst County, July 1861. ANV service: November 1861–April 1865. Assigned: Reserve Artillery Corps, Nelson's Battalion. Commander: Captain Thomas J. Kirkpatrick. Notes: Armed with two 12-pound howitzers and four 6-pound smoothbores in September 1862; with two Napoleons and a 3-inch rifle in December 1865.

Amherst–Nelson Light Artillery Formed: Amherst and Nelson Counties, September 1861. ANV service: January 1862, October 1863–April 1865. Assigned: Cocke's Brigade, Henry's/Haskell's Battalion, Cabell's Battalion. Commanders: Captains Woodville Latham (September 1861–May 1863), James Nelson Lamkin (May 1862–April 1865). Notes: Unarmed in October 1863; with 26 mortars in December 1865.

Ashby Horse Artillery Formed: Flowing Spring, November 1861. ANV service: November 1861–April 1865. Assigned: 7th Cavalry, Pelham's Beckham's, Breathed's, Chew's Horse Artillery Battalions. Commanders: Captains Robert Preston Chew (November 1861–March 1864), James W. Thomson (March 1864–March 1865), John W. Carter (March–April 1865). Notes: Armed with a 3-inch rifle, a 12-pound howitzer and a 3. 1-inch Blakely rifle from March 1862 until April 1865.

Ashland Artillery Formed: Hanover County, August 1861. ANV service: January 1862–September 1863, April 1864–April 1865. Assigned: Richardson's, Lee's, Alexander's, Huger's Battalions. Commander: Captain Pichegru Woolfolk, Jr. Notes: Armed with two 20-pound Parrotts and two Napoleons in July 1863–December 1864.

Bath Artillery (Co. C, 12th Battalion) Formed: Bath, March 1862. ANV service: August 1862–September 1863, April 1864–April 1865. Assigned: Lee's, Alexander's, Huger's Battalions. Commanders: Captains John L. Eubank (August 1862–March

1863), Osmond B. Taylor (March 1863–April 1865).

Bedford Artillery Formed: By conversion of Co. C, 28th Infantry to artillery, August 1861. ANV service: January–October 1862 (disbanded with some men transferred into the Purcell Battery and others into the Lynchburg Artillery). Assigned: Taylor's Brigade, Ewell's Divisional artillery. Commanders: Captains Thomas M. Bowyer (May 1861–April 1862), John R. Johnson (April–October 1862).

Bedford Light Artillery Formed: Bedford County, January 1861. ANV service: June 1862–September 1863, April 1864–April 1865. Assigned: Cobb's, Early's Brigades; Lee's, Alexander's, Huger's Battalions. Commanders: Captains Tylor C. Jordan (January 1861–March 1864), John Donnell Smith (March 1864–April 1865). Notes: Armed with three 24-pound howitzers and a Napoleon in June 1862; with four 3-inch rifles from July 1863 to December 1864.

Botetourt Artillery Formed: Botetourt County, May 1861. ANV service: March–April 1865. Assigned: King's Battalion. Commander: Captain Henry Clay Douthat (September 1863–April 1865). Notes: Armed with six guns in March 1864.

Centerville Rifles Artillery (Wise Legion Artillery Battalion) Formed: As Co. C, Wise Legion, May 1862. ANV service: June 1864–March 1865 (unit disbanded then). Assigned: King's, McLaughlin's Battalions. Commander: Captain William M. Lowrey.

Branch Field Artillery (Lee's Life Guard) Formed: From conversion of Co. K, 16th Regiment to artillery, March 1862. ANV service: June 1862–January 1863, October 1864–April 1865. Assigned: Ransom's Brigade, Branch's/Coit's Battalion. Commanders: Captains James R. Branch (March 1862–May 1863), Richard G. Pegram (May 1863–April 1865). Notes: Armed with a 10-pound Parrott, two 3-inch rifles, and three 12-pound howitzers in August–September 1862; with four Napoleons in December 1864.

Charlottesville Artillery Formed: Charlottesville, March 1862. ANV service: June 1862–May 1864 (captured at Spotsylvania). Assigned: Taylor's Brigade; Ewell's/Early's Divisional artillery; Nelson's, Jones's, Cutshaw's Battalions. Commander: Captain James M. Carrington. Notes: Armed with two 3-inch rifles, two 12-pound howitzers and two 6-pound smoothbores in September 1862; with four Napoleons in July 1863.

Charlottesville Horse Artillery Formed: Charlottesville, May 1863. ANV service: June–August 1863, March–April 1865. Assigned: Jenkins' Brigade, Johnston's Battalion. Commander: Captain Thomas E. Jackson.

Chesterfield Artillery (Johnston Artillery) Formed: Dinwiddie County, September 1861. ANV service: October 1864–April 1865. Assigned: F. W. Smith's Battalion. Commander: Captain Branch J. Epes.

Cockade Mounted Battery (Co. C, 18th Battalion, Heavy Artillery)

Formed: Petersburg, May 1861. ANV service: January–February 1862 (became Co. C, 18th Battalion, Heavy Artillery), April 1865. Assigned: Carter's Command, Department of the Peninsula; Crutchfield's Brigade. Commanders: Captains Gilbert V. Rambaut (May 1861–May 1862), Bernard J. Black (May 1862–April 1863), John Stoop (April 1863–August 1864), John G. Orgain.

Courtney Battery (Henrico Artillery) Formed: Henrico County, July 1861. ANV service: January 1862–May 1864. Assigned: Trimble's Brigade; Ewell's/Early's, Jackson's Divisional artillery; Jones's/Cutshaw's Battalion. Commanders: Captains Alfred R. Courtney (July 1861–July 1862), Joseph W. Latimer (July 1862–May 1863), William A. Tanner (May 1863–February 1865). Notes: Armed with four 3-inch rifles in July 1863.

Crenshaw Battery Formed: Richmond, March 1862. ANV service: July 1862–April 1865. Assigned: A. P. Hill's Divisional artillery; J. R. Anderson's Brigade; Peagram's Battalion. Commanders: Captains William G. Crenshaw (March 1862–April 1863), Thomas Ellet (April 1863–April 1865). Notes: Armed with two 10-pound Parrotts, two 12-pound howitzers, and two 6-pound smoothbores in March 1862; with four Napoleons in July 1863–December 1864.

Dabney Battery (Game Point Battery) Formed: Early 1862. ANV service: June–July 1862 (Became Co. E, 20th Artillery Battalion *c.* November 1863). Assigned:

Artillery Reserve. Commander: Captain William J. Dabney.

Danville Artillery Formed: Pittsylvania County, April 1861. ANV service: June 1862–April 1865. Assigned: Shumaker's, Hardaway's, McIntosh's Battalions. Commanders: Captains Lindsay M. Shumaker (April 1861–April 1862), George Washington Wooding, Robert S. Rice, Berryman Z. Price. Notes: Armed with two 10-pound Parrotts, a 3-inch rifle and a Napoleon in September 1862; with four Napoleons in July–December 1863.

Dixie Artillery Formed: Page County, June 1861. ANV service: October 1861–October 1862 (disbanded, men transferred to Purcell Artillery). Assigned: Rain's Divisional artillery, Longstreet's Divisional artillery, Featherston's Brigade, ANV artillery reserve. Commanders: Captain John K. Booton (October–November 1861), William H. Chapman (November 1861–October 1862). Notes: Armed with four 6-pound smoothbores June–July 1862.

Dixie Artillery Formed: Monroe County, April 1862. ANV service: June 1864–April 1865. Assigned: King's, McLaughlin's Battalions. Commander: Captain George B. Chapman (April 1862–September 1864).

Eighth Star Artillery (New Market Artillery) Formed: New Market, April 1861. ANV service: September 1862 (merged into Danville Artillery). Assigned: ANV reserve artillery. Commander: Captain Robert S. Rice.

Fayette Artillery (Co. B, 38th

Battalion, Light Artillery)
Formed: Richmond, June 1862.
ANV service: June–September
1863, October 1864–April 1865.
Assigned: Dearing's, Read's, Stribling's Battalions. Commander:
Captain Miles C. Macon. Notes:
Armed with two 10-pound Parrotts
and two Napoleons in July 1863;
with two 10-pound Parrotts and
two 3-inch rifles in December
1864.

**Fauquier Artillery (Co. A, 38th
Battalion, Light Artillery)**
Formed: Fauquier County as Co.
G, 49th Infantry, June 1861; converted to artillery September/October 1861. ANV service:
June–December 1863, October
1864–April 1865. Assigned: Dearing's, Read's, Stribling's Battalions.
Commanders: Captains Robert M.
Stribling (July 1861–February
1864), William C. Marshall (February 1864–April 1865). Notes:
Armed with two 20-pound Parrotts
and four Napoleons, August
1862–December 1864.

Fluvanna Artillery Battery
Formed: June 1861 as two separate
batteries designated as above,
which were merged as single battery October 1862. ANV service:
November 1861–March 1865 (no
subsequent records). Assigned:
ANV reserve artillery; Nelson's Battalion. Commanders: Captains
William Henry Holman and
Charles T. Huckstep (Battery No.
1); Cary Charles Cocke and John J.
Ancell (Battery No. 2); John L.
Massie (October 1862–September
1864), Charles G. Snead (September 1864–March 1865). Notes:
Armed with a 3-inch rifle and

three Napoleons in July 1863;
with two 12-pound howitzers in
December 1864.

Fredericksburg Artillery Formed:
Fredericksburg, April 1861. ANV
service: January 1862–April 1865.
Assigned: French's, S. R. Anderson's, Hatton's Brigades: A. P.
Hill's Divisional artillery; Archer's
Brigade: Peagram's, M. Johnson's
Battalions. Commanders: Captains
Thomas A. Curtis (April–May
1861), Carter M. Braxton (May
1861–March 1863), Edward A.
Marye (March 1863–October
1864), John G. Pollock (October
1864–April 1865). Notes: Armed
with two Napoleons and two
10-pound Parrotts in July 1863;
with four Napoleons in December
1864.

**Giles Light Artillery (McComas
Artillery, Pearlsburg Reserves)**
Formed: From Co. B, Wise Legion,
early 1862. ANV service: October
1864–April 1865. Assigned: Stark's
Battalion. Commander: Captain
David A. Martin (April 1862–April
1865). Notes: Armed with four
Napoleons in December 1864.

Goochland Artillery Formed:
From Co. D, Wise Legion Artillery,
March/April 1862. ANV service:
June–October 1862. Assigned:
Armistead's Brigade; R. H. Anderson's Divisional artillery; Jones's
Battalion. Commander: Captain
William H. Turner. Notes: Armed
with four guns in July 1862.

Goochland Light Artillery
Formed: Goochland County, June
1861. ANV service: March–April
1865. Assigned: Crutchfield's
Brigade. Commander: First Lieutenant John Guerrant (December

1864–April 1865). Notes: Served as infantry during the Appomattox Campaign.

Halifax Heavy Artillery Battalion (Co. C, 12th Louisiana Heavy Artillery Battalion) Formed: Halifax County, March 1862. ANV service: October 1864–April 1865. Assigned: Branch's, Coit's Battalions. Commander: Captain Samuel T. Wright. Notes: Armed with rocket–launchers for a time; with four Napoleons in December 1864.

Halifax Light Artillery (Mount Vernon Guards, Yorktown Artillery, Co. C 1st Regiment Artillery) Formed: By conversion of Co. G, 14th Infantry to artillery, May 1862. ANV service: April–October 1862, October 1864–April 1865. Assigned: MeLaw', Toombs' Brigades; Brown's, Moseley's, Caskie's, Blount's Battalions. Commander: Captain Edward R. Young. Notes: Armed with two Napoleons in June 1862; with four Napoleons in December 1864.

Hampden Artillery (Co. C, 38th Battalion, Light Artillery) Formed: Richmond, April 1861. ANV service: April 1861–September 1863, October 1864–April 1865. Assigned: Shumaker's, Dearing's, Read's, Stribling's Battalions. Commanders: Captains Lawrence S. Marye (April 1861–April 1862), William H. Caskie (April 1862–April 1864), John E. Sullivan (April 1864–April 1865). Notes: Armed with four Napoleons, two 8-inch mortars, seven 12-pound mortars and five 24-pound Coehorn mortars in December 1864.

Hanover Light Artillery Formed: Hanover Junction, April 1861. ANV service: January–July 1862 (disbanded, men transferred to Amherst and Ashland Batteries). Assigned: Rain's, D. H. Hill's Divisions. Commander: Captain William Nelson.

Henrico Artillery, Co. B. (Co. C, 1st Regiment, Artillery) Formed: Henrico County, autumn 1861. ANV service: October 1861–October 1862 (disbanded, men assigned to other 1st Artillery Regiment companies). Assigned: Griffith's, Toombs' Brigades; Cabell's Battalion; Brown's Regiment. Commanders: Captains Johnson H. Sands (to April 1862), William B. Ritter (April–October 1862). Notes: Armed with a 10-pound Parrott and three 6-pound smoothbores in June 1862.

Jackson's Flying Artillery Formed: Richmond, March 1862. ANV service: June 1862–April 1865. Assigned: A. P. Hill's Divisional artillery, Hardaway's, McIntosh's, Johnson's Battalions. Commanders: Captains Marmaduke Johnson (March 1862–March 1864), Valentine J. Clutter (March 1864–April 1865). Notes: Armed with two 3-inch rifles and two 12-pound howitzers in September 1862; with two 3-inch rifles and two Napoleons in July 1863–December 1864.

James City Artillery (Co B, 1st Regiment & 1st Battalion) Formed: By assignment of Co. H, 32nd Regiment to artillery, September 1861. ANV service: October 1861–October 1862, April 1865. Assigned: Toomb's Brigade;

Lee's Battalion; Brown's Regiment; Crutchfield's Brigade. Commanders: Captains Alex Hamilton Hankins, Lucien W. Richardson. Notes: Served as heavy artillery, with two 32-pound smoothbores in June–July 1862.

King William Artillery Formed: King William County, June 1861. ANV service: January 1862–April 1865. Assigned: Rodes' Brigade; D. H. Hill's/Rodes' Divisional artillery; Carter's, Page's, Cutshaw's Battalions. Commanders: Captains Thomas H. Carter (June 1861–December 1862), William P. Carter (December 1862–April 1865). Notes: Armed with a 10-pound Parrott, two 12-pound howitzers and two 6-pound smoothbores in August–September 1862; with two 10-pound Parrotts and two Napoleons in July 1863.

Lee Battery Formed: Lynchburg, May 1861. ANV service: May 1862–April 1865. Assigned: Ewell's, Jackson's, Trimble's, Johnson's Divisional artillery; Andrews', Braxton's Battalions. Commanders: Captains Pierce B. Anderson (May–December 1861), Charles I. Raine (December 1861–November 1863), First Lieutenant Charles W. Stratham (November 1863–March 1864), Captain William W. Hardwicke (March 1864–April 1865). Notes: Armed with a 12-pound howitzer and three 3-inch rifles in August–September 1862; with a 10-pound Parrott, a 3-inch rifle and two Napoleons in December 1864.

Letcher Artillery Formed: Richmond, February 1862. ANV service: June 1862–April 1865. Assigned: A. P. Hill's Divisional artillery; Gregg's Brigade; Pegram's Battalion. Commanders: Captains Greenlee Davidson (February 1862–May 1863), Thomas A. Brander (May 1863–April 1865). Notes: Armed with two 3-inch rifles, two 6-pound smoothbores, two 12-pound howitzers in June–July 1862; with two Napoleons and two 10-pound Parrotts in July 1863; with four Napoleons in December 1864.

Long Island Light Artillery Formed: Campbell County, March 1862. ANV service: June–October 1862 (disbanded, men transferred to Orange and Morris Artillery Batteries). Assigned: Jones's Battalion; Reserve Artillery. Commander: Captain Patrick Henry Clark.

Loudoun Artillery Formed: Leesburg, December 1859. ANV service: July 1861–October 1862 (disbanded, men transferred to Fauquier Artillery). Assigned: Evans', Longstreet's, Clark's, Griffith's, Ewell's, A. P. Hill's, Kemper's Brigades; D. R. Jones's artillery. Commander: Captain Arthur L. Rogers. Notes: Armed with four 6-pound smoothbores in July 1861.

Lynchburg Beauregards (Beauregard Rifles) Formed: Campbell County, April 1861. ANV service: June 1862–April 1865. Assigned: Mahone's Brigade; R. H. Anderson's Divisional artillery; Horse Artillery Battalion, Cavalry Division, Cavalry Corps, Rosser's Cavalry Division. Commanders: Captains Marcellus N. Moorman (April 1861–February 1864), John

J. Shoemaker (February 1864–April 1865). Notes: Armed with four guns in July 1863.

Magruder Light Artillery Formed: Richmond, March 1862. ANV service: May–October 1862 (disbanded, men transferred to Bedford Light Artillery). Assigned: Cobb's, Toombs' Brigades; Magruder's Command; ANV reserve artillery. Commander: Captain Thomas Jefferson Page, Jr. Notes: Armed with a 6-pound smoothbore and a 3-inch rifle in June–July 1864.

Manchester Artillery Formed: Manchester, May 1861. ANV service: July–August 1862 (Merged with Courtney Artillery). Assigned: Trimble's Brigade. Commander: Captain Emmet W. Weisiger. Notes: Armed with four guns in July 1862.

Martin's Battery Formed: Richmond, April 1862. ANV service: October 1864–April 1865. Assigned: Bogg's, Sturdivant's Battalions. Commander: Captain S. Taylor Martin. Notes: Armed with three Napoleons and a 12-pound howitzer in December 1864.

Mathews Light Artillery Formed: Mathews County, July 1861. ANV service: October 1864–April 1865. Assigned: Stark's Battalion. Commander: Captain Andrew D. Armistead.

Middlesex Artillery Formed: By converting Co. B, 55th Regiment, to artillery, early 1862. ANV service: July–October 1862 (disbanded, men assigned to Ashland and Johnson Artillery batteries). Assigned: Field's Brigade;, A. P. Hill's Divisional artillery. Commander: Captain William C. Fleet.

Morris Artillery (Davis Artillery) Formed: Louis County, August 1861. ANV service: January 1862–April 1865. Assigned: Nelson's Battalion; D. H. Hill's/ Rodes' Divisional artillery; Carter's, Page's, Cutshaw's Battalions. Commanders: Captains Lewis M. Coleman (August 1861–May 1862), Richard C. M. Page (May 1862–February 1864), Charles R. Montgomery (February 1864–April 1865). Notes: Armed with two 3-inch rifles, a 12-pound howitzer and three 6-pound smoothbores in August–September 1862; with four Napoleons in July 1863.

Neblett's/Coleman's Heavy Artillery Formed: March 1862. ANV service: March–April 1865. Assigned: Smith's Battalion. Commander: Captain Wiley G. Coleman.

Nelson Light Artillery (Nelson Light Artillery, Co. B) Formed: Nelson County, August 1861. ANV service: January–July 1862, April 1865. Assigned: Wise's Brigade, Lightfoot's Battalion. Commander: Captain James H. Rives.

Norfolk Artillery Formed: From Norfolk Light Artillery Blues, June 1861. ANV service: April 1862–April 1865. Assigned: Huger's, R. H. Anderson's, Heth's Divisional artillery; Garnett's, Richardson's Battalions. Commanders: Captain Frank Huger (June 1861–March 1863), Joseph D. Moore (March 1863–April 1865). Notes: Armed with a 3-inch rifle, a 10-pound Parrott and two 6-pound smoothbores in August–September 1862; with a 3-inch rifle, a 10-pound Parrott and two Napoleons in July 1863; with four Napoleons in December 1864.

Norfolk Light Artillery Blues
Formed: Norfolk, September 1829. ANV service: December 1862–April 1865. Assigned: Anderson's, Heth's Divisional artillery; Garnett's, Richardson's Battalions. Commander: Captain Charles R. Grandy. Notes: Armed with two Napoleons, two 12-pound howitzers and two 3-inch rifles in May 1862; with two Napoleons and two 3-inch rifles in July 1863–December 1864.

Orange Light Artillery (Cos. D, F, 1st Confederate Light O'Neal's Artillery) Formed: Richmond, May 1861. ANV service: October 1861–April 1865. Assigned: Reserve Artillery; Jones's, Carter's, Page's, Cutshaw's Battalions. Commanders: Captains Thomas Jefferson Peyton (May 1861–October 1862), Charles W. Fry (October 1862–April 1865. Notes: Armed with a 3-inch rifle, a 12-pound howitzer, and three 6-pound smoothbores in September 1862; with two 3-inch rifles and two 10-pound Parrotts in October 1862; with two 12-pound howitzers in December 1864.

Otey Artillery (Co. A, 13th Battalion, Light Artillery) Formed: Richmond, late 1863. ANV service: May 1864–April 1865. Assigned: Gibbes's, Owen's, Walker's Battalions. Commander: Captain David N. Walker. Notes: Armed with four Napoleons and three Coehorn motars in December 1864; served as infantry during the Appomattox Campaign.

Pamunkey Artillery (Pamunkey Guards, Pamunkey Rescuers)
Formed: New Kent County, May 1861. ANV service: April 1865. Assiged: Crutchfield's Brigade. Commander: Captain Andrew J. Jones. Notes: Armed with nine heavy guns in December 1864.

Parker's Battery Formed: Richmond, March 1862. ANV service: August 1862–September 1863, April 1864–April 1865. Assigned: Lee's, Alexander's, Huger's Battalions. Commander: Captain William W. Parker. Notes: Armed with two 3-inch rifles and two 12-pound howitzers in August–September 1862; with three 3-inch rifles and a 10-pound Parrott in July 1863; with four 3-inch rifles in December 1864.

Peninsula Artillery (Co. G, 1st Regiment, Artillery) Formed: York County, May 1861. ANV service: October 1861–June 1862 (disbanded, men transferred to other regimental companies). Assigned: McLaws' Division; Griffith's Brigade; Cambell's Battalion; Anderson's Brigade. Commanders: Captain Joseph B. Cosnahan, William B. Jones. Notes: Armed with a Napoleon in June 1862.

Pittsylvania Battery Formed: Pittsylvania County, April 1862. ANV service: September 1862–April 1865. Assigned: Heath's Divisional artillery; Garnett's, Richardson's, Poague's Battalions. Commanders: Captains John W. Lewis (April–July 1862), Nathan Penick (July 1862–April 1865). Notes: Armed with two 3-inch rifles and two 10-pound Parrotts in September 1862–December 1864; supposed to have fired last artillery round of Lee's Army.

Portsmouth Light Artillery Formed: Portsmouth, 1808. ANV service: April–October 1862 (disbanded, men transferred to Beauregard and Norfolk Batteries. Assigned: Mahone's Brigade; R. H. Anderson's Divisional artillery. Commanders: Captains Cary F. Grimes (April–September 1862), John H. Thompson (September–October 1862).

Powhatan Battery Formed: Powhatan County, July 1861. ANV service: November 1861–April 1865. Assigned: Reserve Artillery, Brown's, Hardaway's Battalions. Commander: Captain Willis J. Dance. Notes: Armed with a 3-inch rifle, a 6-pound smoothbore, and two 12-pound howitzers in August–September 1862; with four 3-inch rifles in July 1863–December 1864.

Purcell Artillery Formed: Richmond, April 1861. ANV service: July 1861–April 1865. Assigned: Reserve Brigade; Walker's Brigade, A. P. Hill's Divisional artillery; Field's Brigade, Pegram's Battalion. Commanders: Captains Reuben Lindsay Walker (April 1861–April 1862), William J. Pegram (April 1862–March 1864), George M. Cayce (March 1864–April 1865). Notes: Armed with four Napoleons in July 1863–December 1864.

Rebel Artillery (Co. F, 2nd Regiment, Artillery) Formed: Lunenburg County, January 1862. ANV service: April 1865. Assigned: Crutchfield's Brigade. Commander: Captain Cornelius T. Allen. Notes: Served as heavy artillery.

Richmond Howitzers, 1st Company Formed: Richmond, November 1859. ANV service: July 1861–April 1865. Assigned: Bonham's, Griffith's, Barksdale's Brigades; McLaws' Divisional artillery, Cabell's Battalion. Commanders: Captains John C. Shields (July–November 1861), Edward S. McCarthy (May 1862–June 1864), Robert M. Anderson (June 1864–April 1865). Notes: Armed with two 10-pound Parrotts and two 6-pound smoothbores in August–September 1862; with two 3-inch rifles and two Napoleons in July 1863; with four Napoleons in December 1864.

Richmond Howitzers, 2nd Company Formed: Richmond, before May 1861. ANV service: June 1861–April 1865. Assigned: Reserve Artillery, Brown's, Hardaway's, Cutshaw's Battalions. Commander: Captain Lorraine F. Jones. Notes: Armed with two 10-pound Parrotts, a 2. 6-inch Hotchkiss rifle, and a 12-pound Dahlgren howitzer in September–October 1862; with four 10-pound Parrotts in July 1863; with two 10-pound Parrotts and two Napoleons in December 1864.

Richmond Howitzers, 3rd Company Formed: Richmond, before May 1861. ANV service: June 1861–April 1865. Assigned: Reserve Artillery, Brown's, Hardaway's Battalions. Commander: Captain Benjamin H. Smith. Notes: Armed with four 3-inch rifles in July 1863; with two 3-inch rifles and two Napoleons on 10 May 1864; with two 3-inch rifles on 11 May 1864; with four Napoleons in December 1864.

Ringgold Artillery (Co. B, 13th Battalion, Light Artillery) Formed: Danville, February 1862. ANV service: May 1864–April 1865. Assigned: Breckinridge's Division, Gibbes', Owen's, King's Battalions. Commander: Captain Crispin Dickenson. Notes: Armed with three Napoleons and a 3-inch rifle in May 1864; with four Napoleons in December 1864; converted to heavy artillery but served as infantry in 1865.

Roanoke Artillery Formed: By mergers, October 1863. ANV service: June 1864–April 1864. Assigned: Horse Artillery Battalion, Ransom's/Lomax's Cavalry Division; Thomson's Battalion, Horse Artillery. Commander: Captain Warren S. Lurty.

Rockbridge Artillery, 1st Battery Formed: Rockbridge County, April 1861. ANV service: July 1861–April 1865. Assigned: Stonewall Brigade, Jackson's Divisional artillery, Brown's/Hardaway's Battalion. Commanders: Captains John A. McCausland (April 1861), William N. Pendleton (April–July 1861), William McLaughlin (July 1861–April 1862), William T. Poague (April 1862–March 1863), Archibald Graham (March 1863–April 1865). Notes: Armed with three 6-pound smothbores and a 12-pound howitzer in June 1861; two 10-pound Parrotts added in April 1862; with two 6-pound smoothbores, two 12-pound howitzers and two 10-pound Parrotts in August–October 1862; with four 20-pound Parrotts in June 1863; with two 3-inch rifles and two 10-pound Parrotts in December 1864.

Rockbridge Artillery, 2nd Battery Formed: By conversion of Co. B, 52nd Infantry to artillery, September 1861. ANV service: May 1862–April 1865. Assigned: Ewell's, Jackson's Divisional artillery, Hardaway's, McIntosh's Battalions. Commanders: Captains John Miller (September 1861–May 1862), John A. M. Lusk (May 1862–June 1863), William K. Donald (June 1863–April 1865). Notes: Armed with two 6-pound smoothbores, a 3-inch rifle, and a 10-pound Parrott in August–September 1862; with four 3-inch rifles in July 1863; with three 24-pound howitzers in December 1864.

Salem Flying Artillery Formed: By conversion of Co. A, 9th Infantry to artillery, May 1862. ANV service: July 1862–April 1865. Assigned: Brown's, Hardaway's Battalions. Commanders: Captains Abraham Hupp (May 1862–September 1863), Charles B. Griffin (September 1863–April 1865). Notes: Armed with two 12-pound howitzers and two 6-pound smoothbores in August–October 1862; with two 3-inch rifles and two Napoleons in July 1863.

Southside Heavy Artillery Battery Formed: Chesterfield County, January 1862. ANV service: March–April 1865. Assigned: Smith's Brigade. Commander: Captain John W. Drewry.

Stafford Light Artillery Formed: Stafford County, August 1861. ANV service: June–July 1862,

August 1862–January 1863, April 1864–April 1865. Assigned: Holmes' Divisional artillery; Walker's/Cooke's Brigades; Braxton's Battalion. Commanders: Captains John R. Cooke (August 1861–April 1862), Thomas B. French (August–November 1862), Raleigh L. Cooper (November 1862–April 1865). Notes: Armed with three 12-pound howitzers, two 3-inch rifles, and a 10-pound Parrott in June–July 1862; with three 10-pound Parrotts and three 12-pound howitzers in August–September 1862; with two 10-pound Parrotts in December 1864.

Staunton Artillery Formed: Augusta County, November 1859. ANV service: July 1861–April 1865. Assigned: Bee's/Whiting's Brigade, Whiting's Divisional artillery, Texas Brigade, Jones's/Cutshaw's Battalion. Commanders: Captains John D. Imboden (April 1861–June 1862), William L. Balthis (June–December 1862), Asher W. Garber (December 1862–April 1865). Notes: Armed with four 6-pound smoothbores in August–September 1862; with four Napoleons in July 1863; with two 3-inch rifles in December 1864.

Staunton Horse Artillery Formed: By conversion of Co. A, 62nd Infantry (Mounted) to artillery, February 1863. ANV service: March 1863–April 1865. Assigned: North–western Virginia Brigade, Valley District Cavalry Horse Artillery, Lomax's Division Horse Artillery Battalion, McGregor's Horse Artillery Battalion. Commander: Captain John H.

McClanahan. Notes: Armed with six guns in July 1863–May 1864.

Stuart Horse Artillery, 1st Battery Formed: From part of Pelham's Battery, August 1862. ANV service: August 1862–April 1865. Assigned: Cavalry Division Horse Artillery Battalion; Rosser's, Lomax's Cavalry Divisional artillery; Breathed's Battalion. Commanders: Captains James Breathed (August 1862–February 1864), Philip P. Johnson (February 1864–February 1865), Daniel Shanks (February–April 1865). Notes: Armed with four 3-inch rifles in July 1863.

Stuart Horse Artillery, 2nd Battery Formed: From men of Henry's Battery, August 1862. ANV service: August 1862–April 1865. Assigned: Cavalry Divisional Horse Artillery, McGregor's and Thomson's Battalions. Commanders: Captains M. W. Henry (August 1862–February 1863), William M. McGregor (February 1863–February 1865), G. Wilmer Brown (February–April 1865). Notes: Armed with two Napoleons and two 3-inch rifles in July 1863; with four 3-inch rifles in December 1864.

Surry Light Artillery Formed: By conversion of Co. I, 3rd Infantry to artillery, early 1862. ANV service: April 1865. Assigned: Lightfoot's Battalion. Commander: Captain James D. Hankins.

Thomas Artillery Formed: Richmond, May 1861. ANV service: July 1861–October 1862 (disbanded, men to Caskie's Battery). Assigned: Wilcox's Brigade, Reserve Artillery. Commanders: Captains Philip B. Standard (May

1861–July 1862), Edwin J. Anderson (July–October 1862). Notes: Armed with four 6-pound smoothbores in July 1861.

Turner Artillery Formed: Goochland County, August 1861. ANV service: August–October 1862 (disbanded, men transferred to King William Artillery). Assigned: D. R. Jones's Divisional artillery. Commander: Captain Walter D. Leake.

United Artillery Formed: By conversion of Co. E, 41st Infantry to artillery, April 1862. ANV service: April–June 1862, March–April 1865. Commander: Captain Thomas Kevill. Notes: A detachment served guns aboard CSS *Virginia* in March 1862.

Warrenton Artillery Formed: Fauquier County, March 1862. ANV service: September 1862–April 1865. Assigned: Brown's, Poague's Battalions. Commanders: Captains James V. Brooke (March 1862–July 1863), Addison W. Utterback (July 1863–April 1865). Notes: Armed with a Napoleon, a 12-pound howitzer and two 6-pound smoothbores in August–September 1862; with two Napoleons and two 12-pound howitzers in July 1863; with two Napoleons in December 1864.

Washington Artillery (Hampton Artillery) Formed: By conversion of Co. K, 32nd Infantry to artillery, September 1861. ANV service: September 1861–July 1862. Assigned: Brown's Regiment, Reserve Artillery. Commander: Captain William W. Fraser.

West Augusta Artillery (West Augusta Guards) Formed: By conversion of Co. L, 5th Infantry to artillery, November 1861. ANV service: November 1861–April 1862 (disbanded, converted to Co. L, 5th Infantry). Assigned: Stonewall Brigade. Commander: Captain James H. Waters.

Williamsburg Artillery (Lee Artillery, Co. F, 1st Regiment, Artillery) Formed: James City County, May 1861. ANV service: October 1861–October 1862 (disbanded, men transferred to 1st Artillery Regiment companies). Assigned: McLaws' Brigade, Brown's Battalion. Commander: Captain James A. Coke.

Winchester Artillery (Jackson Artillery) Formed: Winchester, March 1862. ANV service: May–September 1862 (merged with Alleghany Artillery). Assigned: Jackson's Division, ANV reserve artillery. Commander: Captain Wilfred E. Cutshaw. Notes: Armed with four rifled guns in May–June 1862.

Wise Artillery (Co. B, 1st Regiment, Artillery) Formed: April 1861. ANV service: July 1861–October 1862 (disbanded, men assigned to S. D. Lee's Battalion). Assigned: Bartow's/S. Jones's, Anderson's, D. R. Jones's, Semmes', G. T. Anderson's Brigades, D. R. Jones's Divisional artillery. Commanders: Captains Ephraim G. Alburtis (April 1861–April 1862), James S. Brown (April–October 1862). Notes: Armed with four 6-pound smoothbores in July 1861; with two 6-pound smoothbores and two 12-pound howitzers in June–July 1862.

VIRGINIA: CAVALRY

1st Regiment Formed: In the field, July 1861. ANV service: July 1861–April 1865. Brigades assigned: ANV Cavalry, Fitzhugh Lee's, Wickham's, Munford's. Commanders: Colonels James E. B. Stuart (July–September 1861), Fitzhugh Lee (August 1861–July 1862), William E. Jones (July–September 1862), James H. Drake (September 1862–July 1863), Richard W. Carter (July–December 1863, August–December 1864), William A. Morgan (December 1863–August 1864, December 1864–April 1865). Notes: Initially armed with sabres and pistols, then with Hall's carbines, later with Sharps (Co. K, May 1862), and Merrill carbines and Adams and Colt Army and Navy calibre revolvers.

2nd Regiment Formed: Lynchburg, May 1861. ANV service: July 1861–April 1865. Brigades assigned: ANV Cavalry, Robertson's, Fitzhugh Lee's, Wickham's, Munford's. Commanders: Colonels Richard C. W. Radford (May 1861–April 1862), Thomas T. Munford (April 1862–February 1865), Lieutenant Colonel Cary Breckinridge (February–April 1865). Notes: Initially armed with shotguns, a few carbines, pistols and sabres; band received instruments captured at Haymarket.

3rd Regiment Formed: In the field, September 1861. ANV service: September 1861–April 1865. Brigades assigned: ANV Cavalry, Fitzhugh Lee's, Wickham's, Munford's. Commanders: Colonels Robert Johnston (September

1861–April 1862), Thomas F. Goode (April–November 1862), Thomas H. Owen (November 1862–April 1865). Notes: Initially armed with shotguns, some carbines, revolvers, sabres and bowie knives.

4th Regiment Formed: Sangster's Crossroads, September 1861. ANV service: November 1861–April 1865. Brigades assigned: ANV Cavalry, Wickham's, Munford's. Commanders: Colonels Beverly H. Robertson (September 1861–June 1862), Williams C. Wickham (June 1862–September 1863), William H. F. Payne (September 1863–November 1864), William B. Wooldridge (November 1864–April 1865). Notes: Initially six companies armed with revolvers and sabres, two with sabres only.

5th Regiment Formed: In the field, May 1862. ANV service: June 1862–November 1864 (disbanded, men merged with 15th Regiment into 5th Consolidated Cavalry Regiment). Brigades assigned: ANV Cavalry, Fitzhugh Lee's, Lomax's, Payne's. Commanders: Colonels Thomas L. Rosser (May 1862–October 1863), Henry Clay Pate (October 1863–May 1864), Reuben B. Boston (May–November 1864). Notes: In December 1862 armed with double–barrelled shotguns and sabres; in 1863 issued with Austrian and Sharps rifles, carbines, revolvers and sabres.

5th Consolidated Regiment Formed: From 5th and 15th Regiments, November 1864. ANV service: November 1864–April 1865. Brigade assigned: Payne's. Commander: Colonel Reuben B. Boston.

6th Regiment Formed: In the field, September 1861. ANV service: September 1861–April 1865. Brigades assigned: ANV Cavalry, Robertson's, Jones's, Lomax's, Payne's. Commanders: Colonel Charles W. Field (September 1861–March 1862), Lieutenant Colonel Julien Harrison (March–July 1862), Colonel Thomas S. Flournoy (July–October 1862), Lieutenant Colonel John S. Green (October 1862–September 1863), Colonel Julien Harrison (September–October 1863), Lieutenant Colonel Daniel T. Richards (October 1863–April 1865). Notes: Armed with Hall, Sharps and Burnside carbines.

7th Regiment (Laurel Brigade) Formed: spring 1861. ANV service: August 1862–April 1865. Brigades assigned: Robertson's, Jones's, Rosser's, Dearing's. Commanders: Colonels Angus W. McDonald (spring–November 1861), Turner Ashby (November 1861–May 1862), William E. Jones (May–October 1862), Richard H. Dulaney (October 1862–April 1865). Notes: Armed with M1841 and Enfield rifles and sabre bayonets; Burnside, Sharps, Smith and Merrill carbines; single–shot pistols and Kerr, Savage, and Colt Army and Navy calibre revolvers; and sabres; wore a brigade cap badge consisting of a heart–shaped piece of cloth, edged with gold lace, with an embroidered laurel twig in its centre.

8th Regiment Formed: January 1862. ANV service: May–August

1863, February–April 1865. Brigades assigned: Jenkins', Payne's. Commanders: Colonels Walter H. Jenifer (January–May 1862), James M. Corns (May 1862–April 1865).

9th Regiment Formed: Aquia District, January 1862. ANV service: June 1962–April 1865. Brigades assigned: ANV Cavalry, W. H. F. Lee's, Chambliss', Beale's. Commanders: Colonels John E. Johnson (January–April 1862), W. H. F. Lee (April–October 1862), Richard L. T. Beale (October 1862–December 1864), Thomas C. Waller (December 1864–April 1865).

10th Regiment (Laurel Brigade) Formed: By merger of 8th Battalion and Wise Legion Cavalry, May 1862. ANV service: May 1863–April 1865. Brigades assigned: Jones's, Lomax's, Rosser's, Dearing's. Commanders: Colonel James L. Davis (May 1862–July 1863, March 1864–February 1865), Lieutenant Colonel Robert A. Caskie (July 1863–March 1864, February–April 1865). Notes: Wore same cap badge as the 7th Regiment.

11th Regiment (Laurel Brigade) Formed: June 1862. ANV service: May 1863–April 1865. Brigades assigned: Jones's, Lomax's, Rosser's, Dearing's. Commanders: Colonels Lunsford L. Lomax (June 1862–July 1863), Oliver R. Funsten, Sr. (July 1863–April 1865). Notes: Armed with Enfield rifled muskets and Gallagher, Burnside, Merrill, Smith, and Hall carbines, and Kerr and Colt Army and Navy calibre revolvers; wore same brigade cap badge as the 7th Regiment.

12th Regiment (Laurel Brigade)
Formed: From the 7th Regiment,
June 1862. ANV service: August
1862–April 1865. Assigned: ANV
Second Corps, Robertson's,
Jones's, Rosser's, Dearing's
Brigades. Commanders: Colonel
Asher W. Harman (June 1862–July
1863), Lieutenant Colonel
Emanuel Sipe (July 1864–April
1865). Notes: Armed with M1841
and Colt revolving rifles and Burn-
side, Hall, Sharps and Smith car-
bines, and Kerr and Colt Army and
Navy calibre revolvers and sabres;
wore same cap badge as the 7th
Regiment.

13th Regiment Formed: From
16th Battalion and 5th Regiment,
July 1862. ANV service: December
1862–April 1865. Brigades
assigned: W. H. F. Lee's, Chambliss', Beale's. Commanders:
Colonels John R. Chambliss (July
1862–December 1863), Jefferson
C. Phillips (January 1864–February
1865), Lieutenant Colonel Alexander Savage (February–April 1865).

**14th Battalion (Chesapeake Bat-
talion)**Formed: May 1862. ANV
service: June–July 1862 (merged
with 15th Regiment, September
1862). Brigade assigned: Ransom's.
Commander: Major Edgar Bur-
roughs.

14th Regiment Formed: September 1862. ANV service:
May–August 1863, March–April
1865. Brigade assigned: Jenkins'.
Commanders: Colonels Charles E.
Thorburn (September 1862–1863),
James Cochran (1863–April 1865).
Notes: Armed with double–barrelled shotguns, M1841 rifles, Merrill carbines, and Colt Army and
navy calibre revolvers.

**15th Battalion (Northern Neck
Rangers)** Formed: spring 1862.
ANV service: June–July 1862
(merged with 15th Regiment, Sep-
tember 1862). Brigade assigned:
ANV Cavalry. Commander: Major
John Critcher.

15th Regiment Formed: By
merger of 14th and 15th Battalions, September 1862. ANV service: November 1862–November
1864 (merged with 5th Consolidated Regiment, November 1864).
Brigades assigned: W. H. F Lee's,
Lomax's, Payne's. Commanders:
Colonel William B. Ball (September–December 1862), Lieutenant
Colonel John Critcher (December
1862–May 1863), Colonel Charles
R. Collins (May 1863–May 1864).
Notes: Armed with Colt Army
revolvers.

16th Regiment Formed: By
merger of Ferguson's and Cald-
well's Battalions, January 1863.
ANV service: May–August 1863,
March–April 1865. Brigades
assigned: Jenkins', McCausland's.
Commanders: Colonel Milton J.
Ferguson (January 1863–February
1864), Lieutenant Colonel William
L. Graham (February–August
1864), Major James H. Nounnan
(August 1864–April 1865). Notes:
Armed with Richmond–made
M1855 rifled muskets.

17th Battalion Formed: From
superfluous men of the 7th Regiment, June 1862. ANV service:
August 1862–February 1863
(merged with 11th Regiment, February 1863). Brigades assigned:
Jackson's Command Cavalry,

Robertson's, Jones's. Commander: Lieutenant Colonel Oliver R. Funsten, Sr.

17th Regiment Formed: By growth of 33rd Battalion, January 1863. ANV service: May–August 1863, March–April 1865. Brigades assigned: Jenkins', McCausland's. Commanders: Colonel William H. French (January 1863–September 1864), Lieutenant Colonel William C. Tavenner (September–July 1864). Notes: Armed with Colt Army and Navy calibre revolvers.

18th Regiment Formed: December 1862. ANV service: June 1864–April 1865. Brigade assigned: Imboden's. Commander: Colonel George W. Imboden (December 1862–April 1865).

19th Regiment Formed: From 3rd Infantry Regiment, State Line, April 1863. ANV service: June 1864–May 1865 (surrendered). Brigade assigned: Jackson's (Valley). Commander: Lieutenant Colonel William P. Thompson.

20th Regiment Formed: August 1863. ANV service: June 1864–April 1865. Brigade assigned: Jackson's (Valley). Commander: Colonel William W. Arnett.

21st Regiment Formed: From State Line, August 1863. ANV service: March–April 1865. Brigade assigned: McCausland's. Commander: Colonel William E. Peters.

22nd Regiment (Bowen's Regiment Virginia Mounted Riflemen) Formed: From Baldwin's Partisan Rangers, October 1863. ANV service: March–April 1865. Brigade assigned: McCausland's. Commander: Colonel Henry S. Bowen.

24th Regiment Formed: By merger of 32nd and 40th Battalions and two companies of the 8th Regiment, June 1864. ANV service: January–April 1865. Brigade assigned: Gary's. Commander: Colonel William T. Robins.

25th Regiment Formed: By merger of 27th Partisan Rangers and Lyle's Company, July 1864. ANV service: November 1864–April 1865. Brigade assigned: Imboden's. Commander: Colonel Warren M. Hopkins.

34th Battalion (1st Battalion, Mounted Rifles, Witcher's Mounted Rifles) Formed: June 1862. ANV service: May–August 1863. Brigade assigned: Jenkins'. Commander: Major Vincent A. Witcher. Notes: Armed with M1841 rifles and and Savage and Colt Army and Navy revolvers.

35th Battalion (Laurel Brigade) Formed: Informally in January 1862, officially in February 1863. ANV service: November 1862–April 1865. Brigades assigned: Jones's, Rosser's, Dearing's. Commander: Lieutenant Colonel Elijah V. White. Notes: Armed with M1841 rifles; Burnside, Smith, and Sharps carbines; Kerr, Savage, and Colt Army and Navy revolvers and sabres; wore same brigade cap badge as the 7th Regiment.

36th Battalion Formed: February 1863. ANV service: May–August 1863. Brigade assigned: Jenkins'. Commander: Major James W. Sweeney. Notes: Armed with M1841 rifles.

37th Battalion Formed: From Dunn's Partisan Rangers, November 1862. ANV service: May–July 1863. Brigade assigned: Jenkins'. Commander: Lieutenant Colonel Ambrose C. Dunn.

39th Battalion (Richardson's Battalion of Scouts, Guides and Couriers) Formed: September 1864. ANV service: September 1864–April 1865. Assigned: Provost Guard, Army Headquarters. Commander: Major John H. Richardson.

43rd Battalion (Mosby's Rangers) Formed: Behind enemy lines, March 1863. ANV service: March 1863–April 1865 (as partisan rangers). Assigned: Unattached. Commander: Colonel John S. Mosby. Notes: Each man armed with a pair of revolvers.

VIRGINIA: INFANTRY

1st Battalion Provisional (Irish Battalion, 1st Regulars) Formed: Richmond, May 1861. ANV service: June 1861–April 1865. Brigades assigned: Campbell's, Cunningham's, J. R. Jones's, Provost Guard. Commanders: Major John D. Munford (May 1861–May 1862), Captain Benjamin W. Leigh (May–summer 1862), First Lieutenant Charles A. Davidson (summer–October 1862), Major David B. Bridgford (October 1862–April 1865).

1st Battalion Reserves Formed: Richmond, May 1864. ANV service: April 1865. Brigade assigned: Barton's. Commander: Lieutenant Colonel Richard T. W. Duke.

1st Regiment (Williams Rifles) Formed: Richmond, May 1851. ANV service: June 1861–February 1863, May–September 1863, May 1864–April 1865. Brigades assigned: Terrett's, Longstreet's, Clark's, Griffith's, Ewell's, A. P. Hill's, Kemper's, Terry's. Commanders: Colonel Patrick T. Moore (1860–July 1861), Lieutenant Colonel William H. Fry (July–November 1861), Colonels Lewis B. Williams, Jr. (April 1862–July 1863), Frederick G. Skinner (July 1863–February 1865), Lieutenant Colonel Francis H. Langley (February–April 1865; in fact commanded much of the time from July 1863 on). Notes: Armed with M1855 rifled muskets; had a band and corps of drums.

2nd Battalion Reserves Formed: Richmond, August 1864. ANV service: April 1865. Brigade assigned: Burton's. Commander: Lieutenant Colonel John H. Guy.

2nd Regiment Organized: Charleston, June 1860. ANV service: July 1861–April 1865. Brigade assignments: 1st Brigade, Second Corps; Stonewall, Terry's Consolidated. Commanders: Colonel James W. Allen (April 1861–June 1862), Lieutenant Colonels (commanding) Botts Lawson (April–August 1861), Raleigh T. Colston Jr. (June–November 1862), Colonels John Quincy Adams Nadenbousch (November 1862–April 1864), William W. Randolph (April–May 1864), Major Charles H. Stewart (May 1864–April 1865) (Captain Joseph J. Jenkins actually commanded most of 1865). Notes: Armed with percussion muskets.

3rd Battalion Reserves Organized: Petersburg, June 1864. ANV service: April 1865. Brigade assign-

ment: Barton's. Commander: Lieutenant Colonel Fletcher H. Archer.
3rd Regiment Organized: Portsmouth, April 1861. ANV service: April 1862–February 1863, May–September 1863, May 1864–April 1865. Brigade assignments: Colston's, Pryor's, Kemper's, Terry's. Commanders: Colonels Roger Atkinson Pryor (April 1861–April 1862), Joseph Mayo Jr (April 1862–April 1865). Notes: Initially armed with flintlock and percussion smoothbore muskets.
3rd Regiment Reserves Organized: Richmond, September 1864. ANV service: January–March 1865. Brigade assignment: Walker's. Commander: Colonel Richard A. Booker.
4th Regiment Organized: April 1861. ANV service: July 1861–April 1865. Brigade assignments: 1st Brigade, Second Corps; Stonewall Brigade; Terry's Consolidated. Commanders: Colonels James F. Preston (April 1861–January 1862), Lewis T. Moore (January–April 1862), Charles A. Ronald (April 1862–September 1863), William Terry (September 1863–May 1864), Major Matthew D. Bennett (May–September 1864), Captain Hamilton D. Wade (September 1864–April 1865). Notes: Co. F issued M1855 rifles and sabre bayonets in 1861; took 53. 8 percent losses at Manassas and 48. 3 percent losses at Chancellorsville.
5th Battalion Organized: April 1861. ANV service: April–September 1862 (disbanded then). Brigade assignment: Armistead's. Commander: Lieutenant Colonel

Fletcher H. Archer (April 1861–May 1862), Majors William R. Foster (May–June 1862), John P. Wilson Jr, (June–September 1862). Notes: Initially issued flintlock musket, replaced with percussion muskets in 1862; saw heavy artillery service.
5th Battalion Reserves (Henry's Infantry Regiment Reserves) Organized: September 1864. ANV service: January–April 1865. Brigade assignment: Walker's. Commander: Lieutenant Colonel Patrick M. Henry.
5th Regiment Organized: Augusta County, May 1861. ANV service: July 1861–April 1865. Brigade assignments: 1st Brigade, Second Corps; Stonewall Brigade; Terry's Consolidated. Commanders: Colonels Kenton Harper (May–September 1861), William H. Harman (September 1861–April 1862), William S. H. Baylor (April–August 1862), John H. S. Funk (August 1862–September 1864), Lieutenant Colonel Hazel J. Williams (September–October 1864), Captain Peter E. Wilson (October 1864–April 1865). Notes: Had a band.
6th Regiment Organized: Norfolk, May 1861. ANV service: April 1862–April 1865. Brigade assignments: Mahonels, Weisiger's. Commanders: Colonels William Mahone (May–November 1861), Thomas Jefferson Corprew (November 1861–May 1862), George T. Rogers (May 1862–April 1865). Notes: Initially armed with flintlock and conversion percussion muskets except for Co. C which carried percussion rifles

made at Harper's Ferry, either M1841 or M1855.

7th Infantry Organized: Camp Wigfall, May 1861. ANV service: June 1861–February 1863, May–September 1863, May 1864–April 1865. Brigade assignments: Early's, Longstreet's, Clark's, Griffith's, Ewell's, AP Hill's, Kemper's, Terry's. Commanders: Colonels James L. Kemper (May 1861–June 1862), Waller T. Patton (June 1862–July 1863), Charles C. Floweree (July 1863–April 1865), Captain William 0. Fry (April 1865). Notes: Initially armed largely with converted muskets, but Co. H received M1855 rifled muskets; Co. H drawn from the District of Columbia and Maryland.

8th Regiment (Old Bloody Eighth) Organized: May 1861. ANV service: June 1861–February 1863, May–September 1863, May 1864–April 1865. Brigade assignments: Cockers, Evans', Pickett's, Garnett's, Hunton's. Commanders: Colonels Eppa Hunton (May 1861–August 1863), Norbonne Berkeley (August 1863–April 1865). Notes: Initially armed mostly with converted muskets.

9th Regiment Organized: July 1861. ANV service: April 1862–February 1863, May–September 1863, May 1864–April 1865. Brigade assignments: Armistead's, Barton's, Steuart's. Commanders: Colonel Francis H. Smith (July 1861–May 1862), Lieutenant Colonel James S. Gilliam (May 1862–June 1863), Colonel James J. Philips (June 1863–April 1865), Captain John Parke Wilson Jr.

(April 1865). Notes: Co. D initially armed with pikes, exchanged for flintlocks, then converted muskets; Co. G armed with M1841 rifles; wore regimental badges after 15 December 1864.

10th Regiment Organized: Harper's Ferry, May 1861. ANV service: July 1861–April 1865. Brigade assignments: EK Smith's, Elzey's, Taliaferrols, Fulkerson's, Warren's, Hampton's, Colston's, Steuart's, Terry's Consolidated. Commanders: Colonels Simeon B. Gibbons (May 1861–May 1862), Edward T. H. Warren (May 1862–May 1864), Lieutenant Colonel Dorilas H. Martz (May 1864–April 1865).

11th Regiment Organized: May 1861. ANV service: June 1861–February 1863, May–September 1863, May 1864–April 1865. Brigade assignments: Longstreet's, Clark's, Griffith's, Ewell's, AP Hill's, Kemper's, Terry's. Commanders: Colonels Samuel Garland, Jr. (May 1861–May 1862), David Funsten (May–June 1862), Maurice S. Langhorne (June 1862), Kirkwood Otey (June 1862–April 1865).

12th Regiment Organized: July 1861. ANV service: April 1862–April 1865. Brigade assignments: Mahonels, Weisiger's. Commanders: Colonels David A. Weisiger (May 1861–May 1864), Everard M. Field (May 1864–April 1865). Notes: Initially issued percussion muskets and Enfield rifled muskets.

13th Regiment Organized: May 1861. ANV service: July 1861–April 1865. Brigade assignments: Elzey's, EK Smith's, Early's, Smith's,

Pegram's, Walker's. Commanders: Colonels A. P. Hill (May 1861–February 1862), James A. Walker (February 1862–May 1863), James B. Terrill (May 1863–May 1864), Major Charles T. Critten (May–June 1864), Captain George Cullen (June 1864–April 1865).

14th Regiment Organized: May 1861. ANV service: April 1862–February 1863, May–September 1863, May–April 1865. Brigade assignments: Armistead's, Barton's, Steuart's. Commanders: Colonels James G. Hodges (May 1861–July 1863), William White (July 1863–1865), Major William D. Shelton (1865). Notes: Initially armed mostly with converted flintlock muskets; wore a regimental badge after 15 December 1864.

15th Regiment Organized: May 1861. ANV service: April 1862–February 1863, May–September 1863, May 1864–April 1865. Brigade assignments: McLaws', Semmes', Corsels. Commanders: Colonel Thomas P. August (May 1861–July 1862), Lieutenant Colonel Emmett M. Morrison (July 1862–April 1865). Notes: Mostly initially armed with converted flintlock muskets, Co. D issued converted Virginia Manufactory flintlocks; took 58. 5 percent losses at Sharpsburg.

16th Regiment Organized: As 26th Regiment, May 1861. ANV service: April 1862–April 1865. Brigade assignments: Mahone's, Weisiger's. Commanders: Colonels Raleigh E. Colston (May–December 1861), Charles A. Crump (December 1861–May 1862), Joseph H. Ham (May 1862–May

1864), Lieutenant Colonel Richard O. Whitehead (May 1864–April 1865). Notes: Arms in 1861 reported in good condition.

17th Regiment Organized: Manassas Junction, June 1861. ANV service: June 1861–February 1863, May–September 1863, May 1864–April 1865. Brigade assignments: Terry's, Longstreet's, Clark's, Griffith's, Ewell's, A. P. Hill's, Kemper's, Corse's. Commanders: Colonel Montgomery D. Corse (June 1861–November 1862), Lieutenant Colonel Morton Marye (November–August 1862), Colonel Arthur Herbert (August 1862–April 1865). Notes: Initially mostly armed with percussion muskets, Co. A carried rifles, either M1855 or M1841, from Harper's Ferry; took 56. 3 percent losses at Sharpsburg.

18th Regiment Organized: May 1861. ANV service: June 1861–February 1863, May–September 1863, May 1864–April 1865. Brigade assignments: Cock's, Pickett's, Garnett's, Hunton's. Commanders: Colonel Robert E. Withers (May 1861–June 1862), Lieutenant Colonel George C. Cabell (June 1862–May 1864), Colonel Henry A. Carrington (May 1864–April 1865). Notes: Initially mostly armed with converted flintlocks.

19th Regiment Organized: Manassas Junction, May 1861. ANV service: June 1861–February 1862, May–September 1863, May 1864–April 1865. Brigade assignments: Cocke's, Pickett's, Garnett's, Hunton's. Commanders: Colonels Philip St. George Cocke (May–October 1861),

Armistead T. M. Rust (October 1861–April 1862), James B. Strange (April–September 1862), Henry Gantt (September 1862–April 1865).

20th Regiment Organized: June 1861. ANV service: June–July 1862 (disbanded October 1862). Brigade Assignment: Wise's. Commander: Lieutenant Colonel John Pegram.

21st Regiment Organized: April 1861. ANV service: May 1862–April 1865. Brigade assignments: J. R. Jones's, J. M. Jones', Terry's Consolidated. Commanders: Colonel William Gilham (April 1861–January 1862), John M. Patton Jr. (January–August 1862), William A. Witcher (August 1862–April 1865).

22nd Battalion Organized: From 2nd Regiment, Artillery, May 1862. ANV service: June 1862–January 1865, April 1865. Brigade assignments: Pender's, Field's, Walker's, Mayo's, Barton's. Commanders: Lieutenant Colonel James C. Johnson (May–November 1862), Edward P. Tayloe (November 1862–April 1865).

22nd Regiment (1st Kanawha Infantry) Organized: April 1861. ANV service: May–June 1864. Brigade assignment: Echol's. Commander: Colonel George S. Patton.

23rd Battalion Organized: January 1862. ANV service: May–June 1864. Brigade assignment: Echols'. Commander: Major William Blessing.

23nd Regiment Organized: Richmond, May 1861. ANV service: June 1862–April 1865. Brigade assignments: Taliaferro's, Warren's, Hampton's, Terry's Con-

solidated. Commanders: Colonels William B. Taliaferro (May 1861–March 1862), Alexander G. Taliferro (March 1862–July 1863), Lieutenant Colonel John P. Fitzgerald (July 1863–May 1864), Major Andrew Jackson Richardson (May 1864–April 1865). Notes: Initially armed with smoothbore muskets and M1841 rifles while Co. H received M1855 rifles; by 1863 carried Enfield rifled muskets.

24th Regiment Organized: Richmond, May 1861. ANV service: June 1861–February 1863, May–September 1863, May 1864–April 1865. Brigade assignments: Early's, Garland's, Kemper's, Terry's. Commanders: Colonels Jubal A. Early (May–August 1861), William R. Terry (August 1861–May 1864), Lieutenant Colonel Richard L. Maury (May 1864–April 1865).

25th Battalion (Richmond City Battalion) Organized: Richmond, August 1862. ANV service: April 1865. Brigade assignment: Barton's. Commander: Lieutenant Colonel Wyatt M. Elliott.

25th Regiment Organized: June 1861. ANV service: June 1862–May 1864, December 1864–April 1865. Brigade assignments: Early's, J. M. Jones', Terry's Consolidated. Commanders: Lieutenant Colonel John C. Higginbotham (May 1862–May 1864), Colonel Robert D. Lilley (May–June 1864), Major Wilson Harper (June 1864–April 1865). Notes: Initially armed with converted 0. 69 calibre flintlock muskets.

26th Battalion Organized: May 1862. ANV service: May–June

1864. Brigade assignment: Echol's. Commander: Lieutenant Colonel George M. Edgar (1862–September 1864).

26th Regiment Organized: June 1861. ANV service: July 1861–August 1862, October 1864–April 1865. Brigade assignments: Crump's Command, Rodes', Wise's. Commanders: Colonels Charles A. Crump (July 1861–May 1862), Powhatan R. Page (May 1862–June 1864), Major William K. Perrin (June 1864–April 1864).

27th Regiment Organized: May 1861. ANV service; July 1861–April 1865. Brigade assignments: 1st of the Second Corps, Stonewall, Terry's Consolidated. Commanders: Colonels William F. Gordon (May–October 1861), Andrew Jackson Grigsby (October 1861–November 1862), James K. Edmondson (November 1862–December 1863), Lieutenant Colonel Charles L. Haynes (December 1863–April 1865).

28th Regiment Organized: June 1861. ANV service: June 1861–February 1863, May–September 1863, May 1864–April 1865. Brigade assignments: Cocke's, Pickett's, Garnett's, Hunton's. Commanders: Colonels Robert T. Preson (June 1861–April 1862), Robert C. Allen (April 1862–July 1863), William Watts (July 1863–April 1865).

29th Regiment Organized: May 1861. ANV service: May–September 1863, May 1864–April 1865. Brigade assignment: Corse's. Commander: Colonel James Giles.

30th Regiment Organized: June 1861. ANV service: September 1862–February 1863, May–September 1863, May 1864–April 1865. Brigade asignments: Walker's, Corse's. Commanders: Colonels Harrison A. Taylor (April 1862–November 1864), Robert S. Chew (November 1864–April 1865—but actually commanded most of the time).

31st Regiment Organized: June 1861. ANV service: June 1862–April 1865. Brigade assignments: Elzey's, Early's, Smith's, Pegram's, Walker's. Commanders: Colonel John S. Hoffman (May 1862–February 1865), Captain Nathan Clawson (February–April 1865).

32nd Regiment Organized: May 1861. ANV service: May 1862–February 1863, May–September 1863, May 1864–April 1865. Brigade assignments: Pryor's, Semmes', Corse's. Commanders: Colonels Benjamin S. Ewell (July 1861–May 1862), Edgar B. Montague (May 1862–April 1865). Notes: Took 45.5 percent losses at Sharpsburg.

33rd Regiment Organized: June 1861. ANV service: July 1861–April 1865. Brigade assignments: 1st of the Second Corps, Stonewall, Terry's Consolidated. Commanders: Colonels Arthur C. Cummings (July 1861–April 1862), John F. Neff (April–August 1862), Edwin G. Lee (August 1862–December 1863), Frederick W. M. Holliday (December 1863–March 1864), George Huston (March 1864–February 1865), Abraham Spengler (February–April 1865). Notes: Initially armed mostly with flintlock and converted flintlock muskets.

34th Regiment Organized: As 4th Regiment, Heavy Artillery, May 1862. ANV service: October 1864–April 1865. Brigade assignment: Wise's. Commander: Colonel John T. Goode.

37th Regiment Organized: June 1861. ANV service: June 1862–April 1865. Brigade assignments: Taliaferro's, Warren's, Hampton's, Colston's, Steuart's, Terry's Consolidated. Commanders: Colonels Samuel V. Fulkerson (June 1861–June 1862), Titus Vespasian Williams (June 1862–April 1865), Captain John A. Preston (actual field commander in 1865). Notes: Initially armed with converted flintlock muskets.

38th Regiment (Pittsylvania Regiment) Organized: June 1861. ANV service: June 1861–February 1863, May–September 1863, May 1864–April 1865. Brigade assignments: Toombs', Early's, Garland's, Armistead's, Barton's, Steuart's. Commanders: Colonel Edward C. Edmonds (June 1861–July 1863), Lieutenant Colonel Joseph R. Cabell (July 1863–May 1864), Colonel George K. Griggs (May 1864–April 1865). Notes: Wore a regimental badge consisting of a blue heart from 15 December 1864.

40th Regiment Organized: May 1861. ANV service: October 1861–January 1865, April 1865. Brigade assignments: Field's, Walker's, Barton's. Commanders: Colonel John M. Brockenbrough (May 1861–January 1864), Lieutenant Colonel Arthur S. Cunningham (January 1864–April 1865).

41st Regiment Organized: July 1861. ANV service: April 1862–April 1865. Brigade assignment's, Mahone's, Weisiger's. Commanders: Colonels John R. Chambliss, Jr. (July 1861), William A. Parham (July 1861–March 1865), Lieutenant Colonel Joseph P. Mineteree (field commander, July 1862–may 1864), Major William H. Etheredge (field commander, May 1864–April 1865).

42nd Regiment Organized: July 1861. ANV service: June 1862–April 1865. Brigade assignments: Campbell's, J. R. Jones', J. M. Jones', Terry's Consolidated. Commanders: Colonel Jesse S. Burks (July 1861–July 1862), Lieutenant Colonel William Martin (July–August 1862), Colonel Robert W. Withers (August 1862–August 1864), Major Jesse M. Richardson (August 1864–march 1865). Notes: Initially armed mostly with converted flintlock muskets.

44th Battalion (Petersburg City Battalion) Organized: Petersburg, November 1863. ANV service: March–April 1865. Assignment: Archer's Battalion, Provost Guard (Co. B). Commander: Major Peter V. Batte.

44th Regiment Organized: June 1861. ANV service: May 1862–April 1865. Brigade assignments: Elzey's, Early's, J. R. Jones', J. M. Jones', Terry's Consolidated. Commanders: Colonels William C. Scott (June 1861–January 1863), Norvell Cobb (January 1863–April 1865). Notes: Initially armed with converted flintlock muskets, replaced in July 1861 with M1855 rifled muskets; Co. E (Richmond

Zouaves) in unique zouave dress.
45th Battalion Organized:
April–December 1863. ANV service: September 1864–March 1865
(disbanded). Brigade assignment:
Smith's. Commander: Major Blake
L. Woodson.

45th Regiment Organized: May
1861. ANV service: May–June
1864. Brigade assignment: Wharton's. Commander: Colonel
William H. Browne (1862–June
1864), Lieutenant Colonel Alexander M. Davis (June 1864).

**46th Regiment (1st Regiment
Wise Legion)** Organized: August
1861. ANV service: April–August
1862, October 1864–April 1865).
Brigade assignment: Wise's. Commanders: Colonels John H.
Richardson (May–September
1862), Randolph Harrison (March
1864–April 1865). Notes: Initially
mostly armed with converted
flintlock muskets; a drum corps of
12 boys organized in January
1862.

47th Regiment Organized: June
1861. ANV service: November
1861–January 1865, April 1865.
Brigade assignments: Field's, Barton's. Commanders: Colonels
George W. Richardson (June
1861–May 1862), Robert M. Mayo
(May 1862–April 1865). Notes: Co.
H was the Maryland Zouaves,
mustered out in June 1862.

48th Regiment Organized: August
1861. ANV service: June
1862–April 1865. Brigade assignments: Campbell's, J. R. Jones', J.
M. Jones', Terry's Consolidated.
Commanders: Colonels John A.
Campbell (August 1861–October
1862), Thomas S. Garnett (October

1862–May 1863), Robert H. Dungan (May 1863–April 1865).

49th Regiment Organized: August
1861. ANV service: July 1861–April
1865. Brigade assignments:
Cocke's, Manassas Garrison, G. B.
Anderson's Special, Featherston's,
Mahone's, Early's, Smith's,
Pegram's, Walker's. Commanders:
Colonels William Smith (August
1861–January 1863), Jonathan C.
Gibson (January 1863–may 1864),
Captain William D. Moffett (May
1864 April 1865). Notes: Took 52.
8 percent losses at Fair Oaks.

50th Regiment Organized: July
1861. ANV service: June
1863–June 1864. Brigade assignments: J. M. Jones', Terry's Consolidated. Commander: Colonel
Alexander S. Vandeventer (January
1863–March 1865).

51st Regiment Organized:
Wytheville, August 1861. ANV service: May–June 1864. Brigade
assignment: Wharton's. Commander: Colonel Augustus Forsberg
(July 1863–March 1865).

52nd Regiment Organized:
August 1861. ANV service: June
1862–April 1865. Brigade assignments: Scott's, Steuart's, Elzey's,
Early's, Smith's, Pegram's,
Walker's. Commanders: Colonels
Michael G. Harman (May
1862–June 1863), James H. Skinner (June 1863–March 1865).

53rd Regiment Organized:
Through merger of Montague's
and Tomlin's Battalions and Waddill's Independent Company,
December 1861. ANV service: June
1862–February 1863, May–September 1863, May 1864–April 1865.
Brigade assignments, Armistead's,

Barton's, Steuart's. Commanders: Colonels Harrison B. Tomlin (December 1861–January 1863), John G. Grammer, Jr., (January–March 1863), William R. Aylett (March 1863–April 1865). Notes: Wore a regimental badge from 15 December 1864.

55th Regiment Organized: By enlargement of the Essex and Middlesex Battalion, September 1861. ANV service: May 1862–January 1865, April 1865. Brigade assignments: Field's, Walker's, Barton's. Commanders: Colonels Francis Mallory (September 1861–May 1863), William S. Christian (May 1863–March 1865).

56th Regiment Organized: September 1861. ANV service: June 1862–February 1863, May–September 1863, May 1864–April 1865. Brigade assignments: Pickett's, Garnett's, Hunton's. Commanders: Colonels William D. Stuart (September 1861–July 1863), Philip P. Slaughter (July 1863–May 1864), William E. Green (May 1864–April 1865). Notes: Initially armed with converted M1822 flintlock muskets.

57th Regiment Organized: Through growth of Keen's Battalion, September 1861. ANV service: April 1862–February 1863, May–September 1863, May 1864–April 1865. Brigade assignments: Armistead's, Barton's, Steuart's. Commanders: Colonel Lewis A. Armistead (September 1861–April 1862), Ford K. Keen (April–July 1862), David Dyer (July 1862–January 1863), John B. Magruder (January–July 1863), Clement R. Fontaine (July 1863–April 1865).

Notes: Wore a regimental badge from 15 December 1865.

58th Regiment Organized: October 1861. ANV service: June 1862–April 1865. Brigade assignments: Elzey's, Early's, Smith's, Pegram's, Walker's. Commanders: Colonels Edmond Goode (October 1861–March 1862), Samuel H. Letcher (March–October 1862), Francis H. Board (October 1862–July 1864), John G. Kasey (July 1864–April 1865).

59th Regiment (2nd Regiment, Wise Legion) Organized: August 1861. ANV service: May–July 1862, October 1864–April 1865. Brigade assignment: Wise's. Commanders: Colonels Charles F. Henningsen (August 1861–November 1862), William B. Tabb (November 1862–April 1865). Notes: Co. A armed with M1855 rifled muskets, Co. K armed with 'Virginia Mountain Rifles,' other companies with flintlocks, converted flintlock muskets and M1855 rifled muskets.

60th Regiment (3rd Regiment, Wise Legion) Organized: August 1861. ANV service: June–July 1862. Brigade assignment: Field's. Commander: Colonel William E. Starke (September 1861–August 1862).

61st Regiment Organized: Through enlargement of 7th Battalion, May 1862. ANV service: September 1862–April 1865. Brigade assignments: Mahone's, Weisiger's. Commanders: Lieutenant Colonel William F. Niameyer (May–October 1862), Colonel Virginius Despeaux Groner (October 1862–April 1865).

10
Lee's Army:
A Chronology

1861

28 May P. G. T. Beauregard ordered to take command of Confederate troops around Richmond
8 June Virginia's forces transferred to the Confederacy
10 June Skirmish at Big Bethel, Virginia
17 June Skirmish at Vienna, Virginia
20 June Army divided into two corps; brigades assigned
7 July Skirmish at Great Falls, Virginia
21 July Battle at Manassas, Virginia
5 August Skirmish at Point of Rocks, Maryland
27 August Skirmish at Ball's Cross Roads, Virginia
31 August J. E. Johnston appointed to command the army
2 September Skirmish at Beher's Mills, Virginia
11 September Skirmish at Lewinsville, Virginia
16 October Skirmish at Bolivar Heights, Virginia
21 October Battle at Ball's Bluff, Virginia
26 November Cavalry skirmish at Drainesville, Virginia
26 November Cavalry skirmish at Hunter's Mills, Virginia
3 December Cavalry skirmish at Vienna, Virginia

1862

5 March Skirmish at Occoquan, Virginia
April Army re-organized, new officers chosen
5 April Opening of Siege of Yorktown, Virginia
3 May Retreat from Yorktown
5 May Battle of Williamsburg, Virginia
7 May Skirmish at West Point, Virginia
15 May Skirmish at Linden, Virginia
24 May Battle at Chickahominy, Virginia
27 May Minor battle at Hanover Court House, Virginia
31 May Opening of battles at Seven Pines, Fair Oaks
1 June Fighting at Seven Pines, Fair Oaks diminishes
1 June R. E. Lee assumes command of the Army of Northern Virginia
11 June Stuart ordered on his Ride Around McClellan
13-15 June Stuart's Ride Around McClellan
18 June Skirmish on Williamsburg Road, Virginia
24 June Jackson's Valley command joins the army
26 June Lee opens Seven Days battles
26 June Battle of Mechanicsville, Virginia

27-8 June Battle of Gaines' Mill, Virginia
29 June Battle of Savage's Station, Virginia
29 June Battle of Peach Orchard, Virginia
30 June Battle of White Oak Swamp, Virginia
1 July Battle of Malvern Hill, Virginia
1 July Seven Days ends
31 July US Navy bombardment, Coggin's Point, Virginia
2 August Cavalry skirmish at Orange Court House
4 August Cavalry skirmish at White Oak Swamp, Bridge
5 August Battle at Malvern Hill
9 August Battle of Cedar Mountain, Virginia
20 August Cavalry action at Brandy Station, Virginia
21 August Cavalry action at Kelley's Ford, Rappahannock River, Virginia
27 August Battle at Manassas, Virginia
27 August Battle at Kettle Run, Virginia
28-9 August Battle at Groveton, Gainesville, Virginia
30 August Battle at Manassas (Second Manassas)
1 September Battle at Chantilly, Virginia
2 September Skirmish at Vienna
7 September Cavalry skirmish at Poolesville, Maryland
9 September Cavalry skirmish at Nolansville, Maryland
10 September Cavalry skirmish at Sugar Loaf Mountain, Maryland
12-15 September Capture of Harper's Ferry, Virginia

14 September Battle at South Mountain, Maryland
15 September Cavalry skirmish at Boonsboro, Maryland
17 September Battle of Sharpsburg, Maryland
20 September Battle at Sheppardstown, Virginia
9 October Cavalry skirmish at Aldie, Virginia
11 October Skirmish at Mouth of Monocacy, Maryland
24 October Skirmish at Manassas Junction, Virginia
31 October Cavalry skirmish at Aldie
2 November Cavalry skirmish at Bloomfield, Virginia
3 November Cavalry skirmish at Upperville, Virginia
5 November Cavalry skirmish at Manassas Gap.
6 November Army organized into two corps
9 November Cavalry skirmish at Fredericksburg, Virginia
17 November Skirmish at Gloucester, Virginia
28 November Cavalry skirmish at Hartwood Church, Virginia
2 December Cavalry skirmish at Franklin, Virginia
13 December Battle of Fredericksburg
19 December Raid on Union wagon train, Occoquan, Virginia
27 December Minor battle at Dumfries, Virginia
28 December Skirmish at Suffolk, Virginia

1863
10 January Skirmish at Catlett's Station, Virginia
7 February Cavalry skirmish at

Williamsburg

10 February Skirmish at Gloucester Point, Virginia

13 February Cavalry skirmish at Smithfield, Virginia

18 February Longstreet's Corps ordered to North Carolina

25 February Cavalry skirmish at Hartwood Church

17 March Cavalry skirmish at Blackwater, Virginia

17 March Cavalry battle at Kelly's Ford, Virginia

29 March Cavalry skirmish at Williamsburg

1 April Cavalry skirmish at Broad Run, Virginia

11 April Cavalry skirmish at Whittaker's Mills

27 April Beginning of Stoneman's Raid in Virginia

30 April Skirmishing along the Rappahannock River

1-4 May Battle of Chancellorsville, Virginia

8 May Return of Stoneman's Cavalry

14 May Skirmish at Warrenton Junction, Virginia

30 May Army re-organized into three corps

5 June Skirmish on Rappahannock River

6 June Longstreet's entire Corps rejoins the army

9 June Cavalry battle of Brandy Station, Virginia

17 June Cavalry skirmish at Aldie

24 June Cavalry skirmish at McConnellsburg, Pennsylvania

26 June Cavalry skirmish at Hanover Court House

30 June Cavalry skirmish at Hanover, Pennsylvania

30 June Skirmish at Sporting Hill, Pennsylvania

1-3 July Battle of Gettysburg, Pennsylvania

5 July Cavalry skirmish at Fairfield, Pennsylvania

6 July Cavalry skirmish at Hagerstown, Maryland

6 July Cavalry skirmish at Williamsport, Maryland

7-9 July Cavalry skirmishes at Boonsboro, Maryland

12 July Skirmish at Funkstown, Maryland

14 July Cavalry skirmish at Falling Waters, Maryland

21 July Cavalry skirmish at Manassas Gap.

21-2 July Cavalry skirmishes at Chester Gap, Virginia

23 July Skirmish at Manassas Gap.

1-3 August Cavalry skirmishes, Rappahannock River

24 August Cavalry skirmish at Coyle Tavern, Virginia

29 August Skirmish at Bottom's Bridge, Virginia

6 September Cavalry skirmish at Brandy Station

9 September Longstreet's Corps begins move to Tennessee

13 September Cavalry skirmish at Culpepper, Virginia

15 September Cavalry skirmish at Smithfield, Virginia

19 September Cavalry skirmish at Racoon Ford, Virginia

21 September Cavalry skirmish at White's Ford, Virginia

10 October Cavalry skirmish at the Rapidan

10 October Cavalry skirmish at Robertson's Run, Virginia

12 October Cavalry skirmish at Jeffersonton, Virginia

14 October Skirmish at Auburn, Virginia
14 October Minor battle at Bristoe Station, Virginia
15 October Skirmish at McLean's Ford, Virginia
15 October Skirmish at Blackburn Ford, Virginia
17 October Cavalry skirmish on the Rapidan
19 October Cavalry battle at Buckland Mills, Virginia
22 October Cavalry skirmish at Beverly Ford
7 November Skirmish at Rappahannock Station
7 November Skirmish at Kelly's Ford
7 November Cavalry skirmish at Stevensburg, Virginia
26-8 November Operations at Mine Run, Virginia
15 December Skirmish at Sangster's Station, Virginia

1864
(Henceforth all fighting in Virginia)
14 January Skirmish at Bealton
6 February Skirmish at Morton's Ford
7 February Cavalry battle at Barnett's Ford
1 March Cavalry skirmishes on the Rapidan
7 April Longstreet's Corps ordered back to Virginia
10 April Skirmish at Little Cacapon
15 April Cavalry skirmish at Bristoe Station
29 April Lee reviews Longstreet's returned Corps
5-7 May Battle of the Wilderness
8-18 May Battle of Spottsylvania Court House
9 May Cavalry battle at Beaver Dam Station
10 May Cavalry battle at Ground Squirrel Church Bridge
11 May Cavalry skirmish at Ashland
11 May Cavalry battle at Yellow Tavern
16-20 May Battle on Fredericksburg Road
20 May Cavalry battle at Milford Station
23-7 May Battle on the North Anna River
28 May Cavalry battle at Hawe's Shop, Virginia
29-31 May Battle at Tocopotomy
30 May Battle at Hanover Court House
30 May Cavalry battle at Ashland
30 May Cavalry battle at Old Church
1-12 June Battles at Cold Harbor
2 June Cavalry battles at various points along the line
10-11 June Cavalry battle at Old Church
12 June J. A. Early and Corps sent to the Valley
15 June Cavalry battle at Samaria Church
15 June-31 December Siege of Petersburg
20 June Skirmish at White House
21 June Cavalry skirmish at Salem
21 June Cavalry skirmish at White House Landing
4 July Early captures Harper's Ferry
9 July Battle of Monocacy, Maryland
11-12 July Skirmishes outside

Washington, DC
12 July Cavalry skirmish at Lee's Mills
17 July Early's men recross the Shenandoah
30 July Mine exploded in Petersburg defences
31 July Early's men burn Chambersburg, Pennsylvania
10 August Cavalry skirmish at Berryville Pike
14 August Cavalry skirmish at Gravel Hill
21 August Cavalry battle at Summit Point
29-30 August Cavalry skirmishes at Arthur's Swamp.
3 September Cavalry skirmish at Darksville
10 September Loss of 'Fort Hell', Petersburg Lines
16 September Cavalry skirmish at Sycamore Church
17 September Cavalry skirmish at Fairfax Station
17 September Cavalry battle at Belcher's Mills
28 September Battle at Fort Sedgwick, Petersburg Lines
1 October Battle at Prebel's Farm

1-5 October Defence of the Weldon Railroad
8 October Skirmishes on Boydtown Plank Road
27-8 October Cavalry skirmishes at Fair Oaks
5 November Battle at Fort Sedgwick, Petersburg Lines
7-11 December Defence of the Weldon Railroad
8-9 December Battle at Hatcher's Run
20 December Cavalry skirmish at Lacey's Springs

1865
1 January-2 April Siege of Petersburg
5-7 February Battle of Hatcher's Run
29 March Battle at Quaker Road
31 March Defence of Boydton, White Oak Roads
1 April Battle of Five Forks
2 April Fall of Petersburg
5 April Battle of Amelia Springs
6 April Skirmish on High Bridge
7 April Battle of Farmville
8-9 April Battle, surrender at Appomattox Court House

11
Orders of Battle

ARMY OF THE POTOMAC
(Brig. Gen. P. G. T. Beauregard)
(Afterwards, First Corps)

INFANTRY

First Brigade (Brig. Gen. M. L. Bonham)
11th North Carolina
2nd South Carolina
3rd South Carolina
7th South Carolina
8th South Carolina

Second Brigade (Brig. Gen. R. S. Ewell)
5th Alabama
6th Alabama
6th Louisiana

Third Brigade (Brig. Gen. D. R. Jones)
17th Mississippi
18th Mississippi
5th South Carolina

Fourth Brigade (Brig. Gen. J. Longstreet)
5th North Carolina
1st Virginia
11th Virginia
17th Virginia

Fifth Brigade (Col. P. St. George Cocke)
1st Louisiana Battalion
8th Virginia (seven companies)
18th Virginia
19th Virginia
28th Virginia
49th Virginia (three companies)

Sixth Brigade (Col. J. A. Early)
13th Mississippi
4th South Carolina
7th Virginia
24th Virginia

Troops not brigaded
7th Louisiana Infantry
8th Louisiana Infantry
Hampton Legion (South Carolina) Infantry
30th Virginia Cavalry
Harrison's Battalion Cavalry
Independent companies (10) cavalry
Washington (Louisiana) Battalion Artillery

Artillery
Kemper's Battery
Latham's Battery
Loudoun Battery
Shield's Battery
Camp Pickens Companies

ARMY OF THE SHENANDOAH
(Brig. Gen J. E. Johnston)

JOHNSTON'S DIVISION

First Brigade (Col. T. J. Jackson)
2nd Virginia Infantry
4th Virginia Infantry
5th Virginia Infantry
27th Virginia Infantry
Pendleton's Battery

Second Brigade (Col. F. S. Bartow)
7th Georgia Infantry
8th Georgia Infantry
9th Georgia Infantry
Duncan's Kentucky Battalion

Pope's Kentucky Battalion
Alburtis' Battery

Third Brigade (Brig. Gen. B. E. Bee)
4th Alabama Infantry
2nd Mississippi Infantry
11th Mississippi Infantry
1st Tennessee Infantry
Imboden's Battery

Fourth Brigade (Col. A. Elzy)
1st Maryland Infantry
3rd Tennessee Infantry
10th Virginia Infantry
13th Virginia Infantry
Grove's Battery

Not brigaded
1st Virginia Cavalry
33rd Virginia Infantry

THE SEVEN DAYS (23 JULY 1862)

JACKSON'S COMMAND
(Maj. Gen. T. J. Jackson)

JACKSON'S DIVISION (Maj. Gen. T. J. Jackson)

First Brigade 'Stonewall Brigade'
(Brig. Gen. C. S. Winder)
2nd Virginia
4th Virginia
5th Virginia
27th Virginia
33rd Virginia

Second Brigade (Brig. Gen. JR Jones)
21st Virginia
42nd Virginia
48th Virginia
1st Virginia Battalion

Third Brigade (Brig. Gen. W. B. Taliaferro)
47th Alabama
48th Alabama
10th Virginia
23rd Virginia

37th Virginia

Fourth Brigade (Brig. Gen. A. R. Lawton)
13th Georgia
26th Georgia
31st Georgia
38th Georgia
60th Georgia
61st Georgia

EWELL'S DIVISION (Maj. Gen. R. S. Ewell)

Fourth Brigade (Brig. Gen. J. A. Early)
12th Georgia
13th Georgia
25th Virginia
31st Virgina
44th Virginia
52nd Virginia
58th Virginia

Seventh Brigade (Brig. Gen. I. R. Trimble)
15th Alabama
21st Georgia
21st North Carolina

Eighth Brigade (Brig. Gen. Richard Taylor)
6th Louisiana
7th Louisiana
8th Louisiana
9th Louisiana
1st Louisiana Special Battalion

Maryland Line (Col. B. T. Johnson)
1st Maryland

LONGSTREET'S COMMAND
(Maj. Gen. James Longstreet)

LONGSTREET'S DIVISION (Maj. Gen. James Longstreet)

First Brigade (Brig. Gen. J. L. Kemper)
1st Virginia
7th Virginia

11th Virginia
17th Virginia
24th Virginia
Loudoun Artillery (Virginia)

Second Brigade (Brig. Gen. M. Jenkins)
2nd South Carolina Rifles
5th South Carolina
6th South Carolina
Palmetto Sharpshooters
Mattison's Battalion (South Carolina)
Fauquier Artillery (Virginia)

Third Brigade (Brig. Gen. G. E. Pickett)
8th Virginia
18th Virginia
19th Virginia
28th Virginia
56th Virginia
Lynchburg Artillery (Virginia)

Fourth Brigade (Brig. Gen. C. M. Wilcox)
8th Alabama
9th Alabama
10th Alabama
11th Alabama

Fifth Brigade (Brig. Gen. R. A. Pryor)
14th Alabama
2nd Florida
14th Louisiana
Coppen's Louisiana Battalion
3rd Virginia

Sixth Brigade (Brig. Gen. W. S. Featherston)
12th Mississippi
16th Mississippi
19th Mississippi
2nd Mississippi Battalion

Artillery Brigade
Washington Artillery Battalion (Louisiana)
Dixie Artillery (Virginia)

A. P. HILL'S DIVISION (Maj. Gen. A. P. Hill)

First Brigade (Brig. Gen. C. W. Field)
40th Virginia
47th Virgina
55th Virginia
60th Virginia
2nd Virginia Heavy Artillery
Middlesex Artillery (Virginia)
Purcell Artillery (Virginia)

Second Brigade (Brig. Gen. M. Gregg)
1st South Carolina
12th South Carolina
13th South Carolina
14th South Carolina
1st South Carolina Rifles
Letcher Artillery (Virginia)

Third Brigade (Brig. Gen. J. R. Anderson)
14th Georgia
35th Georgia
45th Georgia
49th Georgia
3rd Louisiana Battalion
Crenshaw's Battery (Virginia)
Pee Dee Artillery (South Carolina)

Fourth Brigade (Brig. Gen. L. O'B. Branch)
7th North Carolina
18th North Carolina
28th North Carolina
33rd North Carolina
37th North Carolina
Branch Artillery (North Carolina)
Johnson's Battery (Virginia)

Fifth Brigade (Brig. Gen. J. J. Archer)
5th Alabama
19th Georgia
1st Tennessee
7th Tennessee
14th Tennessee
Fredericksburg Artillery (Virginia)

Sixth Brigade (Brig. Gen. W. D. Pender)
16th North Carolina
22nd North Carolina
34th North Carolina

38th North Carolina
German Artillery (South Carolina)

Jones's Division (Brig. Gen. D. R. Jones)
Toombs' Brigade (Brig. Gen. R. Toombs)
2nd Georgia
15th Georgia
17th Georgia
20th Georgia
Madison Artillery (Louisiana)

Anderson's Brigade (Col. G. T. Anderson)
1st Georgia (Regulars)
7th Georgia
8th Georgia
9th Georgia
11th Georgia
Brown's Battery (Virgina)
Hart's Battery (South Carolina)

HILL'S DIVISION (Maj. Gen. D. H. Hill)

First Brigade (Brig. Gen. R. E. Rodes)
3rd Alabama
5th Alabama
6th Alabama
12th Alabama
26th Alabama

Second Brigade (Col. C. A. Colquitt)
13th Alabama
6th Georgia
23rd Georgia
27th Georgia
28th Georgia

Third Brigade (Brig. Gen. S. Garland, Jr.)
5th North Carolina
12th North Carolina
13th North Carolina
20th North Carolina
23rd North Carolina

Fourth Brigade (Brig. Gen. G. B. Anderson)
2nd North Carolina
4th North Carolina

14th North Carolina
30th North Carolina

Fifth Brigade (Brig. Gen. R. S. Ripley)
4th Georgia
48th Georgia
1st North Carolina
3rd North Carolina

Sixth Brigade (Brig. Gen. H. A. Wise)
4th Virginia Heavy Artillery
20th Virginia
26th Virginia
46th Virginia
59th Virginia

Divisional Artillery
Bondurant's Battery (Alabama)
Carter's Battery (Virginia)
Clark's Battery (Virginia)
Hardaway's Battery (Alabama)
Nelson's Battery (Virginia)
Peyton's Battery (Virginia)
Rhett's Battery (South Carolina)

ANDERSON'S DIVISION (Maj. Gen. R. H. Anderson)

First Brigade (Brig. Gen. W. Mahone)
6th Virginia
12th Virginia
16th Virginia
41st Virginia
49th Virginia

Second Brigade (Brig. Gen. A. R. Wright)
44th Alabama
3rd Georgia
22nd Georgia
44th Georgia
1st Louisiana

Third Brigade (Brig. Gen. L. A. Armistead)
9th Virginia
14th Virginia
38th Virginia
53rd Virginia
57th Virginia
5th Battalion

Artillery Brigade
Girardey's Battery (Louisiana)
Grimes' Battery (Virginia)
Huger's Battery (Virginia
Moorman's Battery (Virginia)
Moseley's Battery (Virginia)
Turner's Battery (Virginia)

McLaws' Division (Maj. Gen. L. McLaws)

First Brigade (Brig. Gen. P. J. Semmes)
10th Georgia
53rd Georgia
5th Louisiana
10th Louisiana
15th Virginia
32nd Virginia
Manly's Battery (North Carolina)

Second Brigade (Brig. Gen. H. Cobb)
16th Georgia
24th Georgia
Cobb Georgia Legion
2nd Louisiana
15th North Carolina
Carlton's Battery (Georgia)

Third Brigade (Col. W. Barksdale)
13th Mississippi
17th Mississippi
18th Mississippi
21st Mississippi
McCarthy's Battery (Virginia)

Fourth Brigade (Brig. Gen. J. B. Kershaw)
2nd South Carolina
3rd South Carolina
7th South Carolina
8th South Carolina
Alexandria Artillery (Virginia)

Hill's Command (Maj. Gen. D. H. Hill)

First Brigade (Brig. Gen. J. G. Martin)
17th North Carolina
44th North Carolina
47th North Carolina

52nd North Carolina

Second Brigade (Brig. Gen. R. Ransom, Jr.)
24th North Carolina
25th North Carolina
26th North Carolina
35th North Carolina
49th North Carolina
Burrough's Battalion, Virginia Cavalry
North Carolina Cavalry (two companies)
Graham's Battery (North Carolina)

Third Brigade (Col. J. Daniel)
32nd North Carolina
43rd North Carolina
45th North Carolina
50th North Carolina
53rd North Carolina

Fourth Brigade (Brig. Gen. J. G. Walker)
3rd Arkansas
2nd Georgia Battalion
27th North Carolina
46th North Carolina
48th North Carolina
30th Virginia

Unattached Troops
61st Virginia Infantry
13th Virginia Cavalry

Light Artillery
Branch's Battery (Virginia)
Coit's Battery (South Carolina)
French's Battery (Virginia)
Graham's Battery (Virginia)
Grandy's Battery (Virginia)
Lloyd's Battery (North Carolina)
Ruffin's Battery (Virginia)

Whiting's Division (Brig. Gen. W. H. C. Whiting)

Third Brigade (Brig. Gen. W. H. C. Whiting)
4th Alabama
2nd Mississippi

279

11th Mississippi
6th North Carolina
Reilly's Battery (North Carolina)

Texas Brigade (Brig. Gen. J. B. Hood)
18th Georgia
Hampton Legion
1st Texas
4th Texas
5th Texas
Balthis' Battery (Virginia)

CAVALRY (Brig. Gen. J. E. B. Stuart)
1st Virginia
3rd Virginia
4th Virginia
5th Virginia
9th Virginia
10th Virginia
Cobb Georgia Legion
Jeff Davis Legion
Hampton Legion
1st North Carolina
Critcher's Battalion (Virginia)
Stuart Horse Artillery

RESERVE ARTILLERY (Brig. Gen. W. N. Pendleton)

First Virginia Light Artillery (Col. J. T. Brown)
Coke's Company
Dance's Company
Hupp's Company
Macon's Company
Richardson's Company
Ritter's Company
Smith's Company
Watson's Company
Wyatt's Company
Young's Company

First Battalion Georgia Reserve Artillery (Lt. Col. A. S. Cutts)
Blackshear's Company
Crawford's Company
Lane's Company
Price's Company
Ross' Company

Second Battalion Reserve Artillery (Maj. C. Richardson)
Ancell's Company
Milledge's Company
Woolfolk's Company

Third Battalion Reserve Artillery (Maj. W. Nelson)
Carrington's Company
Huckstep's Company
Kirkpatrick's Company
Page's Company

Fourth Battalion Reserve Artillery (Maj. H. P. Jones)
Clark's Company
Peyton's Company
Rhett's Company
Turner's Company

Not brigaded
1st Virginia Cavalry
33rd Virginia Infantry

SHARPSBURG (September 1862)

LONGSTREET'S CORPS (Maj. Gen. James Longstreet)

McLAWS' DIVISION (Maj. Gen. Lafayette McLaws)

Kershaw's Brigade (Brig. Gen. J. B. Kershaw)
2nd South Carolina
3rd South Carolina
7th South Carolina
8th South Carolina

Cobb's Brigade (Brig. Gen. Howell Cobb)
16th Georgia
24th Georgia
Cobb's (Georgia) Legion
15th North Carolina

Semmes' Brigade (Brig. Gen. Paul J. Semmes)
10th Georgia
53rd Georgia

280

15th Virginia
32nd Virginia

Barksdale's Brigade (Brig. Gen.
William Barksdale)
13th Mississippi
17th Mississippi
18th Mississippi
21st Mississippi

Artillery (Maj. S. P. Hamilton)
Manly's (North Carolina) Battery
Pulaski (Georgia) Artillery
Richmond (Fayette) Artillery
Richmond Howitzers (1st Company)
Troup (Georgia) Artillery

ANDERSON'S DIVISION (Maj. Gen.
Richard Anderson)

Wilcox's Brigade (Col. Alfred Cumming)
8th Alabama
9th Alabama
10th Alabama
11th Alabama

Mahone's Brigade (Col. William A.
Parham)
6th Virginia
12th Virginia
16th Virginia
41st Virginia
61st Virginia

Featherston's Brigade (Brig. Gen.
Winfield S. Featherston)
12th Mississippi
16th Mississippi
19th Mississippi
2nd Mississippi Battalion

Armistead's Brigade (Brig. Gen.
Lewis A. Armistead)
9th Virginia
14th Virginia
38th Virginia
53rd Virginia
57th Virginia

Pryor's Brigade (Brig. Gen. Rodger A.
Pryor)

14th Alabama
3rd Georgia
22nd Georgia
48th Georgia

Artillery (Maj. John S. Saunders)
Donaldsonville (Louisiana) Artillery
(Maurin's Battery)
Huger's (Virginia) Battery
Moorman's (Virginia) Battery
Thompson's (Grimes') (Virginia) Battery

JONES'S DIVISION (Brig. Gen. David R.
Jones)

Toombs' Brigade (Brig. Gen. Robert
Toombs)
2nd Georgia
15th Georgia
17th Georgia
20th Georgia

Drayton's Brigade (Brig. Gen.
Thomas F. Drayton)
50th Georgia
51st Georgia
15th South Carolina

Pickett's Brigade (Col. Eppa
Hunton)
8th Virgina
18th Virginia
19th Virginia
28th Virginia
56th Virginia

Kemper's Brigade (Brig. Gen. J. L.
Kemper)
1st Virginia
7th Virginia
11th Virginia
17th Virginia
24th Virginia

Jenkins' Brigade (Col. Joseph
Walker)
1st South Carolina (Volunteers)
2nd South Carolina
5th South Carolina
6th South Carolina

4th South Carolina Battalion
Palmetto (South Carolina) Sharpshooters

Anderson's Brigade (Col. George T.
Anderson)
1st Georgia (Regulars)
7th Georgia
8th Georgia
9th Georgia
11th Georgia

Artillery (assigned at brigade level)
Fauquier (Virginia) Artillery (Strib-
ling's Battery)
Loudoun (Virginia) Artillery (Rogers'
Battery)
Turner (Virginia) Artillery (Leake's
Battery)
Wise (Virginia) Artillery (J. S. Brown's
Battery)

WALKER'S DIVISION (Brig. Gen. John
G. Walker)

Walker's Brigade (Col. Van H. Manning)
3rd Arkansas
27th North Carolina
46th North Carolina
48th North Carolina
30th Virginia
French's (Virginia) Battery

Ransom's Brigade (Brig. Gen. Robert
Ransom, Jr.)
24th North Carolina
25th North Carolina
35th North Carolina
49th North Carolina
Branch's (Virginia) Field Artillery

HOOD'S DIVISION (Brig. Gen. John B.
Hood)

Hood's Brigade (Col. W. T. Wofford)
18th Georgia
Hampton (South Carolina) Legion
(Infantry)
1st Texas
4th Texas

5th Texas

Law's Brigade (Col. E. M. Law)
4th Alabama
2nd Mississippi
11th Mississippi
6th North Carolina

Artillery (Maj. B. W. Frobel)
German (South Carolina) Artillery
Palmetto (South Carolina) Artillery
Rowan (North Carolina) Artillery

Evans' Brigade (Brig. Gen. Nathan
G. Evans)
17th South Carolina
18th South Carolina
22nd South Carolina
23rd South Carolina
Holcombe (South Carolina) Legion
Macbeth (South Carolina) Artillery

Artillery
Washington (Louisiana) Artillery
(Col. J. B. Walton)
1st Company
2nd Company
3rd Company
4th Company

Lee's Battalion (Col. S. D. Lee)
Ashland (Virginia) Artillery
Bedford (Virginia) Artillery
Brooks (South Carolina) Artillery
Eubank's (Virginia) Battery
Madison (Louisiana) Light Artillery
Parker's (Virginia) Battery)

JACKSON'S CORPS (Maj. Gen. T. J. Jackson)

EWELL'S DIVISION (Brig. Gen. A. R.
Lawton)

Lawton's Brigade (Col. M. Douglass)
13th Georgia
26th Georgia
31st Georgia
38th Georgia
60th Georgia
61st Georgia

Early's Brigade (Brig. Gen. Jubal A. Early)
13th Virginia
25th Virginia
31st Virginia
44th Virginia
49th Virginia
52nd Virginia
58th Virginia

Trimble's Brigade (Col. James A. Walker)
15th Alabama
12th Georgia
21st Georgia
21st North Carolina
1st North Carolina Battalion

Hays' Brigade (Brig. Gen. Harry T. Hays)
5th Louisiana
6th Louisiana
7th Louisiana
8th Louisiana
14th Louisiana

Artillery (Maj. A. R. Courtney)
Charlottesville (Virginia) Artillery (Carrington's Battery)
Chesapeake (Maryland) Artillery (Brown's Battery)
Courtney (Virginia) Artillery (Latimer's Battery)
Johnston's (Virginia) Battery
Louisiana Guard Artillery (D'Aquin's Battery)
1st Maryland Battery (Dement's Battery)
Staunton (Virginia) Artillery (Balthis' Battery)

HILL'S LIGHT DIVISION (Maj. Gen. A. P. Hill)

Branch's Brigade (Brig. Gen. O'B Branch)
7th North Carolina
18th North Carolina
28th North Carolina
33rd North Carolina
37th North Carolina

Gregg's Brigade (Brig. Gen. Maxey Gregg)
1st South Carolina (Provisional Army)
1st South Carolina (Orr's) Rifles
12th South Carolina
13th South Carolina
14th South Carolina

Field's Brigade (Col. J. M. Brockenbrough)
40th Virginia
47th Virginia
55th Virginia
22nd Virginia Battalion

Archer's Brigade (Brig. Gen. J. J. Archer)
5th Alabama Battalion
19th Georgia
1st Tennessee (Provisional Army)
7th Tennessee
14th Tennessee

Pender's Brigade (Brig. Gen. William D. Pender)
16th North Carolina
22nd North Carolina
34th North Carolina
38th North Carolina

Thomas's Brigade (Brig. Gen. Edward L. Thomas)
14th Georgia
35th Georgia
45th Georgia
49th Georgia

Artillery (Maj. R. L. Walker)
Branch (North Carolina) Artillery (A. C. Latham's Battery)
Crenshaw's (Virginia) Battery
Fredericksburg (Virginia) Artillery (Braxton's Battery)
Letcher (Virginia) Artillery (Davidson's Battery)
Middlesex (Virginia) Artillery (Fleet's Battery)
Pee Dee (South Carolina) Artillery (McIntosh's Battery)

Purcell (Virginia) Artillery (Pegram's Battery)

JACKSON'S DIVISION (Brig. Gen. John R. Jones)

Winder's (Stonewall) Brigade (Col. A. J. Grigsby)
2nd Virginia
4th Virginia
5th Virginia
27th Virginia
33rd Virginia

Taliaferro's Brigade (Col. E. T. H. Warren)
47th Alabama
48th Alabama
10th Virginia
23rd Virginia
37th Virginia

Jones's Brigade (Col. B. T. Johnson)
21st Virginia
42nd Virginia
48th Virginia
1st Virginia Battalion

Starke's Brigade (Brig. Gen. William E. Starke)
1st Louisiana
2nd Louisiana
9th Louisiana
10th Louisiana
15th Louisiana
Coppen's (Louisiana) Battalion

Artillery (Maj. L. M. Shumaker)
Alleghany (Virginia) Artillery (Carpenter's Battery)
Brockenbrough's (Maryland) Battery
Danville (Virginia) Artillery (Wooding's Battery)
Hampden (Virginia) Artillery (Caskie's Battery)
Lee (Virginia) Battery (Raines Battery)
Rockbridge (Virginia) Artillery (Poague's Battery)

HILL'S DIVISION (Maj. Gen. Daniel Harvey Hill)

Ripley's Brigade (Brig. Gen. Roswell S. Ripley)
4th Georgia
44th Georgia
1st North Carolina
3rd North Carolina

Rodes' Brigade (Brig. Gen. R. E. Rodes)
3rd Alabama
5th Alabama
6th Alabama
12th Alabama
26th Alabama

Garland's Brigade (Brig. Gen. Samuel Garland, Jr.)
5th North Carolina
12th North Carolina
13th North Carolina
20th North Carolina
23rd North Carolina

Anderson's Brigade (Brig. Gen. George B. Anderson)
2nd North Carolina
4th North Carolina
14th North Carolina
30th North Carolina

Colquitt's Brigade (Col. A. H. Colquitt)
13th Alabama
6th Georgia
23rd Georgia
27th Georgia
28th Georgia

Artillery (Maj. S. F. Pierson)
Hardaway's (Alabama) Battery
Jeff Davis (Alabama) Artillery (Bondurant's Battery)
Jones's (Virginia) Battery
King William (Virginia) Artillery (Carter's Battery)

Reserve Artillery (Brig. Gen. William N. Pendleton)

Brown's (Virginia) Battalion (Col. J. Thompson Brown)
Powhatan Artillery (Dance's Battery)

Richmond Howitzers, 2nd Company (Watson's Battery)
Richmond Howitzers, 3rd Company (Smith's Battery)
Salem Artillery (Hupp's Battery)
Williamsburg Artillery (Coke's Battery)

Cutts' Battalion (Lt. Col. A. S. Cutts)
Blackshears' (Georgia) Battery
Irwin (Georgia) Artillery (Lane's Battery)
Lloyd's (North Carolina) Battery
Patterson's (Georgia) Battery
Ross' (Georgia) Battery

Jones's (Virginia) Battalion (Maj. H. P. Jones)
Morris Artillery (R. C. M. Page's Battery)
Orange Artillery (Peyton's Battery)
Turner's Battery
Wimbish's Battery

Nelson's Battalion (Maj. William Nelson)
Amherst (Virginia) Artillery (Kirkpatrick's Battery)
Fluvanna (Virginia) Artillery (Ancell's Battery)
Huckstep's (Virginia) Battery
Johnson's (Virginia) Battery
Milledge (Georgia) Battery

Miscellaneous
Cutshaw's (Virginia) Battery
Dixie (Virginia) Artillery (Chapman's Battery)
Magruder (Virginia) Artillery (T. J. Page's Battery)
Rice's (Virginia) Battery
Thomas (Virginia) Artillery (E. J. Anderson's Battery)

Cavalry (Maj. Gen. J. E. B. Stuart)

Hampton's Brigade (Brig. Gen. Wade Hampton)
1st North Carolina
2nd South Carolina
10th Virginia

Cobb's (Georgia) Legion
Jeff Davis Legion

Lee's Brigade (Brig. Gen. Fitzhugh Lee)
1st Virginia
3rd Virginia
4th Virginia
5th Virginia
9th Virginia

Robertson's Brigade (Brig. Gen. B. H. Robertson)
2nd Virginia
6th Virginia
7th Virginia
12th Virginia
17th Virginia

Horse Artillery (Capt. John Pelham)
Chew's (Virginia) Battery
Hart's (South Carolina) Battery
Pelham's (Virginia) Battery

CHANCELLORSVILLE (MAY, 1863)

First Corps
(Missing Lt. Gen. James Longstreet with Hood's and Pickett's Divisions and Dearing's and Henry's Artillery Battalions)

McLaws' Division (Maj. Gen. L. McLaws)

Wofford's Brigade (Brig. Gen. W. T. Wofford)
16th Georgia
18th Georgia
24th Georgia
Cobb's Georgia Legion
Phillips' Georgia Legion

Semme's Brigade (Brig. Gen. P. J. Semmes)
10th Georgia
50th Georgia
51st Georgia
53rd Georgia

Kershaw's Brigade (Brig. Gen. J. B. Kershaw)
2nd South Carolina
3rd South Carolina
7th South Carolina
8th South Carolina
15th South Carolina

Barksdale's Brigade (Brig. Gen. W. Barksdale)
13th Mississippi
17th Mississippi
18th Mississippi
21st Mississippi

Divisional Artillery (Col. H. C. Cabell)
Carlton's (Georgia) Battery (Troup Artillery)
Fraser's (Georgia) Battery
McCarthy's (Virginia) Battery (1st Richmond Howitzers)
Manly's (North Carolina) Battery

ANDERSON'S DIVISION (Maj. Gen. R. H. Anderson)

Wilcox's Brigade (Brig. Gen. C. M. Wilcox)
8th Alabama
9th Alabama
10th Alabama
11th Alabama
14th Alabama

Wright's Brigade (Brig. Gen. A. R. Wright)
3rd Georgia
22nd Georgia
48th Georgia
2nd Georgia Battalion

Mahone's Brigade (Brig. W. Mahone)
6th Virginia
12th Virginia
16th Virginia
41st Virginia
61st Virginia

Posey's Brigade (Brig. Gen. C. Posey)
12th Mississippi

16th Mississippi
19th Mississippi
48th Mississippi

Perry's Brigade (Brig. Gen. E. A. Perry)
2nd Florida
5th Florida
8th Florida

Divisional Artillery (Lt. Col. J. J. Garnett)
Grandy's (Virginia) Battery
Lewis's (Virginia) Battery
Maurin's (Louisiana) Battery
Moore's (Virginia) Battery

ARTILLERY RESERVE

Alexander's Battalion (Col. E. P. Alexander)
Eubank's (Virginia) Battery
Jordan's (Virginia) Battery
Moody's (Louisiana) Battery
Parker's (Virginia) Battery
Rhett's (South Carolina) Battery
Woolfolk's (Virginia Battery)

Washington (Louisiana) Artillery (Col. J. B. Walton)
1st Company
2nd Company
3rd Company
4th Company

SECOND CORPS (Lt. Gen. T. J. Jackson)

HILL'S DIVISION (Maj. Gen. A. P. Hill)

Heth's Brigade (Brig. Gen. Henry Heth)
40th Virginia
47th Virginia
55th Virginia
22nd Virginia Battalion

Thomas's Brigade (Brig. Gen. E. L. Thomas)
14th Georgia
35th Georgia
45th Georgia
49th Georgia

McGowan's Brigade (Brig. Gen. S. McGowan)
1st South Carolina (Provisional Army)
1st South Carolina Rifles
12th South Carolina
13th South Carolina
14th South Carolina

Lane's (Fourth) Brigade (Brig. Gen. J. H. Lane)
7th North Carolina
18th North Carolina
28th North Carolina
33rd North Carolina
37th North Carolina

Archer's (Fifth) Brigade (Brig. Gen. J. J. Archer)
13th Alabama
5th Alabama Battalion
1st Tennessee (Provisional Army)
7th Tennessee
14th Tennessee

Pender's Brigade (Brig. Gen. W. D. Pender)
13th North Carolina
16th North Carolina
22nd North Carolina
34th North Carolina
38th North Carolina

Divisional Artillery (Col. R. L. Walker)
Brunson's (South Carolina) Battery
Crenshaw's (Virginia) Battery
Davidson's (Virginia) Battery
McGraw's (Virginia) Battery
Marye's (Virginia) Battery

D. H. HILL'S DIVISION (Brig. Gen. R. E. Rode)

Rode's Brigade (Brig. Gen. R. E. Rodes)
3rd Alabama
5th Alabama
6th Alabama
12th Alabama
26th Alabama

Colquitt's Brigade (Brig. Gen. A. H. Colquitt)
6th Georgia
19th Georgia
23rd Georgia
27th Georgia
28th Georgia

Ramseur's Brigade (Brig. Gen. S. D. Ramseur)
2nd North Carolina
4th North Carolina
14th North Carolina
30th North Carolina

Doles's Brigade (Brig. Gen. George Doles)
4th Georgia
12th Georgia
21st Georgia
44th Georgia

Iverson's Brigade (Brig. Gen. A. Iverson)
5th North Carolina
12th North Carolina
20th North Carolina
23rd North Carolina

Divisional Artillery
Jeff Davis Artillery (Alabama)
King William Artillery (Virginia)
Orange Artillery (Virginia)
Morris Artillery (Virginia)

EARLY'S DIVISION (Maj. Gen. J. A. Early)

Gordon's Brigade (Brig. Gen. J. B. Gordon)
13th Georgia
26th Georgia
31st Georgia
38th Georgia
60th Georgia
61st Georgia

Hoke's Brigade (Brig. Gen. R. F. Hoke)
6th North Carolina
21st North Carolina

54th North Carolina
57th North Carolina
1st North Carolina Battalion

Smith's Brigade (Brig. Gen. W. Smith)
13th Virginia
49th Virginia
52nd Virginia
58th Virginia

Hays' Brigade (Brig. Gen. Harry T. Hays)
5th Louisiana
6th Louisiana
7th Louisiana
8th Louisiana
9th Louisiana

Divisional Artillery (Lt. Col. R. S. Andrews)
Chesapeake Artillery (Maryland)
Alleghany Artillery (Virginia)
Dement's Battery (Maryland)
Lee Artillery (Virginia)

TRIMBLE'S DIVISION (Brig. Gen. R. E. Colston)

Paxton's (First) Brigade (Stonewall Brigade) (Brig. Gen. E. F. Paxton)
2nd Virginia
4th Virgina
5th Virginia
27th Virginia
33rd Virginia

Jones's (Second) Brigade (Brig. Gen. J. R. Jones)
21st Virginia
42nd Virginia
44th Virginia
48th Virginia
50th Virginia

Colston's (Third) Brigade (Col. E. T. H. Warren)
1st North Carolina
3rd North Carolina
10th Virginia
23rd Virginia

37th Virginia

Nicholls' (Fourth) Brigade (Brig. Gen. F. T. Nicholls)
1st Louisiana
2nd Louisiana
10th Louisiana
14th Louisiana
15th Louisiana

Divisional Artillery (Lt. Col. H. P. Jones)
Charlottesville Artillery (Virginia)
Courtney Artillery (Virginia)
Louisiana Guard Artillery
Staunton Artillery (Virginia)

ARTILLERY RESERVE (Col. S. Crutchfield)

Brown's Battalion (Col. J. T. Brown)
Brooke Artillery (Virginia)
Powhatan Artillery (Virginia)
Richmond Howitzers, 2nd Company (Virginia)
Richmond Howitzers, 3rd Company (Virginia)
Rockbridge Artillery (Virginia)
Salem Artillery (Virginia)

McIntosh's Battalion (Maj. D. G. McIntosh)
Danville Artillery (Virginia)
Hurt's Battery (Alabama)
Johnson's Battery (Virginia)
Lusk's Battery (Virginia)

Reserve Artillery (Brig. Gen. W. N. Pendleton)

Sumter Battalion (Georgia) (Lt. Col. A. S. Cutts)
Patterson's Battery
Ross's Battery
Wingfield's Battery

Nelson's Battalion (Lt. Col. W. Nelson)
Amherst Artillery (Virginia)
Fluvanna Artillery (Virginia)
Milledge's Battery (Georgia)

CAVALRY (Maj. Gen. J. E. B. Stuart)

First Brigade (Brig. Gen. W. Hampton)
1st North Carolina
1st South Carolina
2nd South Carolina
Cobb's Georgia Legion
Phillips' Georgia Legion

Second Brigade (Brig. Gen. F. Lee)
1st Virginia
2nd Virginia
3rd Virginia
4th Virginia

Third Brigade (Brig. Gen. W. H. F. Lee)
2nd North Carolina
5th Virginia
9th Virginia
10th Virginia
13th Virginia
15th Virginia

Fourth Brigade (Brig. Gen. W. E. Jones)
2nd Maryland Battalion
6th Virginia
7th Virginia
11th Virginia
12th Virginia
34th Virginia Battalion
35th Virginia Battalion

Horse Artillery (Maj. R. F. Beckham)
Lynchburg Beauregards (Virginia)
Stuart Horse Artillery (Virginia)
McGregor's (Virginia) Battery
Washington Artillery (South Carolina)

GETTYSBURG (JULY 1863)

FIRST CORPS (Lieut. Gen. James Longstreet)

McLAWS' DIVISION (Maj. Gen. Lafayette McLaws)

Kershaw's Brigade (Brig. Gen. Joseph B. Kershaw)
2nd South Carolina
3rd South Carolina
7th South Carolina
8th South Carolina
15th South Carolina
3rd South Carolina Battalion

Semmes' Brigade (Brig. Gen. Paul J. Semmes)
10th Georgia
50th Georgia
51st Georgia
53rd Georgia

Barksdale's Brigade (Brig. Gen. William Barksdale)
13th Mississippi
17th Mississippi
18th Mississippi
21st Mississippi

Wofford's Brigade (Brig. Gen. William T. Wofford)
16th Georgia
18th Georgia
24th Georgia
Cobb's (Georgia) Legion
Phillips' (Georgia) Legion

Artillery Battalion (Col. Henry C. Cabell)
1st North Carolina Artillery, Co. A (Manly's Battery)
Pulaski (Georgia) Artillery (Fraser's Battery)
1st Richmond (Virginia) Howitzers (McCarthy's Battery)
Troup (Georgia) Artillery (Carlton's Battery)

PICKETT'S DIVISION (Maj. Gen. George Pickett)

Garnett's Brigade (Brig. Gen. Richard B. Garnett)
8th Virginia
18th Virginia
19th Virginia
28th Virginia
56th Virginia

Armistead's Brigade (Brig. Gen. Lewis A. Armistead)
9th Virginia
14th Virginia
38th Virginia
53rd Virginia
57th Virginia

Kemper's Brigade (Brig. Gen. James L. Kemper)
1st Virginia
3rd Virgina
7th Virginia
11th Virginia
24th Virginia

Artillery Battalion (Maj. James Dearing)
Fauquier (Virginia) Artillery (Stribling's Battery)
Hampden (Virginia) Artillery (Caskie's Battery)
Richmond Fayette (Virginia) Artillery (Macon's Battery)
Blount's (Virginia) Battery

HOOD'S DIVISION (Maj. Gen. John B. Hood)

Law's Brigade (Brig. Gen. E. McIver Law)
4th Alabama
15th Alabama
44th Alabama
47th Alabama
48th Alabama

Anderson's Brigade (Brig. Gen. George T. Anderson)
7th Georgia
8th Georgia
9th Georgia
11th Georgia
59th Georgia

Robertson's Brigade (Brig. Gen. Jerome B. Robertson)
3rd Arkansas
1st Texas
4th Texas
5th Texas

Benning's Brigade (Brig. Gen. Henry L. Benning)
2nd Georgia
15th Georgia
17th Georgia
20th Georgia

Artillery Battalion (Maj. M. W. Henry)
Branch (North Carolina) Artillery (Latham's Battery)
German (South Carolina) Artillery (Bachman's Battery)
Palmetto Light (South Carolina) Artillery (Garden's Battery)
Rowan (North Carolina) Artillery (Reilly's Battery)

RESERVE ARTILLERY (Col. J. B. Walton)

Alexander's Battalion (Col. E. Porter Alexander)
Madison Light (Louisiana) Artillery (Moody's Battery)
Brooks (South Carolina) Artillery (Gilbert's Battery)
Ashland (Virginia) Artillery (Woolfolk's Battery)
Bedford (Virginia) Artillery (Jordan's Battery)
Parker's (Virginia) Battery
Taylor's (Virginia) Battery

Washington (Louisiana) Artillery (Maj. B. F. Eshleman)
1st Company (Squires' Battery)
2nd Company (Richardson's Battery)
3rd Company (Miller's Battery)
4th Company (Norcom's Battery)

SECOND CORPS (Lieut. Gen. Richard S. Ewell)

EARLY'S DIVISION (Maj. Gen. Jubal Early)

Hays' Brigade (Brig. Gen. Harry T. Hays)
5th Louisiana
6th Louisiana
7th Louisiana

8th Louisiana
9th Louisiana

Hoke's Brigade (Col. Isaac E. Avery)
6th North Carolina
21st North Carolina
57th North Carolina

Smith's Brigade (Brig. Gen. William Smith)
31st Virginia
49th Virginia
52nd Virginia

Gordon's Brigade (Brig. Gen. John B. Gordon)
13th Georgia
26th Georgia
31st Georgia
38th Georgia
60th Georgia
61st Georgia

Artillery Battalion (Lt. Col. H. P. Jones)
Charlottsville (Virginia) Artillery (Carrington's Battery)
Courtney (Virginia) Artillery (Tanner's Battery)
Guard (Louisiana) Artillery (Green's Battery)
Staunton (Virginia) Artillery (Garber's Battery)

JOHNSON'S DIVISION (Maj. Gen. Edward Johnson)

Steuart's Brigade (Brig. Gen. George H. Steuart)
2nd Maryland Battalion
1st North Carolina
3rd North Carolina
10th Virginia
23rd Virginia
37th Virginia

Nicholls' Brigade (Col. J. M. Williams)
1st Louisiana
2nd Louisiana
10th Louisiana

14th Louisiana
15th Louisiana

Stonewall Brigade (Brig. Gen. James A. Walker)
2nd Virginia
4th Virginia
5th Virginia
27th Virginia
33rd Virginia

Jones's Brigade (Brig. Gen. John W. Jones)
21st Virginia
25th Virginia
42nd Virginia
44th Virginia
48th Virginia
50th Virginia

Artillery Battalion (Maj. J. W. Lattimer)
1st Maryland (Dement's) Battery
Alleghany (Virginia) Artillery (Carpenter's Battery)
Chesapeake (Maryland) Artillery (Brown's Battery)
Lee (Virginia) (Raine's) Battery

RODE'S DIVISION (Maj. Gen. Robert E. Rode)
Daniel's Brigade (Brig. Gen. Junius Daniel)
32nd North Carolina
43rd North Carolina
45th North Carolina
53rd North Carolina
2nd North Carolina Battalion

Iverson's Brigade (Brig. Gen. Alfred Iverson)
5th North Carolina
12th North Carolina
20th North Carolina
23rd North Carolina

Doles' Brigade (Brig. Gen. George Doles)
4th Georgia
12th Georgia

21st Georgia
44th Georgia

Ramseur's Brigade (Brig. Gen. Stephen D. Ramseur)
2nd North Carolina
4th North Carolina
14th North Carolina
30th North Carolina

O'Neal's Brigade (Col. Edward A. O'Neal)
3rd Alabama
5th Alabama
6th Alabama
12th Alabama
26th Alabama

Artillery Battalion (Lt. Col. Thomas H. Carter)
Jeff Davis (Alabama) Artillery (Reese's Battery)
King William (Virginia) Artillery (Carter's Battery)
Morris (Virginia) Artillery (Page's Battery)
Orange (Virginia) Artillery (Fry's Battery)

RESERVE ARTILLERY (Col. J. Thompson Brown)

Brown's Battalion (Capt. Willis J. Dance)
2nd Richmond (Virginia) Howitzers (Watson's Battery)
3rd Richmond (Virginia) Howitzers (Smith's Battery)
Powhatan (Virginia) Artillery (Cunningham's Battery)
Rockbridge (Virginia) Artillery (Graham's Battery)
Salem (Virginia) Artillery (Griffin's Battery)

Nelson's Battalion (Lt. Col. William Nelson)
Amherst (Virginia) Artillery (Kirkpatrick's Battery)
Fluvanna (Virginia) Artillery (Massie's Battery)

Milledge's (Georgia) Battery

THIRD CORPS (Lieut. Gen. Ambrose P. Hill)

ANDERSON'S DIVISION (Maj. Gen. Richard H. Anderson)

Wilcox's Brigade (Brig. Gen. Cadmus H. Wilcox)
8th Alabama
9th Alabama
10th Alabama
11th Alabama
14th Alabama

Mahone's Brigade (Brig. Gen. William Mahone)
6th Virginia
12th Virginia
16th Virginia
41st Virginia
61st Virginia

Wright's Brigade (Brig. Gen. Ambrose R. Wright)
3rd Georgia
22nd Georgia
48th Georgia
2nd Georgia Battalion

Perry's Brigade (Col. David Lang)
2nd Florida
5th Florida
8th Florida

Posey's Brigade (Brig. Gen. Carnot Posey)
12th Mississippi
16th Mississippi
19th Mississippi
48th Mississippi

Sumter (Georgia) Artillery Battalion (Maj. John Lane)
Company A (Ross' Battery)
Company B (Patterson's Battery)
Company C (Wingfield's Battery)

HETHS' DIVISION (Maj. Gen. Henry Heth)

First Brigade (Brig. Gen. J. Johnston
Pettigrew)
11th North Carolina
26th North Carolina
47th North Carolina
52nd North Carolina

Second Brigade (Col. J. M. Brockenbrough)
40th Virginia
47th Virginia
55th Virginia
22nd Virginia Battalion

Third Brigade (Brig. Gen. James J.
Archer)
13th Alabama
5th Alabama Battalion
1st Tennessee (Provisional Army)
7th Tennessee
14th Tennessee

Fourth Brigade (Brig. Gen. Joseph R.
Davis)
2nd Mississippi
11th Mississippi
42nd Mississippi
55th North Carolina

Artillery Battalion (Lt. Col. John J.
Garnett)
Donaldsonville (Louisiana) Artillery
(Maurin's Battery)
Huger (Virginia) Artillery (Moore's
Battery)
Lewis' (Virginia) Battery
Norfolk (Virginia) Light Artillery
Blues (Grandy's Battery)

PENDER'S DIVISION (Maj. Gen. William
Dorsey Pender)

First Brigade (Col. Abner Perrin)
1st South Carolina (Provisional
Army)
1st South Carolina (Rifles)
12th South Carolina

Second Brigade (Brig. Gen. James H.
Lane)
7th North Carolina

18th North Carolina
28th North Carolina
33rd North Carolina
37th North Carolina

Third Brigade (Brig. Gen. Edward L.
Thomas)
14th Georgia
35th Georgia
45th Georgia
49th Georgia

Fourth Brigade (Brig. Gen. Alfred M.
Scales)
13th North Carolina
16th North Carolina
22nd North Carolina
34th North Carolina
38th North Carolina

Artillery Battalion (Maj. William T.
Poague)
Albemarle (Virginia) Artillery
(Wyatt's Battery)
Charlotte (North Carolina) Artillery
(Graham's Battery)
Madison (Mississippi) Light Artillery
(Ward's Battery)
Brooke's (Virginia) Battery

RESERVE ARTILLERY (Col. R. Lindsay
Walker)

McIntosh's Battalion (Maj. D. G.
McIntosh)
Hardaway (Alabama) Artillery (Hurt's
Battery)
Danville (Virginia) Artillery (Rice's
Battery)
2nd Rockbridge (Virginia) Artillery
(Wallace's Battery)
Johnson's (Virginia) Battery)

Pegram's Battalion (Maj. W. J.
Pegram)
Pee Dee (South Carolina) Artillery
(Zimmerman's Battery)
Crenshaw's (Virginia) Battery
Fredericksburg (Virginia) Artillery
(Marye's Battery)
Letcher (Virginia) Artillery (Brander's

Battery)
Purcell (Virginia) Artillery (McGraw's Battery)

CAVALRY CORPS (Maj. Gen. James E. B. Stuart)

Fitzhugh Lee's Brigade (Brig. Gen. Fitzhugh Lee)
1st Maryland Battalion (serving with Ewell's Corps)
1st Virginia
2nd Virginia
3rd Virginia
4th Virginia
5th Virginia

Hampton's Brigade (Brig. Gen. Wade Hampton)
1st North Carolina
1st South Carolina
2nd South Carolina
Cobb's (Georgia) Legion Cavalry
Jeff Davis Legion
Phillip's (Georgia) Legion Cavalry

Lee's Brigade (Col. John R. Chambliss, Jr.)
2nd North Carolina
9th Virginia
10th Virginia
13th Virginia

Jenkins' Brigade (Brig. Gen. Albert G. Jenkins)
14th Virginia
16th Virginia
17th Virginia
34th Virginia Battalion
36th Virginia Battalion
Jackson's (Virginia) Battery

Robertson's Brigade (Brig. Gen. Beverly H. Robertson)
4th North Carolina
5th North Carolina
6th Virginia
7th Virginia
11th Virginia
35th Virginia Battalion

Stuart's Horse Artillery (Maj. R. E. Beckham)
Brethed's (Virginia) Battery
Chew's (Virginia) Battery
Griffin's (Maryland) Battery
Hart's (South Carolina) Battery
McGregor's (Virginia) Battery
Moorman's (Virginia) Battery

Imboden's Command (Brig. Gen. John D. Imboden)
18th Virginia Cavalry
62nd Virginia (Mounted Infantry)
McNeill's (Virginia Partisan) Rangers
McClanahan's (Virginia) Battery

PETERSBURG (31 DECEMBER 1864)

HEADQUARTERS (Gen. Robert E. Lee)

Provost Guard
1st Virginia Battalion
39th Virginia Cavalry Battalion

Engineers (Col. T. M. R. Talcott)
1st Engineers

FIRST CORPS (Lt. Gen. James Longstreet)

PICKETT'S DIVISION (Maj. Gen. George E. Pickett)

Steuart's Brigade (Brig. Gen. George H. Steuart)
9th Virginia
38th Virginia
53rd Virginia
57th Virginia

Corse's Brigade (Brig. Gen. Montgomery D. Corse)
15th Virginia
17th Virginia
29th Virginia
30th Virginia
32nd Virginia

Hunton's Brigade (Brig. Gen. Eppa
Hunton)
8th Virginia
18th Virginia
19th Virginia
28th Virginia
56th Virginia

Terry's Brigade (Brig. Gen. William
R. Terry)
1st Virginia
3rd Virginia
7th Virginia
11th Virginia
24th Virginia

Field's Division (Maj. Gen. Charles
W. Field)

Anderson's Brigade (Brig. Gen. G. T.
Anderson)
7th Georgia
8th Georgia
9th Georgia
11th Georgia
59th Georgia

Law's Brigade (Col. W. F. Perry)
4th Alabama
15th Alabama
44th Alabama
47th Alabama
48th Alabama

Gregg's Brigade (Col. F. S. Bass)
3rd Arkansas
1st Texas
4th Texas
5th Texas

Benning's Brigade (Brig. Gen. H. L.
Benning)
2nd Georgia
15th Georgia
17th Georgia
20th Georgia

Bratton's Brigade (Brig. Gen. John
Bratton)
1st South Carolina
5th South Carolina
6th South Carolina

2nd South Carolina Rifles
Palmetto (South Carolina) Sharpshooters

KERSHAW'S DIVISION (Maj. Gen. J. B.
Kershaw)

Wofford's Brigade (Brig. Gen. Dudley M. DuBose)
16th Georgia
18th Georgia
24th Georgia
3rd Georgia Battalion Sharpshooters
Cobb's (Georgia) Legion
Phillip's (Georgia) Legion

Humphreys' Brigade (Brig. Gen. B.
G. Humphreys)
13th Mississippi
17th Mississippi
18th Mississippi
21st Mississippi

Bryan's Brigade (Brig. Gen. Goode
Bryan)
10th Georgia
50th Georgia
51st Georgia
53rd Georgia

Conner's Brigade (Brig. Gen. James
Conner)
2nd South Carolina
3rd South Carolina
7th South Carolina
8th South Carolina
15th South Carolina
20th South Carolina
3rd South Carolina Battalion

Artillery (Brig. Gen. E. Porter Alexander)

Cabell's Battalion (Col. H. C. Cabell)
Anderson's (Virginia) Battery
Callaway's (Georgia) Battery
Carlton's (Georgia) Battery
Manly's (North Carolina) Battery

Huger's Battalion (Lt. Col. F. Huger)
Fickling's (South Carolina) Battery
Moody's (Louisiana) Battery

Parker's (Virginia) Battery
Smith's (Virginia) Battery
Taylor's (Virginia) Battery
Woolfolk's (Virginia) Battery

Hardaway's Battalion (detached
from Second Corps) (Lt. Col. R. A.
Hardaway)
Dance's (Virginia) Battalion
Graham's (Virginia) Batttery
Griffin's (Virginia) Battery
Smith's (Virginia) Battery

Haskell's Battalion (Maj. John C.
Haskell)
Flanner's (North Carolina) Battery
Ramsay's (North Carolina) Battery
Garden's (South Carolina) Battery
Lamkin's (Virginia) Battery

Stark's Battalion (Lt. Col. A. W.
Stark)
Green's (Louisiana) Battery
Armistead's (Virginia) Battery
French's (Virginia) Battery

SECOND CORPS (Maj. Gen. John R.
Gordon)

RODE'S DIVISION (Brig. Gen. Bryan
Grimes)
Battle's Brigade (Brig. Gen. Cullen
Battle)
3rd Alabama
5th Alabama
6th Alabama
12th Alabama
61st Alabama

Grimes' Brigade (Brig. Gen. Bryan
Grimes)
32nd North Carolina
43rd North Carolina
45th North Carolina
53rd North Carolina
2nd North Carolina Battalion

Cox's Brigade (Brig. Gen. William R.
Cox)
1st North Carolina
2nd North Carolina

3rd North Carolina
4th North Carolina
14th North Carolina
30th North Carolina

Cook's Brigade (Brig. Gen. Philip
Cook)
4th Georgia
12th Georgia
21st Georgia
44th Georgia

Early's Division (Brig. Gen. John
Pegram)

Johnston's Brigade (Brig. Gen.
Robert D. Johnston)
5th North Carolina
12th North Carolina
20th North Carolina
23rd North Carolina
1st North Carolina Battalion

Lewis' Brigade (Brig. Gen. William
G. Lewis)
6th North Carolina
21st North Carolina
54th North Carolina
57th North Carolina

Pegram's Brigade (Brig. Gen. John
Pegram)
13th Virginia
31st Virginia
49th Virginia
52nd Virginia
58th Virginia

GORDON'S DIVISION (Brig. Gen.
Clement A. Evans)

Evans' Brigade (Brig. Gen. Clement
A. Evans)
13th Georgia
26th Georgia
31st Georgia
38th Georgia
60th Georgia
61st Georgia
12th Georgia Battalion

Terry's (Stonewall) Brigade (Brig. Gen. William Terry)
2nd Virginia
4th Virginia
5th Virginia
10th Virginia
21st Virginia
23rd Virginia
25th Virginia
27th Virginia
33rd Virginia
37th Virginia
42nd Virginia
44th Virginia
48th Virginia

York's Brigade (Vacant)
1st Louisiana
2nd Louisiana
5th Louisiana
6th Louisiana
7th Louisiana
8th Louisiana
9th Louisiana
10th Louisiana
14th Louisiana
15th Louisiana

Artillery (absent, 'in the Valley')

THIRD CORPS (Lieut. Gen. A. P. Hill)

HETH'S DIVISION (Maj. Gen. Henry Heth)

Davis' Brigade (Brig. Gen. Joseph R. Davis)
1st Confederate Battalion (later to Archer's Brigade)
2nd Mississippi
11th Mississippi
26th Mississippi
42nd Mississippi

Cooke's Brigade (Brig. Gen. J. R. Cooke)
15th North Carolina
27th North Carolina
46th North Carolina
48th North Carolina
55th North Carolina

MacRae's Brigade (Brig. Gen. William MacRae)
11th North Carolina
26th North Carolina
44th North Carolina
47th North Carolina
52nd North Carolina

Archer's Brigade (Col. R. M. Mayo, also below)
(then consolidated with Johnson's Brigade under Col. McComb)
13th Alabama
1st Tennessee (Provisional Army)
7th Tennessee
14th Tennessee

Walker's Brigade (Col. R. M. Mayo)
2nd Maryland Battalion (later to Archer's Brigade)
22nd Virginia Battalion
40th Virginia
47th Virginia
55th Virginia

Johnson's Brigade (Col. William McComb)
17th/23rd Tennessee
25th/44th Tennessee
63rd Tennessee

WILCOX'S DIVISION (Maj. Gen. Cadmus M. Wilcox)

Thomas's Brigade (Brig. Gen. E. L. Thomas)
14th Georgia
35th Georgia
45th Georgia
49th Georgia

Lane's Brigade (Brig. Gen. James H. Lane)
7th North Carolina
18th North Carolina
28th North Carolina
33rd North Carolina
37th North Carolina

McGowan's Brigade (Brig. Gen. Samuel McGowan)

1st South Carolina (Provisional
Army)
12th South Carolina
13th South Carolina
14th South Carolina
Orr's (South Carolina) Rifles

Scales' Brigade (Brig. Gen. Alfred M.
Scales)
13th North Carolina
16th North Carolina
22nd North Carolina
34th North Carolina
38th North Carolina

MAHONE'S DIVISION (Maj. Gen.
William Mahone)

Sanders' Brigade (Brig. Gen. J. C.
Sanders)
8th Alabama
9th Alabama
10th Alabama
11th Alabama
13th Alabama
14th Alabama

Weisiger's Brigade (Brig. Gen. D. A.
Weisiger)
6th Virginia
12th Virginia
16th Virginia
41st Virginia
61st Virginia

Harris's Brigade (Brig. Gen.
Nathaniel H. Harris)
12th Mississippi
16th Mississippi
19th Mississippi
48th Mississippi

Sorrel's Brigade (Brig. Gen. G. M.
Sorrel)
3rd Georgia
22nd Georgia
48th Georgia
64th Georgia
2nd Georgia Battalion
10th Georgia Battalion

Finegan's Brigade (Brig. Gen. Joseph
Finegan)
2nd Florida
5th Florida
8th Florida
9th Florida
10th Florida
11th Florida

ARTILLERY (Col. R. L. Walker)
Reserve
Hunt's (Alabama) Battery
Dement's (Maryland) Battery
Chew's (Maryland) Battery
Donald's (Virginia) Battery
Clutter's (Virginia) Battery

Pegram's Battalion (Col. W. J.
Pegram)
Richards' (Mississippi) Battery
Gregg's (South Carolina) Battery
Braxton's (Virginia) Battery
Brander's (Virginia) Battery
Cayce's (Virginia) Battery
Ellett's (Virginia) Battery

Poague's Battalion (Col. W. T.
Poague)
Williams' (North Carolina) Battery
Johnston's (Virginia) Battery
Utterback's (Virginia) Battery

Eshleman's (Louisiana) Battalion
(Washington Artillery)
(Lt. Col. B. F. Eshleman)
Owen's Battery (1st Company)
Richardson's Battery (2nd Company)
Hero's Battery (3rd Company)
Norcom's Battery (4th Company)

Richardson's Battalion (Lt. Col.
Charles Richardson)
Landry's (Louisiana) Battery
Moore's (Virginia) Battery.
Grandy's (Virginia) Battery
Penick's (Virginia) Battery

Lane's Battalion (Maj. John Lane)
Wingfield's (Georgia) Battery
Patterson's (Georgia) Battery
Ross' (Georgia) Battery

Owen's Battalion (Maj. W. M. Owen)
Chamberlayne's (Virginia) Battery
Dickenson's (Virginia) Battery
Walker's (Virginia) Battery

ANDERSON'S CORPS (Lt. Gen. Richard H. Anderson)

HOKE'S DIVISION (Maj. Gen. R. F. Hoke) (Left for North Carolina 20 December 1864)

Hagood's Brigade (Brig. Gen. Johnson Hagood)
11th South Carolina
21st South Carolina
25th South Carolina
27th South Carolina
7th South Carolina Battalion

Colquitt's Brigade (Brig. Gen. A. H. Colquitt)
6th Georgia
19th Georgia
23rd Georgia
27th Georgia
28th Georgia

Clingman's Brigade (Brig. Gen. Thomas L. Clingman)
8th North Carolina
31st North Carolina
51st North Carolina
61st North Carolina

Kirkland's Brigade (Brig. Gen. W. W. Kirkland)
17th North Carolina
42nd North Carolina
66th North Carolina

JOHNSON'S DIVISION (Maj. Gen. Bushrod R. Johnson)

Wise's Brigade (Brig. Gen. Henry A. Wise)
26th Virginia
34th Virginia
46th Virginia
59th Virginia

Elliott's Brigade (Brig. Gen. Stephen Elliott, Jr.)
17th South Carolina
18th South Carolina
22nd South Carolina
23rd South Carolina
26th South Carolina
Holcombe (South Carolina) Legion

Gracie's Brigade (Brig. Gen. A. Gracie, Jr.)
41st Alabama
43rd Alabama
59th Alabama
60th Alabama
23rd Alabama Battalion

Ransom's Brigade (Brig. Gen. M. W. Ransom)
24th North Carolina
25th North Carolina
35th North Carolina
49th North Carolina
56th North Carolina

Artillery (Col. H. P. Jones)

Mosley's Battalion (Lt. Col. E. F. Mosley)
Slaten's (Georgia) Battery
Cumming's (North Carolina) Battery
Miller's (Virginia) Battery
Young's (Virginia) Battery

Blount's Battalion (Maj. J. G. Blount)
Dickerson's (Virginia) Battery
Marshall's (Virginia) Battery
Macon's (Virginia) Battery
Sullivan's (Virginia) Battery

Coit's Battalion (Maj. James C. Coit)
Wright's (Louisiana) Battery
Bradford's (Mississippi) Battery
Pegram's (Virginia) Battery

Martin's Battalion (Capt. S. Taylor Martin)
Martin's (Virginia) Battery
Sturdivant's (Virginia) Battery

Cavalry Corps (Maj. Gen. Wade Hampton)

Butler's Division (Maj. Gen. M. C. Butler)

Butler's Brigade (Col. H. K. Aiken)
4th South Carolina
5th South Carolina
6th South Carolina

Young's Brigade (Col. J. F. Waring)
10th Georgia
Cobb's (Georgia) Legion
Phillip's (Georgia) Legion
Jeff Davis (Mississippi) Legion

Lee's Division (Maj. Gen. W. H. P. Lee)

Barringer's Brigade (Brig. Gen. Rufus Barringer)
1st North Carolina
2nd North Carolina
3rd North Carolina
5th North Carolina

Beale's Brigade (Brig. Gen. R. L. T. Beale)
9th Virginia
10th Virginia
13th Virginia

Dearing's Brigade (Brig. Gen. J. Dearing)
8th Georgia
4th North Carolina
16th North Carolina

Horse Artillery (Maj. R. Preston Chew)
Hart's (South Carolina) Battery
Graham's (Virginia) Battery
McGregor's (Virginia) Battery

Richmond and Danville Defences (Brig. Gen. J. A. Walker)

Local Defence Troops (Brig. Gen. W. C. Lee)
1st Battalion, Local Defense Troops
2nd Battalion, Local Defense Troops

3rd Battalion, Local Defense Troops
4th Battalion, Local Defense Troops
5th Battalion, Local Defense Troops
6th Battalion, Local Defense Troops
1st Regiment Reserves

Cavalry Brigade (Brig. Gen. Martin W. Gary)
Hampton Legion
7th South Carolina
24th Virginia

Not brigaded
60th Alabama
25th Virginia Battalion Infantry
1st Battalion Cavalry, Local Defense

Artillery Defences (Lt. Col. John C. Pemberton)

First Division (Richmond Inner Line)
10th Virginia Battalion Heavy Artillery
19th Virginia Battalion Heavy Artillery

Second Division (Richmond Inner Line)
18th Virginia Battalion Heavy Artillery
20th Virginia Battalion Heavy Artillery

Unattached
Louisiana Guard Artillery

Light Artillery (Lt. Col. Charles E. Lightfoot)
Caroline (Virginia) Artillery (Thornton's Battery)
2nd Nelson (Virginia) Artillery (Rives' Battery)
Surry (Virginia) Artillery (Hankins' Battery)

Chaffin's Bluff (Lt. Col. J. M. Maury)
Stark's Battalion, Light Artillery (Maj. Alexander W. Stark)
Mathews (Virginia) Artillery (Armistead's Battery)
McComas (Virginia) Artillery (French's Battery)

Chapter Notes

Chapter 1. The Mission of Lee's Army
1. Wallace, introduction, p. 1
2. Dowdey and Manarin, *Wartime Papers*, p. 33
3. Wallace, op. cit., pp. 88-9
4. *Official Records of the War of the Rebellion* (hereinafter 'OR'), Series IV, Vol. I, pp. 380-386
5. OR, IV, 1, pp. 381-4
6. Richardson, I, p. 117
7. Jones, p. 25
8. Ibid., p. 30

Chapter 2. Robert E. Lee
1. Jones, p. 13
2. Howard, p. 24
3. Watkins, p. 27
4. Horn, *The Lee Reader*, pp. 131-2
5. Sorrel, pp. 50-1
6. Dowdey and Manarin, op. cit., p. 197
7. Fremantle, pp. 197-8
8. Davis, Burke, *To Appomattox*, p. 361
9. Porter, Horace, *Campaigning With Grant*, p. 474
10. Dowdey & Manarin, p. 428
11. Ibid., p. 616
12. Sorrel, p. 215
13. Lee, Robert E., Jr., p. 79
14. Ibid., pp. 105-8
15. Dowdey & Manarin, p. 401
16. Taylor, Richard, p. 112
17. Alexander, pp. 91-2
18. Sorrel, p. 99
19. Thomas, p. 176
20. Alexander, p. 110
21. Lee, Fitzhugh, p. 270
22. Haskell, pp. 55-6
23. Longstreet, p. 332
24. Nolan, p. 113

Chapter 3. Lee's Generals
THOMAS J. JACKSON
1. Douglas, pp. 236-7
2. Taylor, Walter, p. 85
3. Worsham, p. 102
4. Taylor, Richard, p. 89
5. Davis, Jefferson, p. 119
6. Dowdey and Manarin, p. 484

JAMES LONGSTREET
1. Longstreet, p. 13
2. Fremantle, p. 189
3. Sorrel, pp. 4-5
4. Kean, R. G. H., p. 10
5. Taylor, Walter, p. 99
6. McKim, pp. 175-6
7. Haskell, p. 58
8. Longstreet, p. 262
9. Alexander, p. 362
10. Fremantle, p. 198

A.P. HILL
1. Haskell, Alexander, pp. 16-17
2. Sorrell, pp. 64-5
3. Seymour, p. 89
4. Gordon, p. 379

RICHARD S. EWELL
1. Gordon, pp. 38-9
2. Taylor, p. 36-40
3. Ibid., p. 88
4. Gordon, p. 153
5. Douglas, p. 246
6. Alexander, p. 353
7. Dowdey & Manarin, p. 776

JUBAL EARLY
1. Douglas, pp. 33
2. Sorrel, pp. 33-4
3. Alexander, p. 397

RICHARD H. ANDERSON
1. Sorrel, p. 107
2. Alexander, p. 364
3. Sorrel, pp. 213-14

JAMES EWELL BROWN STUART
1. Cooke, John Esten, 'General Stuart in Camp and Field' in *The Annals of the War*, p. 666
2. Mosby, p. 31
3. Lee, Fitzhugh, p. 151
4. Douglas, p. 193
5. Ibid., pp. 281
6. Thomason, p. 3

WILLIAM N. PENDLETON
1. Alexander, p. 336
2. Sorrel, p. 94
3. Dowdey and Manarin, p. 783
4. Fremantle, p. 197

Chapter 4. Lee's Staff
1. Alexander, p. 236

2. *Army Regulations*, p. 51
3. Horn, p. 352
4. Ibid., pp. 112-13
5. Sorrell, pp. 51-2
6. OR, IV, 2, pp. 446-7
7. Ibid., 3, p. 352
8. Ibid., p. 498
9. Dowdey & Manarin, p. 374
10. Ibid., p. 340
11. OR, IV, 1, p. 129
12. Ibid., 3, p. 497

Chapter 5. Lee's Soldiers
1. Stampp, pp. 29-30
2. Hinton, p. 241
3. Stevens, p. 7

RECRUITING
1. OR, IV, 1, pp. 866-7
2. Ibid., p. 585
3. 'Boy Officer of the Washington Artillery', in *Civil War Times Illustrated*, May 1975, p. 21
4. Ibid., p. 833
5. Official, *Army Regulations*, pp. 385-6
6. Mixson, p. 18
7. Official, op. cit., p. 387
8. Ibid., p. 386
9. OR, IV, 1, p. 825
10. Livermore, p. 42
11. OR, III, 1, p. 301
12. OR, IV, 1, pp. 1095-7
13. Ibid., pp. 976-7
14. Miers, p. 189
15. Ibid., p. 110
16. Kean, p. 64
17. Jones, p. 107
18. Kean, pp. 80-1
19. Jones, p. 179
20. Mosby, p. 98
21. Dowdey and Manarin, p. 698
22. Ibid., pp. 843-4

THE OFFICER CORPS
1. OR, IV, 1, p. 126
2. Ibid., p. 128
3. Ibid., p. 302
4. Ibid., pp. 594-5
5. Mosby, pp. 101-2
6. Dawson, p. 54
7. Blackford, p. 62
8. Krick, p. 16
9. Ibid., pp. 19-21
10. OR, IV, 1, p. 1128
11. OR, I, X, 2, p. 501
12. OR, IV, 2, pp. 205-6
13. OR, I, LI, 2, p. 756
14. Dowdey and Manarin, p. 669
15. OR; IV, 2, p. 189
16. Sorrel, p. 30
17. OR, IV, 3, p. 1034

NON-COMMISSIONED OFFICERS
1. *Army Regulations*, p. 72
2. Squires, Charles, 'The "Boy Officer" of the Washington Artillery', in *Civil War Times Illustrated*, May 1975, p. 113. Howard, p. 63
4. Mixson, pp. 111-12

TRAINING
1. Worsham, p. 7
2. OR, IV, 2, p. 207
3. Ibid., p. 437
4. OR, IV, 3, pp. 490-1
5. Dowdey and Manarin, p. 693

DISCIPLINE
1. McKim, p. 29
2. Scheibert, p. 36
3. OR, IV, 1, p. 835
4. OR, I, XIX, Part 1, p. 143
5. OR, IV, 2, p. 7
6. Dowdey and Manarin, p. 591
7. Ibid., p. 886
8. Smith, Edward, 'Friendly Enemies', in *Civil War Times Illustrated*, Issue XXV
9. Sorrel, p. 228

CLOTHING
1. OR, IV, 1, p. 229
2. Pember, p. 75
3. Harwell, p. 37
4. OR, IV, 1, p. 534
5. Yearns, W. Buck, and Barrett, John G., *North Carolina Civil War Documentary*, Chapel Hill, North Carolina, pp. 1-2
6. Townsend, George A., *Rustics In Rebellion*, Chapel Hill, North Carolina, 1950, p. 84
7. Miers, p. 49
8. OR, IV, 3, p. 674
9. McDonald, Bob, 'Standard-issue Confederate Slouch Hat', in *North-South Trader's Civil War*, Christmas, 1991, pp. 32-7
10. Martin, David, 'Heightstown, N. J.'in *Camp Chase Gazette*, November 1982, p. 15
11. Kimmell, Ross M., 'The Confederate Infantryman at Antietam' in *Military Illustrated*, February/March 1989, pp. 8-9
12. Fremantle, p. 180
13. Summer, p. 77
14. 'Resources of the Confederacy in February, 1865', in *Southern Historical Society Papers*, Vol. 2, No. 1, p. 118
15. Ibid., p. 117
16. Lewis, pp. 61-2
17. Pember, p. 75
18. Foote, Frank H., 'Recollections of Army Life with General Lee' in *Southern Historical Society Papers*, Vol. 31, p.

244
19. Dowdey and Manarin, pp. 664-5
20. Foote, op. cit., p. 244
21. 'Resources', op. cit., pp. 118, 120

RATIONS
1. McCarthy, pp. 55-7
2. Sorrell, p. 235
3. Letter, private collection
4. Gordon, Richard F., Jr., 'Letters To Emeline', in *Soldiers*, August 1988, p. 29
5. Mixson, pp. 82-3
6. McCarthy, p. 59
7. Mixson, p. 34
8. Sorrel, p. 236
9. Ibid., pp. 191-2
10. Alexander, pp. 339-40

MORALE
1. Alexander, p. 139
2. Ibid., p. 222
3. Cunningham, p. 211
4. Jones, J. William, p. 155
5. Ibid., p. 349
6. McCarthy, p. 208
7. Gordon, Richard F., op. cit., p. 31
8. McCarthy, p. 152

GETTING OUT
1. *Army Regulations*, p. 17
2. Richardson, Vol. II, pp. 684-5
3. OR, IV, 2, p. 231
4. Ibid., p. 499

Chapter 6. The Combat Arms
INFANTRY
ORGANIZATION
1. Livermore, pp. 27-9
2. OR, IV, 1, p. 127-8
3. Ibid., p. 278
4. Ibid., p. 529
5. Livermore, p. 27

TACTICS
1. Ross, p. 37
2. Benson, p. 22
3. Ibid., p. 23

WEAPONS
1. Resources, Vol. 2, p. 64
2. Albaugh and Simmonds, p. 155
3. OR, I, XXV, part 1, p. 819

EQUIPMENT
1. Benson, p. 12
2. McCarthy, p. 22
3. Worsham, pp. 8-9
4. OR, I, XXV, part 1, p. 819
5. Ibid.
6. Ibid.
7. McCarthy, p. 27

INSIGNIA
1. Howard, pp. 251-2
2. Frassanito, p. 60

3. Survivor's Association, *History of the 118th Pennsylvania Volunteers*, Philadelphia, 1686, p. 332
4. Menge, W. Springer, and Shimrak, J. August, *The Civil War Notebook of Daniel Chisholm*, New York, 1989, p. 85
5. OR, I, XI, part 3, p. 564

FLAGS
1. Time-Life Books, p. 242
2. Ashe, S. A., 'Unusual Experiences as Soldier and Prisoner', in *Confederate Veteran*, September 1927, p. 341

PAY
1. OR, IV, 1, p. 129
2. Miers, p. 390

SHARPSHOOTERS
ORGANIZATION
1. OR, IV, 1, p. 1127
2. OR, IV, 2, p. 288
3. Dunlop, p. 17

TACTICS
1. Dunlop, p. 19

WEAPONS
1. Dunlop, p. 22

EQUIPMENT/UNIFORMS/INSIGNIA
1. Menge and Shimrak, p. 74

ARTILLERY
1. OR, IV, 1, p. 128
2. Ibid., pp. 580-1
3. Ibid., p. 687
4. Ibid., pp. 964-5
5. Ibid., p. 1045
6. Ibid., p. 1096
7. OR, IV, 2, p. 153
8. Alexander, pp. 104-5
9. Ross, p. 131
10. Wise, p. 419
11. OR, I, 36, part 3, pp. 881-2
12. OR, IV, 3, pp. 293-4
13. Wise, pp. 911-16
14. Ibid., p. 949

TACTICS
1. Andrews, p. 5
2. Moore, p. 36
3. Alexander, p. 483

WEAPONS
1. Miller, Francis, Vol. 5, p. 60
2. OR, I, 2, p. 477
3. Ross, pp. 129-30
4. Wise, p. 571
5. Ibid., p. 917
6. OR, I, IV, pp. 674-5
7. OR, I, XXXVI, part 3, pp. 809-11
8. McCarthy, p. 67

INSIGNIA
1. Laswell, Mary, p. 130

PAY
1. OR, IV, 1, pp. 129-30

2. Ibid., p. 1076
CAVALRY
ORGANIZATION
1. OR, IV, 1, pp. 127-8
2. Ibid., p. 1096
TACTICS
1. Blackford, p. 26
2. Fremantle, pp. 199-200
3. Ibid., p. 227
4. OR, IV, 2, p. 568
5. Taylor, Richard, pp. 65-6
WEAPONS
1. Redfield, H. V., 'Characteristics of the Armies', in *Annals of The War*, p. 361
2. Mosby, p. 30
3. Fremantle, p. 200
4. *Ordnance Field Manual*, p. 54
EQUIPMENT
1. *Ordnance Field Manual*, p. 45
2. Dowdey and Manarin, p. 504
INSIGNIA
1. Summer, pp. 55, 68
2. Ibid., p. 81
PAY
1. OR, IV, 1, pp. 129-30
PARTISAN RANGERS
1. OR, IV, 1, p. 1030
2. OR, IV, 2, p. 304
3. OR, I, LI, 2, p. 609
4. Ibid., 2, p. 82
5. Ibid., p. 585
6. Ibid., p. 48
7. Ibid., p. 499
8. Ibid., p. 1003
9. Dowdey and Manarin, pp. 688-9
10. OR, IV, 3, p. 194

Chapter 7. The Support Arms
CORPS OF ENGINEERS
ORGANIZATION
1. OR, IV, 1, p. 127-8
2. Ibid., p. 226
3. Ibid., p. 331
4. Ibid., p. 821
5. Ibid., p. 1080
6. OR, IV, 3, p. 898
7. Official, *General Orders for 1863*, p. 70
8. OR, IV, 3, pp. 190-1
TACTICS
1. 'Diary of Captain James K. Boswell', in *Civil War Times Illustrated*, April 1976, p. 37
2. Official, *General Orders for 1863*, p. 124
3. Reid, p. 116
WEAPONS
1. Reid, p. 108
PAY
1. OR, IV, 1, p. 130
2. Ibid., p. 331

3. Official, *General Orders for 1863*, p. 70
4. OR, IV, 3, p. 191
SIGNAL CORPS
ORGANIZATION
1. Alexander, p. 38
2. OR, I, 21, p. 446
3. Alexander, p. 61
4. OR, IV, 1, p, 1132
5. OR, IV, 2, p. 199
6. Ibid., p. 289
7. Ross, pp. 91-2
TACTICS
1. OR, IV, 2, p. 47
2. Taylor, Charles E., pp. 6-7
INSIGNIA
1. Gaddy, David E., 'Confederate States Army Signal Corps Insignia', in *Military Collector & Historian*, summer 1973, p. 87
PAY
1. OR, IV, 1, pp. 1131-2
MEDICAL DEPARTMENT
ORGANIZATION
1. OR, IV, 1, p. 115
2. Ibid., pp. 326-7
3. Ibid., p. 1024
4. Ross, pp. 132-3
5. Time-Life Books, p. 219
6. Nisbet, James Cooper, p. 78
TACTICS
1. Miller, Vol. 7, pp. 248-50
2. Tapert, p. 77
3. Miller, pp. 262-4
EQUIPMENT
1. OR, IV, 2, p. 13
2. Ibid., p. 467
3. Ibid., p. 569
4. Ibid., p. 1024
5. OR, IV, 3, p. 712
6. Miller, Vol. 7, pp. 248, 260
7. *Army Regulations*, p. 253
INSIGNIA
1. Miller, Vol. 7, p. 350
2. Stevenson, p. 134
3. Fremantle, p. 186
PAY
1. OR, IV, 1, p. 129
BANDS
1. *Army Regulations*, p. 8
2. 'A Month's Visit to the Confederate Headquarters', in *Blackwood's Edinburg Magazine*, American ed., Vol. LVI, January-June 1863, p. 23
3. OR, IV, 1, p. 1059
4. Ross, p. 40
5. Mathews, Horace, 'Inflation Grips The South', in *Civil War Times Illustrated*, March 1983, p. 45
6. Fremantle, p. 208

7. Time-Life Books, p. 218
8. Manarin, Louis, and Wallace, Lee, Jr., *Richmond Volunteers, 1861-1865*, Richmond, 1969, p. 194
9. Time-Life Books, p. 219

PROVOST MARSHAL GUARD
1. OR, XI, 3, pp. 576-7
2. Ibid., XIX, I, pp. 1006-7
3. Ibid., XXVII, 2, p. 599
4. Ibid., LI, 2, pp. 785-6
5. Tower, R. L. (ed.), *A Carolinian Goes To War*, Columbia, South Carolina, 1983, p. 166

INVALID CORPS
1. OR, IV, 3, p. 214

CHAPLAINS
1. OR, IV, 1, p. 275
2. OR, IV, 3, p. 496
3. McKim, pp. 215-16
4. Jones, J. William, p. 358
5. Ibid., p. 522
6. Buckley, C. M., *A Frenchman, A Chaplain, A Rebel*, Chicago, 1981, pp. 61-2

PAY
1. OR, IV, 1, p. 327
2. Ibid., p. 595
3. Ibid., p. 1076

SUTLERS
1. OR, IV, 1, p. 887
2. Howard, p. 253

CIVILIAN SUPPORT ORGANIZATIONS
1. Jones, J. William, p. 280
2. Miers, Diary, p. 344

Chapter 8. Combined Arms in Action

CHANCELLORSVILLE: COMBINED ARMS IN THE FIELD
1. 'J. K. Boswell's Diary', in *Civil War Times Illustrated*, April 1976, p. 36
2. Dowdey and Manarin, p. 449
3. Casler, John O., p. 151
4. Lee, Fitzhugh, p. 245
5. Alexander, p. 197
6. Scheibert, Justus, 'General Robert E. Lee, Ober-Commander der ehemaligen Sudstaadlechen Armee in Nord Amerika', in *Jarbucher für die Deutsche Armee und Marine*, XVI (September 1875), pp. 208-09
7. OR, I, XXV, 1, p. 805
8. Ibid.
9. Ibid., pp. 818-19
10. Lord, Francis (ed.), *The Fremantle Diary*, p. 176

PETERSBURG: COMBINED ARMS IN THE DEFENCE
1. OR, I, XL, part 2, p. 669
2. 'Colonel Talcott', in Miller, Vol. V, p. 262
3. Ripley, p. 60
4. Alexander, p. 441
5. Ibid., pp. 443-4
6. Miller, p. 262
7. Blackford, pp. 269-70
8. Miller, p. 264

Bibliography

BOOKS

Anon. *Prayers and Other Devotions for the Use of the Soldiers of the Army of the Confederate States*, Charleston, South Carolina, n.d.

Albaugh, William A. III. *Confederate Edged Weapons*, New York, 1960

— and Simmons, Edward N. *Confederate Arms*, New York, 1957

Alexander, Edward Porter. *Fighting for the Confederacy*, Chapel Hill, North Carolina, 1989

Andrews, R. Snowden. *Andrews' Mounted Artillery Drill*, Charleston, South Carolina, 1863

Bailey, D. W. *British Military Longarms 1715-1865*, London, 1986

Bennett, William W. *A Narrative of The Great Revival Which Prevailed In the Southern Armies*, Harrisonburg, Virginia, 1989

Benson, Susan W. (ed.). *Berry Benson's Civil War Book*, Athens, Georgia, 1962

Bergeron, Arthur W. Jr. *Guide to Louisiana Confederate Military Units 1861-1865*, Baton Rouge, Louisiana, 1989

Bill, Alfred H. *The Beleaguered City*, New York, 1946

Blackford, W. W. *War Years With JEB Stuart*, New York, 1945

Boatner, Mark M. III. *The Civil War Dictionary*, New York, 1988

Buckley, C. M. (trans.). *A Frenchman, A Chaplain, A Rebel*, Chicago, 1981

Burton, Joseph Q., and Botsford, Theophilus F. *Historical Sketches of the Forty-Seventh Alabama Infantry Regiment*, CSA, Montgomery, Alabama, 1909

Canon, Devereaux D., Jr. *The Flags of the Confederacy*, Memphis, Tennessee, 1988

Caster, John O. *Four Years in the Stonewall Brigade*, Guthrie, Oklahoma, 1893

Chisholm, Daniel. *The Civil War Notebook of Daniel Chisholm*, New York, 1989

Coates, Earl J., and Thomas, Dean S. *An Introduction To Civil War Small Arms*, Gettysburg, Pennsylvania, 1990

Connelly, Thomas L. *The Marble Man, Robert E. Lee and His Image In American Society*, Baton Rouge, Louisiana, 1977

Cooling, B.F. *Jubal Early's Raid on Washington*, Baltimore, Maryland, 1989

Cross, C. Wallace, Jr. *Ordeal By Fire*, Clarksville Montgomery County Museum, Clarksville, Tennessee, 1990

Crute, Joseph H., Jr. *Confederate Staff Officers 1861-1865*, Powhatan, Virginia, 1982

— *Emblems of Southern Valor*, Louisville, Kentucky, 1990

— *Units of the Confederate States Army*, Midlothian, Virginia, 1987

Cunningham, H.H. *Doctors In Gray*, Gloucester, Massachusetts, 1970

Davis, Burke. *To Appomattox, Nine April Days, 1865*, New York, 1960

Davis, Jefferson. *Rise and Fall of the Confederate Government*, New York, 1881.

Davis, William C. (ed.). *The Image of War: 1861-1865*, Garden City, New York, 1981-4

Dawson, Francis, W. *Reminiscences of Confederate Service*, Baton Rouge, Louisiana, 1980

Douglas, Henry Kyd. *I Rode With Stonewall*, Chapel Hill, North Carolina, 1940

Dowdey, Clifford. *Experiment in Rebellion*, Garden City, New York, 1946
— *Lee's Last Campaign*, Boston, 1960
— *The Seven Days*, New York, 1964
Dowdey, Clifford, and Manarin, Louis H. (eds.). *The Wartime Papers of R. E. Lee* , New York, 1961
Downey, Fairfax. *The Guns at Gettysburg* , New York, 1958
Dunlop, W. S. *Lee's Sharpshooters*, Dayton, Ohio, 1988
Early, Jubal A. *Narrative of the War Between the States*, New York, 1989
Edwards, William B. *Civil War Guns*, New York,1962
Faust, Patricia L. (ed.). *Historical Times Illustrated Encyclopedia of the Civil War*, New York, 1986
Fieberger, G. J. *The Campaign and Battle of Gettysburg*, West Point, New York, 1915
Fox, William F. *Regimental Losses in The American Civil War*, Dayton, Ohio. 1985
Frassanito, William A. *Antietam*, New York, 1978
— *Gettysburg, A Journey in Time*, New York, 1975
— *Grant and Lee, The Virginia Campaigns 1864-1865*, New York, 1983
Freeman, Douglas Southall. *R. E. Lee*, New York, 1934
— *Lee's Lieutenants*, New York, 1944
Fremantle, Arthur J. L. *The Fremantle Diary*, New York, 1954
Gilham, William. *Manual of Instruction for the Volunteers and Militia of the Confederate States*, Richmond, 1861
Gordon, John B. *Reminiscences of the Civil War*, New York, 1903
Gragg Rod. *The Illustrated Confederate Reader*, New York, 1989
Griffith, Paddy. *Battle Tactics of the Civil War*, New Haven, Connecticut, 1989
Harwell, Richard. *A Confederate Marine*, Tuscaloosca, Alabama, 1063
Harwell, Richard B.(ed.). *The Confederate Reader*, New York, 1992
Haskell, John. *The Haskell Memoirs*, New York, 1960
Heleniak, Roman J., and Hewitt, Lawrence L.(eds.). *The Confederate High Command*, Shippensburg, Pennsylvania, 1990
Hinton, Rowan Helper. *The Impending Crisis of the South*, New York, 1963
Hopkins, Luther W. *From Bull Run to Appomattox*, Baltimore, Maryland, 1908
Horn, Stanley (ed.). *The Robert E. Lee Reader*, Indianapolis, Indiana, 1949
Howard, McHenry. *Recollections of a Maryland Confederate Soldier*, Baltimore, Maryland, 1914
Johnson, Robert U., and Buel, Clarence C. (eds.). *Battles and Leaders of the Civil War*, New York, 1956
Jones, Terry L. (ed.). *The Civil War Memoirs of Captain William J. Seymour, Reminiscences of a Louisiana Tiger*, Baton Rouge, Louisiana, 1991
Jones, J. William. *Army of Northern Virginia Memorial Volume*, Dayton, Ohio, 1976
— *Christ In The Camp*, Harrisonburg, Virginia, 1986
— *Life and Letters of Gen. Robert Edward Lee*, Harrisonburg, Virginia, 1986
Katcher, Philip. *The Army of Northern Virginia*, Reading, England, 1975
— *The American Civil War Sourcebook*, New York, 1992
— *Flags of the American Civil War (1): Confederate*, London, 1992
Krick, Robert K. *Lee's Colonels*, Dayton, Ohio, 1991
Laswell, Mary (ed.). *Rags and Hope*, New York, 1961
Lee, Fitzhugh. *General Lee*, Greenwich, Connecticut, 1961
Lee, R. E. *Recollections and Letters of General Lee*, Garden City, New York, 1904
Lee, Susan P. *Memoirs of William Nelson Pendleton, D.D.*, Harrisonburg, Virginia, 1991
Lewis, John H. *Recollections from 1860 to 1865*, Washington, DC, 1895
Livermore, Thomas L. *Numbers and Losses in the Civil War in America*, Dayton, Ohio, 1986
Longstreet, James. *From Manassas To Appomattox*, New York, 1991
Lord, Francis. *Civil War Sutlers and their Wares*, New York, 1969
Luvaas, Jay, and Nelson, Harold W.

The US Army War College Guide to the Battles of Chancellorsville and Fredericksburg, New York, 1988

McCarthy, Carlton. *Detailed Minutiae of Soldier Life in the Army of Northern Virginia*, Richmond, 1882

McKim, Randolph H. *A Soldier's Recollections*, Washington, DC, 1983

McPherson, James M. *Battle Cry of Freedom*, New York, 1988

Miers, Earl Shenck (ed.) *John B. Jones's A Rebel War Clerk's Diary*, New York, 1958

Miller, Francis T. *The Photographic History of the Civil War*, New York, 1957

Mitchell, Reid. *Civil War Soldiers*, New York, 1988

Mixon, Frank M. *Reminiscences of a Private*, Camden, South Carolina, 1990

Moore, Edward A. *The Story of a Cannoneer under Stonewall Jackson*, New York, 1907

Mosby, John S. *The Memoirs of John S. Mosby* , Bloomington, Indiana, 1959

Nichols, James L. *Confederate Engineers*, Tuscaloosa, Alabama, 1957

Nolan, Alan T. *Lee Reconsidered*, Chapel Hill, North Carolina, 1991

Norton, Herman. *Rebel Religion*, St. Louis, Missouri, 1961

Pember, Phoebe Yates. *A Southern Woman's Story*, St. Simon's Island, Georgia, 1974

Pickett, George E. *The Heart of a Soldier as revealed in the Intimate Letters of Genl. George E. Pickett*, New York, 1913

Polley, J. B. *Hood's Texas Brigade*, Dayton, Ohio, 1976

Porter, Horace. *Campaigning with Grant*, Bloomington, Indiana, 1961

Radley, Kenneth. *Rebel Watchdog*, Baton Rouge, Louisiana, 1989

Reid, J. W. *History of the Fourth Regiment S.C. Volunteers*, Dayton, Ohio, 1975

Richardson, James D. *A Compilation of the Messages and Papers of the Confederacy*, Nashville, 1906

Ripley, Warren. *Artillery and Ammunition of the Civil War*, New York, 1970

Robertson, James I., Jr. *The Stonewall Brigade*, Baton Rouge, Louisiana, 1963

— *Soldiers Blue and Gray*, Columbia, South Carolina, 1989

Rogers, Thomas G., and Harrison, Richard M. *Never Give Up This Field*, Norcross, Georgia, 1989

Roper, Peter W. *Jedediah Hotchkiss*, Shippensburg, Pennsylvania, 1992

Ross, FitzGerald. *Cities and Camps of the Confederate States*, Urbana, Illinois, 1958

Scheibert, Justus. *Seven Months in the Rebel States during the North American War, 1863*, Tuscaloosa, Alabama, 1958

Sears, Stephen W. *Landscape Turned Red*, New Haven, Connecticut, 1983

Sifakis, Stewart. *Compendium of the Confederate Armies*, New York, 1992

Simpson, Harold B. *Gaines' Mill to Appomattox*, Waco, Texas, 1963

Sorrel, G. Moxley. *Recollections of a Confederate Staff Officer*, New York, 1992

Spence, John W. *Corsicana To Appomattox*, Corsicana, Texas, 1984

Stampp, Kenneth M. *The Peculiar Insitution*, New York, 1956

Stevens, Jno. W. *Reminiscences of the Civil War*, Hillsboro, Texas, 1902

Stevenson, William G. *Thirteen Months in the Rebel Army*, New York, 1959

Stewart, George R. *Pickett's Charge*, Greenwich, Connecticut, 1963

Summer, Festus P. *A Borderland Confederate*, Pittsburgh, Pennsylvania, 1962

Symonds, Craig L. *Gettysburg, A Battlefield Atlas*, Baltimore, Maryland, 1992

Tapert, Annette (ed.). *The Brothers' War*, New York, 1989

Taylor, Charles E. *The Signal and Secret Service of the Confederate States*, Harmans, Maryland, 1986

Taylor, Richard. *Destruction and Reconstruction*, New York, 1955

Taylor, Walter H. *Four Years with General Lee*, Bloomington, Indiana, 1962

Thomas, Emory M. *Bold Dragoon*, New York, 1988

Thomason, John. *Jeb Stuart*, New York, 1930

Tidwell, William A. *Come Retribution*, Jackson, Mississippi, 1988

Todd, Frederick P. *American Military Equippage, 1851-1872*, Vol. II, Providence, Rhode Island, 1977

— *American Military Equippage, 1851-1872, State Forces*, New York, 1983

Vandiver, Frank E. *Mighty Stonewall*, New York, 1957

Wallace, Lee A., Jr. *A Guide To Virginia Military Organizations, 1861-1865*, Lynchburg, Virginia, 1986

Warner, Ezra J. *Generals In Gray*, Baton Rouge, Louisiana, 1959

Weinert, Richard P., Jr. *The Confederate Regular Army*, Shippensburg, Pennsylvania, 1991

Wert, Jeffry D. *Mosby's Rangers*, New York, 1990

Wheeler Richard. *On Fields of Fury*, New York 1991

— *Sword Over Richmond*, New York, 1986

— *Witness to Appomattox*, New York, 1989

White, Henry Alexander. *Robert E. Lee and the Southern Confederacy*, New York, 1968

Wiley, Bell Irvin. *The Common Soldier in the Civil War*, New York, 1952

Wise, Jennings Cropper. *The Long Arm of Lee*, Lynchburg, Virginia, 1915

Worsham, John R. *One of Jackson's Foot Cavalry*, Jackson, Tennessee, 1964

Younger, Edward (ed.). *Inside the Confederate Government: The Diary of Robert Garlick Hill Kean*, New York, 1957

Time-Life Books. *Arms and Equipment of the Confederacy*, Alexandria, Virginia, 1991

The War of the Rebellion: A Compilation of the Official Records of the Union and Confederate Armies, Washington, 1880-1900

Civil War Centennial Commission. *Tennesseans in the Civil War*, Nashville, Tennessee, 1964

Official. *Field Manual for the Use of the Officers on Ordnance Duty*, Richmond, 1862

Official. *Regulations of the Army of the Confederate States, 1863*, Richmond, 1863

The Annals of the War, Philadelphia *Weekly Times*, Dayton, Ohio, 1988

PERIODICALS (SPECIFICALLY, ARTICLES CITED)

America's Civil War

Bogue, Hardy Z. III. 'Ordnance', November 1990

Camp Chase Gazette

Fleming, Michael. 'The Daniel Letter', May 1984

Civil War Times Illustrated

Greer, George H. T. 'All Thoughts are Absorbed in the War', December 1978;

Jones, Terry L. 'Going Back into the Union at Last', January-February 1991;

Mathews, Horace. 'Inflation Grips the South', March 1983;

Musick, Michael. 'The Diary of Corporal Westwood James', October 1978;

Squires, Charles W. 'The Boy Officer of the Washington Artillery', May-June 1975;

Sullivan, David M. (ed.). 'Fowler the Soldier, Fowler the Marine', February 1988;

Von Brocke, Heros. 'The Prussian Remembers', February-March 1981

Confederate Veteran Magazine

Maryland Historical Magazine

Hopkins, C. A. Porter. 'The James J. Archer Letters', June, 1961

Mail Call

Dooley, John. 'Fredericksburg: Just a Stone's Throw Away', winter, 1991

Military Images

Index

311